Professional Web Design

Other Prima Computer Books Available Now!

Build a Web Site: The Programmer's Guide to Creating, Building, and Maintaining a Web Presence
The CD-ROM Revolution
CompuServe Complete Handbook and Membership Kit, Second Edition (with CD-ROM)
CorelDRAW! 5 Revealed!
Create Wealth with Quicken, Third Edition
Cruising America Online 2.5
Cruising The Microsoft Network
Data Security
DOS 6.2: Everything You Need to Know
Excel for Windows 95: The Visual Learning Guide
Excel 5 for Windows: The Visual Learning Guide
Excel for the Mac: The Visual Learning Guide
Free Electronic Networks
WINDOWS Magazine Presents: Freelance Graphics for Windows: The Art of Presentation
Harvard Graphics for Windows: The Art of Presentation
IBM Smalltalk Programming for Windows & OS/2 (with 3½-inch disk)
Interactive Internet: The Insider's Guide to MUDs, MOOs, and IRC
Internet After Hours
Internet After Hours, 2nd Edition
Internet for Windows: America Online Edition
Internet for Windows: America Online 2.5 Edition
Internet for Windows: The Microsoft Network Edition
Internet Information Server
The Internet Warp Book: Your Complete Guide to Getting Online with OS/2
Introduction to Internet Security
Macintosh Design to Production: The Definitive Guide
Making Movies with Your PC
Making Music with Your PC
Managing with Microsoft Project
Microsoft Office in Concert, Professional Edition
Microsoft Works for Windows 95: The Visual Learning Guide
Migrating to Windows 95
Moving Worlds (with CD-ROM)
OS/2 Warp: Easy Installation Guide
PageMaker 5.0 for the Mac: Everything You Need to Know
PageMaker 5.0 for Windows: Everything You Need to Know
Paradox 4.5 for DOS Revealed! (with 3½-inch disk)
Paradox for Windows Essential Power Programming (with 3½-inch disk)
PC DOS 6.2: Everything You Need to Know
PowerPoint for Windows 95: The Visual Learning Guide
Quicken 5 for Windows: The Visual Learning Guide
QuickTime: Making Movies with Your Macintosh, Second Edition
Researching on the Internet: The Complete Guide to Finding, Evaluating, and Organizing Information Effectively
Smalltalk Programming for Windows (with 3½-inch disk)
The Software Developer's Complete Legal Companion (with 3½-inch disk)
Symantec C++: Object-Oriented Programming Fundamentals for the Macintosh (with 3½-inch disk)
Think THINK C! (with two 3½-inch disks)
Thom Duncan's Guide to NetWare Shareware (with 3½-inch disk)
The USENET Navigator Kit (with 3½-inch disk)
Visual Basic for Applications Revealed!
The Warp Book: Your Definitive Guide to Installing and Using OS/2 v3
Web Advertising and Marketing
Web After Hours
Web Browsing with America Online
Web Browsing with Netscape Navigator 1.1
Web Browsing with NETCOM NetCruiser
Web Browsing with The Microsoft Network
Web Browsing with Prodigy
WinComm PRO: The Visual Learning Guide
Windows 95: The Visual Learning Guide
Windows 95: A to Z
Windows 95: Easy Installation Guide
The Windows 95 Book: Your Definitive Guide to Installing and Using Windows 95
WinFax PRO 4: The Visual Learning Guide
WinFax PRO 7 for Windows: The Visual Learning Guide
Word for Windows 95: The Visual Learning Guide

How to Order:

For information on quantity discounts contact the publisher: Prima Publishing, P.O. Box 1260BK, Rocklin, CA 95677-1260; (916) 632-4400. On your letterhead include information concerning the intended use of the books and the number of books you wish to purchase.

PROFESSIONAL WEB DESIGN

Theory and Technique on the Cutting Edge

Molly E. Holzschlag

PRIMA PUBLISHING

P is a registered trademark of Prima Publishing, a division of Prima Communications, Inc.
Prima Publishing® is a registered trademark of Prima Communications, Inc.
Prima Publishing, Rocklin, California 95677.

Publisher: Don Roche, Jr.
Associate Publisher: Ray Robinson
Senior Acquisition Editor: Alan Harris
Senior Editor: Tad Ringo
Acquistion Editor: Deborah F. Abshier
Developmental Editor: Tim Huddleston

Project Editor: Jeff Ennis
Copyeditor: Robert Campbell
Technical Reviewer: Tony Schafer
Assistant Acquisitions Editor: Julie Barton
Indexer: Katherine Stimson
Cover Design: Mike Tanamachi
Interior Design/Production: Shawn Morningstar
Illustrations: Matt Straznitskas and Stephen D. Sloan
Cartoon Illustrations: Joe Forkan

ISBN: 1-7615-0759-0
Library of Congress Catalog Card Number: 96-69006
Printed in the United States of America
96 97 98 99 BB 10 9 8 7 6 5 4 3 2 1

For my mother, Dr. Phillipa Kafka, esteemed professor,
author, and cherished friend, and the First Jewish Mother in Cyberspace.
I love you, Mom. Thanks for believing in me.

Table of Contents

Foreword

Talent, Attitude, and Nerve. I often cite these as the main components of "Way New Journalism," a phrase coined by Josh Quittner of *Time* magazine, to describe a new kind of reporting taking place in cyberspace. All three are vital to the survivability and viability of Net-based journalism. How else does one create a product that rises above the vast amounts of digital flotsam and jetsam that comprises most of what passes for "content" on the Net, and on the Web in particular?

These elements are needed to create a "voice," to establish a brand. It is something that I've been able to achieve through my own Net-based publication, CyberWire Dispatch. But these three ingredients also can be applied to Web design.

There are no instant successes here. A great Web page doesn't just happen overnight. There is an online maxim that "content is king" on the Web. And to a large degree, that's true; however, if content is king, then Web design is the crown prince. But it does take time.

This stuff isn't easy. If it were, everyone and their mother would be a Web designer. Um . . . come to think of it, judging by the enormous quantity of bad design out there, it appears that everyone with a Web page and an HTML coding cheat sheet does consider themselves a designer. But just as buying a paint program hardly qualifies you as a computer artist, neither does knowing a few handy HTML tags make you a Web designer.

This book challenges you to do some real work; it provides the down and dirty nuts and bolts of what makes good design, how to achieve it, and what land mines to look for along the way. Buying this book won't make you a hot Web designer; that takes talent and creativity. This book does provide an important road map; that's all it can do. Talent and creativity can't be bought off the shelf . . . at least not yet.

About this time you might be asking yourself why a journalist, whose own home page *PC Magazine*, in its ratings of the Top 100 Web sites, described as "a pencil sketch hanging among the Worhols," is writing the foreword to a book on Web design. Fair question; easy answer. For me, Web design is like obscenity . . . yes, it is. I may not be able to adequately describe it, but I sure know it when I see it. This is why I'm writing the foreword and not the book itself; that task was left in Molly's capable hands.

You might be tossed in jail and left to rot for putting obscene material on your Web page in some parts of the world, but no one is going to toss you in the slammer for bad Web design. There are no "design police" trolling the Web for offenders. At least there were none at the time of this writing. With various attempts by governments worldwide, including the U.S., to regulate the Internet in any way possible, there's no guarantee that some outlaw nation state might not decide to create just such a design police force. Think I'm joking? Think again. Already Web designers are being approached to create pages for foreign countries with the caveat that the morals, customs and religion be given foremost consideration. It is not beyond the pale that some country will issue "design mandates" for Web pages. Just how such edicts would be enforced is for another time.

The Net is a living, breathing organism, full of life and community a global community. The Web is simply a major population hub of that community. Web design and content are the two major "food groups" providing sustenance to this community. Attitude and noise round out the food chain.

Noise is this Web's equivalent of "junk food." Some of it tastes good, satisfies a jones for empty calories, but it provides little else. I would argue such noise doesn't qualify as content, just as a Twinkie doesn't qualify as a part of a well-rounded meal. Is there a place for it? Yes. But it's easy to gorge on it and the Web seems to be on such a junk food binge.

Content, on the other hand, adds substance and quality. There are varying degrees of content, to be sure, and there is content to serve just about anyone's particular taste. You can get the highbrow literary quality of a Salon or Slate, or the hip, in-your-face kind of content when you order up a HotWired or Spiv or Suck with your Web browser. Each of these offers solid, dependable content, geared to a particular readership, or "consumer" if you prefer that term. It's the content that keeps people coming back for more and moves someone to paste a particular site's URL in the browser bookmark.

Attitude applies to a majority of Web content. Not all content is attitude laden. In fact, some sites, such as Slate, bend over backwards to steer away from attitude. Slate's guiding light, Michael Kinsley, is quoted in the *New Yorker* as being skeptical of the Web's bent toward attitude, so much so that Kinsley is quoted as saying he wouldn't go "whoring after twenty-somethings." It remains to be seen if Kinsley can survive, having automatically alienated a large part of the Web's core demographic with that remark. And yet, merely by choosing to deliberately steer clear of attitude, Kinsley is, indeed, exhibiting his own "attitude." It's everywhere, to varying degrees—there's no escaping it. Deal with it; embrace it.

Finally, there is Web design. This is more ambiguous than content, more subtle than attitude, but can certainly slip into the "junk food" category if a designer is not careful. Content rarely carries a site if the design is insufferable. And a bad design can drive people away. This is a crucial fact to keep in mind. In this huge metropolis called the Web, there are few second chances. If you screw up your first impression, if your design turns off a visitor, it may be a long time coming before that visitor returns. Like I said early on, this isn't easy.

And so this book. It will give you the tools, the footpath for "searching for a paradigm" as Molly puts it. This isn't just a quick, "how-to" book for writing a personal home page. Rather, it "examines the professional Web design experience," as Molly writes. That experience is the digital flip-side of Mr. Toad's Wild Ride, I guarantee you. Good Web designers are hard to find; great Web designers are poised to become an industry unto themselves. This book will help you get there.

But first, you'll need talent, attitude and nerve. I wish you well.

Brock N. Meeks

Contributing Editor, *Wired Magazine*

Acknowledgments

As with successful Web design, this book is a result of a team effort. Each individual involved in the process brought insight, direction, and support, without which the project would have been impossible.

Wil Gerken is a brilliant Web engineer, whose vision is tempered only by his ability to do the hard labor to make that vision reality. He has influenced me greatly in my growth as a Web designer, and his contributions to this project and my life are immeasurable. Phil Stevens remains the central catalyst for how I came to be a Web designer. His vast knowledge rings clearly through every page here, and his friendship is an invaluable part of my life. Valerie Rogers deserves the highest praise for diving into uncharted waters and supporting this project with her friendship, warmth, and dedication. Steve Sloan offers powerful, sophisticated illustration to these pages, and I feel very fortunate to have met and befriended him through this project. Joe Forkan has charmed me and will surely do so others when they see the marvelous cartoon illustrations that appear in this book. Read his comic strip, Staggering Heights, appearing every Wednesday evening at: http://desert.net/tw/current/backpage.htm.

To C. Scott Convery for his early contributions to this book, and especially for the memory of what was good between us.

Matt Straznitskas of BrainBug L.L.C. embodies the concept of Web design. His ideas will undoubtedly become foundations of future media. Matt and I met online—for reasons completely unrelated to work—years ago. Thanks for growing up with me and so often guiding the way, M@.

Highlighted appreciation to Dr. Joel Snyder and Jan Trumbo of Opus One, without whom this book or my education as a Web designer would never have happened.

Research assistants Lee Anne Phillips, Lois Patterson, and Deborah D.K. Gerber provided excellent work. I am deeply indebted to them, and to the contributions they made to the organization and preparation of the appendices. Much of their wit and wisdom remain intact in those sections. A special thanks to the Spiderwoman list, and all the Spiderwomen out there weaving Webs. You go, Webgrrls!

For their input and general support, Jason Steed, Julie Boyce, and all the DesertNet denizens. Douglas Biggers, Dan Huff, and John Hankinson and each of the staff members of the Tucson Weekly. Brock Meeks of Wired and HotWired for his tenacity as a pioneer of this brave new world and participation as mentor. To my staff on the Microsoft Network, my original beginnings on GEnie, personal friends Patrick Curley, Claire Wudowsky, Rich Carson, John Kline, Ph.D., Dale and Tina Roose, and to Scott La Rochelle, who each gave me tools to begin the journey. Dr. Patricia Hursh, Cantrell Maryott, and Don Bowes for helping me in body and spirit. Patty Sundberg, Amy Allen, and Sapphire for the music. Michael Metzger for the opportunity to change anger into love through online communications. Susan Lee Benson and Susan Fleming for love and friendship. To all my wonderful friends, I am so blessed that simply naming you one by one would fill an entire book. I am deeply grateful for your love.

Don Roche, Alan Harris, Jeff Ennis, Debbi Abshier and all of the good people at Prima Publishing, I acknowledge for the opportunity, and their confidence in my vision. A very heartfelt thanks to Tim Huddleston, who was the book's shepherd during the actual writing stage and became a trusted mentor and guide through this process. His support is largely the reason this book ever made it to publication. For his quiet wisdom and important contributions I am forever in his debt.

To my brother Linus, who keeps me laughing, my brother Morris for his love, and my step-dad Ollie for his gentle presence in our lives.

Finally, to the memories of Timothy Leary and Frank Zappa—both who influenced me in curious ways, and both who understood the vision and reality of the Web long before it ever was.

Introduction

Just Another Book on How to Write a Home Page?

Professional Web Design: Theory and Methods on the Cutting Edge does not seek to teach people how to write a home page but rather examines the professional Web design experience in detail. There are many excellent books on Hypertext Markup Language (HTML), graphic design, multiple media, programming, systems administration, and Internet marketing. This book addresses the combined needs of the Web design specialist, meeting his or her challenges with theoretical paradigms as well as practical, on-hand methodology and solutions for common problems.

In the first section, "Searching for a Paradigm: New Media and Web Design," we explore components of design as well as fundamental concepts in new media. The intent is to offer background, ideas, and options for Web designers—in both the solo and team model—to use as a means for moving ahead in a profession that is placing increased demands on their knowledge base. The designer with exposure to the history of the Web, new media theory, and more information on where to study such concepts in detail will naturally be better equipped to compete on a practical level with the numerous individuals and companies cropping up during this exciting but unruly time. This section culminates in the offering of a new paradigm for Web designers, offering up a comprehensive model for the interactive age.

The second section, "Building a Foundation: Current Challenges for the Web Designer" more aggressively examines the history, foundations, and philosophy behind the Web and its varied components. HTML standards and a recommended process for speedier implementation of those standards are discussed. Browser technology—perhaps the most challenging current aspect of Web design—is examined in detail. Within this section is a comprehensive selection of common browsers and their related features. At this point in the book we begin moving away from the theoretical background and into more practical points of information.

The third section, "The Process of Creating Web Sites," studies the key areas of the Web design process and offers a virtual tour guide through that process—showing case scenarios in a step-by-step fashion. Problem spots are examined in detail, and many helpful examples are provided for any Web designer to use as a reference in his or her own process.

Finally, *Professional Web Design* focuses intently on the individual areas of the field in the book's fourth section, "Web Design Technology in Practice." By offering an overview of the current environment of such Web disciplines as copy writing, graphics, systems administration, special of such Web disciplines as copy writing, graphics, systems administration, special programming, HTML, and marketing, the reader will learn about trouble spots, find answers to specific, common challenges, and have a hands-on set of resources. With these tools, *Web Design* helps a designer bring any model of virtuoso talent to a state of perfection and grow beyond simply being a designer to becoming a master of the field.

Assumptions about the Reader

Although other resources exist for Web designers, there currently is a pervasive need for new resources that reach right to the heart of problems encountered by professionals in the field. Whether you are a lone Webmaster, one member of a developing team, or someone interested in the field as part of your future, you'll find that this book addresses the comprehensive needs of the professional.

The typical reader of this book will have some knowledge of Web technologies, access to the Web, and plenty of computer hardware and software to do the job. More specifically, you will probably have had some exposure to HTML coding and graphic design, along with some further breadth of experience: perhaps advanced programming skills, or perhaps dynamic marketing experience and ideas. Even without these resources, *Professional Web Design* can be quite helpful, especially in providing a contemporary overview of what the job entails.

What is most important is that readers come to this book as part of a serious study of Web design as a profession, with an interest in learning more about the past, current, and future issues in Web design. Such readers will find *Web Design* an excellent starting point for future study, as well as a practical resource for specific challenges that arise during the process of working in the profession.

A Note From the Author

Most of the web design and team-model paradigm is based on my experiences as the Web Design Director for DesertNet Designs, the design group affiliated with DesertNet, the largest Web content provider in the southwestern United States. We maintain offices in a restored adobe building in the Barrio Viejo District of Tucson, Arizona. With some of the hottest talent around, DesertNet is truly proud of its accomplishments as providers of Web-based entertainment, journalism, and online marketing. This book would have been impossible to write without the distinct experience of the many members of the DesertNet team, who always bring significant insight and tremendous enthusiasm to their Web work.

Part I

Searching for a Paradigm:
New Media and Web Design

chapter 1

A Brave New World

"Cyberspace", "the ethers," "surfing the Net"—all are euphemisms for a fast-moving, computer-based, and publicly accessible technology that, until only recently, was both laughed at and feared. As MIT's famed Nicholas Negroponte says in his book *Being Digital*, "Computing is not about computers any more. It is about living." Computers—particularly as communication tools—are being used daily by people the world over, and from all walks of life. Designing in this new field requires not only technical and creative skills but an understanding of how we as people interact—first with each other, and then with the computer-based environment.

Whether it's in the news, on television, the subject of films, or discussed in the board room, the hot news of the '90s is that computers are a central part of our lives and lifestyles. Even more specifically, the use of communications technology is fast becoming part of millions of people's daily routines—whether it be via commercial services such as America Online or the still-free ranges of the Internet.

From the news hounds searching out the top headlines with their morning espresso, to the lonely hearts seeking romance in the middle of a dark night, society has accepted computers as a means of information exchange and communication. This acceptance is so widespread that PCs and modems are becoming "household objects" as familiar as our televisions, VCRs, and radios. The vast difference with this technology, of course, is that it is interactive. The PC's interactive capabilities grant the individual much more power to exercise free will in deciding what he or she wants served up on that new Pentium or Power PC.

Interactive media are the media of a new culture. The Internet—specifically the World Wide Web—is a popular and expanding matrix for these contemporary media. It is a brand new baby, constantly absorbing material and turning out bright-eyed ideas. It is often irritable as it struggles to comprehend its own existence, and at other times it is joyous with new discovery, inconsistent in routine but always brave as it ventures to take its first steps toward vast, incomprehensible possibilities in a new world.

When World Wide Web technology went public on a grand scale, many people realized that putting up a home page on the Web wasn't difficult. Doing so became a trend among academics and Net heads alike. As time went on and a broader audience heard the electronic surf's enticing call, the Web rapidly became a vast and varied entanglement showcasing everything from the latest medical research to Mildred and Marvin's 75th anniversary announcement.

To draw again from Negroponte, this "pull"—the hunger of the public for interactive, personal media—is creating a demand for the creation of Web documents that not only inform but communicate, sell, and entertain. It has become a virtual juggling act to create the tools, methods, and delivery mechanisms as dynamically and quickly as public pull demands. This is where the concept of Web design as a profession enters.

The days of gray, over-linked, and left-aligned pages on the Web are numbered—left to the text-dominant needs of research institutions and the hallowed halls of academia. Commercial enterprises—themselves motivated by public interest—demand professionally designed and thoughtful sites. Such sites necessitate the leadership of individuals or groups with an increasingly sophisticated balance and range of skills.

The One-Man Band

Currently, many solo Web designers, often referred to as "Webmasters," are responsible for the varied aspects of Web development. Whether due to budgetary concerns or the simple fact that the medium is so new that no model really exists for the act of making Web sites, a great deal of responsibility falls on individual Webmasters. However, recent advances in technology are proving that the One-Man Band model may not be realistic any more.

In an article appearing in *Internet World* magazine, June 1996, Dr. Joel Snyder sheds light on the changing demands being placed on Web designers. "If someone insists that he can do the entire job alone, pass him up" Snyder advises—harsh words to the Webmaster who performs Web weaving daily and does it well. Nevertheless, the point is that the Web and its technologies are evolving so fast as to create new and more complex conditions for the designer.

Snyder suggests a four-person team approach, including a team leader, a programmer, a graphic artist, and the client. Although the suggestions within *Professional Web Design* can be used by the lone Webmaster as well as members of a professional design team, like Snyder, this book strongly favors a progressive, team model for Web design. It is in this spirit that we return time and again to the team paradigm, despite our continued respect for the Webmaster who works alone.

The Orchestral Model

When a symphony orchestra rehearses, it is the job of the conductor to unite the talent into a combined and elegant effort. Each individual may be a virtuoso on a specific instrument, but the symphony itself cannot succeed if the group relationship is not guided with strength and direction. A conductor sets the pace, points out flaws, leads, and guides the instruments of the orchestra toward a full and ultimately interactive expression.

The professional Web designer plays a similar role, albeit in a vastly different medium of expression. He or she must evaluate the big picture, set the stage, and counsel the talent in order for the final outcome to be melodic and in tune.

Furthermore, the challenges imposed by radically and rapidly changing technologies and a lack of agreed-upon standards require the Web designer to pave his or her own highway. In an industry that is at best described as transitional, competitive, and outright explosive, only Web designers with vision can propel virtuoso talent toward the most desired of destinations: an effective and attractive Web site.

Historical Issues as Contemporary Problems

Figure 1-1 show us that the World Wide Web has been absorbed into the realm of commercial media. As many Web professionals are aware, the Internet originally grew out of academic, military, and research-based organizations as a way to trade information quickly and safely. In the United States, agencies such as the National Science Foundation (NSF) made significant contributions to this new and efficient "network of networks" that many now fondly refer to as the "Net."

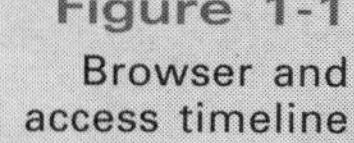

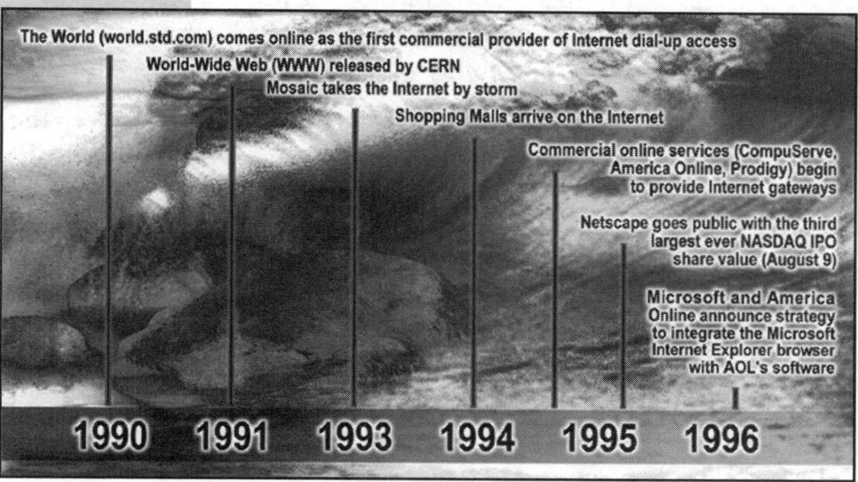
The World (world.std.com) comes online as the first commercial provider of Internet dial-up access
World-Wide Web (WWW) released by CERN
Mosaic takes the Internet by storm
Shopping Malls arrive on the Internet
Commercial online services (CompuServe, America Online, Prodigy) begin to provide Internet gateways
Netscape goes public with the third largest ever NASDAQ IPO share value (August 9)
Microsoft and America Online announce strategy to integrate the Microsoft Internet Explorer browser with AOL's software
1990
1991
1993
1994
1995
1996

Figure 1-1 Browser and access timeline

In the mid-to-late 1980s several commercial online services such as America Online, CompuServe, Prodigy, and GEnie appeared, appealing to business and entertainment needs. As the home PC phenomenon spread, these services became a very profitable marketplace for those with wares to sell. It wasn't long before entrepreneurs figured out that the Internet, which was cheaper and more widespread, was a great alternative to these higher-priced and closed networks. By the early 1990s, commercial Internet Service Providers (ISPs) began appearing, offering text-based services to people at very reasonable prices.

The Internet rapidly became a sexy subject in the traditional media, and people were jumping on for a vast variety of motives. The desire to research, interact, soapbox, or just sate a pervasive curiosity motivated many to find out what a modem really does. By the mid 1990s, the once academic and research-based Internet was overrun—much to the chagrin of the academics—by a new diverse population with wide-ranging needs.

It didn't take long for organizations interested in commerce to notice the changing demographics and growing population of the Internet. In 1993 Mosaic, the first graphic Web browser, hit the mainstream market and caused the initial surge of business activity on the Web. This activity created strains on the funding institutions behind the

Internet—and conflicts of interest. By 1995, the National Science Foundation had pulled most of its support out, and the Web became the responsibility of larger, commercial organizations.

The private networks are still scrambling to keep their competitive edge by providing Internet gateways for their clients. It's a constant battle, sometimes one that is lost, as seen in the case of General Electric's GEnie, which almost succumbed to internal problems and external marketing issues and was sold, nearly defunct, in early 1996. America Online, Prodigy, and CompuServe must constantly find new ways to meet the needs of their clients—many of whom are interested in the quality local, or in-house, content these services provide. These commercial services must also cater to their newer members, who care primarily about the Internet, and specifically the World Wide Web.

What Do These Issues Mean to the Web Designer?

While these issues are interesting historically, they create a specific set of challenges to the field of Web design. The multiple ways various systems handle the growing quantity of data, and the way that the Internet is presented—often erroneously—to the public, weave a very tangled web indeed.

Commercial networks such as CompuServe handle their gatewayed Web data differently than Internet Service Providers, without necessarily explaining to end users what effect that data management will have on bandwidth, speed, and caching. The consumers may not notice, but designers must be aware of such problems in order to best do their work. Traditional media depict different faces of the Internet—sometimes accurately, sometimes reporting information that might be detrimental to the field of professional Web design. A good example is the press's ongoing attempt to provide statistical information about the Web; this information is usually inaccurate because of the high speed changes on the Web or the bias of the particular medium in question. In the end, this type of misinformation is confusing to the public—and to the Web designer's prospective clients—who want solid facts and numbers.

Changes in the telecommunications industry also create challenges for the designer. Corporate machinations occur daily, changing the design environment with a single electronic funds transfer or merger. This process was exemplified when Microsoft, in a concerted effort with America Online, announced that the Microsoft Web browser, Internet Explorer, would be packaged with America Online's software as of early fall 1996.

News of this nature is of paramount importance to the Web designer attempting to surf a tidal wave. In essence, it means that the Netscape Web browser, which currently holds the majority of the free-browser market, will have a heavy competitor. This places the HTML standards issues and browser development—the meat and potatoes of how designers design Web sites—onto the hot plate. How it all pans out is truly anyone's guess, but these events certainly demonstrate that big players with big money are hashing out big issues at the very same moment the Web designer is trying to do his or her job.

Daily Fiber

Another enormous issue is *bandwidth*, which is the amount of data that can pass through a specific space in a given period of time. Bandwidth affects design decisions for a variety of technologies including graphics, special programming, and multiple media additions such as animation and audio. Designers must know their entire audience and consider their audience's access limitations or advantage.

Two years ago home computers did not come with modems as a standard feature. Now they do, but some major manufacturers are still packaging 14.4 bits per second (bps) modems with their computers, which are too slow for the best Web viewing and cause Web designers to be cautious in the choice of graphics and unique functions they will add to particular sites. Conversely, people with more than an avid interest in the Web are able to afford 28.8 bps modems, and those on the high end of the industry often have 56k frame relay access or better.

Even more dramatic is the recent offering in many areas of Integrated Services Digital Network (ISDN) access at affordable rates . Many cities around the world have fiber optic cable already in place. Cable modems, which offer speeds greater than two megabits per second (mbps), are on tomorrow's menu. The impact that increased bandwidth will have on the future of the Web is beyond projection, but it is safe to say that many of the debates regarding graphics, animation, or other multiple media on the Web will rapidly become passé.

As this discussion demonstrates, the Web designer's environment is simultaneously exhilarating and frustrating. Web designers are continually challenged by both internal and external industry issues, as well as the rapid shifts within the technological environment. A designer, to return to the metaphor, begins rehearsal cringing at the mismatched sounds of the untuned orchestra but knowing that its potential is limitless and feeling a profound sense of accomplishment when instruments find their harmonies.

chapter 2

What is Web Design?

"Web Design" means taking advantage of the various elements supported by the World Wide Web—including text, images, audio, and animation—and orchestrating them to create a Web site that embraces the opportunities actualized by Web technology. It is not static; it utilizes multiple media. It is not two-dimensional, but rather it seeks to use images with depth and dimension. It is not verbose, attempting instead to create content that is well-written and extremely concise. Web design is not simply an electronic business card or resume, nor is it traditional advertising. Web design is much more than taking a printed page and scanning it, tossing some HTML tags around it, and placing it on a Web server.

Rather, a successful design incorporates the hypertextual, contextual, and sensory realms and combines them with effective programming and administrative and marketing strategies. Ultimately, Web design is the creation of high-impact presence for companies and organizations seeking representation on the Internet.

Components of Design

In the fourth part of *Professional Web Design,* "Web Design Technology in Practice," the reader will find detailed information regarding the practical uses of each of these ingredients. For the purposes of this foundational chapter, Web design incorporates, but is not limited to, the components described here. It is important to note that—while all of these elements are part of what a Web designer needs to understand—how and when they are to be applied are critical choices a Web designer must make. In many instances, multimedia presentations or complicated programming will extend far beyond the budgetary constraints and practical needs of a given client. In other scenarios, these elements will all be part of a Web site, carefully chosen to provide for an appropriate client need.

- **Content and copy writing.** Content is the most fundamental aspect of Web design because without content to share, the Web would serve little purpose. But what content should be put on a Web site, and how should that content be displayed? Professional Web design honors high writing and copy editing standards, providing streamlined, attractive, appropriate language as part of any well-designed site.

- **Hypertext markup language** (HTML). HTML is the language of the Web—the essential component without which nothing else could exist. It is not a difficult or even highly technical scripting language, which is why so many hobbyists and entrepreneurs have said "Hey, I can do this!" For the professional Web designer, therefore, the challenge is not in the doing, but in doing well. Contemporary Web design demands a thorough knowledge and the skill to use it to cross browser barriers. Experience teaches the professional Web designer when to stick to HTML standards and when to ignore them. Creativity and design sensibilities lead us to push to the cutting edge of HTML design—and even to redefine the cutting edge—without alienating an audience.

- **Graphic design.** Not long ago, graphics weren't even an issue on the Net. Then suddenly, they became a hot issue—under challenge as being superfluous. There are still purists who insist that graphics are a complete waste of Web resources, but these individuals are not in the *business* of making Web sites. Graphic design on the Web has become a necessity in the commercial and competitive realm, and the fact remains that most Web graphics are very poor. Even high-quality print artists make inappropriate design choices for the Web because they do not have an understanding of the simple and unique tools available to them. Quality Web design means using graphics, learning the programs and tools that best create them, and designing cleverly, meeting a variety of browser and bandwidth requirements.

- **Multimedia.** New technologies are making multimedia presentations a reality on the Web. Audio and video are already available as externally viewable media; in fact, they can be viewed right in-line in some browsers. Plug-in technologies such as Real Audio and multimedia players such as Shockwave are creating an atmosphere in which it is very easy to see that the future of the Web not only is graphical but incorporates movement, sound, *and* interactivity simultaneously.

- **Advanced programming.** Common Gateway Interface (CGI) scripts have allowed for fun and unusual things to occur on the Web for some time now. These include fill-out forms for shopping, creation of interactive games, and even in-line animation. With the recent introduction of Java and JavaScript, and upcoming technologies such as Microsoft's ActiveX and Visual Basic Script, new interactive choices are being created for Web users nearly every day. But for Web designers who want to incorporate these interactive features into their Web sites, programming skills are a must. Knowledge of advanced languages is becoming increasingly important for those interested in working on progressive Web sites.
- **Systems administration.** Some might wonder "what on earth does systems administration have to do with designing a Web site?" Well, it follows a theatrical metaphor: If you cannot light the stage, no other aspect of the production will be seen, and therefore it is useless. A Web site must be hosted on a Web server, and the more designers know about how that is done, the better able they are to place or recommend to their clients how and where to place their designs with providers that are stable, secure, and effective at serving up the final product.
- **Marketing.** What if I built a Web site and nobody came? If my goal is to create presence for a client and I do not follow through on strategies to bring people to that site, I have failed that client completely. Strategies ranging from simply knowing how and where to index sites to aggressive online and other marketing options are crucial to the process of successful design.

Fundamental Concepts in New Media

You have doubtless heard the term "new media" used in recent months. But what does the term mean? *New media* means the convergence of more traditional types of media such as text, two- and three-dimensional graphics, audio, video, and animation, into interactivity. The World Wide Web is probably the best example of new media in action, since it incorporates many common aspects of traditional media in a new and different setting. Writing, graphic art, audio and video presentations—all of these are familiar and now thought of as "traditional" media (see Figure 2-1).

The new media concept takes the components of these traditional media, puts them in an interactive setting, and jumbles them up so that they become intertwined. It is this intertwining that creates new media. The result is connected to us personally—an active, choice-driven environment rather than the passive media most people in the latter part of the twentieth century know and understand.

Imagine the following scenario. A child is watching cartoons on television. He laughs at the antics of the characters, he is involved with them on a certain level, but cannot touch them, cannot invoke them at will, and cannot interact with them. Sit another child down at a computer with an educational CD-ROM, and suddenly she can choose her direction, interact with characters, and make decisions on how and when she wants to involve herself with any given idea.

Now, take this model a step further, adding live interaction with other information and people—often at opposite ends of the earth—and an entirely new possibility is born. We have left the domain of passive, directed information absorption and entered a new realm where action, interaction, and reaction exist on demand.

Figure 2-1
Traditional media

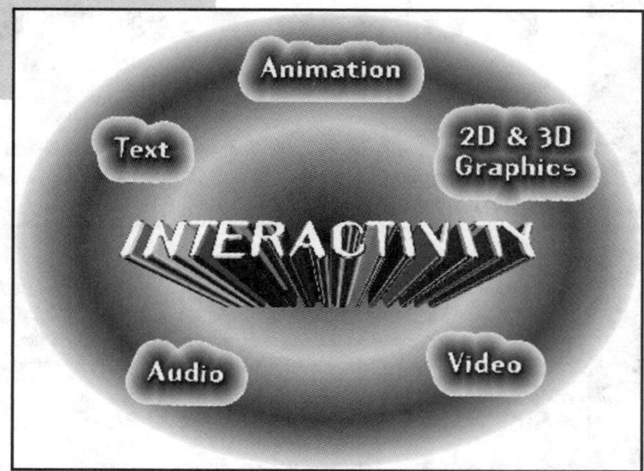

In Web design, interactivity results from the designer providing options for the end user. In some cases this will be as simple as the way a site is navigated, with clickable options and alternatives for individuals to select at will. In more advanced examples, fill-out forms, interactive games, and forum discussion groups might be appropriate for a given site, and it is the Web designer's job to decide when, where, and how to employ such advanced technologies, which are largely dependent on high-level programming. A Web designer must stay ahead of new media concepts and related technologies, and members of his or her team must be ready and capable of implementing such technology for the appropriate Web site.

One exciting place that the new media concept is being put into action is in online journalism. Certain online Web sites are encouraging reader interaction and feedback. For an excellent example of this type of new media in action, visit the *Tucson Weekly* site (see Figure 2-2). Notice how the mature use of text, graphics, and even occasional sound mixes with the opportunity for readers to post to forums related to hot topic areas, as well as the option to write directly to many of the writers, editors, and other staff involved with this alternative weekly newspaper.

Figure 2-2 New media in encouraging reader interaction and feedback action: http://desert.net/tw/

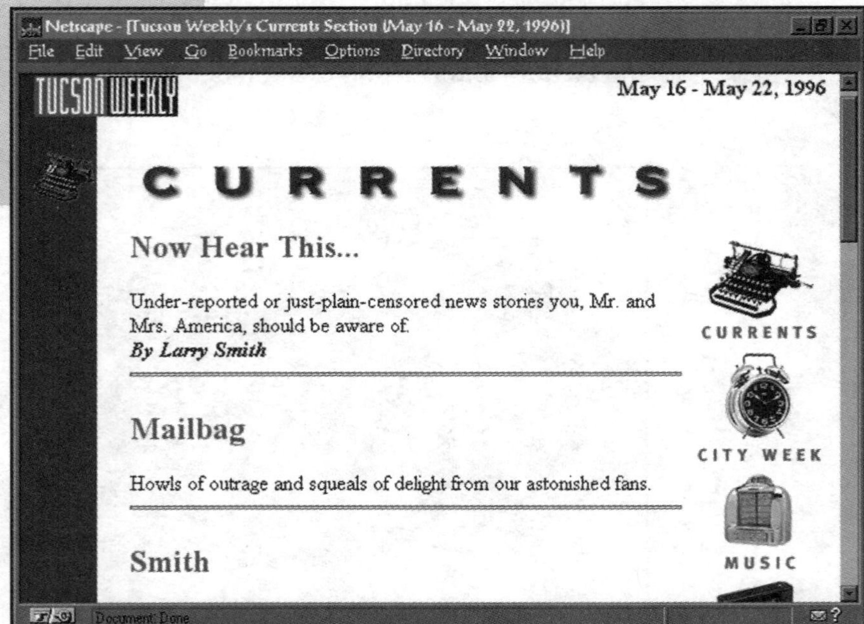

A more commercial application is the use of interactive forums and games on a Web site that sells recreational vehicles. Why on earth would an RV outlet place this kind of interactivity on its site? In this case, the appeal is that there is almost a subculture of RV fans traveling around. In order to make this Web site useful in a practical and fun fashion as well as showcasing products, an interactive forum and ongoing story game add intrigue and appeal. Visit http://desert.net/beaudryrv/ for a look at how interactivity can serve a commercial purpose and complement rather than deter from good site design (Figure 2-3).

Hypermedia and Nonlinear Thought

As discussed earlier, the idea of enabling users to be active rather than passive is inherent in new media experiences, such as CD-ROM and video games. This active-versus-passive notion is also demonstrated on the Web in the Web's fundamental connective tissue: hypertext, hyperlinking, or hypermedia. By using highlighting and colors, and by designating "hot" areas within a Web document, we can navigate the Web and go from one area to another immediately. Sometimes this

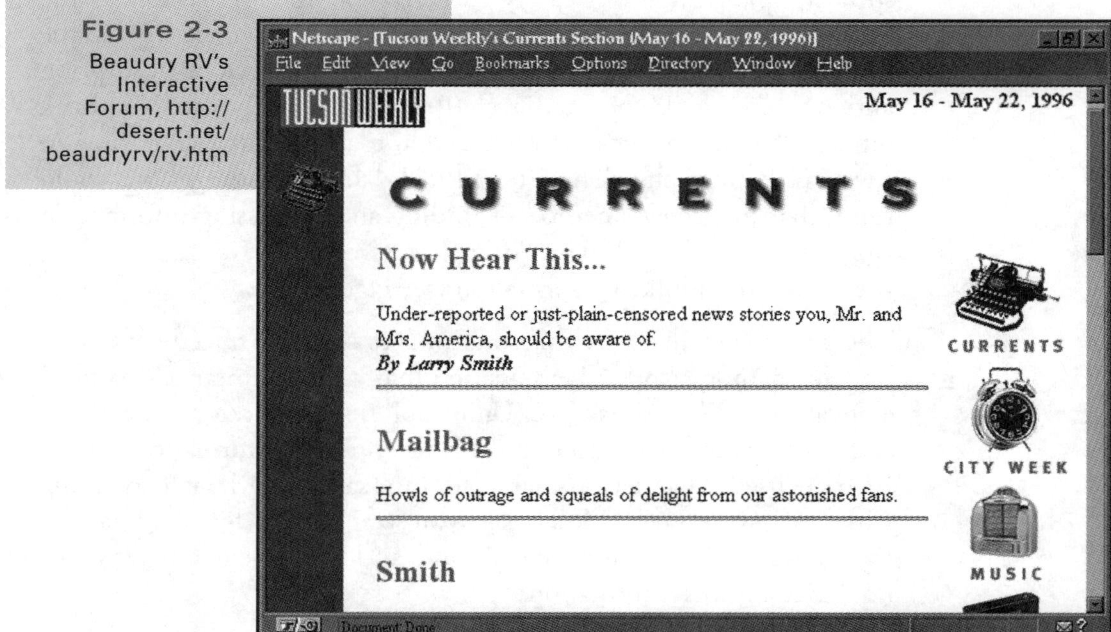

Figure 2-3
Beaudry RV's Interactive Forum, http://desert.net/beaudryrv/rv.htm

means simply moving to a different spot within the same Web site, and other times it means jumping to a site with related information. That information might be on a server half a world away, but to the individual, the important thing is that it is accessible.

It is *hypermedia* that creates the virtual silk strands of information on the Web. Hypermedia is exciting because its content is driven only in part by the designer—it is navigated by individuals, each of whom might choose to go about the task independently. This creates an interactive rather than passive relationship between the user and the content. Users chart their own course through the highways and byways of a site, and the other sites it links to, depending upon the way the links appeal to them. The discovery process within this journey is the essence of new media and exemplifies nonlinear thinking.

What is absolutely fascinating about this interactivity between individuals and hypermedia is that it is completely antithetical to how the contemporary western mind is accustomed to dealing with information. Typically, we have learned to read left-to-right, we receive information passively from a singular source, and process information in a linear fashion. Hypermedia is not linear. It moves tangentially, spirally, spherically, but rarely in a straight line. This idea is the fundamental reason why the Web stands to be a potent element in the future of human development as it pertains to information absorption and processing. Hypermedia challenges the individual to think differently than how he or she was taught to think, but also to think in a way the brain itself will have no difficulty understanding. One would think that this "new" method of finding and processing information would be quite natural to us. After all, neural pathways are not linear; they are webs of linked information (see Figure 2-4).

The best way to analogize this concept is to compare it to the way that human memory works. Let's assume that an acquaintance's name is equivalent to a Web site's URL (Uniform Resource Locator—the virtual address at which it resides), and his face, to the information on the Web site itself. That person's name, for fun's sake, is Earl. I'm conversing with a pal, who says, "Molly, have you seen Earl lately?" An image of Earl comes to the forefront of my mind, and I am able to answer yes or no, based on this information.

Figure 2-4
The Neural Web

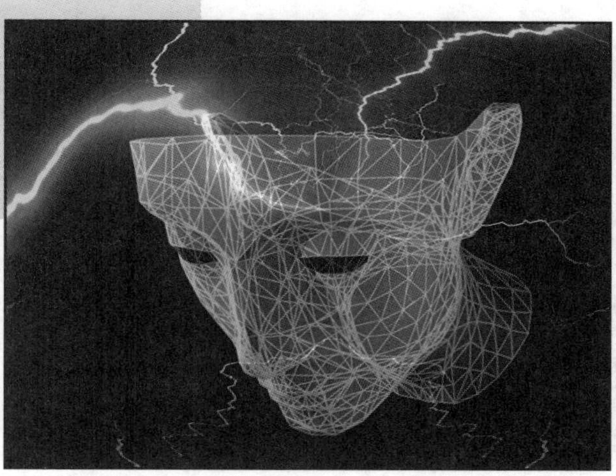

World Wide Web Design Service Agreement

Client Information

But the information that makes up Earl's image is not stored all in one file, or one part of my brain. It is, in fact, broken up into minute pieces of memory data and strewn far and wide in various neural pockets, just as various bits of information on that Web site is located in different files or directories. In order to put together the image of Earl, my brain has to collect all of the bits of data—eyes, nose, mouth, ears, body—by rapidly traveling on a variety of neural pathways and ultimately putting them together in one cohesive piece. If these processes work, I end up with the image of Earl.

This is a nonlinear procedure, as are the data retrieval and circuitry of a Web site. One piece fits into the next piece and so on, but they refer back to one another; connect over other, unrelated masses of information; and run in the tangents, spirals, and spheres described earlier in order to end up on my browser as a fully integrated Web site. It is this process and this parallel that create an opportunity for endless, creative discovery in educational and human growth potential (see Figure 2-5).

Web designers will only benefit from understanding these interesting concepts and theories. Not only will these ideas aid them in deciding how and when to use various interactive, multiple media as part of a given site's design, but they will also enable them to think about how to offer people ways in which to have a lot of fun while visiting a site. Moreover, with this type of knowledge, Web designers essentially plant

Figure 2-5 Pathways of data on the World Wide Web

seeds in fertile ground for high-quality communications. Even in the case of a commercial site, as exemplified by the Beaudry RV design, the opportunity for education, humor, and personal advancement exists. This is the Web at its finest—a fun, informative, effective marketing tool that has the opportunity to stimulate the mind instead of numbing it, as passive media so often have done.

Precision Content

One of the essential elements of new media is the ability to use interactivity as a means to precisely communicate multiple thoughts, ideas, and data. We already have technical ways of accommodating large amounts of text for retrieval from the Internet. A World Wide Web site may contain access to such documents, but within the definition of new media, content presentation demands concise expression.

In a textbook, we are allowed the liberty to explore complicated ideas within hundreds or thousands of pages. This type of written exploration simply cannot occur on the Web, mostly due to the nature of the on-screen environment. In some instances, such as when people use commercial services for access, time online costs money, and that is a consideration as well. Web surfers seem to want to have their ideas snappy, quick, and concise. Ideas must be clear, written much more like headlines than detailed paragraphs. The concept is to catch the reader's eye, quickly get to the point of the site, and then offer greater details as necessary.

Hypermedia can help or hinder this process, depending upon how it is used. If a hyperlink to another document is placed in the first sentence of a Web site introduction, there is a chance of losing a visitor within the first several seconds of his or her visit. At the other extreme, if no hypermedia is used within a site, the strengths of the Web are not being exploited. It takes a strong mix of writing skills and good instinct to combine hypermedia with short, sharp language to get right to, rather than away from, the point of a site.

Sensory Experience

With today's browser and bandwidth capabilities, sites exploiting multiple media have become the norm. At the very least, most sites will use language and graphics to communicate their message. Technologies such as the multimedia Shockwave, or real-time streamed audio from Real Audio, have allowed for the distribution of complete multimedia presentations.

The multiple media concept is currently one of the most difficult issues in Web design. There was a time when a graphical site with large, cumbersome graphics would cause a visitor to leave before accessing the information there. Now, with the Web having shifted from textual information to a visually rich environment with enhanced ability to create quick-loading, attractive graphics, the opposite is often true. Many individuals will avoid a site with no graphics or design, thinking perhaps that it is an information-only site, with no compelling interactive experience available.

Contemporary Web design must then find a way to incorporate multiple media, particularly graphics, and maintain integrity of content without ever losing hold of the site's primary goal. A quality Web design will meet the needs of the diverse population viewing the material and make accommodations for as many browser types and bandwidth access speeds as possible, allowing for simultaneous creativity and functionality.

Weaving It Together

With some theoretical background on the components of design, and how these components interrelate with choices in a changing technology, individuals interested in professionally designing Web sites are better prepared to look at what it takes to be a Web designer. Furthermore, an understanding of the foundations of new media helps a Web designer comprehend the more subtle mechanisms of how the Web actually works, and how he or she as an individual can use technology in creative, positive ways to weave extraordinary, flexible, yet cohesive Web sites.

chapter 3

What is a Web Designer?

Search for the keywords Web designer on any major Web search engine, and you'll find hundreds if not thousands of individuals who are advertising Web design services. Currently there are no existing professional or educational prerequisites that give these individuals certification; anyone can claim the title. Many people who profess to be Web designers actually do have the experience and technique to back up their claim; a vast number of them, however, do not.

Because the current atmosphere of the Web is variegated, this book's model—to have a designer at the core of a full team of varied talents—is undeniably no more than an ideal. Many present designers are responsible for the entirety of site production. This situation may be due to budgetary concerns or a lack of awareness of the multiple skills required of designers. In the case of either the single designer or the evolving design team, knowledge of both the science and art of the Web must be combined with exceptional skill in human and computer-based communications.

Designers and Masters

This book by no means leaves out the single Webmaster, who is more greatly challenged by having to wear many hats and to wear them well. We are examining introductory theory and applying it to a pervasive need to determine the difference between the home page hobbyist and the professional Web design outfit. Our aim is to suggest a paradigm for Web design that embraces all the sophisticated needs of the job. This paradigm points to the fact that HTML script writing, graphic design, technical writing and copy editing, systems administration, marketing, and client relations are best coordinated by the Web designer but carried out by individuals highly trained in those specific and demanding fields.

Look at the newness of the Web itself; it's only a few years old, and, as we've described, conventions change daily and standards do not keep step with convention. Examine the trendiness that surrounds the Internet, and you'll quickly find that many entrepreneurs have jumped on the bandwagon trying to make a quick—and often dirty—buck.

Pick up any book on HTML, and it is obvious that the subject isn't nearly as difficult to master as organic chemistry. Combine these facts with easy and cheap ISP access, and it's easy to see how literally anyone can learn enough about the Web to put up a page and hang out a virtual shingle inviting business (see Figure 3-1).

But design? As Chapter 2 demonstrates, there are many components to Web design that are far more complex than many people who claim to be Web designers understand. As a result, very poor examples of Web design (and Web designers) exist. These examples cast a shadow over progressive and refined designers, including young designers struggling to learn what they can in a serious attempt to become masters of the field. These varied examples have the potential to confuse the consumer and give the Web design field an inconsistent reputation.

Figure 3-1
An example of amateur but prevalent design practice

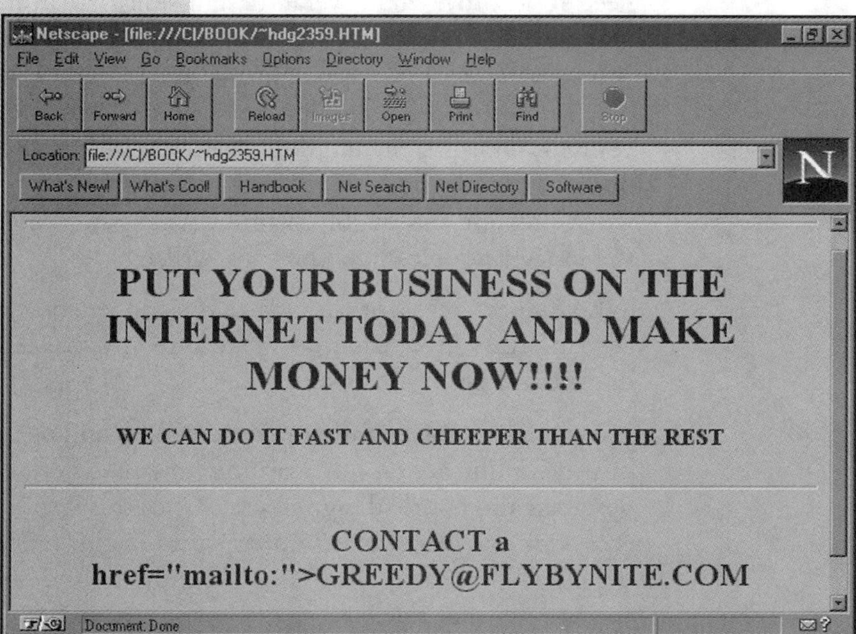

If you are a Web designer and aren't confident that your work is in the professional range, or if you are concerned that it become so, ask yourself some of the following simple questions:

- Do my pages download evenly and with reasonable speed?
- Is the balance between design and content right for my audience?
- Are too many elements not pertinent to the subject matter here?
- Is the text clear and concise, free of spelling errors and grammatical blunders?
- Do all my links work?
- Does all my programming and special scripting function?

Although these are preliminary questions, they are an excellent starting point to examine your site and determine some areas in which you might need to improve your overall design skills. For fun, and to see where you as a designer need the most help, I highly recommend visiting Mirsky's Worst of the Web at http://mirsky.com/wow/ (see Figure 3-2). This humorous site keeps links to the worst Web pages—featuring lousy content, poor design, and foul programming, this site is filled with the opportunity to visit the Web's truly worst examples. Visit any of Mirsky's worst sites and thoroughly examine what you find. Look at the design, the HTML source code, the copy writing.

Where does your work fit in? Is it stronger in some ways? Weak in certain areas? How can you make sure any professional site of yours doesn't end up on this list?

Fortunately, public awareness is increasing, and people who spend a lot of time online are rapidly learning how to differentiate between well-designed and poorly designed sites. Until this is the rule rather than the exception, however, it is imperative to begin defining what the Web designer's ideal background and role truly are, and how you as a designer can best fill that role.

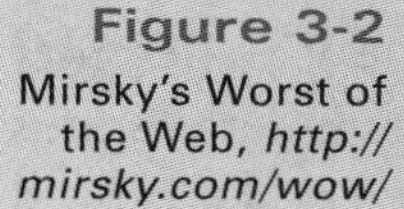

Figure 3-2
Mirsky's Worst of the Web, *http://mirsky.com/wow/*

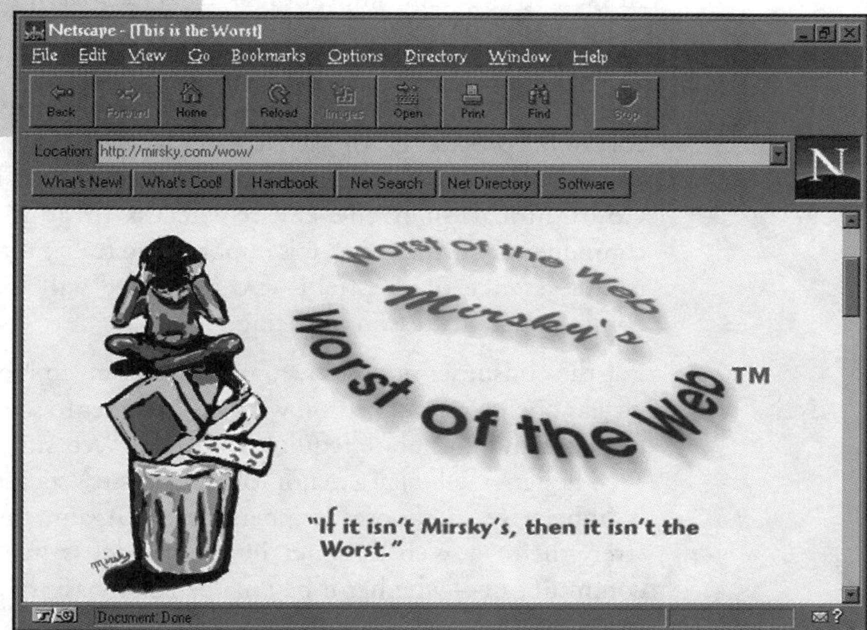

Professional Experience

Most Web designers who are doing the job well come from a variety of backgrounds, including graphic design and multimedia, computer science, and marketing. But a good Web designer is the person, regardless of professional background, who has the ability to integrate diverse concepts—particularly to integrate liberal arts and technological science. This requires a certain amount of experience, which eventually may come from evolving educational programs and appropriate training.

It's an excellent rule of thumb that an aspiring Web designer should become familiar with media in general, emphasizing new media (as defined in the previous chapters) and the concepts that the Web embraces. A Web designer must have conceptual skills, be a good copy writer and editor, and also understand fundamental concepts of human communication.

In fact, strong communication skills are critical for a Web designer. Many aspects of Web design can be outsourced, and the Web designer in an ideal paradigm will be relying on many others to complete various aspects of Web site design. It is the Web designer who is the central core of the process. He or she must be able to deal with clients, Internet Service Providers, staff, and vendors of other, related services. Communication is the key to success in administrating these components. Furthermore, it is important to realize that communication is the essence of the field—no Web site will work if it fails to communicate its reason for being.

For the consumer or employer, it is important to look at portfolios as well as open communication with the designer to see if he or she meets personal and corporate requirements. If a Web site is to succeed, the Web designer will play a major role in that site's success. Accordingly, it is imperative to choose designers wisely. Again, the area of greatest strength for a Web designer in this model is his or her ability to communicate—whether it be on a personal basis or a virtual one.

Few professional development options exist for aspiring Web designers. Most in the field have learned by doing—by taking the throw the baby in the pool and see if it can swim approach. This can very often be an excellent way to learn—lessons from this kind of experience don't come easily—and the dedicated individual will take his or her mistakes and subsequent learning to heart. The person involved in the field to make a quick dollar is rarely going to analyze his or her experiences but will make what money he or she can and move along.

Education

Ambitious Web designers will seek out training of some sort. Currently there aren't many options, but as the field grows, so will related opportunities. Some possibilities for consideration are included in the following discussion. More detailed resources related to specific disciplines are available in part IV of this book, Web Design: Technology in Practice.

Apprenticeships and Internships

The Web itself is an excellent research tool. Industrious Web designers will look for existing design groups that are showing savvy and growth, and they will follow up with e-mail to such companies, asking if there are opportunities available. Many design companies are interested in fostering the virtual office—working with people at a distance—and this approach can really empower designers as well as employees at large. Go to one of the major search engines such as AltaVista (http://www.altavista.digital.com) and search for Web design or Web designers and begin writing to the contacts at the sites that appeal to you.

Conferences

A growing number of seminars and conferences are available in major cities. Attending such conferences can be incredibly helpful, not only because they expose the designer to new ideas, but because the inherent opportunity to meet and speak with people on the cutting edge of the industry can only be a valuable experience. For a list of current conferences related to the Internet, visit Yahoo's list at http://www.yahoo.com/Computers/Internet/Conferences_and_Events. Another good resource is WEBster's conference list at: http://www.tgc.com/websec/65001.html. As always, check regularly with your favorite search engine for upcoming events.

Courses

Several universities have extensive media programs that include Internet and Web-related courses. One such university is the New School for Social Research in New York City, which offers its programs both in person and online, giving unparalleled opportunity for advanced, academic exposure to New Media—something sorely lacking in current programs. Other excellent educational programs include those found at the Multimedia Lab, Brown University (http://www.stg.brown.edu/~mmlab/); the Center for New Media, Columbia University (http://www.cnm.columbia.edu/); the New Media Center, New York University (http://www.nyu.edu/nmc/); and the University of Art and Design, Helsinki, Finland (http://www.uiah.fi/).

The Mind Extension University

Available in the United States on cable television, the Mind Extension University has an untapped wealth of programs dedicated to online theory and technology. The beauty of these programs is that they are offered both as part of a formal educational process through MEU or in free-standing form for the more casual observer. Furthermore, this unique series is attempting to promote fundamental concepts in new media—interactivity and nonlinear education via a progressive medium. Access http://www.meu.edu/meu/meu.html or call 1-800-777-MIND.

Magazines and Industry Net Sites

Keeping up with the industry is a critical part of a Web designer's education and job. It should be required, regular practice to check the following sites:

1. Magazines and Webzines. By no means complete, this list is a good start for the Web designer interested in keeping up with the industry.

   - **Ziff-Davis Net.** This Web site offers daily industry news as well as features online versions of many of this publisher's popular magazines, including PC Magazine, PC Week, Mac Week, PC Computing, Inter@ctive Week, Windows Magazine, Computer Shopper, Computer Gaming, Yahoo! Internet Life, Family PC, and so on. Access http://www.zdnet.com/.

   - **c|net.** A very comprehensive and popular information source devoted to computers, multimedia, online services, and the ongoing digital revolution. Access http://www.cnet.com/.

   - **Hotwired.** The most trend-setting online webzine around. Access http://www.hotwired.com.

   - **Web Developer.** Geared specifically to the Web designer, this magazine can be found at http://www.webdeveloper.com/.

   - **Internet World.** An excellent read for Internet fans and professionals alike. Access http://www.internetworld.com/.

   - **Web Week.** Comprehensive Web-related news. Access http://www.webweek.com/.

2. Net Sites. It is part of a Web designer's job description to check these two sites on a daily basis!

   - **Netscape.** Breaking news on browser, server, and Web-related technology is available by visiting http://home.netscape.com.
   - **Microsoft.** Browser, server, Web-related, and general industry information. Access http://microsoft.com

3. Internet Newsgroups. A wide range of Internet Newsgroups exist for Web designers. Detailed information on specific disciplines is available in section 4 of this book, but here are a few tips for starters:

   - **comp.infosystems.www.authoring.html.** Mostly HTML discussions, but plenty of Web-design related information gets hashed out as well
   - **comp.infosystems.www.authoring.images.** Using images, imagemaps, and other graphic elements on the Web
   - **comp.infosystems.www.advocacy.** Comments and arguments over the best and worst of what is on the Web
   - **comp.infosystems.www.misc.** Miscellaneous World Wide Web discussions

Text Resources for New Media, Cyberculture, and Philosophies of the Mind

Quite a few very fine books on new media and emerging technological thought are available. Again, a more detailed resource listing by discipline is available in part 4 of this book, but here are a few choice titles:

- *Chaos and Cyberculture*, by Timothy Leary (Ronin Publishing). This highly creative, unusual book examines Leary's vision of Cyberia. It includes interesting discussions on media, new media, and evolving techno-cultures.
- *Cyberspace: First Steps*, ed. Michael Benedict (the MIT Press). A selection of excellent essays on the nature, synthesis, paradigm shifts, and creative possibilities of the cultural world created by computer communications

- *Cyber Arts: Exploring Art and Technology*, ed. Linda Jacobson (Miller-Freeman, Inc.). Another selection of essays on both artistic and technological aspects of interactive and new media
- *Mind at Large: Knowing in the Technological Age*, by Paul Levinson, Ph.D. (JAI Press, Inc.). A sophisticated, academic journey into how the human brain relates through technology to the world
- *The Society of Mind*, by Marvin Minsky (Simon and Schuster, Inc.). A series of compelling, sometimes maddening thoughts about the way the mind works, according to one of MIT's artificial intelligence gurus
- *Turing's Man: Western Culture in the Computer Age*, by J. David Bolter (The University of North Carolina Press). An examination of intelligence—both real and artificial—that relates scientific and humanistic studies both logically and creatively

Web Designers in Action

A Web designer does not serve strictly as an HTML script writer, a graphic artist, or a programmer, nor is he or she a systems administrator, although he or she may have come to the field through one of these areas and be completely qualified and often required to fill any of these roles. In our ideal model, a Web designer is instead the point of communication for each of these individuals, providing feedback, support, and direction as development proceeds.

Web design is a complex field, and we can expect it to get even more complicated. Because of this, the cream will rise to the top—and the designer who is ready to commit to the field will do whatever is required to be prepared. People often question whether the Web will even be around in a few years, and this is an excellent question. The fact is that no one really knows, but technology is evolving and one thing is certain: new media concepts are one of today's biggest growth areas, and they certainly form the foundation for tomorrow's evolved media. Learning the components of Web design as described here can only strengthen the possibilities for bright and exciting futures in whatever technology evolves from the current Web matrix.

chapter 4

The Web Design Paradigm

In *Professional Web Design*, one dominant goal: is to convey that, even in the maelstrom that defines the current environment of the World Wide Web, a strong Web design model lays the foundation for future growth of the Web design industry.

This book takes the position that the best-case scenario is a team-oriented model, in which a variety of individuals who perform specific duties are tied not only to each other but centrally to the Web designer. Only a few organizations currently act under the team model; many Web designers are individuals wearing each of the many hats of the field. Although some are managing these many roles with great success, it is difficult and will become even more difficult to do so as the technology, management, and artistic skills necessary to create competitive Web sites become more complicated.

There's something especially strong about the Web design team members who have hashed out and refined the ideas set forth in this book. Each of us, if given the task, could build a fine Web site from start to finish. We each know enough about the aspects of Web design to do it completely on our own, but we also have come to recognize that working alone is by no means an ideal situation.

We find, unanimously, that taking the jobs for which each of us is best suited and concentrating on those individual tasks is really where our Web design begins moving from good to great, from hot to sizzling. There is an undeniable excitement in the co-creative process, and because of this, the entire theory put forth here is meant to suggest such a model for future design groups—if you will, a *Web design paradigm.*

Again, we do not wish to write off the individual Webmaster, for he or she is currently the backbone of the Web. Because of that, we set forth these theories as food for thought—for Webmasters thinking of expanding their horizons, or for the member of the general public who needs to become better educated in the growing intricacies of the field. This is why this book's practical pages offer what we intend to be the best current information available to help *any* Web designer or design team avoid pitfalls and strengthen their design skills.

Nevertheless, we are excited by the potential this model sets forth. Highly creative and communicative individuals working in a nonhierarchical, nonlinear atmosphere are relatively unusual. Even Microsoft Corporation, famed for fostering a progressive ambiance for its employees, still functions through hierarchical structures. We are not suggesting that these structures are wrong, because the proof of their efficacy is in their success. However, because the Web medium cries out for integration and interactivity, we want to suggest that a working environment that nurtures these issues is, in essence, the strongest conceivable foundation for future advancement.

Exploring the Design Paradigm

The paradigm that this book proposes reaches for an ideal, operating in the changing environment that Web weaving demands. Eventually entire departments might substitute for the individuals who now perform the day-to-day tasks of creating Web sites. Although we acknowledge that this scenario is optimistic, our paradigm does offer a very realistic starting point for Web designers who seek to enhance their efficacy by adopting a team-based model.

In this paradigm, the Web designer interacts intimately with every individual or department involved in the design process. The designers are the directorial hub through which data pass and return, but they must remain flexible and open to everyone's input and ideas. Ideally, a Web designer has experience in many areas—enough to speak the language of each unique facet of the process, including HTML scripting, technical and creative writing, computer technology and systems administration, graphic design, marketing and media, business, and (perhaps most importantly) communication. With these facets of the design process spelled out, it is easy to see why Web design is a complicated and highly skilled field that demands experience and a professional demeanor.

Although the Web designer must be able to wear any of these different hats, he or she must also be willing to take that hat off and defer to the expertise of individuals in any given area. A Web designer knows his or her limitations, listens, and interprets incoming information for the rest of the team.

The Web designer is the central axis, the centripetal force. He or she is responsible for finding out the details and directions of a client's site through a rigorous examination of the client's needs and direction. Surrounding the Web designer is a group of team members who interact with one another in the creative process, even though they will carry out aspects of their work alone. The Web designer is, to draw from our metaphor, the conductor. He or she is familiar with the score, has a vision regarding its presentation, and is responsible for helping the following team members realize a fully functional Web site:

- **Copy writers and editor.** These are the individuals who will evaluate and prepare copy for the Web site. Writing for the Web is a technical and creative skill, requiring a sharp eye and occasionally a severe editorial hand.
- **The HTML coder.** Responsible for the HTML coding, the coder must work closely with other team members to help them both understand the constraints arising in each given scenario and realize its possibilities.
- **The graphic designer.** This is the artist on the team, the individual who gives input on appropriate graphic use for a given site, and who works closely with the Web designer and the coder to create the look and feel, layout and navigation, and site schemes. The graphic designer is the individual who will do the actual graphics rendering.
- **The programmer.** Programmers are responsible for any special scripting or programming a given site will demand. In the interactive model, programmers learn to work with the other team members and understand when programming events are required, and when they might detract from a site's true purpose.
- **The systems administrator.** Responsible for knowing the possibilities and limitations of the Web server and maintaining the system hardware, the systems administrator is a critical team member. Even if he or she is not required to be present during creative meetings, the systems administrator's input will be invaluable along the way when it comes to data management.

- **Marketing and sales.** The marketing person is important at two extremes of the Web design process. At the outset, he or she is responsible for bringing the client in. Afterward, it becomes the job of the marketing person to follow up on Web-based marketing on and off the Web, encouraging the client to consider the vast and varied options available to enhance the site's visibility.

We will visit and revisit this paradigm throughout the book (see Figure 4-1), and we will refer to it as a model in our journey throughout the process of creating Web sites. The intent, again, is to offer an idea. There are many interpretations and variations on this theme, from the vision of what this model will offer down the road, to other, current models in existence.

The Dream Team

If someone came to me and said, "Okay Molly, go to it. You have all the money you need, all the resources. Go forth and create the best design team you can possibly imagine," well, I would have a ready answer. I would recommend a team model with the Web designer in

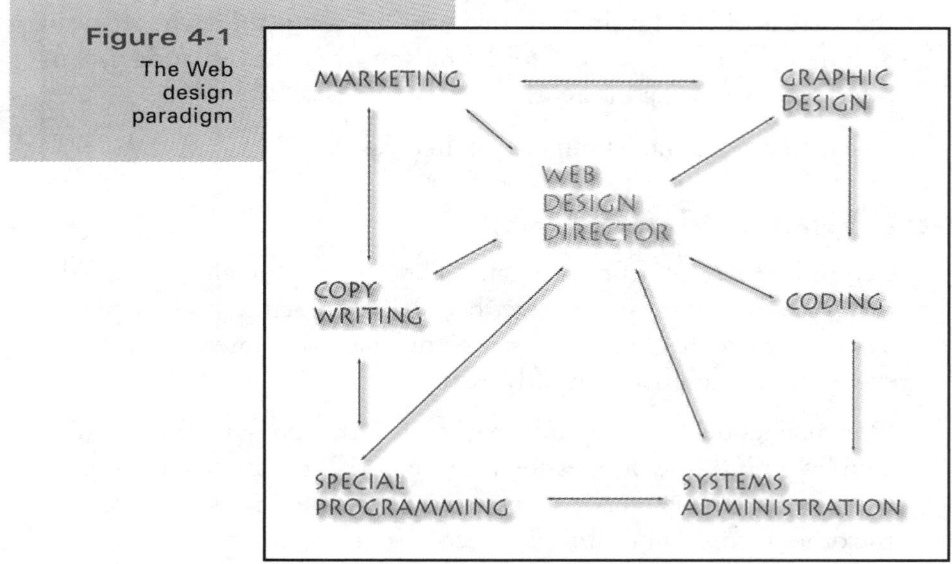

Figure 4-1 The Web design paradigm

the center, as we've already described. Around her are the directors of each of the departments in charge of running the specific tasks, including HTML coders, programmers, graphic designers, systems administrators, and marketing specialists.

Each of these department heads interact with the Web designer on a daily basis, and each is a peer rather than an employee. The Web designer must use her excellent communication skills to lead and guide the team, helping to integrate, direct, and, when necessary, set aside the ideas that evolve in the co-creative process.

The department heads are responsible for similar issues within their own departments. Ideally, although these heads are to direct or lead their department members, conceptually everyone is thought of as a peer within the work circles, since new and important ideas are always emerging from various team members.

I would also exploit virtual offices, allowing much work to be done not only at home, if necessary, but at great distances across the globe. I have read a lot about virtual workplaces, but in this industry they are relatively rare, which is philosophically against the grain of the interactive model set forth in this book for a brave new Web world. So in principle, I would like to challenge others in the field to think about the virtual office, finding creative ways of using the technology to enhance in-house work, and challenging the boundaries of preinteractive media thought.

The dream team model might look like Figure 4-2.

A Current Team Model

I consider myself fortunate because DesertNet is growing toward the dream team I've previously described. It's very exciting to be a part of something like that, but at the same time, I am very interested in other successful models that currently exist.

One such model I've seen quite frequently is the spousal team, in which couples go into the business of Web design. Typically one member is either a graphic designer or a person with marketing experience, and the other focuses on technical aspects (see sidebar.)

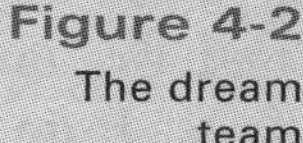

Figure 4-2
The dream team

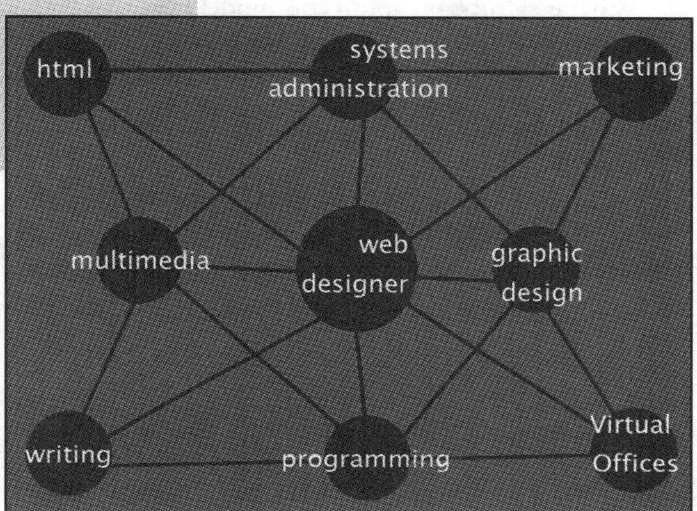

Laurie and Tim McCanna
Owners of Web Diner, Inc.
Author of *Creating Great Web Graphics*

"Working with a spouse is an interesting and challenging balancing act," Laurie says. "What makes it work is that we both are passionate advocates of the Web. Our skills tend to complement each other. He has the patience for details that I often don't."

"I go in with the creative," Laurie continues, "Tim is more technical. He double-checks any HTML I've done. Ideas fly back and forth." With strength in visual organization and graphic design, and Tim's technical expertise, the McCannas have encountered an interesting phenomenon. "He's become more creative, and I find myself becoming more technical. Also, when you are married and working together, you have to work out conflicts in order to get the job done—this strengthens the entire relationship."

Laurie sums it up: "You can stretch yourself in ways with the Web that you've never done before."

What is significant about this model relates to balance of power. Laurie and Tim—through balancing naturally different skills—have shown that such differences can serve to enhance rather than detract from the mutual effort. This effort shows in the quality of their Web weaving, as depicted in Figure 4-4.

Laurie and Tim's ability to understand each other's roles, regarding the changing creative and technical skills of each member of the team, and the deepening of the communication efforts between the two, raises critical issues relating to the ideal paradigm as well. It is interactivity and communication that lie at the heart of the Web, and it is therefore only natural that people who work that way will create strong Web sites. The value-added side effect is felt when that interactivity and communication not only enhance a client's opportunities but create human growth within the Web design team itself.

Figure 4-4 The Web Diner

The Client-Designer Relationship

A most crucial point in Web design is when Web designer and client first meet. The assessment of client need—along with understanding that need—is the focal point for the Web designer and must always be adhered to in order for Web site design to succeed. This is not to suggest that needs don't change—in fact they do, and often. Wherever in the process a shift in direction is needed, it is the Web designer who will manage the organization and redirection of resources.

The Web designer, then, is essentially an interpreter who fits a client's ideas into the Web context using traditional techniques of layout and storyboarding. With the assessment in hand, the Web designer begins to direct other members of the design team, talking about look and feel with the graphics designer, HTML particulars with the scripters. Special programming for forms or multimedia presentations are discussed with various programmers and artists, copy production and enhancement, with writers and copyeditors. Issues involving hosting, directory structures, and domain issues are taken up with systems administrators, and marketing tactics, with the marketing people.

In the best-case scenario, each of these individuals and groups will evaluate the information provided by the Web designer and offer feedback or ideas from that facet's perspective. The Web designer in turn must weigh this input and place it in the design if he or she believes it will be a reasonable and effective part of the site's goal. If new ideas come out of the team and are believed to fit the goal, the Web designer can then return to the client and find out if this new approach or enhancement fits within the bigger picture (see Figure 4-5).

It is often very difficult to judge whether or not to involve a client in every step of the design and production process. As a neurosurgeon is best qualified to operate on a patient, the Web design team is best qualified to meet client needs. However, since Web design very often creates a presence for the client, there must be a certain amount of input from the client beyond the initial design meeting. A Web designer learns to sense intuitively when this is appropriate or not, and how large a part of the team the client becomes once production begins.

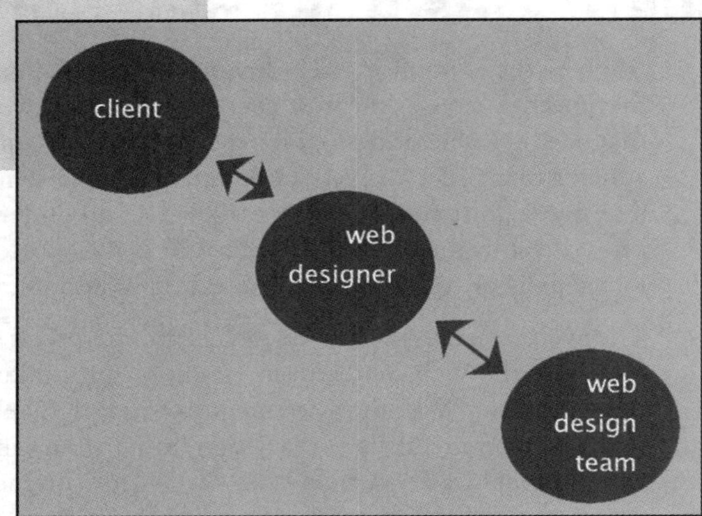

Figure 4-5 The Web designer/director and team relationship

Another factor in this decision is the type of client. A Webmaster managing a single site for a large company is typically not going to have the design freedom a Web design firm will. The sophistication of Web design lies in creating the opportunity for complete Web service firms to act as development as well as marketing agencies for their clients. Often, existing advertising agencies act as representatives for commercial clients, and they too will have input and a vision of what approach is best for the person they represent.

In cases such as these, a Web designer's job is to listen and respond but also to understand enough about the theory behind the Web, how it works, and how certain techniques might not work for a given client. Let's say a small restaurant wants Web presence to advertise its cuisine. The chef has a series of instructional videos she's prepared on several of her recipes. She's heard that video can be placed on the Web and is interested in making video clips the entire thrust of her online presence.

Although a clip or two can conceivably be placed on the Web for download, there are so many current issues regarding bandwidth, platform, and browser capabilities that, in this case, a better method would be to use stills from the video, showcasing the delectable food the restaurant prepares. Content can include sample menus; look and feel can capture the establishment's lovely color schemes. The video content must be used to accentuate but never replace the more accessible value of Web capabilities.

Another, opposite scenario is provided by the client who has a complete print presentation that has been successful in direct mailing or other venues. He or she may wish to simply place that content on the Web, without taking advantage of hypermedia or more aggressive graphic design. It is very easy to think that what has worked in one medium will work in another, but this is, in simplest terms, a mistake. We want people to visit the site, and then visit again, because we've chosen to use the dimension and value available to us instead of creating flat, noninteractive sites that mimic print.

Web designers will often run into challenges like these, and it is part of their responsibility to address the client's ideas tactfully and appropriately. This can only be done if the designer has a very strong sense of what will work for a given scenario. Sometimes, however, the Web designer will only be in a position to agree, allowing the client to call the shots. These are not ideal instances, but they do happen. The designer can often make the most of these circumstances if the client is open to learning a bit about how the Web really works. Otherwise, it's best that the designer do one of two things—give the client what that client needs and expects to work, rather than an ideal solution—or else recommend that the client explore other companies or ways of achieving his or her goal.

Some might say that this approach is very harsh, and it is. Web myths are rampant at this point, so this is not a casual issue. Since this paradigm insists on a balanced, communications-based relationship between everyone involved, it is a good idea to know when a situation is just not a good fit, and to be ready to recommend other options.

A Natural Model for the Interactive Age

We have used words such as "nonlinear," "interactive," and "tangential" many times throughout this introduction, and not frivolously. It is crucial that the Web design team, from the designer to each individual member and over to the client, understand that these concepts are what the Web is fundamentally about. To go against that grain doesn't necessarily equate to failure or a tearing of Web fabric, but it does suppress the possibilities of using the Web for the greater good—be it in the commercial, corporate, personal, or charitable realm (see Figure 4-6). For all these reasons, the Web design paradigm seeks to mimic these spiral and spherical concepts. The objective is to make the business—and the art—of Web design one that draws from integrated media and lends direction to a natural model for a progressive, interactive age.

Figure 4-6
An image of a torn Web

Part II

Building a Foundation: Current Challenges for the Web Designer

chapter 5

Foundational Challenges for the Web Designer

Because the field of Web design is evolving, strong design models that designers can use have yet to emerge. It is primarily for this reason that we are suggesting such a model, but also because Web design disciplines are being applied daily, and creating some stability in the Web designer's work environment can only enhance his or her ability to create powerful Web sites. These disciplines, which we've described earlier as the components of Web design, include copy writing, HTML coding, graphic design, multimedia, computer programming, systems administration, and marketing. They are the essentials of a Web designer's job.

Such disciplines are employed to build a structure, and for a structure to be sturdy, it must have a strong foundation. A foundation requires ,a mold, concrete, and a solid framework. In Web design it is HTML standards and Web browsers that are key components of this foundation.

In a sense, Web design as a definitive profession is akin to the missing link. The Web designer is like our early human—he or she is using a variety of tools and building a rudimentary shelter, but ofttimes the rain leaks in. The Web designer has the ways and the means but does not always understand them or succeed in defining how to employ them.

In order to move from rudimentary structures to the sturdy foundations and ultimately to produce the elegant structures of a mature culture, we must define and then refine our construction material. On the Web, we need to determine and redetermine what our HTML standards are, delimit their problems, and offer solutions to make them stronger. Browser issues—an enormous part of Web design structure—must be better dealt with in order to use these potent tools as a help rather than a hindrance.

An Expanded History and Philosophy of Web Design Foundations

Roger Hurwitz, a research specialist at MIT, draws from philosopher Pascal to claim God's circumference is everywhere but his center is

nowhere, that is the model of the Web. This clever comment points to the fact that the Web's foundation may not be a definitive place; rather, it is either transient or, even more compellingly, nonexistent. This creates a striking paradox: in order to have strong Web sites, one must build a foundation where possibly no center for it exists.

This is perhaps an esoteric notion for the Web designer searching these pages for the tools of his or her trade, but this paradox is an essential, pivotal issue in creating good Web sites. As an artist is stronger knowing the rules before breaking them, so is the Web designer. We've mentioned time and again that the rules are in a constant state of flux, they are in fact being written and rewritten, broken and broken again, in the Web design field on a daily, if not momentary, basis.

Also mentioned time and again are the lack of adherence to Web standards and the conflicting conventions that are evolving in spite of preexisting rules. It's a difficult situation, undeniably. In an effort to meet the pull of the public, to creatively push existing technology to the edge and beyond, the rules—in essence, the centers—that do exist are often ignored.

But what are these foundations, these centers? Who is lord and master of Web design, and if we dare to go against such a one, shouldn't we first know his identity? Exposure to Web history and the evolution of its technologies can be an excellent beginning. It's unlikely that such concepts will be sought out by the fly-by-night designer, and knowing them isn't necessarily going to make a bad designer a good one. But certainly knowing the history and laws of a cultural condition better equips one to make decisions to work within, or, as is often the case in Web design, without, those principles as a guide.

HTML and HTML Standards

The Hypertext Markup Language, HTML (see Figure 5-1), is the language of the Web. HTML coders use this language to create the skeleton of what will ultimately flesh out the content of Web pages, including text, images, hypermedia, and a growing variety of other features.

HTML's linguistic origins are related to the Standard Generalized Markup Language (SGML). SGML is used as a digital document formatting method, offering a variety of control options. HTML uses SGML concepts and allows users to code for formatting components such as paragraphs and line breaks, and for other visually organized situations.

Figure 5-1
HTML in action

```
XOONJFMV.txt - Notepad
File  Edit  Search  Help
<!DOCTYPE HTML PUBLIC "-//IETF//DTD HTML//EN">
<!-- Changed by: Dave Raggett,  18-Mar-1996 -->
<!-- Changed by: Rohit Khare,  15-Mar-1996 -->
<!-- Changed by: Dave Raggett, 05-Apr-1996 -->
<HEAD>
<TITLE>The World Wide Web Consortium (W3C)</TITLE>
</HEAD>

<BODY>

<H1><img align=middle alt="W3C" src="Icons/WWW/w3c_96x67.gif">
The World Wide Web Consortium</H1>

<p>
The World Wide Web is the universe of network-accessible information.
The <a href="Consortium/">World Wide Web Consortium</a>
exists to realize the full potential of the Web.

<p> W3C works with the global community to produce <a
href="#Specifications">specifications</a> and <a
href="#Reference">reference software</a>.  W3C is funded by industrial
<A HREF="Consortium/Member/List.html">members</A> but its products are
freely available to all.  The Consortium is run by <a
href="http://web.mit.edu/">MIT</a> <a
href="http://www.lcs.mit.edu">LCS</a> and by <A
HREF="http://www.inria.fr/">INRIA</A>, in collaboration with <A
HREF="http://www.cern.ch/">CERN</A> where the web originated.  Seed
funding for W3C was provided to MIT LCS by <A
```

HTML standards began with very simple tags, with the focus on presenting documents that were predominantly text-based and used in a research environment. Tim Berners-Lee authored the original HTML specification at the European Laboratory for Particle Physics in Geneva, Switzerland. Known more commonly as CERN, this highly focused physics laboratory has carved its largest niche in history as being the birthplace of the World Wide Web.

Other groups contributed to Berners-Lee's work to form what was eventually published as HTML 2.0. This publication is, at this writing, the true standard for HTML, even though conventions and day-to-day use have grown far beyond the HTML 2.0 specifications, into HTML 3.0 and beyond.

Just as English as a language has evolved, incorporating new words to accommodate new ideas, or embracing common words brought to it from other languages, the Hypertext Markup Language must remain flexible but keep its familiar gloss or appearance. Originally developed under the hand of academia, which guides methodically—and as a result often slowly—HTML is now the backbone of a new medium. It has become public domain, and the public, as it will with any language, is adding its slang, euphemisms, and other components.

HTML versions 1.0 and 2.0 each went through a committee-based standards process. Designers using only HTML 2.0 will run into very few, if any, of the challenges discussed in this book. HTML 3.0 has, as of May 7, 1996, been surpassed by a new specification, HTML 3.2. In actuality, only HTML 2.0 is considered standard, because although 3.0 and above exist, they have not been formally reviewed and accepted by any board. Therefore, browser developers often incorporate their own, sometimes rebellious, ideas into browser software.

This is a disrespectful relationship. Standards need to be acknowledged, but reciprocally the governing boards need to acknowledge the rapid growth of the field and make any necessary accommodations in order to honor new information. To a progressive Web designer, HTML 2.0 is really nothing more than glorified word-processing. Standards committees must begin evaluating the 3.2 specification and its related proposed extensions and to move it from convention into a new, formal standard.

Strengthening Commercial Web Design through Standards

An update of current standards will help the Web designer immeasurably. Browser developers will be forced to embrace the standards, and new renegade ideas can continue to develop, but with a better foundation. The simple truth is that up until recently academics and researchers had not been thinking of commercial needs. There shouldn't be a battle between commerce and academia, but there often is, and it can be an unfortunate one.

It is impossible to think at this point in the evolution of HTML that academic needs are not met. The HTML requirements in an academic environment are satisfied—hypertext documents can be created, navigated, and published without any problems. It is the design elements, the programming advancements, and the commercial needs that are not being looked on as important. Yet, it is the commercial element that now drives the existing environment for HTML—the World Wide Web. Without this element the Web, and possibly the entire Internet, could conceivably die. Educational institutions simply cannot afford to keep it alive, but big business can. And now that there appear to be very viable marketing options through the Internet, large corporations have a significant interest in making sure the Web continues to grow and evolve.

A Recommended Process

The solution lies in the creation of better standards for the standards committees. Because this is a lightning-speed technology, boards in charge of overseeing how HTML evolves should be working 12 months a year and coming out with standards publications at least three, if not four, times per year to meet the demand for them.

Whether such an aggressive committee will ever exist is yet to be seen, but the exciting news as of March 1996 is that an agreement between several major committees and organizations has been reached that may very well lead to resolution of these issues. The World Wide Web Consortium (the W3 Consortium) at the MIT Laboratory for Computer Science has agreed to work with Institut National de Recherche en Informatique et en Automatique (the French National Institute for Research in Computer Science and Control, also referred to as INRIA) and with commercial market leaders to push for more contemporary HTML standards. The W3 Consortium and its member organizations are also interested in creating progressive rules for various Web directions such as the incorporation of multimedia, forms, and tables into the HTML glossary.

It is no accident that Netscape Communications Corporation and Microsoft hold positions among the many commercial members of the Consortium. Every indication is that these two companies will dominate the browser industry, and therefore their input will be of staggering importance to the future development of HTML and browser technology. Also included in this list are IBM, Novell, SoftQuad, Spyglass, and Sun Microsystems. For a complete list of participants, and for regular press releases regarding the status of HTML standards, visit the World Wide Web Consortium's home page (Figure 5-2) at http://www.w3.org/pub/WWW/.

Figure 5-2
The World Wide Web Consortium's home page

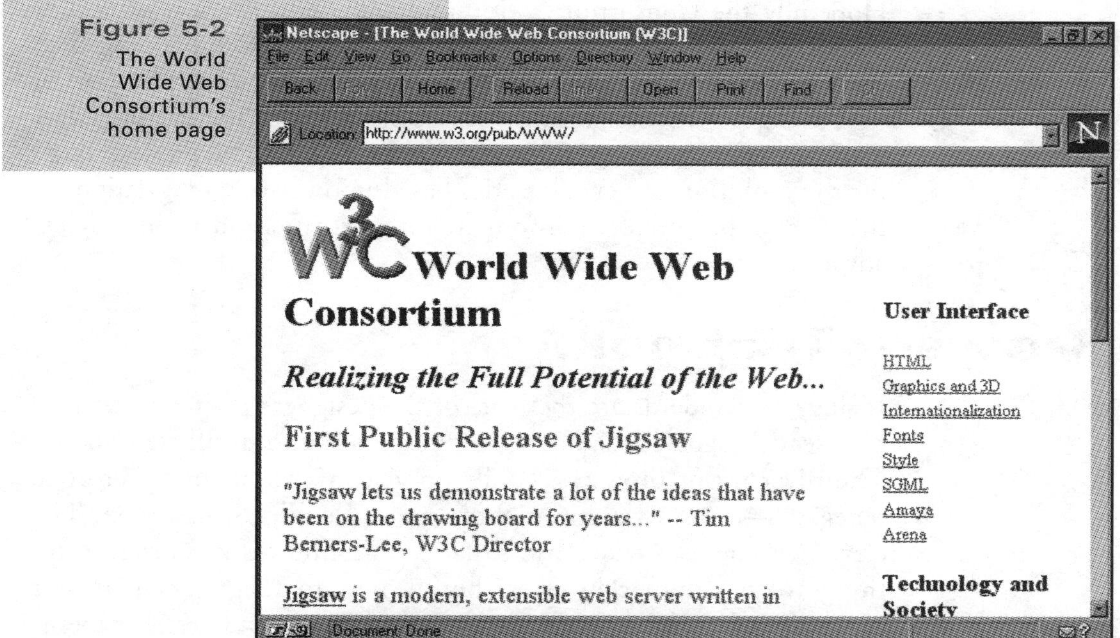

Academically Speaking

Dr. Joel Snyder, contributing editor to Mecklermedia's Internet World and coauthor of the Macintosh Networking Bible, oversimplifies the political stand-off between developers of standards and media-oriented, renegade Web designers. It's not that standards don't exist, he asserts, but that Web designers choose to ignore them.

Snyder and those of his disposition must be respected. It does in fact seem quite aggressive of Web innovators to disregard rules written only

two years ago—rules that are in fact powerful and useful, and that when adhered to allow the designer to avoid the headaches that renegade design causes. Conversely, to tell a Web designer not to use existing technologies to create exciting designs for clients is an insult to progress and creativity, and herein lies the central challenge of contemporary Web design.

Hope for Resolution

Hopefully the Consortium, with academic and historical as well as corporate and progressive representatives, will allow impending Web directives to form a healthy balance between the science and the art of Web design. Web designers must be able to go to the cutting edge, break the rules, make new rules, and start over again. This process allows for the evolution of new glossaries based upon strong foundations—the only appropriate environment for scientific and technological advancement.

Browser Technology

If sluggish standards are the bane of the designer's existence, current browser design practice amounts to rubbing salt into an afflicted wound. The diversity of browsers—built upon conventions or by creative renegades—causes waking nightmares and endless frustration. The clever designer can take a bad situation and find workarounds or fun things to do with rebel browsers, but the need to design for all browser capabilities forces the designer to stay continually on his or her toes.

Until Mosaic entered the scene in early 1993, such design issues didn't even exist, because the Web was a text-based environment viewable only by line browsers such as www and eventually the more popular Lynx (see Figure 5-3). Developed by Marc Andreessen and Eric Bina at the National Center for Supercomputing Applications (NCSA), University of Illinois at Urbana-Champaign, Mosaic has often been referred to as the most important factor in the growth of the Web for one primary reason—its capabilities of displaying graphics, as we see demonstrated in Figure 5-4. A software tool that took three months to develop broke ground for the growth of a new medium, an opportunity for public world commerce, and an environment of challenge and change.

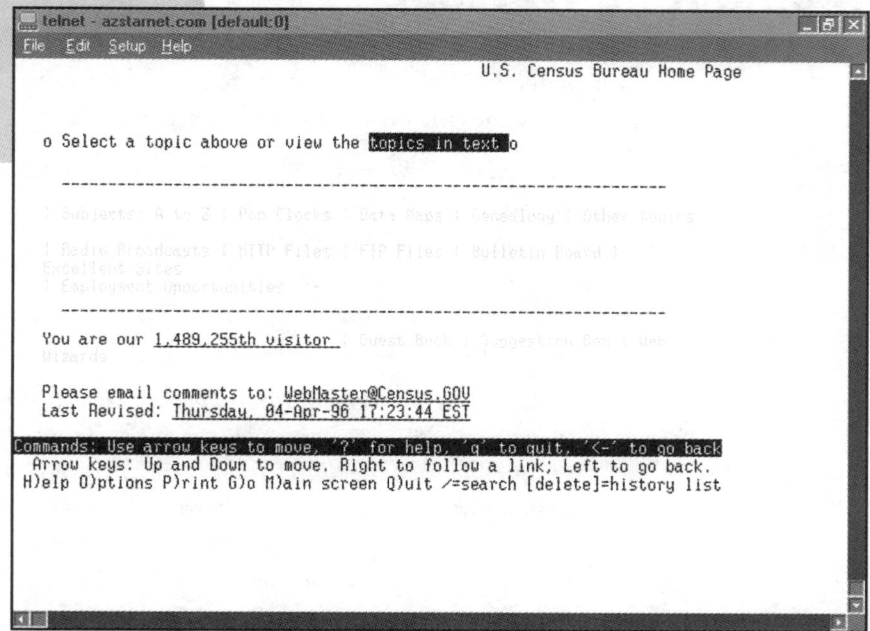

Figure 5-3
A Web page as viewed with Lynx

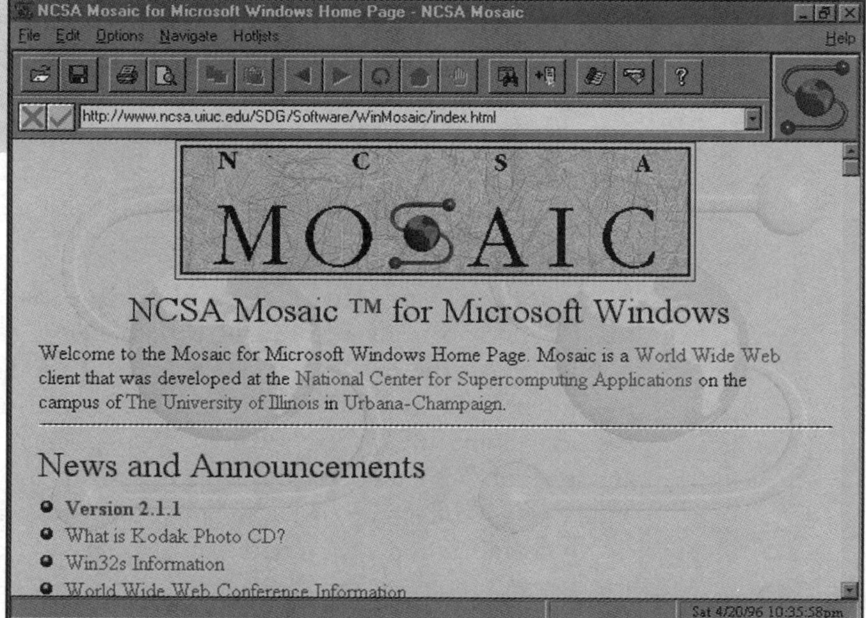

Figure 5-4
The Mosaic browser and home page

Blame It on Netscape

A medley of Web browsers began to pop up, including Cello and eventually Netscape Navigator, released in its first version in 1994. Netscape shares the following words with readers of its 1995 annual report:

> *The market had spoken. With the help of Jim Clark, founder of Silicon Graphics, a core team of the people who had originally developed NCSA Mosaic and related Internet technologies moved to California. In April 1994, this team founded a company which a few months later became formally known as Netscape Communications Corporation.*
>
> *By the end of 1994, Netscape shipped its flagship product, Netscape Navigator. The first commercially available Internet client software product to include built-in security features for facilitating commercial transactions and encrypted communications over the Internet, Netscape Navigator is notable for its high-speed performance and ease of use. In addition, Netscape Navigator's adherence to open standards and cross-platform interoperability provides users with significant compatibility and connectivity advantages.*

From the conservative perspective, the blame for designer departure from strict standards to so-called open standards falls wholly on the shoulders of Netscape Communications Corporation and lies in the contribution of their Netscape Navigator browsers to the mien of the Web. The Netscape browsers have embodied renegade behavior from the moment of their birth—their designers have intentionally ventured, and continue to venture, beyond the rules.

From the design perspective, Netscape has created amazing opportunities for designers to really experiment with the edge of Web technology. Netscape bears the weight of this rebellion but also holds the honorable position of being innovative in the face of conservatism. This innovation has been immeasurably exploited by Web designers—one cannot visit any series of Web sites before reaching one that boasts that it is Netscape enhanced and offers the visitor an opportunity to immediately leave the site to download the most recent Netscape version (see Figure 5-5).

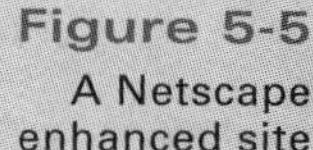

Figure 5-5
A Netscape enhanced site

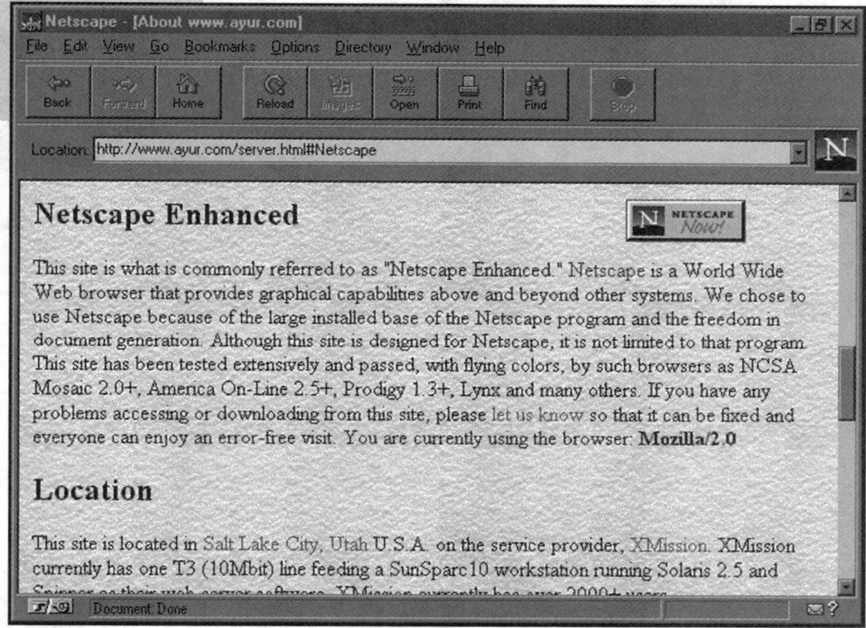

Essentially Netscape took Mosaic's gift of visual—and therefore commercially inviting— Web browsing potential and exploited it beyond imagination. Suddenly the Web became aggressively focused on designing the applications Netscape had allowed. In enabling features from the use of background colors and graphics, to plug-in technology such as Virtual Reality Modeling Language (VRML), to scripting and language capabilities as found with Java, it is Netscape that has caused major quakes in the Web universe (see Figure 5-6).

Enter Microsoft

Now enter Microsoft, that most hated, feared, and brilliant of developers. Penetrating the browser market quietly at first, more recently with an aggressive attack, Microsoft has devised a Web strategy of such inherent intelligence that any designer who hasn't sat up and noticed it is not paying close attention. Intentionally embracing current Netscape conventions in version 2.0 of the Internet Explorer browser, Microsoft has added its own dissident functions, including in-line video, support for background sound, the marquee effect, and the FONT FACE tags (see Figure 5-7).

Figure 5-6 Netscape's home page as viewed through Netscape Navigator 2.0

Figure 5-7 Microsoft's Internet Explorer and the I.E. home page

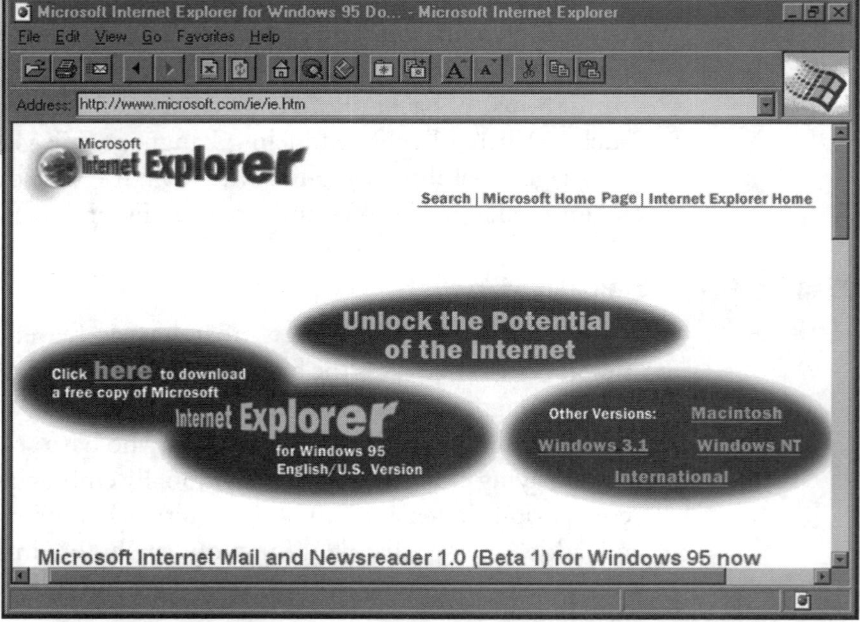

Currently Netscape Navigator claims the dominant market share of Web browsers. However, lured by access to the Internet combined with ease of use, many people venture onto the Web via their online service, particularly America Online, which boasts the largest population of commercial service members. The soon-to-be-defunct America Online Web browser has been a thorn in the side of designers, largely because it is a poorly written and presented product.

Not six months after Microsoft's own competitive entrance into the online network service realm with the Microsoft Network (MSN), the two companies most obviously in a position to be aggressive competitors—Microsoft and AOL—are now keeping close company when it comes to Web browser development. Obviously interested in keeping members, America Online has sought to improve the Web browser it commonly packages with its popular access software.

The politics have been complicated, but suffice it to say that somehow these two computer and communications industry giants have joined forces to thrust the Internet Explorer browser dead into the face of Netscape Navigator. As of fall 1996, AOL's online service software will be packaged and distributed with Microsoft's Internet Explorer version 3.0 as its Web browser.

Microsoft also appears to be working closely with another huge market—CompuServe. The primary advantage that Microsoft has in promoting its Web browser is that it is a completely free product. This gives an undeniable edge in the business realm, and Netscape is going to have to really scramble in order to match the competition.

The Battle of the Browsers

Although many fear the dominance of large corporations—and reasonably so—news of this competition couldn't be better for the Web designer. As the two giants occupy the battlefield, the focus goes to their fight, and smaller competitors die off or leave the field altogether, knowing that any attempts to compete will most likely fail.

Until this battle is played out—until the W3 Consortium and its members approve standards more readily—and until the dust from the browser wars settles, the challenge in a Web designer's existence continues to center on the issue of nonadherence to standards and the subsequent creation of HTML conventions. It is these conventions that most designers are following, and this fact gives rise to many challenges for browser developers, designers, and recreational users of the Web alike.

Empowering the Web Designer

In the following chapter, we'll look more closely at the way current browsers handle information. The intention is to enable the Web designer by giving him or her a very concise idea of features that can be used across platforms, along with features that a Web designer will want to avoid in certain instances. Using learned techniques, one can create Web sites that span browser capabilities, and although a given site might not look its best in one browser or another, the wise designer has made certain that it is viewable—at least in part—in all browsers. This is no small feat, but it is essential for Web designers in current practice to be aware of, understand, and employ such a measure of compatibility as a rule, despite whatever rebellious stances they might wish to embrace.

The history we see unfolding here is actually the natural course of discovery—taking known entities and experimenting with them in unique and often chaotic environments. If the hypotheses upon which these experiments are based pan out, then the next logical course is to incorporate that knowledge into the realm of what is considered standard. Then developers and designers will have the opportunity to learn the newest rules and break them all over again, launching themselves into uncharted but thrilling new territories.

chapter 6

Browser Technology: A Closer Look

In this chapter we will first take a look at browser technology in general and then closely examine several of the most popular browsers, considering what they can or cannot do. It is the intent of this chapter to expose the Web designer to the current trends in this important technology—since it is browsers that often determine the way that designers must design.

While reading this chapter, bear in mind that sometimes it is the differences rather than the similarities that cause challenges for the designers. The main point is to be broadly familiar with the popular browser functions, giving you as a Web designer an accessible resource that can serve to enhance your own unique experiences designing with various browsers in mind.

As mentioned in Chapter 5, Mosaic was the first graphical Web browser; it changed the Web's primary use from information alone to entertainment and commerce. Recent events have shown that Microsoft and Netscape Communications Corporation are poised to enter into what trade magazines are already calling a "war" over their respective browsers, and the battle is beginning for dominant market share among Web surfers. This so-called war is highly reminiscent of the Macintosh-versus-Windows debate—or to take an analogy from another technology, the Beta-versus-VHS videotape wars. In the end, one technology usually dominates over others.

In many ways, it may be a very good thing if one vendor emerges as the dominant force in browser technology. This argument relates back to the issue of standards and the need to create a sturdy platform upon which new ideas and applications can be developed. Currently, both Netscape's and Microsoft's Web browsers have very attractive features, but because the standards situation is far from settled, both of these relatively young products are already off and running on different tracks. As was mentioned in Chapter 5, this is causing more, not fewer, problems for designers, who can appreciate the need for competition within the browser industry, but who also long for some guidance to make the design job easier.

A Selection of Current Browsers

Because browser technology is driving many of the requirements being placed on designers, we can most fairly evaluate those challenges if we first examine the current crop of browsers. In this chapter, we'll look primarily at today's most popular browsers, because these browsers create the greatest concerns for designers.

The following lists of Web browsers represent a fair cross-section of the browsers that are available for current use, as well as of the browsers that are either currently popular or destined to be popular in the coming months. Table 6-1 offers a detailed look at their features. For purposes of our discussion, remember that the critical issue is that these browsers significantly affect the way a Web designer will do his or her job, depending on their common features and individual idiosyncrasies.

- **Netscape Navigator 2.1.** Created by Netscape Communications Corporation, this is currently the most feature-diverse browser available. To download, visit:

  http://home.netscape.com/comprod/mirror/client_download.html

- **Internet Explorer 2.0.** Microsoft's excellent current addition to the browser market, this version is available at:

  http://www.microsoft.com/ie/ie.htm

- **Mosaic 2.1.1.** Mosaic is the original graphic browser. It has some interesting features, so it's worth a look.

  http://www.ncsa.uiuc.edu/SDG/Software/Mosaic/

- **Lynx 2.4.** A text-only browser, this browser can be viewed through most Internet-connected, UNIX-based shell accounts. It is a powerful browser for pure text environments, but it appears, unfortunately, that there will be no more releases due to a shift in consumer demand away from text environments. It is important to discuss Lynx as many people still rely on text-based browsing. It is worth noting that Lynx is also the most accessible format for blind individuals and thus has a unique reason for being.

The following browsers are currently in beta at this writing, but they will soon be available as full commercial products. No matter what a browser's stage of development, it is important for Web designers to download and become familiar with the new enhancements for each popular browser. Growing familiar with a browser in its beta stage gives the Web designer a certain amount of lead time in learning what to expect in trends and changes.

- **Netscape 3.0.** Netscape's next generation browser is available in its beta version at this writing. It has enhancements including in-line sound and background color attributes for tables.
- **Internet Explorer 3.0.** Like Netscape 3.0, the Internet Explorer next-generation browser, which will support many advanced features, is currently in the beta testing phase. We have used the beta version as a model and projected features that will be included with its final release.

Note

The America Online Browser. AOL's current, proprietary browser has been purposely left out of the following table. A very problematic browser, It has caused untold suffering for Web designers. In mid-June of 1996, AOL released a PC-based version of an enhanced browser that has many improved features. A Macintosh version has yet to be released, and as already stated, AOL will be improving its browser service globally by offering Microsoft's Internet Explorer as part of the AOL package, as well as the option to use Netscape should the customer prefer. These circumstances stand as a powerfully descriptive example of the difficulties currently faced by Web designers, and how shifts in policies as well as the technology affect day-to-day issues in Web design.

Current Web Browser Features

As you can see from Table 6-1, browsers vary greatly in their abilities. How these abilities relate to the field of Web design is critical, and the following discussion of browser features will help a designer to understand individual traits. Although this description is comprehensive, it is by no means complete. The primary intent is to name the special features that browsers have, thereby demonstrating their individual importance in Web design.

Table 6-1 Features of Popular Browsers

	Netscape 2.1	Internet Explorer 2.0	Mosaic 2.1.1	LYNX	Netscape 3.0	Internet Explorer 3.0
Access and Platforms						
DOS				Can be viewed on any text-based dialup platform		
Macintosh	*	*	*		*	*
UNIX	*		*		Projected	
VMS			*			
Windows 3.1	*	*	*			
Windows 95	*	*	*		*	*
Windows NT	*	*	*		Projected	*
TCP/IP Stack	*	With Win95 or NT			*	*
Functions and Features						
Bookmarking	*	*	*	*	*	*
Caching	*	*	*		*	*
Helper Applications	*	*	*		*	*
In-line Sound		*	*		*	*
Plug-Ins	*				*	*
View Source	*	*	*	*	*	*
Graphics						
Images	*	*	*		*	*
GIF	*	*	*		*	*
Animated GIF	*				*	?
JPEG (JPG)	*	*	*		*	*
Progressive JPEG (JPG)	*	*			*	*

Table 6-1 Features of Popular Browsers (continued)

	NETSCAPE 2.1	INTERNET EXPLORER 2.0	MOSAIC 2.1.1	LYNX	NETSCAPE 3.0	INTERNET EXPLORER 3.0
HTML AND RELATED ATTRIBUTES						
Body Attributes	*	*	*	*	*	*
Background Color	*	*	*		*	*
Text Color Attributes (link, vlink, alink, etc.)	*	*	*		*	*
Fonts						
Font Color	*	*			*	*
Font Size	*	*	*		*	*
Font Face		*				*
Client-Sided Image Mapping	*	*	*		*	*
Frames	*				*	*
Image Attributes						
Floating Images	*	*			*	*
Width and Height	*	*			*	*
Tables	*	*	*		*	*
Table Attributes						
Background Color		*			*	*
Background						*
Width	*	*			*	*
Programming						
ActiveX						*
Java	*				*	*
JavaScript	*				*	*
Visual Basic Script						*
VRML	*	*			*	*
Special Scripting Features						
Client-Sided Cookies	*	*			*	*

Table 6-1 Features of Popular Browsers (continued)

	Netscape 2.1	Internet Explorer 2.0	Mosaic 2.1.1	LYNX	Netscape 3.0	Internet Explorer 3.0
Support Services and Applications						
Access to other Internet Clients						
E-mail	*	*	*	modified	*	*
FTP	*	*	*		*	*
Gopher	*	*	*		*	*
News	*	*	*		*	*
Telnet	*	*	*		*	*
Documentation	*	*	*	*	*	*
Security	*	*			*	*

Access and Platforms

The first platform consideration is the *operating system* (OS). This relates to the software that runs the computer itself. These are the principal operating systems in use today, with particular attention to how they relate to the structure of the Internet or access to it:

- **DOS.** The principal OS for IBM PCs and compatible computers for over ten years, it is strictly text-based, with a command-line interface (no graphics).
- **Macintosh.** A machine-specific OS developed by Apple for the machine of the same name, it is the first operating system to use a graphic user interface (GUI) exclusively.
- **UNIX.** This venerable system is called the "operating system of the Internet" because it runs on most of the minicomputers, mainframes, and LANs at educational institutions, large corporate installations, and scientific and research concerns. UNIX

commands, including directory structure, are case sensitive. This has created some unique problems in accessing Web sites. For example, the Uniform Resource Locator (URL) http:// MYwoRld.CoM/ is distinct in the UNIX environment from http:/ /myworld.com.

- **VMS.** Developed by Digital Equipment Corporation as a rational alternative to UNIX, VMS has much better security. A critical note to Web designers—it is not case-sensitive.
- **Windows 3.1.** Really an operating *environment* rather than a system, Windows 3.1 runs under DOS and gives full GUI capabilities to the IBM PC world.
- **Windows 95 and NT.** The newest 32-bit incarnations of Windows, these are functionally complete operating systems that no longer require DOS and that offer enhanced networking ability.

The *TCP/IP stack* constitutes an additional platform consideration. Most browsers require a direct Internet connection. The stack is the set of network drivers that actually set up and maintain this connection. Although there are shareware and OS-based TCP/IP stacks available, a browser may have its own in order to optimize performance.

Functions and Features

These features are usual in the present generation of browsers:

- **Bookmarking.** Allows a user to keep a log of URLs in order to return to them later. A well-organized set of bookmarks can be a way to get to your favorite sites quickly, or to document research sessions. A random, sprawling list of Web addresses becomes analogous to a desk covered with business cards, sticky notes, and receipts—a resource, but a clumsy one.
- **Caching.** Most browsers will cache (store in memory or on disk) frequently retrieved documents and images. This allows the browser to load pages faster by getting the information from the local system instead of across the network. An advantage is the resulting decrease in network traffic. However, frequently updated

pages can be "missed" by users if their browsers do not check the documents for revision dates but use the stale cached pages instead.

- **Helper applications.** When a browser visits a site with options that it cannot play in-line, it will offer to launch a software application that runs locally on the user's machine. An example of a helper application is Netscape's Audio Player (Naplayer). If we visit a site and click on a sound file, Naplayer will be launched and play the sound.
- **In-line sound.** This is the ability to play audio without spawning an external viewer or a plug-in.
- **Plug-ins.** A helper application is a standalone program that the browser opens in order to execute or display a file, but a plug-in is a browser-dependent but separate program that is designed to look and act like part of the browser environment.
- **View Source.** This allows viewers to see the HTML coding behind any document on the Web.

Graphics

Graphics, or images, may include graphical art for Web use such as header graphics, rules, buttons, navigation bars, and stylized photography. Image types include these:

- **GIF.** GIF refers to the CompuServe graphics interchange format. It is a platform-independent graphics format that is compressed and includes a pallet of up to but no more than 256 colors. GIF was the original Web graphics standard. Its special features include interlacing, which allows for progressive rendering of the image.
- **Animated GIF.** A series of GIFs stacked into a single GIF, with enclosed data on looping, speed, and loading, can be animated. The final product is a single GIF with movement that can be interpreted by certain browsers.
- **JPEG or JPG.** JPEG is the acronym for Joint Photographic Experts Group. JPEGs are in a compressed, 24-bit graphics format that

allows for over 16 million colors. It is an especially good format for photographic and true color images.

- **Progressive JPEG.** Like the interlacing feature in GIFs, progressive JPEG progressively renders the graphic image by rearranging data into a series of scans of increasing clarity. Browsers decode the low-quality images first, and then the quality is increased as each scan comes in.

HTML and Related Attributes

Body attributes are a series of extensions to the <body> tag that will create certain attributes on a Web page when viewed through the browser. These are some of them:

1. **Colors.** A selection of hexadecimal color values exists within certain browsers and enables the designer to choose a color to match his or her design scheme.
   - **Background Color.** This is the color that appears on the background of a page.
   - **Text Color.** This is the color chosen for static text.
   - **Link Color.** This is the hotlink color, indicating that the text or medium utilizing this color is linked to another section or external document.
   - **Vlink Color.** Links that have been followed will appear in this color.
   - **Alink Color.** Links that are active (being clicked on) turn this color.
2. **Fonts.** Font arguments allow for various font attributes to appear on the page via the browser.
   - **Font Color.** This feature forces a color for static fonts. It will override a text color attribute.
   - **Font Size.** This allows a designer to use larger or smaller fonts than a browser's default.

- **Font Face.** Currently a limited feature, this allows for the choice of font style, as in Times New Roman, Courier, and so on.

Functional attributes can enhance the overall design of a site. Two of these attributes are:

1. **Client-side image mapping.** This feature allows the coder to place image mapping coordinates into the HTML, to be read by the browser. Contrary to the ISMAP convention, client-sided image mapping doesn't require extra visits to the server. This speeds up navigation and is an excellent design feature.

2. **Frames.** Frames allow the designer to break up screen space into different sections, allowing for different activities to take place in each area. An animation can be active in one area, with text information in another, and navigation in yet another (see Figure 6-1).

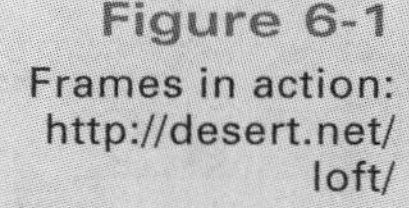

Figure 6-1
Frames in action: http://desert.net/loft/

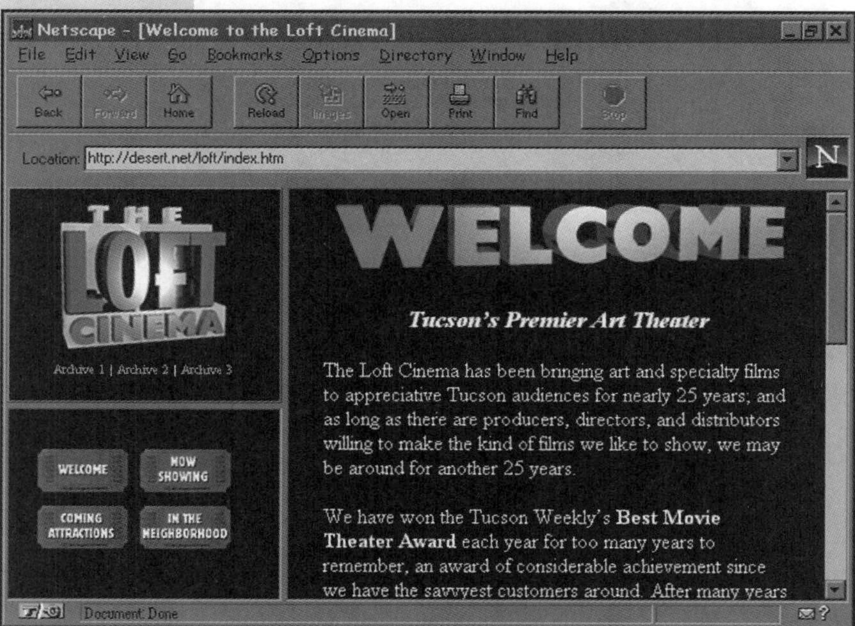

Image attributes are specific arguments that can be given to an image, and are highly important in terms of controlling the images within a design.

1. **Floating Images.** This feature offers the ability to place an image within text to the right, center, or left along a horizon. Text will dynamically wrap around a floating image, creating a look familiar to us from newspapers and magazines (see Figures 6-2 and 6-3).
2. **Image width and height.** These arguments are specifically important to a designer because they help to optimize graphics for speed and sensible loading.
3. **Tables.** One of the most effective ways of viewing comparative information is in a row/column format. Table support in browsers gives the designer a visually effective means of presentation akin to the common spreadsheet.
   - **Bgcolor.** This allows the table (or cell) background color to be set independent of the page.

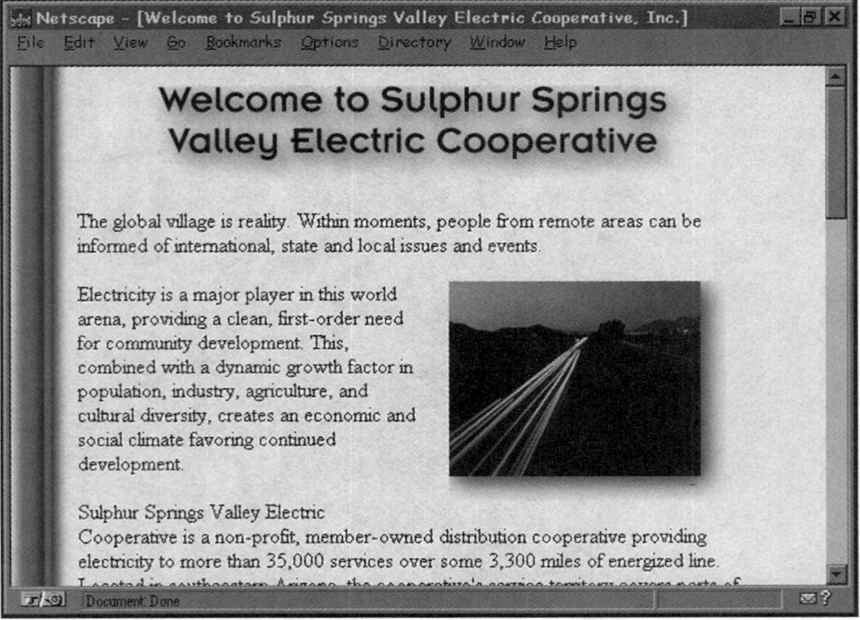

Figure 6-2 An example of a floating image as viewed through Netscape 2.1: http://ssvec.org/ssvec/

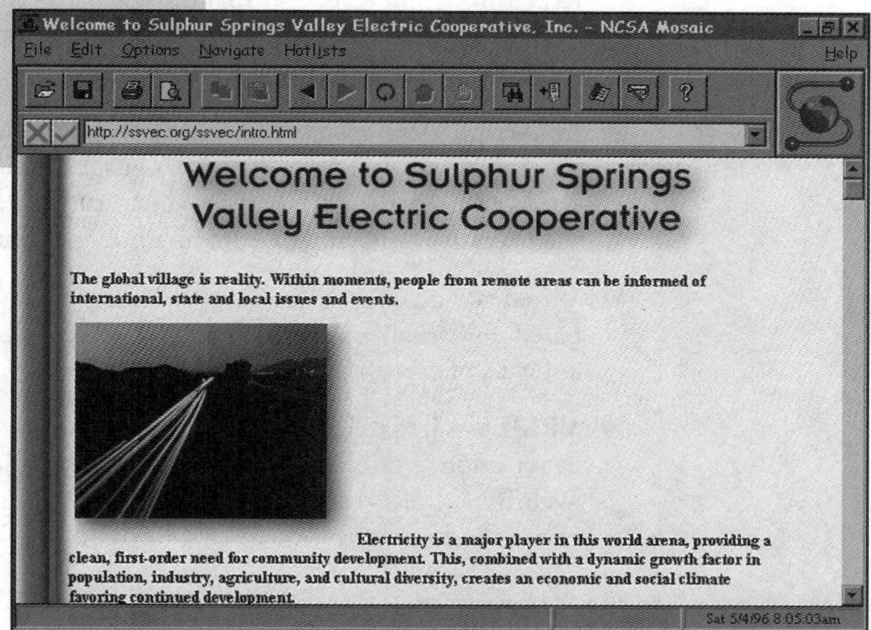

Figure 6-3
The same image as viewed through Mosaic 2.1.1

- **Background.** This allows the table (or cell) background image to specified.
- **Width.** This value is somewhat problematic: there are screen percentage definitions and actual pixel definitions of the displayed width of columns supported by different browsers.

Programming

These programming environments now (or soon will) figure strongly in Web site development:

- **ActiveX.** Microsoft's major development kit will assist in the development of Internet applications and content. ActiveX technologies will allow for a wide variety of multimedia and programming functions. They will be fully available upon release of Internet Explorer 3.0.
- **Java.** Developed by Sun Microsystems, this language allows "applets," or little applications—in this case executable programs—

to be run within a browser that has a Java interpreter as part of its design. Popular uses for Java include animations and other, multiple media applications.

- **JavaScript.** Developed by Netscape Communications Corporation, JavaScript is based on the Java language. It allows designers to create a variety of active multimedia features, but simply, without the necessity of having to learn an entire programming language.
- **Visual Basic Script.** Microsoft has created this scripting language, based on Visual Basic and often referred to as the "Java Killer," as a means of creating in-line Web applications.
- **VRML—Virtual Reality Modeling Language.** VRML allows for the creation of three-dimensional scenes and inclusive World Wide Web hyperlinks. It was born of a desire to move beyond static images and into sense-oriented worlds on the Web.

Special Scripting Features: Cookies

No, *cookies* aren't a batch of hot chocolate chips served up over your modem! The term refers to *client-side persistent information*, implemented as a bite (byte?) of data in which a Common Gateway Interface (CGI) script stores information from the Web browser on the Web server and can later read it again. This is useful for having the browser keep data from page to page—like a virtual shopping cart visiting pages and keeping the information throughout the visit, or between different dates a visitor comes to a site.

Support Services and Applications

Support services and applications commonly assume these forms:

1. **Access to other Internet clients.** Whether it be through a plug-in, a helper application, or an in-line method, the following clients are often associated with a browser, making the Web browser a central apparatus for Internet navigation:
   - **E-mail.** Allows a user to access a standard POP server without launching a separate application. E-mail can be read and sent

from the browser, and such features as images and links can be incorporated in messages.

- **FTP—File Transfer Protocol.** Access to FTP servers enables downloads of documents and programs from directly within the browser.
- **Gopher.** Once embracing the most highly used central research servers on the Internet, Gopher has now largely been absorbed by the World Wide Web. Existing Gopher services can be accessed through Web browsers.
- **News.** Allows Internet newsgroups to be read and posted to from the browser environment.
- **Telnet.** This is a mechanism that allows individuals to directly access the internal workings of a given server, if they have access. From there, they can manage a wide range of processes including file and data transfers, and they can access other services.

2. **Documentation.** Any good software package will come with documentation of some sort, describing the features and options the given product has. Often, there will be a hard-copy version and an online help resource.
3. **Security.** In terms of browsers, "security" refers to the availability of secure transaction transmission over the Net. At this writing, SSL is the most common security scheme; however, several other proposed forms of browser-supported security schemes are under discussion.

   - **SSL(Secure Socket Layer).** This is a low-level encryption scheme that encrypts transactions. It was developed by Netscape Communications Corporation.
   - **SHTTP (Secure HTTP).** This is the scheme proposed by CommerceNet, a group of businesses interested in developing the Internet for commercial use. It is a higher-level security option that works only with the HTTP protocol.
   - **PCT Protocol.** Microsoft's entry in the stakes, this security protocol is backward compatible with SSL.

This Site Is Not Enhanced

No matter the quality of a specific site's design, a good design director will go into spasms when viewing a site that advertises its enhancements. A good designer should never, and I mean never, have to justify his or her choices. Certainly if one is *choosing* to give options such as text or no text, frames or no frames, that's an honorable thing. But having to use browser A or browser B to get to the content should not occur. Even if certain design elements are employed, such as a server push-pull animation that is only handled by Netscape or a marquee that is only viewable by Internet Explorer, the thrust of the site's content should be intact.

I didn't always feel that way, I'll confess. I once believed that it didn't matter who saw or didn't see my site. That attitude is well and good for a personal home page or highly artistic project, but it is tantamount to the death of a commercial site. The one exception we see is when a company is interested only in the image that having a Web site offers. Even so, the site can be designed so that the content is *at the very least* textually accessible regardless of the visitor's chosen browser.

This is not to say that courtesies such as allowing visitors to know what to expect on a given site aren't encouraged. Some Web designers feel this is an imperative, and I won't argue that having a choice is a bad thing. After all, choice is in step with the interactive, new media model upon which the World Wide Web is built. Many sites using frames, tables, animations, and other nonstandard features will offer alternative options for their visitors, and this is a great courtesy (see Figures 6-4 and 6-5). It must be stressed, however, that such options be offered as part of the design, with sensibility and style.

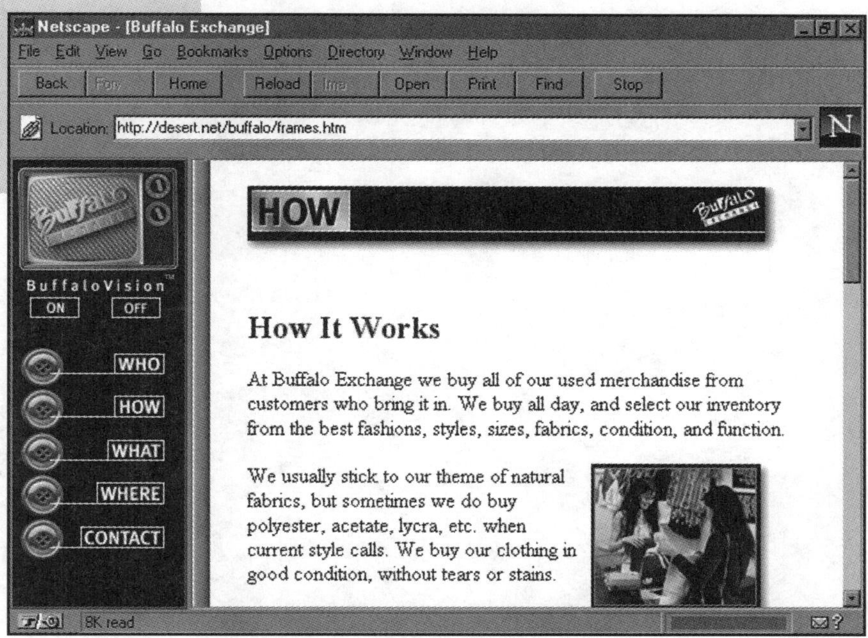

Figure 6-4 The Buffalo Exchange (http://desert.net/buffalo/) viewed with frames

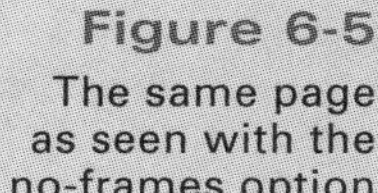

Figure 6-5 The same page as seen with the no-frames option

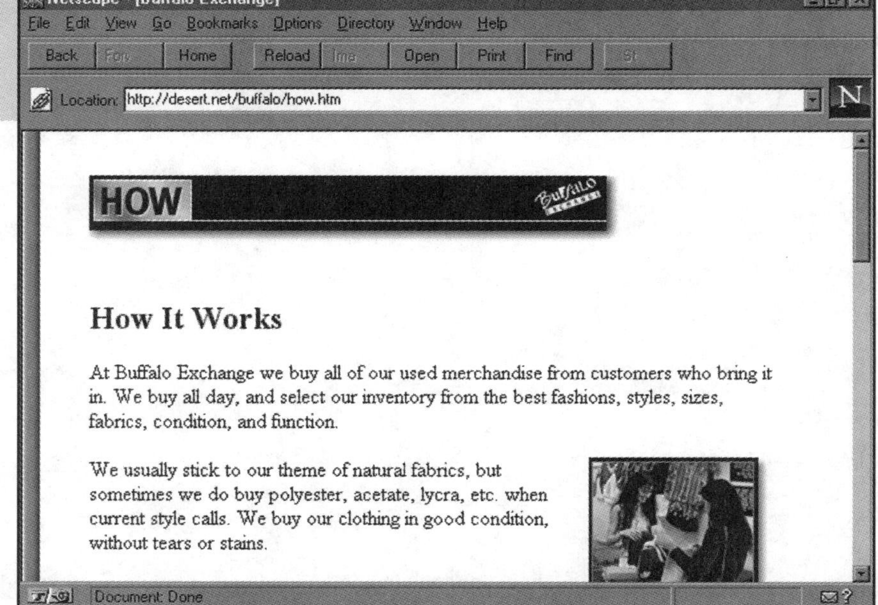

Part III

The Process of Creating Web Sites

chapter 7

An Overview of the Web Design Process

Perhaps the most important pieces of any creative or interactive endeavor are the base elements. In cooking it is the quality, freshness, and type of the ingredients; in human relations it is trust, honesty, and communication. With Web design, it is the preproduction work that, if not well-organized and arranged, can lead to the first and most deadly failing of a site's design.

Because the field is so new and no model exists, it becomes imperative for the designer to think about his or her role in the preproduction phase very carefully. There are highly specific questions that a designer can ask him or herself before beginning, and there are techniques than can be borrowed from other media to make the process easier. As we examine the process, we will refer to the team model, but these techniques and challenges can also be applied by the individual who must go about the task alone.

In this section of *Professional Web Design*, we will be taking a look at the process of creating Web sites. I want to first describe the process as a whole and then go into the individual disciplines. The intent is to demonstrate the theoretical complexity of the Web design process, then to look at the process in action, and finally to examine fundamental applications within the various disciplines. In this section we begin to depart from the theoretical as we explore issues applying to the act of creating Web sites.

The process of creating Web sites can be broken down into a several areas and subareas, such as the following:

- Preproduction (including evaluation)
- Production
- Publication
- Postproduction (including expansion)

Each of these areas focuses on very specific types of responsibilities within the Web design process. Not everyone is going to approach Web design in specifically this fashion, or in this order, but again—here we are seeking to offer an ideal. This section of *Professional Web Design* examines theoretical and often practical guidelines that a Web designer can use as a helpful, organized model by which to work.

In this section, we will discuss many disciplines within Web design, including HTML and graphic design, and we will even take two virtual guided tours through the process. The central idea in this section of *Professional Web Design* is to give the designer a model to follow rather than teach the disciplines, which are described in detail in section 4 of the book, "Web Design Technology in Practice."

From client-designer meeting, through placement of the site on a server, and even further ahead to potential growth and change, the following chapters, then, will provide a model that designers can use as a guide. Our virtual tour guides will take us through difficult as well as simple site design examples, offering insight into the things that worked or did not work in these particular case scenarios.

Preproduction

There is an old saying among programmers—"The sooner you start to code, the longer it's going to take you." In other words, if you start working without a well-thought-out plan, it's going to take more time. In fact, in media production in general, preproduction is considered about two-thirds of the process. Do your homework in this part of the process and end up with a better product all around! Preproduction in Web design can include the following steps:

The Client-Designer Meeting

The client-designer meeting is crucial for a number of reasons. First, and most important, it gives each party an opportunity to learn about the other's intentions and directions. In an ideal situation, this meeting is in a comfortable, relaxed atmosphere, where the client can be at ease and the Web designer has the tools of his or her trade at hand—Net connectivity, a good monitor, and perhaps a chalkboard where preliminary ideas can be sketched out. And of course, we recommend a pot of excellent coffee. The designer, by virtue of her profession, requires it, and the client may very well appreciate it. In all seriousness, the client's comfort (and the designer's) is paramount to providing an environment where trust, and ultimately strong communications, can best be realized.

Obtaining Content

Although some initial planning can occur without all of the content, it is wise to have as much data—copy, logos, photography, or other existing marketing and information materials the client has used—as possible. In fact, content in preproduction is a more-is-more situation.

This may seem odd at first, because designing for the Web often requires a less-is-more approach. However, having detailed data as well as insight and direction from the design meeting allows the Web designer to synthesize ideas to best meet the needs of the client. Besides, it's always easier to cut than to add. It's going to be to the Web designer's benefit if he or she can begin with too much information and set aside the parts deemed repetitive or unnecessary. Having little to start with and trying to flesh it out later to make a site work is much more difficult and can result in a weak presentation.

Assessment of Client Need

After the design meeting, and when the Web designer has received a significant portion of the data, the designer will sit down and evaluate the important facts drawn from the conversation. The designer will address critical questions and concerns in order to begin planning the site. Needs from client to client will be very different, and it is at this point that decisions regarding the major thrust of the site will be evaluated.

Planning

After defining the client's needs and examining the data received, the Web designer can begin planning for the site. This involves determining size and related navigation options, general look and feel, content and graphic layout and design, programming features, and interactive elements. The Web designer working in the team model will begin thinking about which graphic designers will be best suited to the job, what type of programming and programmers will be necessary, and what some of the long-term goals of the site are. This is an excellent time to consider maintenance and growth issues, what we like to refer to as *open-ended design.*

Storyboarding

Borrowed from a technique used regularly in film and television, the use of storyboards that map out each section of the site is an extremely effective way of getting concepts and data organized. As suggested in Figure 7-1, the unique aspect of storyboarding for the Web lies in the interactive element. It is essential to remember that Web storyboards are not hierarchical; rather, each aspect relates to other pieces of the site—and other sites on the Web—via hypermedia. The Web designer begins to assign specific tasks, based on the storyboard, to various members of the team.

Site Mock-Up

Once the storyboard is in place, it is helpful to begin setting up a simple example of the site. At this point, it's important to remain flexible enough that changes can be readily implemented. As shown in Figure 7-2, use dummy text, preliminary colors and graphics, and examples of applicable programs and special features instead of creating full-fledged final items. This approach saves time and trouble if a client has concerns with elements of the direction the Web designer has taken, and it also allows for new ideas to be implemented along the way.

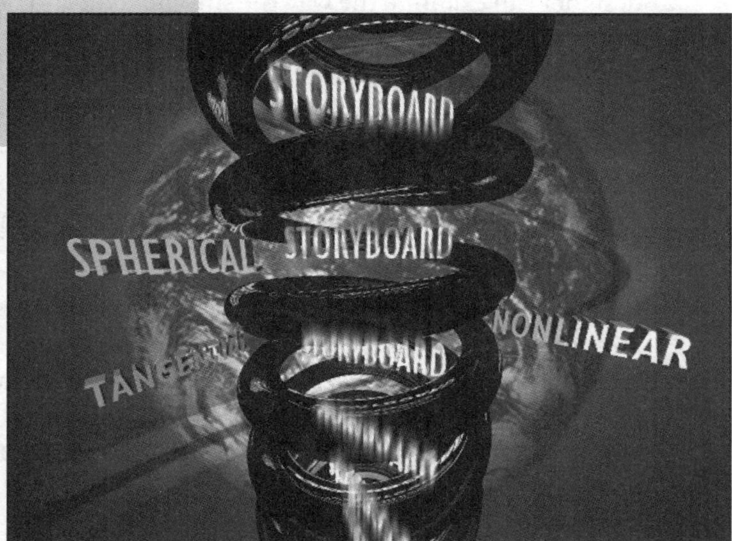

Figure 7-1
Storyboarding for the Web

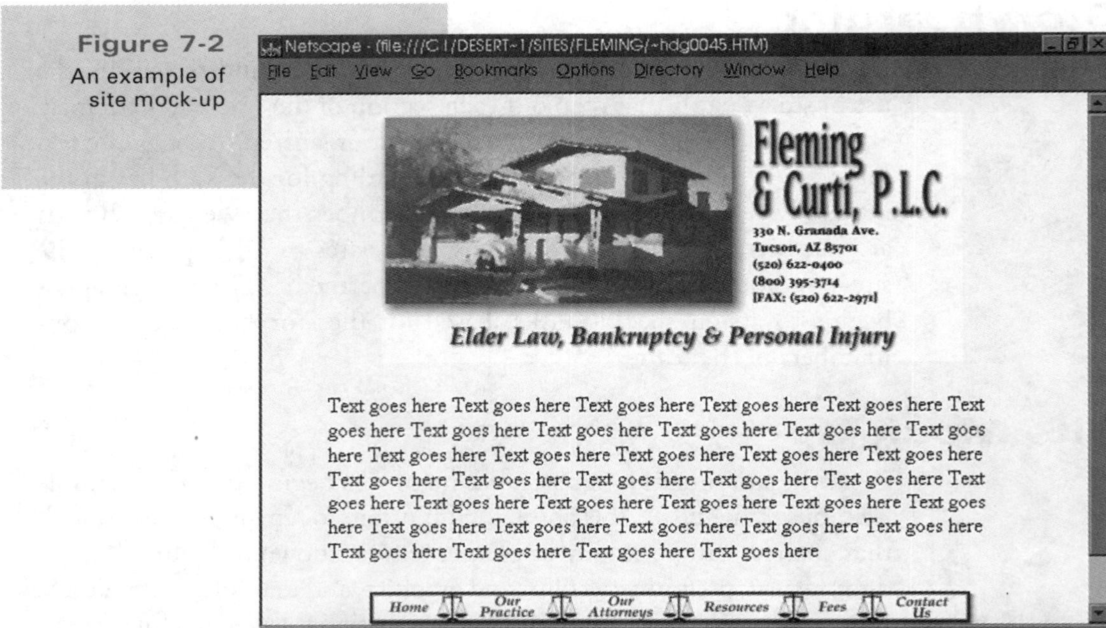

Figure 7-2 An example of site mock-up

Evaluation

Now that there is a visual example of the site's direction, the Web designer can examine the way the site will look and how it will interact, and an initial determination can be made regarding the site's overall match with client need and direction. The Web designer should encourage input from all team members at this point, seeking out criticism, new ideas, and fresh input as to the realization of the site. This is typically a time when specific problems, solutions, and new directions will occur—and it's better to have them occur now than down the road when the site is fully developed.

Once the Web designer and development team have evaluated the site and implemented their ideas, a second client-designer meeting should take place. At this point, the client can respond to the direction of the site, the look and feel, and the interactive elements. This is a very critical and sensitive meeting, since we want to keep the client's interaction on a very directed path. As we will see, giving the client too much weight in the process can make more work for everyone, and it is the designer's responsibility to respond to reasonable, applicable requests but gently explain why certain decisions were made about the site at this point. If the designer has really done his or her preproduction work, client feedback will typically be positive and the process can continue smoothly.

Reevaluation

With new feedback from the client, the designer now can reevaluate the site design and direction. The designer gathers all of the information and feedback received so far, reevaluates the site, and makes decisions as to what needs to be changed, altered, and redirected.

Production

Ideally the preproduction work was done thoroughly enough to make the actual site development smooth. The Web designer now firmly picks up the orchestral baton and begins to orchestrate the final production of the site. The following list gives a brief overview of the production elements and process, but it is very important to bear in mind the original, interactive team model. Although individual team members may need to work in isolation for certain developmental aspects of production, interaction with the team is imperative. It falls on the Web designer to do a lot of over-the-shoulder peering into the various activities and to help everyone get involved on an interactive level as the following pieces of the puzzle are pulled together:

- **Content and copy writing.** The Web designer works with writers and editors to flesh out and refine the site's copy.
- **HTML.** Once the copy, graphic, programming, and media elements are in place, the HTML coders code the pages and add various structures and elements.
- **Graphic design.** Graphic designers begin the final renderings of the varied graphic elements, including headers, backgrounds, image maps, navigation bars and buttons, and any special graphic elements.

- **Multimedia.** If audio, video, plug-in, or other multimedia technologies are going to be used, they are developed at this time.
- **Advanced programming.** Special programming elements including forms, Java, Visual Basic, or any other advanced programming options are created and debugged.
- **Systems administration.** Web server administrators are contacted and advised as to what will be required to house the site. If the design company runs its own servers, the systems administrators will begin developing directory structures and preparing for any special scripts or other programming required. Extra services such as domain names and the like will be implemented at this time.
- **Marketing and sales.** Sales staff should be aware of the site's progress and be working on unique internal and external marketing ideas to reach both broad-based and target audiences.

Publication

If all has gone according to plan, at the end of this process we should have a fully designed interactive site ready to place on the Web. Actual placement is referred to as *publication,* when the Web site will be "officially" online.

Even after it is in its fully designed, active home, the Web site should be reviewed very carefully for any and all problems that may have been missed during production. This step can also be referred to as *editorial review.* Review of copy, code, and graphics, along with thorough browser testing, are performed at this point.

Postproduction

The Web designer must now coordinate postproduction activities. These include such items as:

- **Site indexing.** The site is registered with major Web search engines and indexes.

- **Search key tagging.** Elements to assist in making sure the site gets multiple listings are added to the site.
- **Marketing strategies: on the Net.** Some options include purchase of banner advertising on widely used sites, favorable sharing of links, and announcements to relevant and appropriate newsgroups and lists of interest to the potential product market.
- **Marketing strategies: off the Net.** The client is encouraged to use its Web site in all aspects of other marketing, in-house, and general communications—this is an extremely effective offline marketing enhancement to bring the best to the Web site.

Expansion

Very often clients will return for expansion or redesign of their sites, depending upon their varied needs. This is why it is always wise to design sites with the future in mind, so that extra content, new technologies, and new ideas can be easily and readily implemented for a client.

Organization Equals a Strong Foundation

From this overview, it is easy to see how professional Web design is a fairly complex procedure. As with any business undertaking, excellent organization as well as straightforward communication skills will give the designers a strong foundation upon which to produce the product and service. Furthermore, although individual talents and independent work must be respected, in the team model it is imperative that interactivity be kept uppermost in order to enhance every aspect of a site's design, implementation, and ultimate success.

Shamanism, Music, Coffee, the 'Net

Phil Stevens

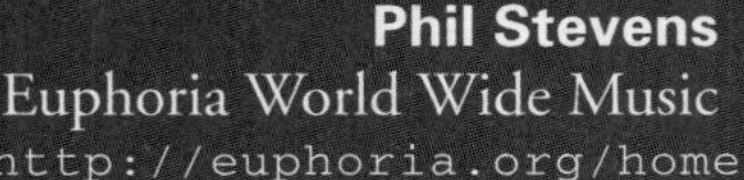

Euphoria World Wide Music

http://euphoria.org/home/

Phil Stevens has a remarkable way of blending music, audio engineering, computer programming and technology, humor, and musicianship—all manifest in his web work as the web Shaman of Euphoria. Whether the drive is a result of too much good coffee or genetics is yet to be discovered.

"I'm a lifelong musician who's always had an interest in how things work. I used to take apart radios and tape decks when I was a kid and try to make them sound different. My first brush with computers was in the late 1970s, and since then I've used the infernal machines in some fashion.

In 1993 I was exploring gopherspace and had the bright idea of creating a site devoted to music and indie labels, with artist bios and downloadable sound files. The web was brand new, and it appeared to be the direction things were heading. The seeds of Euphoria were planted. 1994 was the year that the Courage Sisters were recording their CD in my studio. A series of caffeine-fueled brainstorms with Molly led to talks with my childhood orchestra pal Joel, and by January of 1995 we had a web server to play on.

Molly and I started working on the Euphoria site with a vision and little else. Within a couple of months, we had other organizations interested in our abilities, and were officially in the web design business."

The Healing Web

Rebecca Ryan Hunter

Results Direct Internet Marketing

http://www.resultsdirect.com

One of the often overlooked activities of web designers is their involvement in creating web services that exist to help and support people worldwide. It's extremely important for the public to know that web designers in general are drawn to the field because of a love of not only design, but human interactivity. Because of this and their access to vast resources humanitarian efforts are a major part of a web designer's role and responsibility.

"I have been working for the last 15 months to design web sites that are useful for people, that bringing information to people who need it.

My greatest pride is not one of the corporate designs I have done but a web site designed to provide information for women who have been diagnosed with cervical dysplasia. Since the creation of that site, I have received a large amount of mail from women who have been diagnosed and have received little or no information about their condition. They come to the web to search for information and I am able to comfort them, teach them, and help them be more demanding of their doctors.

I wish there was no need for this site, but there is because doctors aren't being helpful enough. Thankfully, I have a forum where I can help others."

chapter 8

Evaluation and Preproduction

As mentioned in the previous chapter, preproduction may be the most critical aspect of the Web design process. By knowing where the starting gate is, the Web designer and design team are better equipped to look toward the finish line with optimism and confidence. If you or your company doesn't yet have a model for preproduction, it may be a good time to consider creating one. The reason is simple: preproduction is by its very nature the most intensive part of the production process. It requires tremendous organization, very highly developed communications between team members and the client—it is essentially the starting point where the Web site begins. If there is failure at this level, that failure can, as we will later see, be carried into the process and create many challenges for the design team members and client alike.

The following phases of preproduction and evaluation will be discussed in detail:

- The client-designer meeting
- Obtaining content
- Assessment of client and site need
- Planning
- Storyboarding
- Site mock-up
- Evaluation

The Client-Designer Meeting

Whether the client has been brought in by a sales team member, an ad agency, or some other contact, once the client is ready to have a Web site developed, the first step in preproduction is the Web design meeting. This meeting will set the tone, pace, and communication style of any future dealings with the client, so it is never to be taken for granted. A professional, confident demeanor; clear, sincere, and specific communications; and a good dose of enthusiasm are highly recommended for the Web designer going into this meeting.

Introduce yourself, briefly describing your background and current responsibilities, and offer a brief outline of what can be expected during the meeting. It is a good idea to keep your introductions short, because the Web design meeting is going to be much more successful if you allow the client to do a lot of the talking. However, the client may have questions about you and your company, so be ready to ask and answer any questions that the client may have.

Be prepared to take notes and subtly direct the conversation, but once a rhythm and rapport are established, the best thing you as a Web designer can do for the first part of the meeting is be a good listener.

An excellent starting point for the first meeting is to find out how much your client actually knows about the World Wide Web. Ask her about what she's read, if she currently has an Internet account, what type of access she has, how much she's surfed the Web, and what sites she enjoys. Listen very carefully as the client speaks because her answers will give you an idea of her own level of exposure, interests, and possible prejudices.

Then begin asking questions about your client's business. Remember, you know about Web design, but the client knows about bicycles, French food, or recreational vehicles. Let the client tell you what excites her about her work, as this will help you gain direction and gather ideas about what will meet the client's needs.

Things to Bring Along to the Client Meeting

- Your design portfolio highlighting the other sites you've worked on
- Working models of company Web sites on a notebook computer
- A client list and/or detailed references
- Company media kits

Exploring the Client's Needs

Once you've gotten to know a little bit about a particular client and his business, you should ask specific questions about the substance of the proposed site. Consider asking questions like these:

- **What is the primary intent in having a Web site?** The client may want point of sales (see Figure 8-1), or simply the brightest and boldest online presence around. Other clients want precision content geared toward a focus group (see Figure 8-2), and still others simply want a place to provide company or organizational information (Figure 8-3). This first question is a very key one to ask the client—as well as one to keep asking yourself as the Web designer. Ask it continually throughout the process, because it will assist in further clarifying the site's focus and intent.

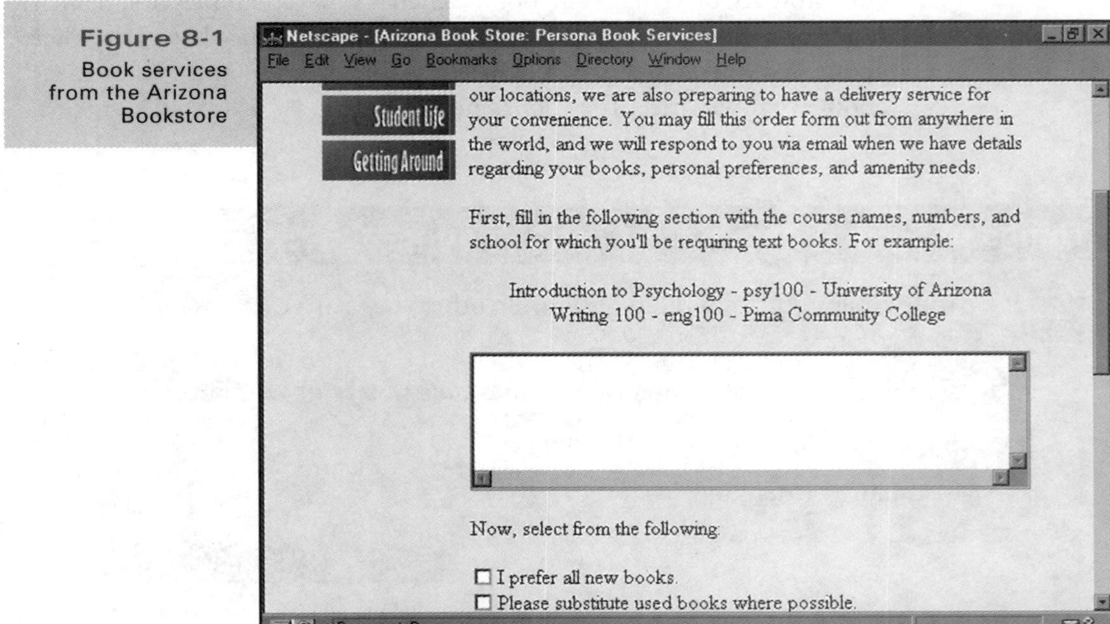

Figure 8-1 Book services from the Arizona Bookstore

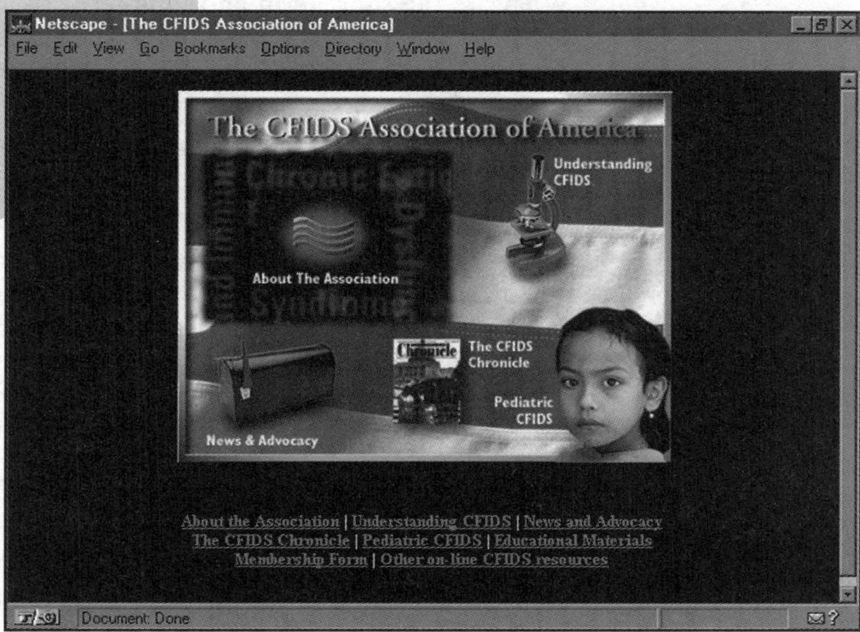

Figure 8-2 The Chronic Fatigue and Immune Dysfunction Syndrome home page

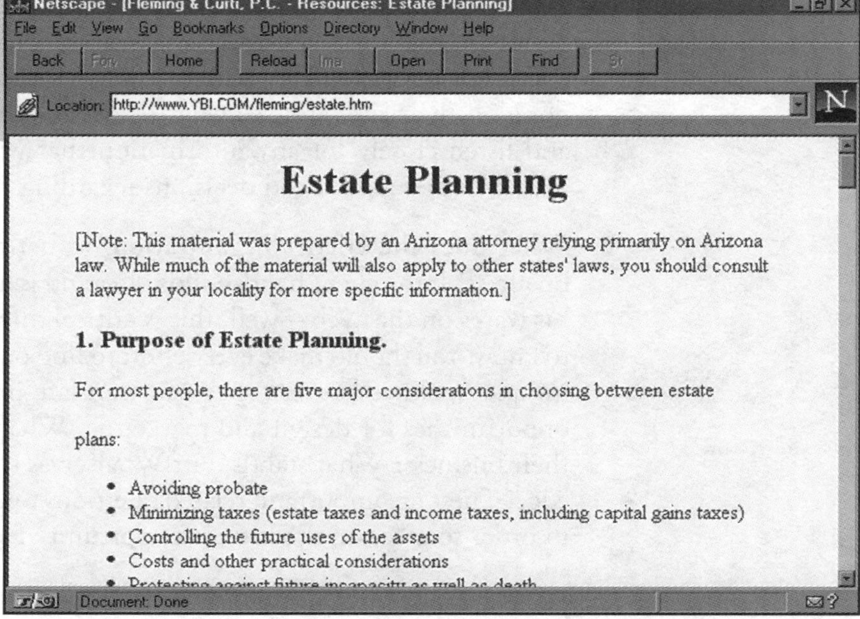

Figure 8-3 Legal benefit information from Fleming and Curti, PC

- **What are the short-term and long-term goals of the site?** It is possible that the client wants only to make static information available on the Web. If that is the case, there is an opportunity to discuss the value of interactive media and how they can enhance the presentation of the client's ideas and information. On the other hand, the client may have ideas that are not realistic for the site's audience. How do these ideas fit in the short term? The long term? Keeping sites fresh and interesting is an important part of site design, and this is an excellent time to recommend that the client develop an ongoing commitment and strategy for updating and maintaining the sites (Figure 8-4).
- **Who is their intended audience?** Who does the client hope to attract to the site? If the client represents senior citizens, then a certain presentation, look and feel, and style of navigation will be appropriate; if a site is designed to appeal to contemporary poets, a different design is called for (see Figure 8-5). It is interesting to keep in mind that, while we can design for a certain target audience, we also want the site to appeal to the broad spectrum of Web surfers. If the client's site is done well, it will be frequented by seniors and others alike.
- **What appeals to the client?** Demonstrate an animation, a high-tech page, a simple page; give the client a sampler of what can be done on their site, and see what tickles his or her fancy. Watch and listen closely for any information that will help you as the Web designer make solid decisions regarding the client's needs.
- **What does the client's organization do better than any other business?** If the client hand-builds kites and is hoping to showcase his wares on the Web—well, this is critical information you need to know. You should make every effort to find out the organization's unique qualities because they can translate into equally unique opportunities for design and marketing. What is different about their business? What stands out? What gives this organization its edge? These are important, related questions to ask and understand in order to give the site its best opportunity for success.

Figure 8-4 The Sulphur Springs Valley Electric Cooperative provides updates of southeastern Arizona events.

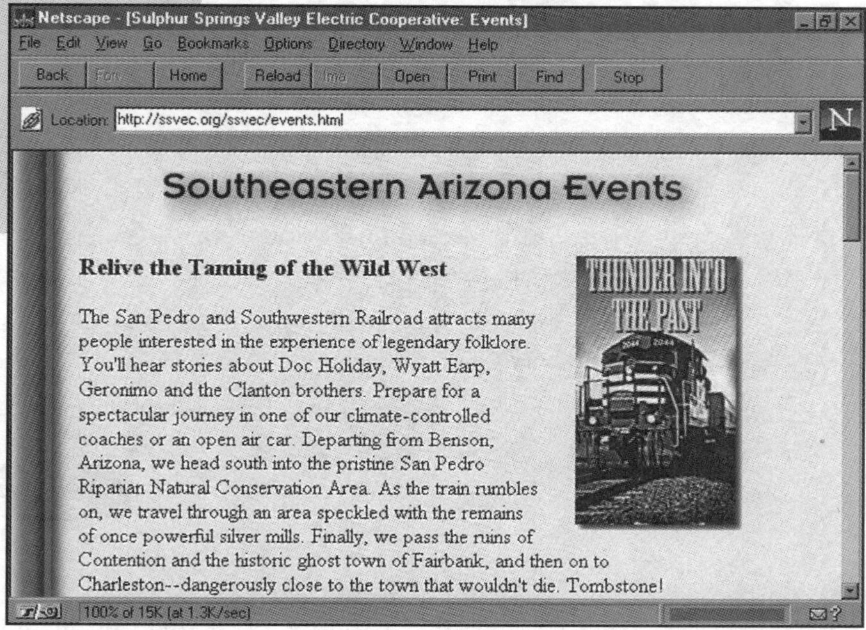

Figure 8-5 A hypermedia poem, designed especially for the contemporary artist, not for the conservative commercial client

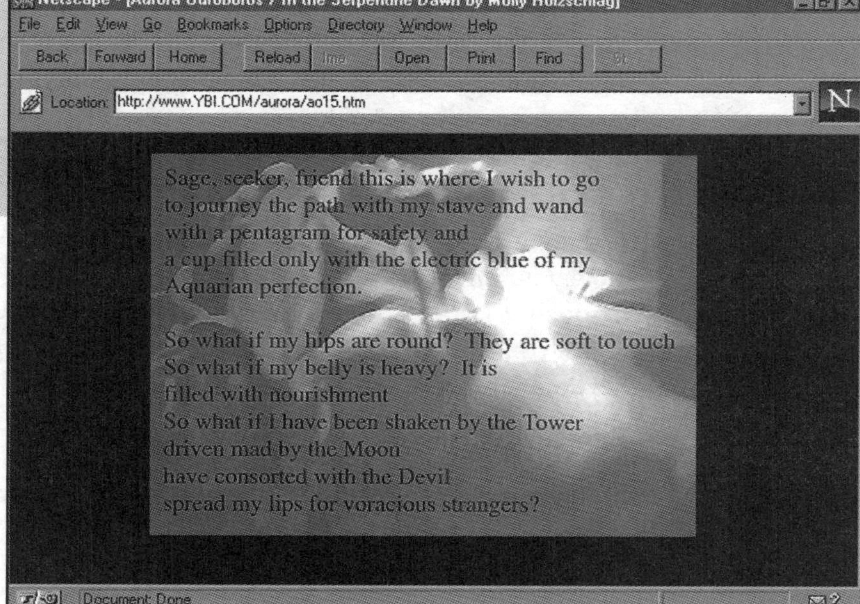

Six Questions a Web Designer Should Ask a Client

- What is your primary intent in having a Web site?
- What are your short- and long-term goals regarding the site?
- Who is the intended audience?
- What, from this demonstration of the World Wide Web, appeals or does not appeal to you?
- What is your current media image, and are you satisfied with that image?
- What does your organization do better than anyone else?

After you've gotten a good sense of what the client's intent, audience, and tastes are, it is a good time to allow for natural brainstorming and conversation to occur. This gives both the client and the designer time to digest all the details. Get a sense of the individual and what interests him or her most about what he or she does. Note any critical observations as to his or her thoughts, opinions, and outlook on how the company is presented.

Managing the Client

In the course of the client-designer meeting, you will be getting to know your client—his or her organization, style of presentation, and personality. Clients come in many different flavors. Some will be very interested in being a team player; others will want to be told what it is they want and need. Still others will be intimidated by the technology, and then there are those clients that will want too much control in the process. Finding a way to work effectively with each individual comes through experience, intuition, and—as always—good communication.

Here are some tips for dealing with clients:

- **Clearly define the terms of your design process to the client.** Explain the process to your client very clearly—from client meeting, through to production and publication. Let the client know at which points he or she will be brought in for consultation, and how long each step of the process will take. Defining the process very clearly gives the client an exact schedule of what to expect. This can potentially set the concerned client at ease or deter the client who wants to steer the ship his or her way from the start.
- **Be confident, firm, and ready to say no.** Although professional courtesy is always paramount, learning to remain confident and in control when dealing with nervous or aggressive clients is a benefit. If clients are becoming too involved, say so. If your company cannot meet a certain need or desire of a client, tactfully learn how to express that those are services that your company does not provide. Although it may feel uncomfortable, a strong stance is always going to gain more respect in general than an insecure, all-too-willing-to-please attitude.
- **Know when to say "I don't know."** For some reason these three simple words are threatening to the brightest and best of us. Whether as a result of our aggressive business culture or a personal fear of failure, most people are very uncomfortable admitting that they don't know something. In my experience, being able to answer honestly that you do not know the answer to a certain question is going to be better received by others—who innately understand that not one of us can possibly know everything! You can always temper the answer by saying you will check the appropriate source right away and have an answer for the client immediately. Either way, by saying "I don't know," you avoid the dangerous experience of saying something on the fly that might be incorrect.
- **Know your boundaries.** If you as the Web designer know how much you will allow a client to be involved in the process, and where you draw the line, you will be much better equipped to get the best participation from the client—without that individual confusing the process. Remember again—you know about Web

design; the client specializes in whatever business he or she represents. Finding a working balance is imperative in creating good sites in a timely fashion, instead of getting bogged down in unimportant or time-consuming details.

- **Provide clients with some hard data about the Web and your Web services.** Make sure you have media that represent your services clearly so that the client can always refer to them should basic questions arise. A brief description of what the Internet and the World Wide Web are, and what they can do for potential clients, can be included in media kits.
- **Be available for questions.** Making sure a company representative is available for questions and concerns is often very helpful. Sometimes clients have a lot of questions or insecurities—and just knowing that someone is available to answer concerns alleviates those tensions.

Obtaining Content

After a comfortable client session, ask the client to collect (if he or she hasn't already) as much data about the organization as possible. Brochures, taped audio and video spots, business cards, existing logos, letterheads, pamphlets, catalogs, informational material, contact information photos—the more you can get, the better. This is, in fact, so critical it must be said again! The more hard information and data you can collect from your client at this point in the process, the better position you will be in to design a comprehensive and powerful site.

The reason having more data is important at this phase is that this is the stuff that will direct you as designer in every way. From marketing spin, to identity, and on to the look and feel of a site, the information gathered now will be used as the starting point for the critical analysis of a site's direction to come.

Interestingly, it seems that collecting all the data necessary for a site is one of the most difficult parts of the process. For this reason, it is recommended that you suggest a date by which the client should have the data ready. It may even be wise to go a step farther and let the client know that your turnaround time on a site begins on the day the complete content is received, rather than the design meeting date. Make your client responsible but do it subtly. If you have sales staff, let them give a call to confirm the date at a reasonable midpoint between the design meeting and the appointed time for retrieval of data; otherwise, a gentle reminder from the Web designer is a very reasonable and often helpful thing to do.

Assessment of Client and Site Needs

Once the content is in hand, the Web designer needs to cloister himself or herself with all of the collected data, including content and any notes from the Web design meetings. This is a good place to start asking that all-important question: what is the intent of this site? Working from that question, expand out to the question of audience. Ask a variety of questions regarding look and feel of the site, and how to balance the client's ideas against the realities of the technology and the market. Think about what kind of interactivity will be appealing to the site. Which technologies should be exploited, and which should be avoided? The answer will vary from case to case, but an exhaustive examination of the data and meeting notes will help a site design direction emerge that is focused and appropriate on the client's needs.

I cannot overstate the importance of this needs-assessment process. Before we even enter the planning stage, it is crucial to have a strong grasp of what is required. If you feel less than confident at any point, *now is the time to go back and ask the client to clarify his intent and need.* To do it later will undoubtedly cause an overburdening of yourself and the team or cause problems with the site's development or end design.

Following these suggestions will lead to a successful assessment:

- **Put aside everything you've read so far regarding interactive teamwork.** *"Why do this?"* you may be thinking—particularly after I've stressed the teamwork aspect so fervently. Assessing client need is a solitary job, at least at this point. Site assessment requires intense critical analysis, and it has been my experience that inviting others into this process can take much more time than presenting the team with a solid idea. Once you as the designer have made your assessment, then pass it on to other team members.
- **Begin by asking, "what is the intent of this site?"** Write the intent down in clear, simple terms. Go back and look at it during every step of this process, as well as later on during the remainder of the site's preproduction and production phases.
- **Ask the next critical question: "who is the intended audience?"** Always bear in mind that what a client's target audience is for other media may be different from that client's potential Web audience. Pinpoint a demographic, but always keep the diverse Web audience and its needs in view as decisions are made.
- **If at any time the intent of the site becomes muddied, go back and figure out why.** If there is missing data, absent content, or an unclear idea of the client's needs or audience *go back now and fill in the gaps.*

Answer each question clearly, and then write out a paragraph or two that summarizes the work within this part of the process. This will be a helpful resource to refer to as we move out of assessment and into planning and ultimately production.

At this point, the Web designer can come out of seclusion and offer the summary around to his or her fellow team members for input and insight. This is a strong way of getting the team familiar with upcoming project development and a fine opportunity to do the team-model brainstorming *from a foundational, directed idea* rather than try to have everyone assess all of the data. The Web designer can then evaluate the feedback and apply it to the summary before embarking on the next stage of the process.

Tips for Successful Assessment

- Work alone with the material until a satisfactory direction emerges.
- Continually ask yourself "What is the intent of this site?"
- Often ask "Who is the intended audience?"
- Fill in missing data *now rather than later!*
- Summarize your assessment in a clearly written paragraph or two.

Planning

Site planning is essentially a preliminary layout of how a site's production will be arranged. The Web designer, based on his or her knowledge of client need and site direction, begins to make decisions regarding the who, what, when, how, and why of the process. Critical steps in the planning process include:

- **Content.** The Web designer has, at this point, collected as much data as possible regarding the site (Figure 8-6). Examine the data and decide what content is critical to the site, and approximate a place for that content within the site's construct.
- **Size of site.** Although this may seem a superfluous issue, the opposite is actually true. The amount of data is critical to deciding layout and feel, and to planning the design style, navigation, and interactivity options. Typically, commercial marketing sites will not be extremely extensive, although sometimes they are, for a variety of reasons. As long as the objectives are well thought out and justified, sites can range in size from one page to thousands. As a rule of thumb, however, commercial marketing sites should stick to their intent and remain streamlined, adding interactive aspects as ways to enhance that intent rather than detract from it. Larger sites will typically be data- or content-heavy, as in the case of online

newspapers or search services. In either case, it is imperative to know what quantity of data is to be managed, and how frequently, in order to plan ahead for those needs (Figure 8-7).

- **Navigation.** Also a critical issue to begin solving early in the process, navigation is essential to any site that requires the visitor to move from page to page. There should always be a variety of navigation options for people because, after all, it is the interactivity that gives the Web a great deal of its power. By offering logical choices for site navigation, the Web designer not only creates a cohesive foundation for data access but aids visitors to the site in easily getting to the data. Matching navigation to size of content creates a strong foundation for further site development (Figure 8-8).
- **Look and feel.** This refers to the presentation of material and relates directly to the questions "what is the site's intent" and "who is the audience." If a client is appealing to a conservative audience, a slick, hip site with monosyllabic words and wild colors is not going to be appropriate. This is a very creative area for the Web designer, who is challenged to match a concept to the summary knowledge he or she has gathered (Figures 8-9 and 8-10).

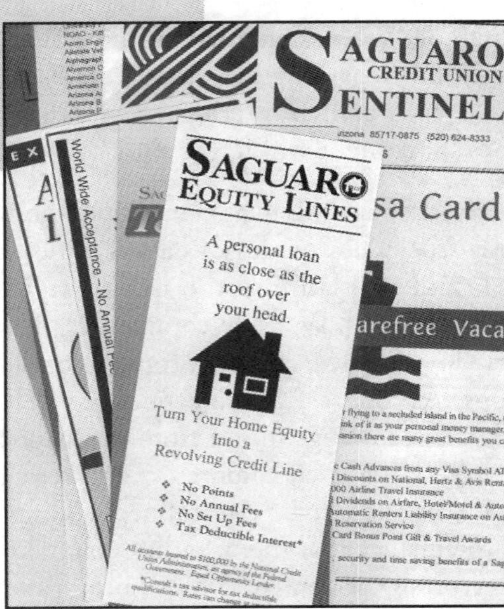

Figure 8-6
A List of content for the Saguaro Credit Union site

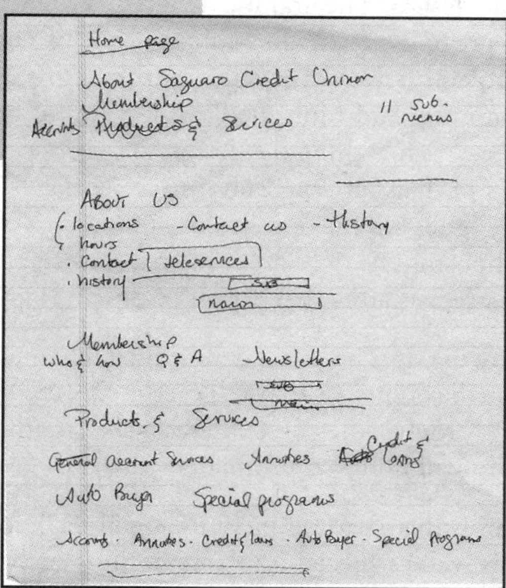

Figure 8-7 Notes on data requirements for Saguaro Credit Union

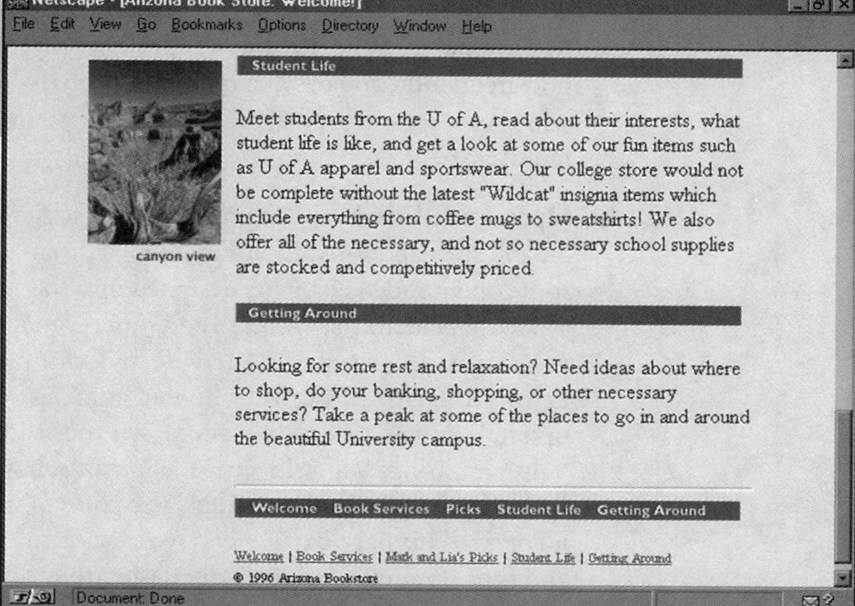

Figure 8-8 Navigation options for the Arizona Bookstore

- **Graphic design.** The graphic design of a site will need to meet all of the previous needs, including extent of content, navigation, and look and feel, as well as other considerations such as programming and multimedia. Most important at this point in the process is matching the design to the conceptual look and feel of the site. It is an especially fun aspect of Web design when a Web designer has the opportunity to match a particular artist to a site. Choosing the right art and artist for a site is as essential to the site's success as any other aspect of design (Figure 8-11).

- **Multimedia.** If it has been determined that audio, video, or other multimedia events are to occur on the site, the Web designer needs to plan for what they are, where in the site they will best reside, and who will do the multimedia work.

- **Programming.** Features including mail-back forms and shopping carts, as well as special implementations such as more advanced gatewayed scripts, Java, Visual Basic script, or other, related applications, may be appropriate for a given site. If they are, then the right programmer, placement of special features, and technical implementation of these features must be planned.

- **Maintenance.** Will this site require ongoing maintenance? If so, how frequently, and of what type? The Web designer will determine what is necessary and plan on ways to meet maintenance requirements.

- **Open-ended design.** It is my sense, as suggested by artist Steve Sloan's surreal doorways in Figure 8-12, that all sites should have some open-ended elements designed into them. This means being aware that clients may want to add more content or special features at a later date. Open-ended design can be very subtle but extraordinarily powerful when it comes to making changes, updates, and additions to a site down the road. For example, the Sulphur Springs Valley Electric Cooperative has a community page that branches out into extended Web content on the communities it covers. This page can easily have new communities added to it, and there is a uniform template design that can be applied to any incoming community (Figures 8-13, 8-14).

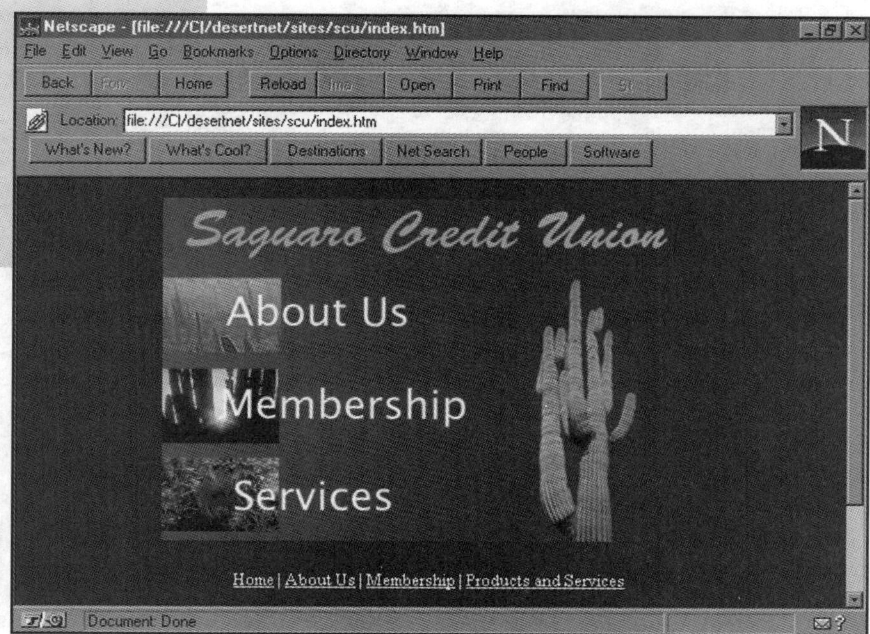

Figure 8-9 Southwestern images for Saguaro Credit Union, a site needing to appeal to a more conservative range of clientele

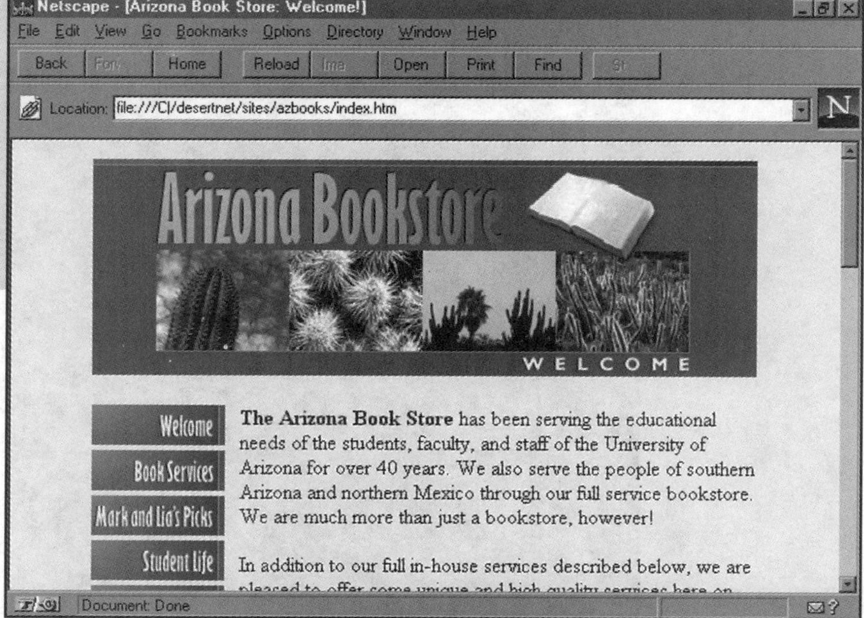

Figure 8-10 A similar design approach for the Arizona Bookstore. This site uses bolder colors and a less conservative layout, appealing to University of Arizona students.

Figure 8-11 Graphic artist Matthew Bardram captures the sensual and wild feel of the Hotel and Club Congress sites

Figure 8-12 Open-ended design

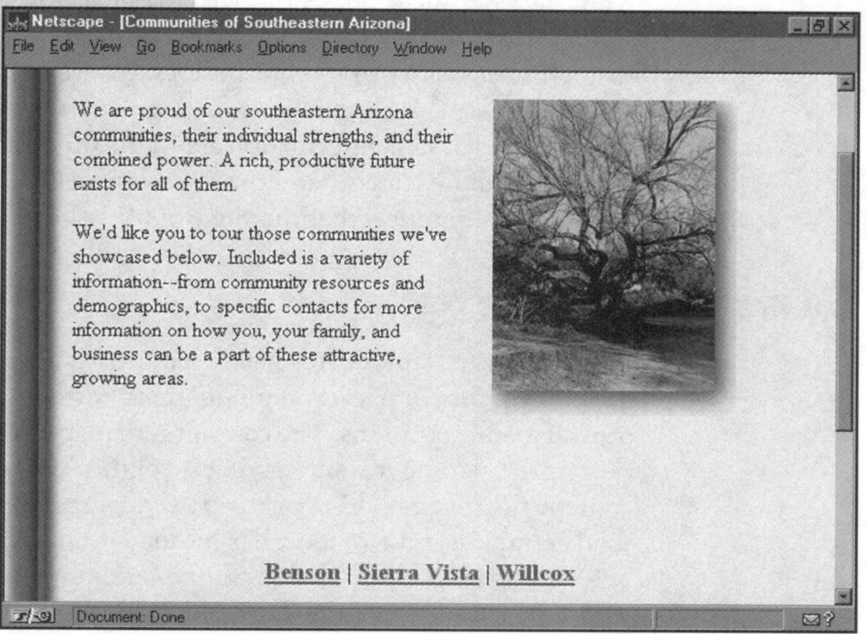

Netscape - [Communities of Southeastern Arizona]
File Edit View Go Bookmarks Options Directory Window Help
We are proud of our southeastern Arizona communities, their individual strengths, and their combined power. A rich, productive future exists for all of them.
We'd like you to tour those communities we've showcased below. Included is a variety of information--from community resources and demographics, to specific contacts for more information on how you, your family, and business can be a part of these attractive, growing areas.
Benson | Sierra Vista | Willcox
Document: Done

Figure 8-13 The Sulphur Springs Valley Community Page

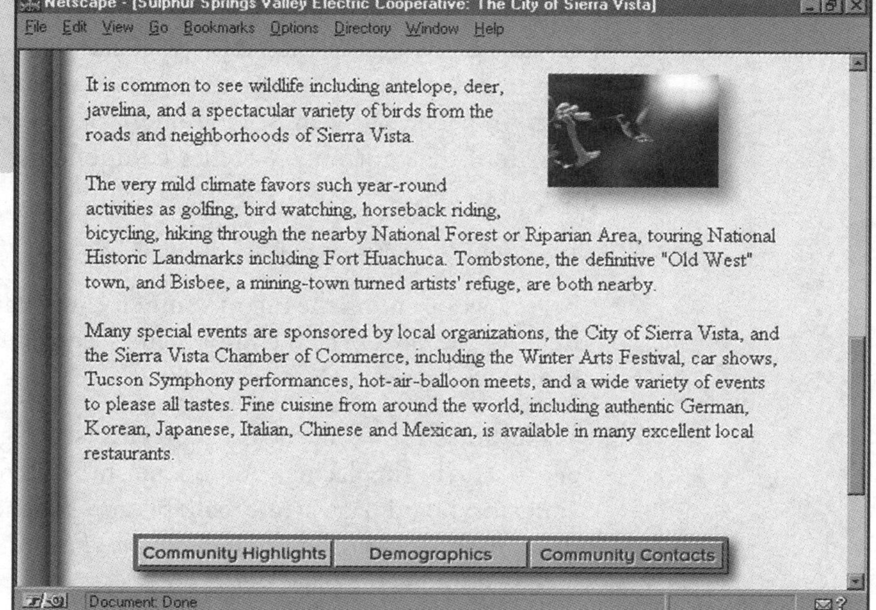

Netscape - [Sulphur Springs Valley Electric Cooperative: The City of Sierra Vista]
File Edit View Go Bookmarks Options Directory Window Help
It is common to see wildlife including antelope, deer, javelina, and a spectacular variety of birds from the roads and neighborhoods of Sierra Vista.
The very mild climate favors such year-round activities as golfing, bird watching, horseback riding, bicycling, hiking through the nearby National Forest or Riparian Area, touring National Historic Landmarks including Fort Huachuca. Tombstone, the definitive "Old West" town, and Bisbee, a mining-town turned artists' refuge, are both nearby.
Many special events are sponsored by local organizations, the City of Sierra Vista, and the Sierra Vista Chamber of Commerce, including the Winter Arts Festival, car shows, Tucson Symphony performances, hot-air-balloon meets, and a wide variety of events to please all tastes. Fine cuisine from around the world, including authentic German, Korean, Japanese, Italian, Chinese and Mexican, is available in many excellent local restaurants.
Community Highlights
Demographics
Community Contacts
Document: Done

Figure 8-14 Community Pages navigational options on the SSVEC site

As in the assessment phase, the Web designer now can write a concise summary of the answers to his or her efforts at this point. It is helpful to use bulleted lists to define specifics, or even to create a template form that the Web designer can use regularly to streamline his or her process. At each step, information about the site's direction is becoming clearer and more concise, and the Web designer has a growing sense of confidence regarding what the site will likely be in completed form.

Storyboarding

For many years, storyboards have been used as a way to sketch out the direction of film or television productions, cartoons, commercials, and other dynamic creations. The concept is to map out the components of every page within the site, giving a solid, physical example of how content fits together. One of the powers of storyboarding is that this solid example is still a lot more flexible than the matrix of film, television, or—in this case—Web design. Storyboarding is akin to doing math with a pencil; if you make a mistake, you can erase it and start again without having to redo the entire problem.

The benefit of Web storyboards goes beyond providing a physical yet flexible sketch of a Web site. Web site storyboards enable the Web designer to play with the interactivity of individual components. A Web storyboard, as shown in Figure 8-15, may appear two-dimensional and linear on paper, but it must be thought of as a three-dimensional, nonlinear tool that not only sketches components, but defines their unique relationships.

The storyboarding process can be done as follows:

- Begin by examining the intent summary and planning evaluation. Refer to the site's design components—copy, images, animation, forms, multimedia.
- Make notes on a storyboard template (see Figure 8-16). Use a pencil, and begin placing components into different sections. Keep your storyboard page areas small, because this helps in organizing the components of the site in a concise fashion, leading to more precise content per page.

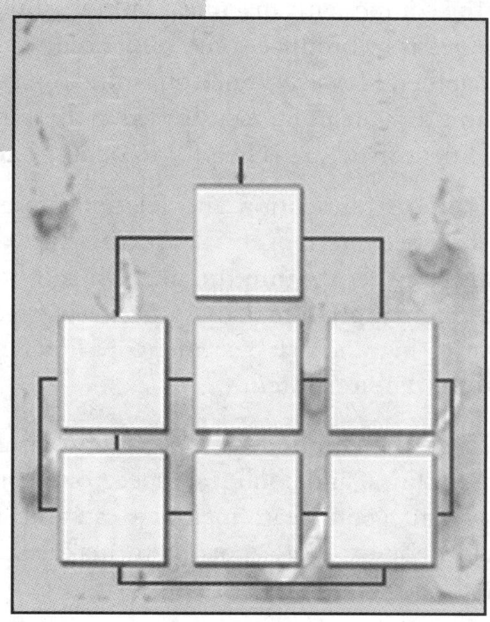

Figure 8-15
A Web storyboard template

Figure 8-16
The Web designer at the chalkboard

- Lay out the components in a linear fashion, but always remember that the idea is to produce something nonlinear by tying certain things together. However, since our minds—and our clients' and visitors' minds—are more accustomed to thinking linearly, having a strong linear structure is helpful to quality site construction.

Once a strong linear foundation and relationship are built, evaluate what aspects can become tangential. Ask if items on page 1 can be linked to items elsewhere within the site. Or, is it better to link them outside of the site? Apply interactivity between pages and other sites cautiously, bearing in mind that placement of a link is meant to enhance, not detract from, the site's intent.

- Now that all the components have found an appropriate place, and both the linear and nonlinear aspects of the site are clear, review the storyboard again. Team members can and should be brought in to help define trouble spots or to make suggestions that will enhance the structure in accordance with their areas of expertise.

- It is often very helpful now to draw the storyboard onto a large chalkboard. The Web designer and design team will refer to this drawing on a regular basis throughout production of the Web site.

Storyboarding

- Refer to all of your prepared summary information.
- Using a storyboard template (see Figure 8-16), place elements in different sections.
- Tie elements together interactively.
- Review the storyboard.
- Draw the final storyboard out onto a chalkboard.

Site Mock-Up

Now that the site has been rendered two-dimensionally and visualized three-dimensionally, it is time to provide an example of the site. It's important to keep things fluid enough that changes can be made immediately and easily. For this reason, it's wise to use dummy text, preliminary graphic ideas, basic forms, and placeholders for multimedia applications. The goal of a mock-up is to see how the site will function in its living form (Figure 8-17). It also provides a ready example for the client at this stage, so if the Web designer has missed elements, or if the client is unhappy with a particular aspect of the mock-up, directions can be shifted without major upheaval.

Furthermore, as the design team's client list and portfolio grow, keeping these mock-ups can actually provide a library of templates for designing in a specific style. The Web designer can then apply or reuse aspects of existing mock-ups for new sites, modifying graphics, links, and code where applicable.

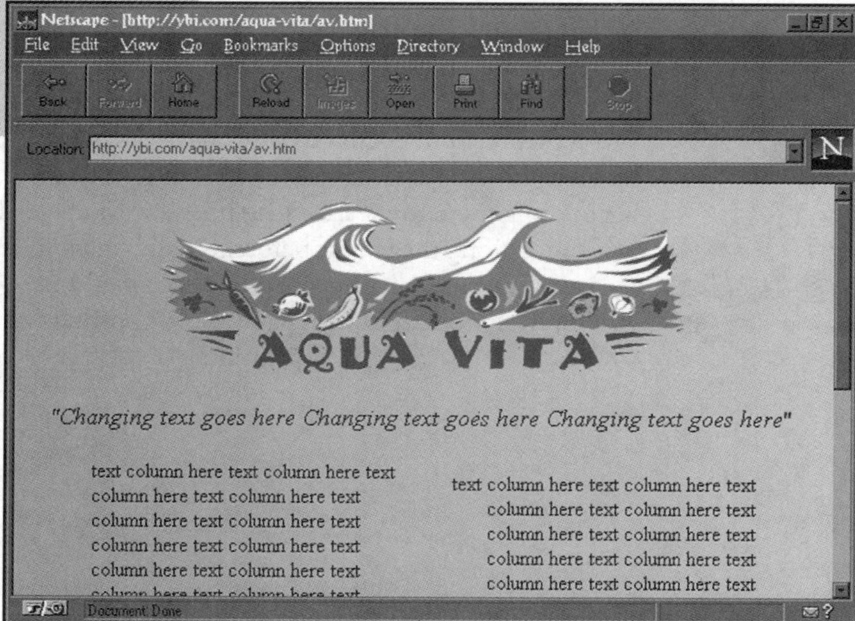

Figure 8-17 A mock-up of the site for Aqua Vita

Evaluation and Reevaluation

Have as many team members as possible examine the mock-up, and then let the client review it. If the Web designer has done his or her preproduction work thoroughly, chances are pretty good that the site will be very close to the client's goal. This is a good time for problem spots to be very easily noticed, and solutions can be provided now rather than later in production, when even more exhaustive work has taken place.

With team and client feedback in hand, the Web designer will know whether it is time to return to the storyboard or move into the next phase of the process. Sometimes—and this is not always the fault of the designer—certain intentions will have been missed or misinterpreted. The value of preproduction is obvious in this situation. When the time for a mock-up is reached, much work will have been done, but it will largely have consisted in the Web designer's planning rather than full-out graphic design, content and copy writing, programming, and multimedia applications production. This approach saves tremendous time, effort, and expense, because if changes must be implemented, they will not entail redesigning a completed site.

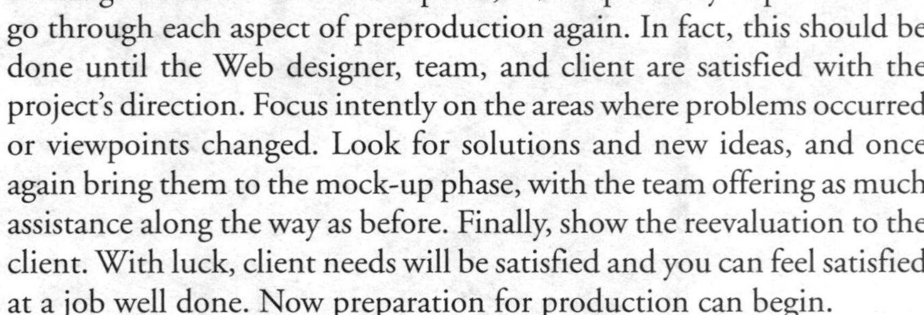

If changes must be made at this point, the simplest way to proceed is to go through each aspect of preproduction again. In fact, this should be done until the Web designer, team, and client are satisfied with the project's direction. Focus intently on the areas where problems occurred or viewpoints changed. Look for solutions and new ideas, and once again bring them to the mock-up phase, with the team offering as much assistance along the way as before. Finally, show the reevaluation to the client. With luck, client needs will be satisfied and you can feel satisfied at a job well done. Now preparation for production can begin.

The Big Picture

Eric J. Andersen
Creative Director, Edge City Media
http://www.novia.net/~ejanders

What really scares Eric is the average guy who found how easy it is to throw together an HTML page.

"Boom, he's a web designer. It's a stampede to get on the web. I put nothing out on that server until there was a site. Nothing irritates me more than a company that this is "under construction." I don't care. It reminds me of going to an all you can eat buffet, and I feel like everyone else is getting my food. My competitor is out there so I have to throw a picture out. Itís a feeding frenzy, and people will throw out anything they can get, when they wouldnít think for a minute sending something like that to a client, wouldnít in a million years send off a piece of paper that says 'buy our stuff, hey we're not finished with this yet, but buy our stuff.'

My biggest concern is that these people are going to make some quick profits with companies that have no idea about the technology but are getting caught up in the web hype.

What is a web designer? No certification needed, but you've got to be not just graphics, and not just technology, but the user interface and human factor. That portion is sorely neglected—because it is so new, and since it is so technology-heavy right now. A lot of people who would be excellent web designers are not in the field because they are scared of it.

I think the most important thing for a web designer to do is to look at the big picture—what the site is going to look at entirely rather than just the front page with a company logo and mission statement. The big picture interface from top to bottom."

Women Online Designs

Amy Goodloe
http://www.wodesigns.com

"I went online for the first time in 1989, back when I was a professional graduate student, and I've been hooked ever since (well, more so since Netscape was first released!). In June, 1994 I decided to quit the graduate program I was in and move to San Francisco to seek my fortune, which turned out to be in Macintosh and Internet consulting. In February, 1995, I started doing business as Women Online, armed with the belief that the Internet is a new frontier, and that, unlike any other time in history, women can have a major influence on the shape of this new terrain.

In February, 1995 I created my first web site and began the process of building a comprehensive index of "women's resources on the Internet." By June, however, the number of women's resources had more than tripled and it was becoming clear that "comprehensive" was no longer an attainable goal, so I turned my attention towards specifically lesbian resources instead, starting with the creation of a not-for-profit web site called Lesbian.org.

Now I devote myself full time to collecting and maintaining resources for women and lesbians, and to enabling lesbian organizations and women-owned businesses to establish a presence in the "online world." In order to better fund this worthy cause, however, I am also doing contract work and looking for ways to grow my small business."

Team Work

Annette Loudon
Construct Internet Design
http://www.construct.net

Finding the space in between the technical and creative is the web designer's goal. In that space, we can balance science and art, and there is something extraordinarily empowering about that. Annette sees this as coming through the combining of artistic and talented individuals within the team model:

"I hope that more creative people team up with tech people and begin to really push the limits of what we know the web to be. VRML and some genetic algorithms could really spice this place up.

Construct's projects benefit from the input of talented people from widely varied backgrounds. We really feel like there is no point making something pretty that doesn't work, nor is there any point making something that works which is unpleasant to navigate.

There are drawbacks to team work as well. In drawing on so many different talents the production process becomes very complicated and takes a great deal of organization and communication. Although we're all getting very good at communication, it can be difficult to get things done when there are so many aspects of production that only a couple of us can do.

I look forward to a time when the web ceases to hip and groovy and that international communication and information sharing becomes something that people take for granted."

The Art of Interface

hUe andresonne
Graphic Design, User Interface Programmer, Tribal Voice
http://www.tribal.com/

Bringing a new voice, and unique way of being to the web is Hue's trademark. His work at Tribal Voice seems totally in step with that new voice, and individual way of relating to others.

"I've been working at Tribal Voice since August, 1995. Since then I've been adding tons of graphics to Tribal Voice's Internet Communicator, the PowWow. Also, writing lots of C code for general improvements to PowWow's User Interface. Before I was working here, I did a lot of rendering stills and animation targeted for the world wide web. My main interest at that time was to get myself on the net and to get prospective employers looking at my site 2see what I could do.

It gives me some real satisfaction to know that there are a whole lot of people out there playing around with the tools/toys that I have made, interacting and communicating with friends and strangers in the way I have dreamed up! I'm fortunate to work in a place which has given me plenty of creative freedom. Sometime I can just come up with an off-the-wall idea and run with it. It's cool to see a gadget or a communication tool go from the idea, through the development process, getting sculpted and tuned, then polished and released and fixed.

Often there isn't much similarity between the spark of idea and the outcome, but as long as the outcome kicks butt then it doesn't matter, it exists as a THING on its own. It's the Creation Process and I'm really hooked on it!"

chapter 9

Production and Publication

It's time for the Web designer to tap his or her baton on the music stand and demand the attention of the instrumentalists. If the Web designer has communicated to his or her team well, not only will they have tuned their instruments—having grown familiar with the agenda and prepared themselves to begin working on the production—but they will also know the score. They will have been apprised of the preproduction summaries and storyboards, and they will be familiar with the direction of the project.

Production and publication are the nuts-and-bolts work of Web site development. If the team has strong skills and has been well prepared, this phase should also be the easiest, most harmonious, and best organized part of the performance. In preproduction, we have had to deal with many varying factors, including clients, who often differ greatly in the ways that they interact and communicate. Hopefully we were able to meet the challenge with strong strategies and production values.

A formal team meeting is the ideal place to begin production, but some people work in "virtual" (long-distance) situations, and some designers use outsourced talent, so a face-to-face launch meeting isn't always practical for the team. Either way, this is another instance where the Web designer must be an expert communicator. At the crucial start of production, he must be prepared to delegate various tasks to the team's members and solicit their input regarding the best ways to interact and refine each part of the individual and team process to come. Ideally, the Web designer has chosen or hired the individuals involved and has found people with high levels of skill in their specific disciplines, who have the ability to work well in a team environment—whether in close quarters or at a distance from one another. For more information on how to find qualified individuals in every aspect of Web design production, visit the Web Developer's Virtual Library, http://www.stars.com/Vlib/Misc/Resumes.html.

This chapter discusses the production process in detail and describes each of the disciplines (copy writing, HTML coding, and so on) that are involved in the physical creation of a Web site. In our team model, the Web designer is charged with directing each of these disciplines; that is, he must manage the team members who are responsible for the various categories of work. The Web designer should know enough about each discipline to communicate his direction to the person in charge of that task. For our one-man-band leader, understanding how each of these disciplines will be managed can lead to a highly streamlined, organized process.

Part IV of *Professional Web Design* details these disciplines more specifically and offers practical guidelines that can help you manage each of them. In this chapter, we seek to describe the Web designer's relationship to the logic and process of these disciplines, and to the people who will actually carry out the required tasks within each discipline.

Content and Copy Writing

Content is the most important element of any Web site. Attractive and fun graphics are significant as well, but content—including *copy*, or text—is the site's true substance. It is important that the team give serious consideration to the site's content and the way it is presented. The Web designer, having examined the needs of a given client, now must decide how to implement the copy within the site's layout. Very often, copy will have been prepared by the client or a representative of the client, and the Web designer will have asked enough questions to ensure that everyone is heading down the right road. Now the job is to refine the content to be consistent with the needs of the Web site while addressing the needs of the site's visitors.

The Web designer and copy writer should ask the following questions:

- **How much freedom do the Web designer and copy writer have with the copy?** Can they change it to meet their specific vision of the site, or has the client expressed concern that the copy provided remain largely intact?

- **Is the copy complete enough?** In other words, does it thoroughly describe the needs of the client and fulfill the site's intent? If not, the copy writer will need to fill in the gaps. This once again speaks to the idea that more is more when it comes to obtaining information from the client.

- **Is the copy too verbose?** People often write more than is necessary. Look at the copy and determine what can be cut, if anything. This will streamline the communication and make it concise enough for the Web environment and the short attention spans of many Web denizens.
- **Does the copy read well and appropriately for the intended audience?** Voice is as important on the Web as anywhere in writing, and perhaps even more so, since the Web is a new medium without too many cues from other sources. Make sure the voice is appropriate for the audience. If it is cocky and youthful but the intended audience is conservative, this is a good time to bring the copy to a better balance.
- **Is the copy free of spelling and grammatical errors?** There is nothing less attractive than a Web site that has poor grammar and misspelled words. The copy writer must ensure that the copy content is clean and free of any problems that will later detract from the strength of the site. Web designers would be wise to recruit experienced writers for their team, or on a consultant basis. Such writers should have experience in newspaper or broadcast writing, as these persons will be skilled at making sure text is both concise and readable.

Questions about the Copy

- Do I have freedom to change the client's copy in any way?
- Is there enough copy?
- Is the copy too wordy?
- Is the copy appropriate for the audience?
- Are there any spelling or grammatical errors that need repair?

HTML

Without our skeletons, our bodies would have no structure; they would be amorphous—unable to move or even survive. HTML is the skeleton of the Web. It supports *every* aspect of a Web site. Without it, we would have no Web.

But HTML does not require genius to understand. It is a very straightforward, logical scripting language, and with so many easy-to-read, informative books on the market, just about anyone can use it and do so fairly well.

However, a Web designer must go beyond knowing HTML or having a coder on the team who knows HTML. Coders must know how to use HTML as creatively as possible, while still keeping the code as clean and legal as is feasible. This is not an easy task and requires much more than knowledge of the language. Coders who understand that HTML is an important part of a Web site—but that it is indeed a *part* and must be treated as such—will fare much better in the business of Web design. HTML must interact with all these other elements of Web design, and that is where the chasm exists between amateur hobbyist and professional.

In a production setting, this requirement translates to the ability to be able to look at the big picture—the flesh, features, and appearance of a site. The HTML coder must be able to do that and find a way to create solid, clean code that supports that structure well. It is for this reason that the HTML coder must be able to communicate well with other members of the team—but most especially with other components of the Web site.

Questions the HTML Coder Should Ask

- What is the most effective way to code for this site?
- Are there clever ways to link pages within the site via hypertext that do not detract from but enhance the power of the site?
- Are there any special tricks I can use to optimize the way this site appears in various browsers?

Graphic Design

Choosing the right graphic designer for a given project is often the key to the artistic success of that project. Unlike the copy writer or HTML coder, who should be so skilled at his or her special area that flexing to meet a specific style is possible, graphic designers are by nature typically bound to certain styles. Certainly this does not mean they cannot create images that are diverse enough to meet a variety of needs, but the phenomenon of a particular artistic touch and temperament is widely known.

For these reasons, the ideal Web design team has an art director. The art director's job may very well be to work on day-to-day graphic designs for the company, but in a larger company seeking diversity in design, having a number of freelance artists to choose from can help both the Web designer and the art director choose artists who are most appropriate for a particular site.

A good example of this involves some of DesertNet's regular artists, Laura Valentino of Valentino Designs, Matt Straznitskas of BrainBug Graphics, and Jason Steed, who works in-house. Laura specializes in a very distinct illustrative style, by contrast with the slick, high-tech work we receive from Matt or the more subtle designs Jason has done (Figure 9-2). Each touch, each style is immeasurably important to creating the diverse textures of our Web sites, but one artist is not always going to be the appropriate choice for a given project. It is part of the Web designer's job to ensure that the client's image needs are appropriately met, and this is often best done by choosing the right designer for the job.

Once the graphic artist has been chosen to create images for the site, it is important to consider the following issues:

- **What artistic image does the client want to present?** Is it high-tech? Sophisticated? Personal and warm? A regional flavor versus a cosmopolitan one? Look at other examples of any marketing that the client has done and is pleased with. These examples may very often be excellent starting points for coming up with elements for a client's Web image, both as a source of logos and artwork to reuse (with the owner's permission), and as inspiration for custom graphics for the site.

Figure 9-1 Examples of art work from three separate artists

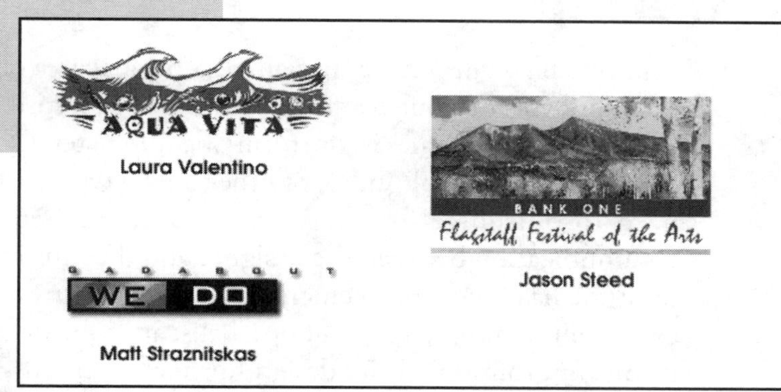

- **Who is the client's audience?** This is important to ask in the realm of graphic design because it will enable the Web and graphic designers to determine what types of graphics they can use. If the client wants a Web site largely because having cutting edge design is important to the client's company and having an URL is part of its corporate image, , then the designer will meet with fewer constraints based on browser and bandwidth access. On the other hand, if the audience is very broad and the content is critical, then it is imperative to keep graphics geared toward more conservative choices.
- **Are there graphic elements that can be reused throughout the site?** This is a very helpful question to ask, particularly when a large amount of data is involved. Using and recycling graphics in a site is a good way to speed up the site as well as keep workload and costs down because less graphic art is actually rendered.

Questions for the Graphic Designer

- What image does the client wish to project?
- Who is the audience?
- Where can I reuse and recycle graphic elements within the site?

Multimedia

Multimedia is currently a specialized, optional area of Web design, and therefore you or your team may not have expertise in a given media area. Whether it comes in the form of audio bytes, Quick Time Virtual Reality, VRML, Real Audio, or other media types, quite often you will need to outsource for the work. Again, this requires very strong communication between the designer and the multimedia artist. Is the multimedia choice complementary to the site's directives? Very often, a client will want to have the hoops, bells, and whistles just for the fun of it. But in professional site design for marketing purposes, this *may* be detrimental. Very carefully examine the choice of multimedia.

Check out the following URLs to see some good examples of multimedia used appropriately on the Web:

- **Euphoria World Wide Music (http://euphoria.org/home/).** Dedicated to independent musicians and labels, the site makes invaluable use of downloadable audio (Figure 9-2). Also featured is a Netscape animation by animator Hugh Anderson. A frame shot of this animation can be seen in Figure 9-3. Since the audience is perceived as progressive and innovative, these multimedia features are absolutely appropriate for a site of this nature.

- **The Brink (http://brink.com/brink/).** An on-the-edge Web 'zine, the Brink regularly incorporates multimedia features, including Shockwave and Netscape animations. In Figure 9-4, we see the opening page of the Suction Issue. For people who have the correct version of Netscape and the appropriate Shockwave plug-in, the plunger is enhanced with both animation and sound. Again, we have an example of audience support and interest in unconventional, on-the-edge use of Web technology.

- **The Club Congress Club Cam and Quick Time Virtual Reality (http://hotcong.com/congo/club/index.htm).** The trendiest club in Tucson, Arizona, the Club Congress knows its audience is hip to fun! Featuring two unusual multimedia choices, a live action-camera and Quick Time Virtual Reality, the Club Congress site (see Figure 9-5) is an extremely appropriate example of rational multimedia use.

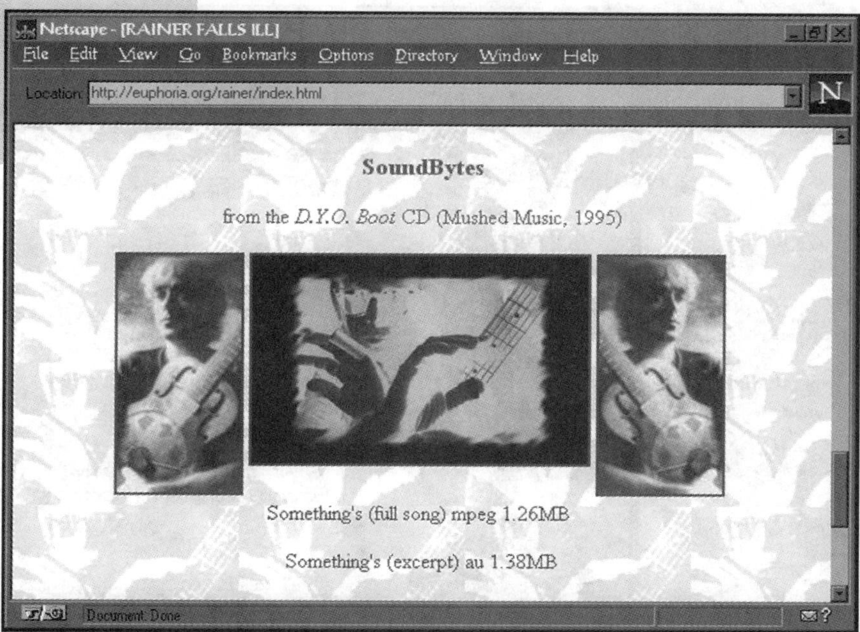

Figure 9-2 Downloadable sound bytes from musician Rainer Ptacek

Figure 9-3 Euphoria World Wide Web's Nanimation

Figure 9-4
A still image of Shockwave multimedia on the Brink

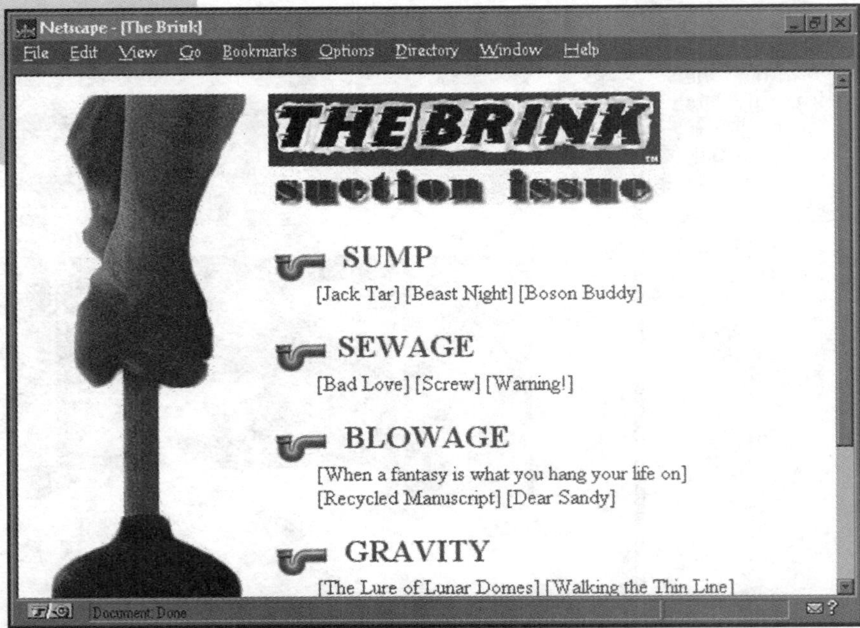

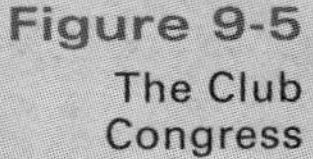

Figure 9-5
The Club Congress

As demonstrated in these examples, multimedia options in Web design are largely determined by the audience. In a conservative commercial or informational site, multimedia options of this nature are rarely going to be in the client's best interest. It is up to the Web designer to continually challenge his or her decisions with those original, important questions regarding the site's intent and the site's audience. Doing so ultimately gives the designer more creative options when faced with the opportunity to design sites as described in this section.

Questions for the Multimedia Designer

- Are any multimedia options applicable to this site?
- If so, what and where would they be appropriate?

Programming

Very much as with multimedia, the choice of using programming on a site is quite often going to depend on your audience. Sometimes, programming simply refers to Common Gateway Interface scripts, which are relatively common and important for interactive feedback forms, such as the one shown in Figure 9-6.

However, as time goes on and technologies develop, programming is really becoming the foundation for a wide range of interactive and multiple media options. Examples can include live chat rooms or interactive forums, as shown in Figure 9-7. Other programming-based technologies include Java and JavaScript, VRML (as demonstrated by Figure 9-8), QTVR, the upcoming Visual Basic and ActiveX features from Microsoft, and proprietary programs that perform individual routines, as we see in Figure 9-9.

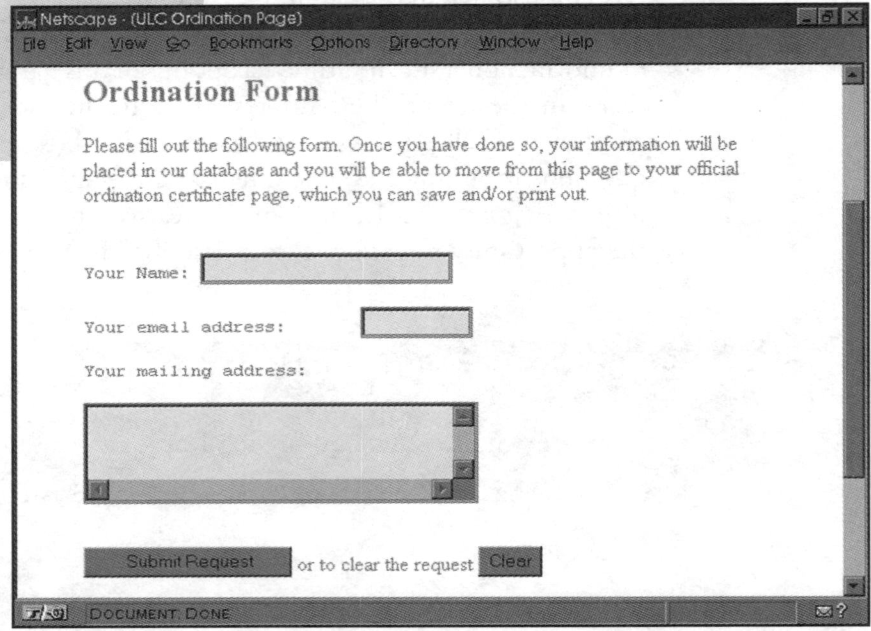

Figure 9-6 A Common Gateway Interface feedback form

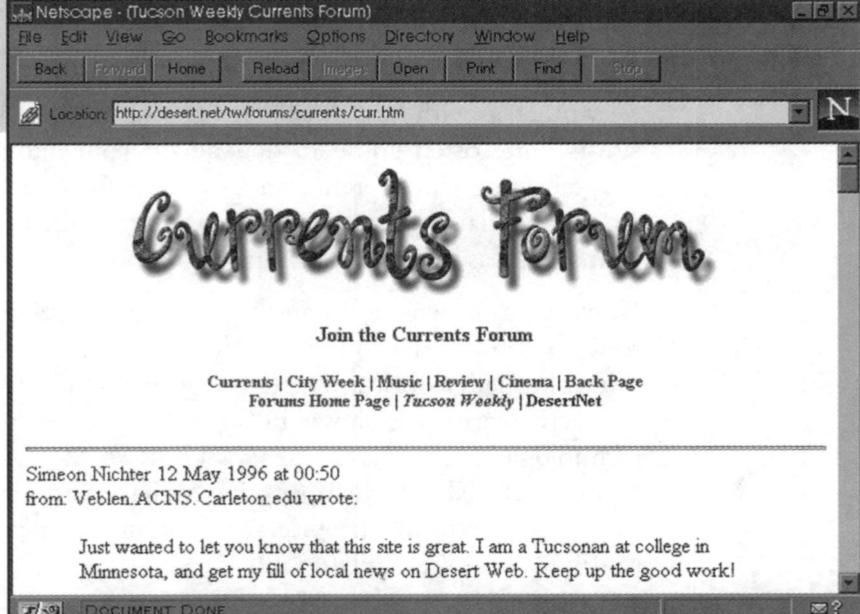

Figure 9-7 Interactive forums on the Tucson Weekly

Figure 9-8
An example of VRML programming code

```
#VRML V1.0 ascii

Separator {
        DEF SceneInfo Info {
                string "Converted by wcvt2pov v2.6c"
        }
        PerspectiveCamera {
                position -60.000000 0.000000 -1000.000000
                orientation 0 1 0 3.14
                focalDistance 5
                heightAngle 0.785398
        }
        PointLight {
                on      TRUE
                intensity       1.0
                color   1.0 1.0 1.0
                location 0.000000 250.000000 1000.000000
        }
        PointLight {
                on      TRUE
                intensity       1.0
                color   1.0 1.0 1.0
                location 0.000000 250.000000 -1000.000000
```

Figure 9-9
Each visit to Buffalo Exchange's Web site offers a unique quote.

Similar questions then, must be asked to determine whether these features enhance a site or detract from its intent. If they enhance the site, help keep it fresh and fun, then by all means use them, as programming is rapidly becoming the most important part of the Web.

Questions for the Programmer

- Are there any applicable programming options for this site?
- If so, what are they and where would they be appropriate?
- What is the most efficient language or script to use to program this site?

Systems Administration

A site cannot exist on the Web without a server to call home. The Web designer will be required either to find a server and systems administrator for each given site or to choose to run a server within the company. Either way, the systems administrator, or *sysadmin*, will be responsible, aside from the general care and feeding of the server, for allocating disk space; providing for domain registration if required; and letting the Web designer know what CGI scripts are available on the server, what limitations a given server might have, and how directory structures will be created.

Again, the need for a Web designer to be an extremely competent communicator and to understand enough about the many hats of the Web design field is exemplified here. Systems administration is a highly technical field in and of itself. Like many of the aspects of Web design, systems administration has its own, mysterious jargon (see Figure 9-10). The Web designer who is equipped to communicate with the sysadmin is going to find that the production of any Web site will go that much more smoothly.

Figure 9-10 Systems administration jargon

Marketing

Currently ignored or not considered a significant part of Web site development, marketing and sales are absolutely critical in the grand scope of the field. Although the marketing department's responsibilities for a completed Web site occurs *after* production, it isn't too early to involve the principals in the production process. Marketing people can be informed at production time of the site's status and direction, and they can be prepared to get down to marketing strategies for the Web site. We'll look more closely at these techniques as we go through the postproduction process, and then we'll give them a more intensive study in part IV of this book.

Publication

After the logistics of production are dealt with and each team member has worked with the Web designer and other members of the team to produce the site's features, the end result should be all the components of a site ready to stitch together. Working alone or with the team members, the Web designer oversees this weaving of the Web fabric—all the components are joined together on the server.

With team feedback, fresh ideas, and helpful criticisms along the way, the site is soon ready to be published. Technically, the site may have been sitting on a server, or on a local network within the company, throughout the production process. Either way, publication simply refers to the site becoming *officially* live online. If all has proceeded well and according to plan, the pieces of the site will all fit together snugly and smoothly.

Publication Review

Before the site moves into postproduction and out to the public, it is imperative that the team exhaustively work the site. Are there misspelled words? Graphics that take too long to load? Does a bit of HTML appear on a page because of a missing angle bracket? Do all the forms, programming features, and multimedia implementations function? The more thorough a review is, the more confident the Web designer and the team members can be that they have, finally, produced and published a very strong product ready for public enjoyment.

chapter 10

Post Production and Expansion

Unlike the case of print or other media, when production of a Web site has been completed, only two-thirds of the job has truly been achieved. Web sites are really like living organisms—they require continued care and feeding throughout their lives. From the point of indexing a Web site, on through to creating ways of marketing the site so that it is visited regularly, to expanding the site to meet growing or changing client need—postproduction is a critical yet often overlooked part of the Web design process.

I recall a young woman visiting our booth in the exhibit hall at an Internet Expo not long ago. She was asking questions regarding DesertNet, and I was telling her about our site design and marketing packages. "But I thought that having a Web page *was* marketing!" she exclaimed. The comment at first struck me as naive, but later I realized that her impression was very likely a natural result of the media's misrepresentation of the Web. Yes, a Web site can in and of itself be a marketing tool, but would you—as my business partner Wil likes to say—open up shop in a dark alley and not put out a sign? Web sites must be marketed, and there are fun and interesting strategies to help the Web designer and the team make the audience aware of the Web site.

If you're working within the team model, ideally a sales and marketing specialist is available to help with the postproduction process. Even solo fliers will appreciate the concepts offered here. Good marketing is an essential element of Web design. Remember when we discussed the theatrical metaphor of how critical it is to light a stage? The same is true with Web design—without the lights, there is no design. For Web designers, marketing is lighting up the stage, and good marketing strategies will also help guide the audience right to the most comfortable seats in the house.

Site Indexing

Indexing refers to making sure that sites are listed with search engines around the globe. These are growing databases that allow people looking for specific information to find references and resources. There are different types of indexes on the Web—some, like Yahoo, list by category. Others, like my current personal favorite shown in Figure 10-1,

AltaVista, are Web "crawlers" or "worms"—basically robots that go out onto the Web searching for new URLs and sites and cataloging the related references.

Web designers, if they do nothing else, should ensure that sites get listed on as many indexes as possible. Most indexes have an area where the designer or marketing person can fill out a form to have the desired URL listed. This is good to do on the Web crawlers as well—even though it is likely they will find your site at some point, giving the robots a nudge never hurts! Sometimes it takes more than one try, and the individual in charge of the process has to be fairly persistent in keeping up with indexing. There are quite a few tricks and advanced indexing and related marketing methods. Let's become familiar with a few of the more popular indexes:

- **AltaVista. http://www.altavista.digital.com.** This is a very comprehensive search engine and Web crawler, sponsored by Digital Equipment Corporation (DEC). AltaVista currently claims access to "30 million pages found on 225,000 servers, and 3 million articles from 14,000 Usenet newsgroups." It is accessed over 10 million times a day and has won several awards for its excellent, stable service. Web designers can submit or delete URLs by following the link, as shown in Figure 10-2, off the main page.

- **Lycos, http://lycos.cs.cmu.edu/.** I am particularly fond of this index, which began as a project at Carnegie Mellon University. It remains housed there, a free service that represents extended Web-related interests. *Lycos* refers to the first few letters of the Greek word for "Wolf Spider," a play on Web crawling. Submit, change, or delete links at: http://www.lycos.com/register.html (see Figure 10-3).

- **Open Text, http://www.opentext.com/.** Open Text Corporation, as shown in its home page in Figure 10-4, is very involved in helping Web organizations find information, develop collaborative efforts, and create efficient, economical, and secure methods of utilizing Web resources. The address http://www.opentext.com/omw/f-omw-submit.html is the URL for submissions and changes.

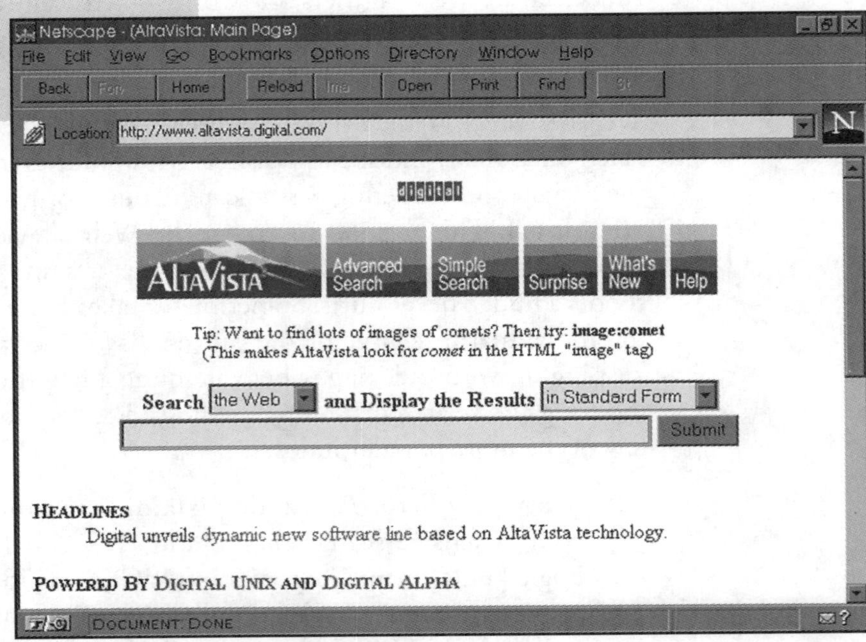

Figure 10-1 The AltaVista home page

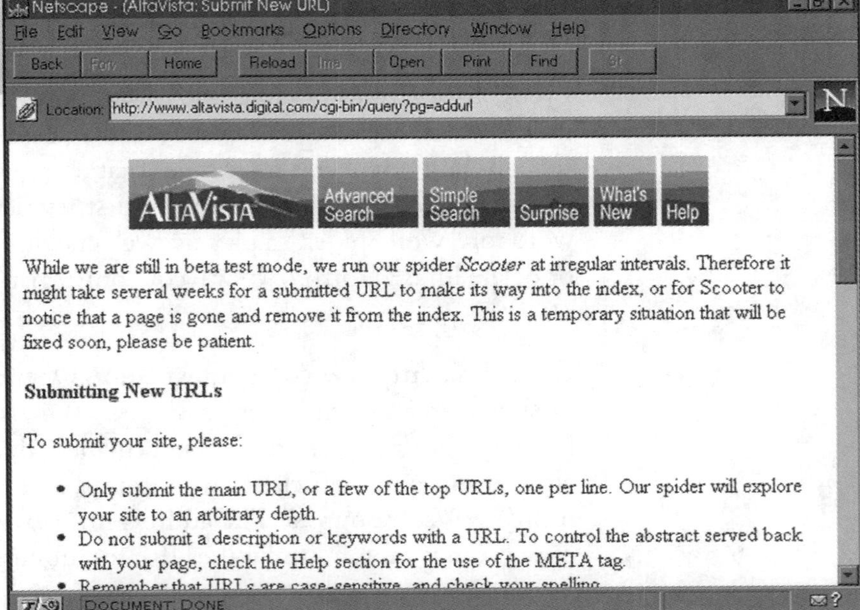

Figure 10-2 Submitting URLs via AltaVista

Figure 10-3
The Lycos home page

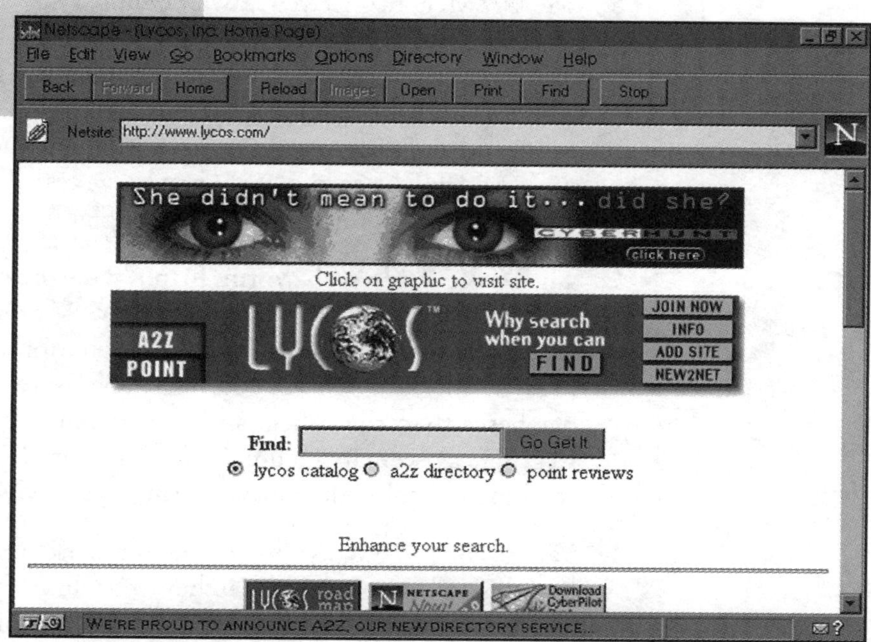

Figure 10-4
Open Text home page

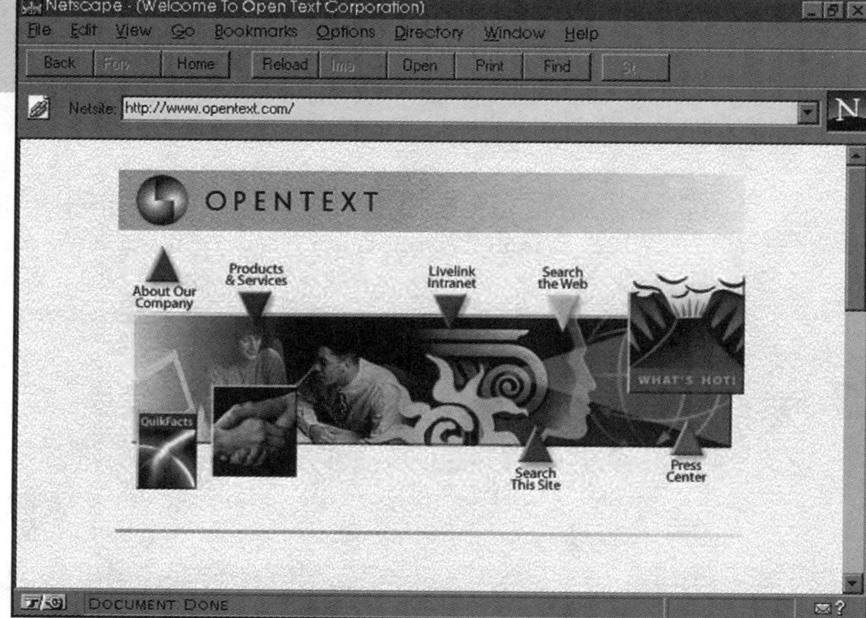

- **WebCrawler, http://webcrawler.com/.** This is a very powerful search engine connected to Global Network Navigator's Select Reviews. Search engines that are combined with commercial services often have added opportunities and benefits, such as banner advertising, awards, picks-of-the-day, and reviews on Web sites. Add URLs to the WebCrawler at http://webcrawler.com/WebCrawler/SubmitURLS.html (see Figure 10-5).

- **The World Wide Web Worm, http://wwwmcb.cs.colorado.edu/home/mcbryan/WWWW.html.** WWWW provides four types of search databases: citation hypertext, citation addresses (URL), HTML titles, and HTML addresses. The last two are much smaller databases than the others and can therefore be searched faster. Register, as seen in Figure 10-6, with the WWWW at http://wwwmcb.cs.colorado.edu/home/mcbryan/WWWWadd.html.

- **Yahoo!, http://www.yahoo.com/.** A hierarchical guide organized by subject, Yahoo! allows searches to be done by category. This is a powerful and popular engine, with related efforts including print magazines, awards, cool sites, and random links, as portrayed in Figure 10-7. Unfortunately Yahoo! can take a very long time in getting sites registered, and Web designers have often complained about this challenge. Yahoo! asks that URL submissions be done by category. To find out more on how to submit URLs to Yahoo!, visit Yahoo!'s main page and select "Add URL."

Another excellent resource for Web designer's concerned with indexing their sites is Submit It. This site contains a form, depicted in Figure 10-8, that allows indexing to be done from one main area. Submit It is a very convenient way to get listed with the best of Web crawlers. Visit http://www.submit-it.com/ for more information.

Search Key Tagging and Keywords

Aside from manually indexing pages or waiting for crawlers to find pages, a Web designer can use certain tags and tricks to assist the crawlers. Crawlers look for specific information, including URLs, titles, and frequent words appearing on a given page. For this reason, it is always

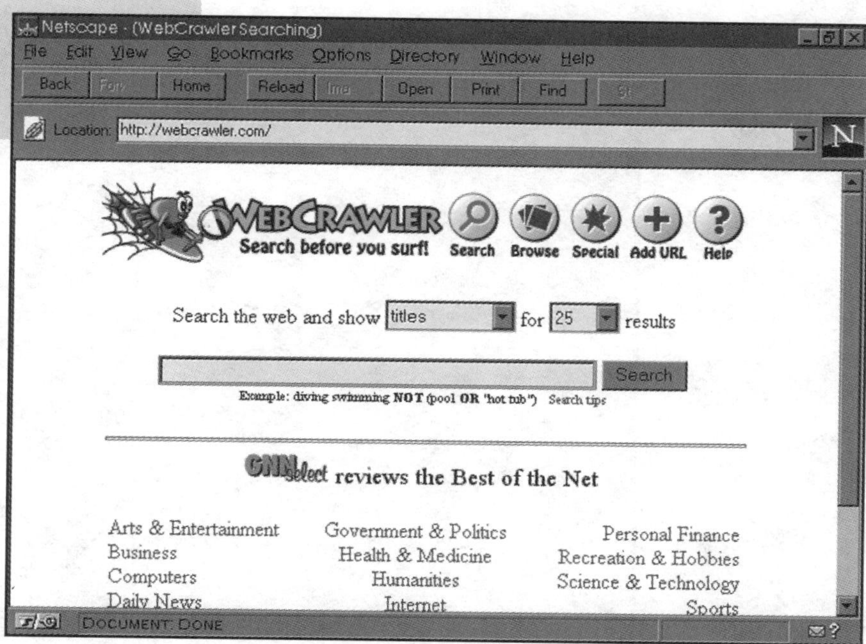

Figure 10-5 The WebCrawler's home page

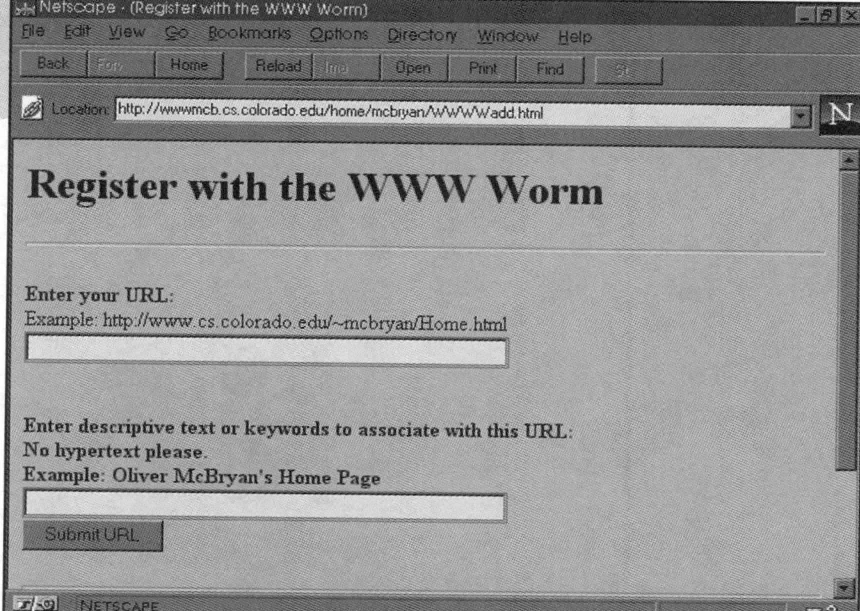

Figure 10-6 Submit URLs via the World Wide Web Worm.

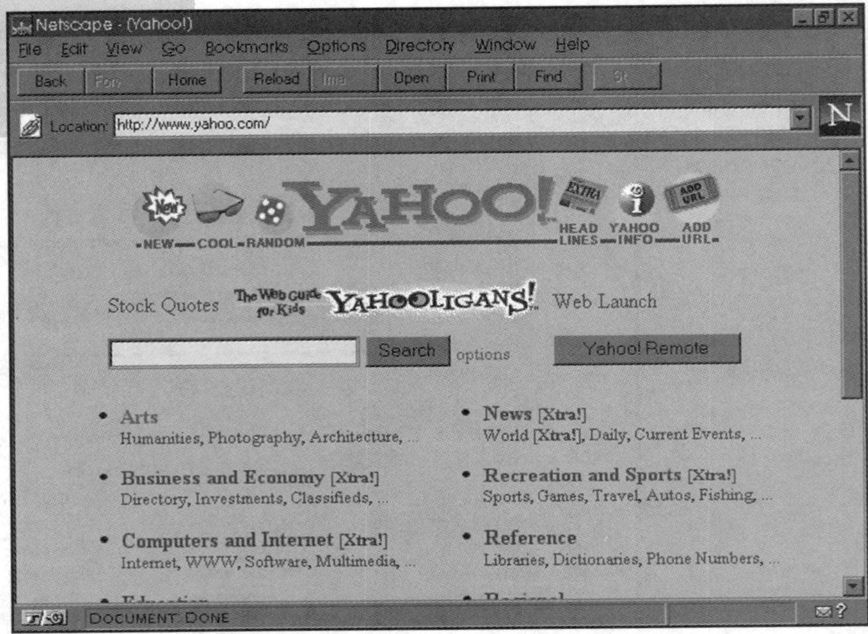

Figure 10-7
The Yahoo! home page

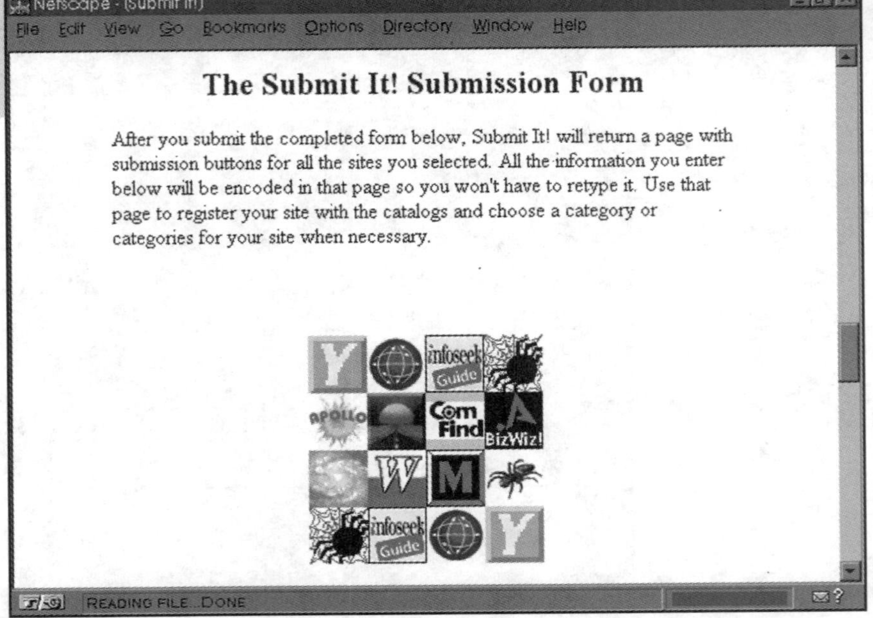

Figure 10-8
Submit URLs using the Submit It form.

a good idea to make sure you title every page you author, using titles that make logical sense. For example, if you are doing a site for Mondo Produce Incorporated, each page should be identified in the <title> tag with both the company name *and* the specific page name:

```
<title>Mondo Produce, Inc.: Best Tomato Awards!</title>
```

Another trick is using the META tag. This tag is used by AltaVista as well as other search engines, and it can be quite helpful in adding your pages to the indexes. There are several specific tag arguments, including *subject, author, content,* and *keywords.* It isn't necessary to place all of these tags, but it can be especially helpful to make sure your information gets cross-referenced. I recommend that, even if you choose to use the META tag, you should carry out aggressive manual indexing to ensure placement.

To use the META tag follow this template:

```
<head>

<title>Mondo Produce, Inc.: Home Plate</title>

<meta name="subject" content="Mondo Produce,
Incorporated. Main Page Info">

<meta name="author" content="DesertNet Designs">

<meta name="keywords" content="Produce, fruit,
vegetables, organic, recipes, diet, eating, health">

<meta name="description" content="Mondo Produce Inc.,
features the finest in organic fruits and vegetables,
healthy eating, and delicious recipes">

</head>
```

Note that the META tag is placed within the HEAD tag and after the TITLE tag. For additional information and resources on how to use search tagging and keywords, refer to part IV of this book.

Domain Registration

One useful method of marketing sites is by registering domains for them. Depending on what type of Web server service you are using, there will be a variety of options for the clients you and your company represent. If your company runs its own servers, the process and details will be easily handled by your sysadmin. Quite often, virtual servers offer domain registration along with their packaging, although this service may only cover your company's personal domain, and additional ones will cost extra. Mileage will vary, but check with the sysadmin you deal with or any ISPs you've chosen to use for specific projects.

Domain names consist of a name and a suffix. Names can be just about any that you can think of that aren't already in use. Typically a name will be the actual name of the company, an acronym that represents it, or some other defining property. Web designers seeking to offer domain names for their clients' sites should use names that are logical and easy to find, to fit into the marketing objective. Mondo Produce, Inc., might be mondo.com or produce.net, for example. To check on whether a domain name has been put into use, log in to a command prompt on your ISP and type **whois** ***so-and-so.net***, where *so-and-so* refers to the name you're looking for and *.net* is replaced by the suffix you are interested in. See Figure 10-9 for an example of whois results.

Domains suffixes for general use fall under three main categories:

- **COM.** The .com domain refers to *commercial* organizations and is most appropriate for any business enterprise on the Internet.
- **ORG.** This domain refers to *organizations* as such and is best used by nonprofit groups or other groups not specifically oriented toward commercial activities.
- **NET.** The *network* domain has a wider interpretation than the preceding types; it can be used by commercial organizations or noncommercial groups. This domain typically includes any organization that is a network in its own right, such as desert.net.

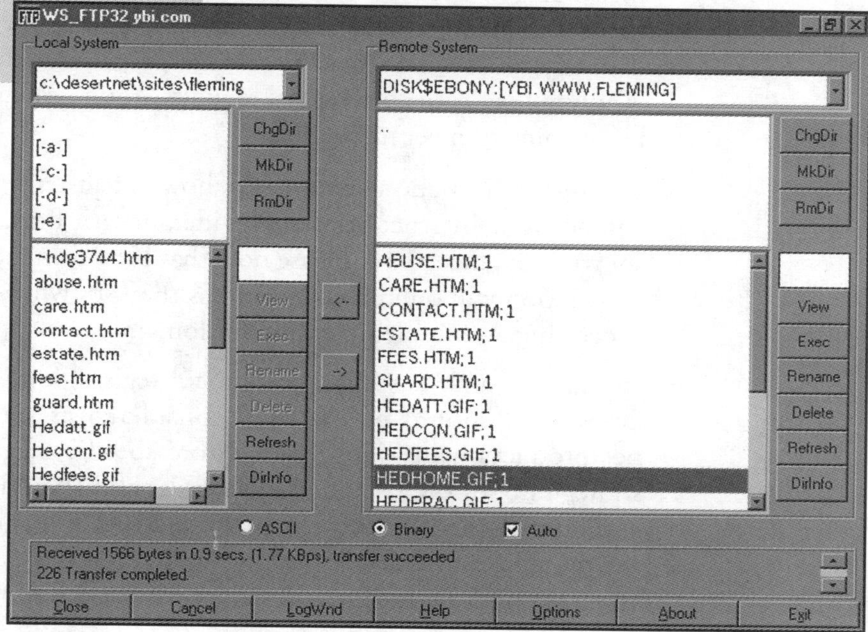

Figure 10-9
Results of a whois search

There are three other domain suffixes Web designers should be aware of, although they rarely, if ever, play into the commercial realm. They are:

- **EDU.** This is the *educational* organization suffix; it is commonly part of the domain name for any school or university.
- **GOV.** *Government* agencies are given this suffix.
- **MIL.** This refers to *military* organizations.

A country suffix appears after many foreign domains. These are two-letter identifications. Examples include .au for Australia and .de for Germany.

Domains used to be free of charge to register, but as the Internet—especially due to Web interests—became absorbed by commercial enterprises, it no longer remained feasible for the organization handling domain registrations to provide the service free. Internic now asks for a registration fee *and* a yearly maintenance fee to keep domains. When this strategy was first announced, it causes quite an uproar from Web users. Personally I have always felt that asking for registration and maintenance fees is not at all unreasonable, particularly because Internic is now able to turn commercial requests around much faster because it has income to meet its overhead.

For more information on domains, how to register, and associated fees, contact your Internet Service Provider, or visit http://internic.net/, as shown in Figure 10-10. Please note that ISPs' fees and Internic fees for registration will often be different, as the ISPs will add on charges for processing and implementation of domains.

Indexing, search tagging, and domain registration, while optional in every case, should be carefully considered as significant parts of postproduction in Web design. More specific, aggressive marketing strategies both on and off the Net exist and should be utilized more and more as the Web becomes saturated with information. It becomes the design team members' responsibility and duty to make sure they shine the light on the great design they've achieved for their clients.

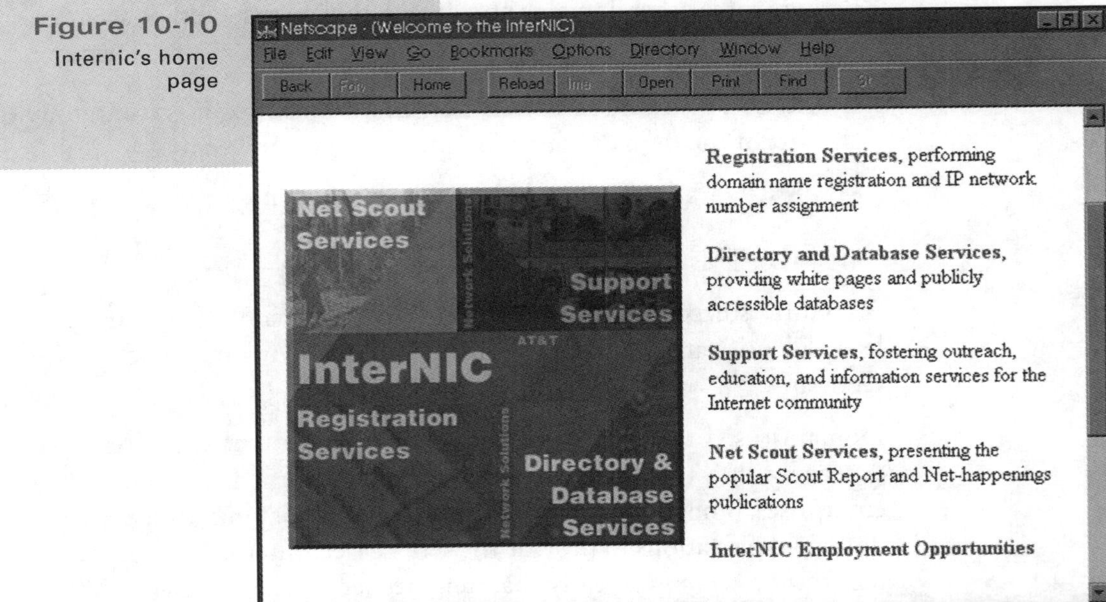

Figure 10-10 Internic's home page

Marketing Strategies: on the Net

The three strategies we've already discussed lay the foundation for any marketing objectives. However, certain options will be reviewed here and discussed in further detail in the marketing portion of part IV of this book. It's good for the Web designer to get a feel for current trends in online marketing, and some of the right—and wrong—ways to go about getting your Web site noticed. As with the rest of this chapter, more specific details and references can be found in Chapter 20, which specializes in providing special tricks and tips. For now, let's sample what some of these options are.

- **Banner advertising.** Much like advertisements in a popular or niche paper, banner ads are rapidly becoming a great way both to attract interest to a site and to enhance a site's usability by providing advertising—if appropriate—within it. Banner ads are typically well-placed on major search engines (see Figure 10-11) and corporate sites, as well as within online newspapers (see Figure 10-12). They are hotlinked to the site itself. The fun part of banner advertising is that it creates an actual area of Web design. Good banner design will help induce individuals to click on that banner in the first place! Banners that are fun and intriguing will get used. The downside of banner ads is that, at least in terms of the *very* well-traveled sites, they can be very expensive.

- **Link sharing.** Linking documents is the essence of what makes the Web a web in the first place! By offering links of interest to related sites, you've opened the door to have return links from their sites to yours. Contact Webmasters in charge of sites you wish to link to, and ask for shared, or trade, links between your sites. Most are delighted to comply, as it assists them in routing highway traffic their way.

- **Announcing to Internet newsgroups and mailing lists.** Quite a broad range of special interest groups exists on the Internet. Do a bit of research and find out which might cater to your client's interests. Some serious issues of netiquette arise over how to appropriately announce commercial ventures on the Net., details appear in Chapter 20. In general, be *absolutely certain* that you

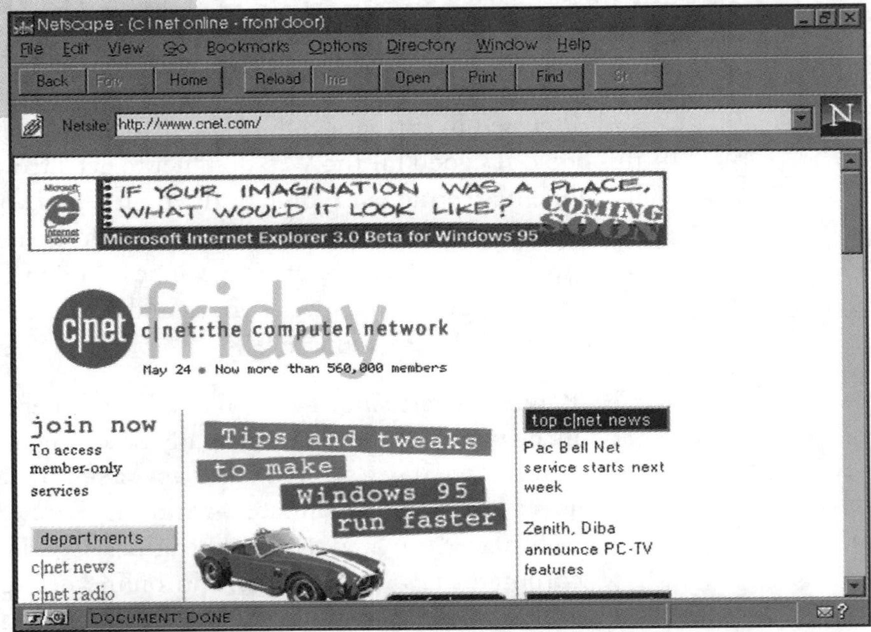

Figure 10-11
A Banner ad on ClNet

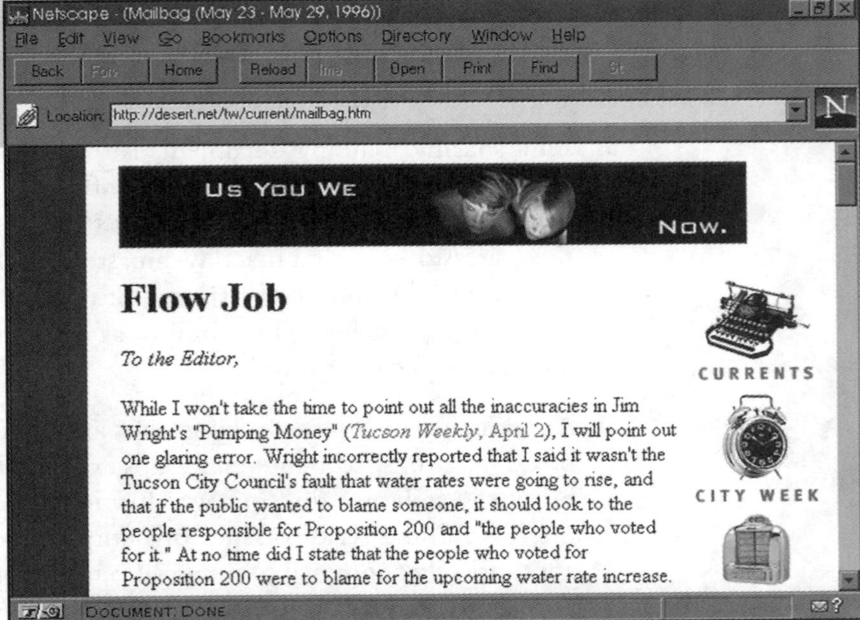

Figure 10-12
A Banner Ad for Gadabout Salons on the *Tucson Weekly*

read the group's rules and regulations before posting, and that you don't inundate the group with inappropriate numbers of posts. This is called "spamming" and it will cause vehement, angry responses from Netizens. If you're going to use newsgroups and lists as a way to advertise, consider the rules before embarking on an effort that may harm rather than help your client.

Marketing Strategies: off the Net

Off-Net marketing is an area that many people don't even think about, although the Web is rapidly filtering into traditional media. As shown in Figure 10-13, URLs are popping up in print ads; on television and radio; in newspaper stories; and even on promotional goods such as coffee mugs, t-shirts, and pencils.

Talk to the clients and find out what their current marketing strategies are. Encourage them to start adding their Web site's URL to literally *everything* they put out regarding their business. From business cards to promotional brochures, radio and television spots, print advertising, giveaways—even their company billing and communications sheets should have that URL prominently placed where people can read it. The reason is simple: the site exists to provide information 24 hours a day, seven days a week, every day of the year. If a client's customers

Figure 10-13
A print ad with URLs for the Congress

wish to find more information, they can browse on in and often have many of their questions answered right there on the site. In some cases, they will learn a lot more about the company with whom they are dealing, and this can be very beneficial all around.

The power of this type of marketing enhancement goes beyond the surface. In fact, its power is global, because although these are *excellent* techniques to enhance the promotion of a Web site, there is also an added, albeit somewhat subversive, element to it. That is, it inundates our culture with the language of the Net, and eventually people will be better aware of what all these goofy colons, slash slashes, and www's are—making our jobs as Web designers better understood, and ultimately, easier when we can spend less time explaining the Web and more time actually getting down to what we do best—design.

Expansion

It has become evident in the past couple of years that enough changes occur on the Web on a regular basis to create a need and a demand for addition of content and even site redesign. Also, many clients have tried their hands at creating Web sites for themselves, and as they see the marketing need for professional handling of sites, they come to designers for expansion and reworking of a site. For these reasons, it is strongly recommended that Web sites be built with the future in mind. This is a vague statement, since the future can hold all kinds of possibilities that none of us can forecast. By the same token, we also can listen to the long-term goals of our clients and work to keep updated content, new technology, design upgrades, and new ideas implemented for our clients.

Designing an open-ended site means that you and your client are working toward adding new content or changing content. New content can be added without much trouble if the Web designer anticipates flexible structures, as we've demonstrated in the planning discussion in Chapter 7. It is in this planning phase—as we determine what amount of data and what type of navigation options are best suited to our client's needs—that we can ensure some flexibility for plugging in future content with relative ease.

Some Web evangelists say that Web content should change daily. Brock Meeks has stated this on more than one occasion, and he has even suggested that hourly changes would be even more effective. Justin Hall, who is well known for his Web site, Links from the Underground (http://www.links.net/nonscape.html), Web evangelism, and his outspoken beliefs since 1994, is a strong advocate of dynamic, changing data on the Web. How this philosophy can be applied to commercial sites is yet to be determined, because costs are prohibitive to the average client seeking a Web site.

Web Times They Are a Changin'

Dynamic content, while not always financially feasible, should still be a designer's goal. Yet, all over the Web surfers will find those obnoxious "under construction" symbols. I have found their use ironic, because ideally *no Web site is ever truly complete.* The living, breathing nature of the Web fosters an environment of constant change, so the "under construction" signs are not only unsightly but actually not necessary. Postproduction embodies change as its fundamental philosophy. By marketing sites both off- and online, we keep an influx of individuals coming to them, which naturally creates a need to keep material fresh. The very nature of the technology begs for open-ended design and expansion, and if the work in postproduction is well done, it will be that much easier to meet the changing demands of the Web, and the shifting needs of clients, in as optimal a fashion as possible.

The Web as Landscape

Biz Kellam
Webbabe Publishing
`http://www.webbabe.com`

"I have a background in Landscape Architecture. Yea, good old dirt pushin, wall buildin', pathway meanderin', Landscape Architecture. A site in cyberspace is really similar to good site planning and development here on planet earth. There must be a reason for people to enter a site, the entry must be attractive enough to draw them in if they were just strolling by. There must be enough interesting and/or informative content to make them want to stay. Or if they were specifically looking for rose bushes and found themselves in the midst of the 'Rare Cactus Sanctuary,' allow them to exit gracefully and leave them with the memory of a good experience anyway. Make it easy for them to get around to where they are going, but throw in little tidbits of surprise and adventure along the way. Think of strolling along a garden path only to turn a corner and glimpse a small waterfall with a statue of a forest sprite along its' pool edge. Like a garden changes with the seasons—keep it refreshing and new."

Biz works solo, although she out-sources for "programming stuff." She has a distinct dislike for cyber-showoffs who overuse all the latest bells and whistles. One of her top peeves: *"Blinking animated java framed-out tables with avi.wav.mpeg counting, hits-elaborating, form-responding search engines for the site you're on pages from hell. I mean, sure all the new stuff is cool and appropriate for certain uses. But it's why my boyfriend doesn't cook—use all the spices in the cabinet at the same time on the same piece of chicken and ain't nobody gonna want to eat it."*

Words are Vision

Danny Vinik
Publisher, The Brink
`http://brink.com/brink/`

As publisher of The Brink, a totally on-the-edge example of new media concepts in action, Danny Vinik is constantly challenging web technology with both creative uses of the medium, and his own unique sense of art.

"A few years ago I traded my motorcycle for a Powerbook. And I saw the web. Everything changed.

All of a sudden I was excited about something: the end of the word. The beginning of the graphic object. Or maybe the beginning of the word and the end of TV?

I had to have my own site.

Then that wasn't enough. I had to have a better site, the latest Netscape. I had to spend every waking moment killing myself with inane code, risking my relationships, wiping out every vestige of the old me. In short, I became a world class nerd, a position I openly despised, but secretly coveted.

Now I'm dreaming of the day when I'll be able to take for granted the damned technology, use it when I need it, ignore it when I don't, and get back to work telling my stories all the best ways I know how."

chapter 11

Virtual Tour Guide I: The Buffalo Exchange

Now that we've explored some of the theory and practice of building Web sites, we're going to take two virtual tours. The idea is to clearly illustrate the process by actually going through it step by step. The tone of these tours will be quite personal, due in large part to the real, individual relationships team members and I have with these clients and their respective sites.

This first tour will focus on a site developed by DesertNet for the Buffalo Exchange. Although both DesertNet and the clients are pleased with the final product, the process was filled with complications. In this chapter, we will look carefully at the problem spots in order to demonstrate how both a solid, progressive design model and good communications are of paramount importance.

The Web Design Team

Let's begin by meeting the Web design team for this project. In the role of Web designer, we have Wil Gerken (see Figure 11-1). Wil comes to DesertNet with formidable programming, layout, and management skills, as well as a very mature understanding of the World Wide Web. He is a very easygoing, friendly person. He was, however, a reluctant commercial Web designer, and he filled those shoes for this project mostly due to shifts and changes within the company. In this case, he also wore his more comfortable hats of coding and programming. He approached the project with enthusiasm and, no matter the lessons learned, ultimately designed a wonderful site.

Figure 11-1 Wil Gerken, Web engineer, DesertNet Designs

In the role of art director was Matt Straznitskas, whom we call "Straz" around the office. Straz is unquestionably one of the finest Web graphic designers around, and his Connecticut-based company, BrainBug (see Figure 11-2), works on some of the largest corporate accounts in the country. We are especially proud of our relationship with Straz and BrainBug, whose quality design work has undeniably given DesertNet part of its edge. Working along with Straz was Michelle Carrier, a fine artist and at that time a new member to BrainBug, who offered input on colors and layout and designed some of the collage work.

The Buffalo Exchange is represented by Pollock and Associates Advertising, a Tucson ad agency with significant talent and experience. Much of the original copy and image data came through Pollock. I was personally responsible for thematic development and layout of the site. Marketing was covered by John Hankinson, DesertNet's marketing manager. Finally, DesertNet runs its own Web servers, so we are responsible for systems administration.

Figure 11-2
The BrainBug home page, *http://brainbug.com/*

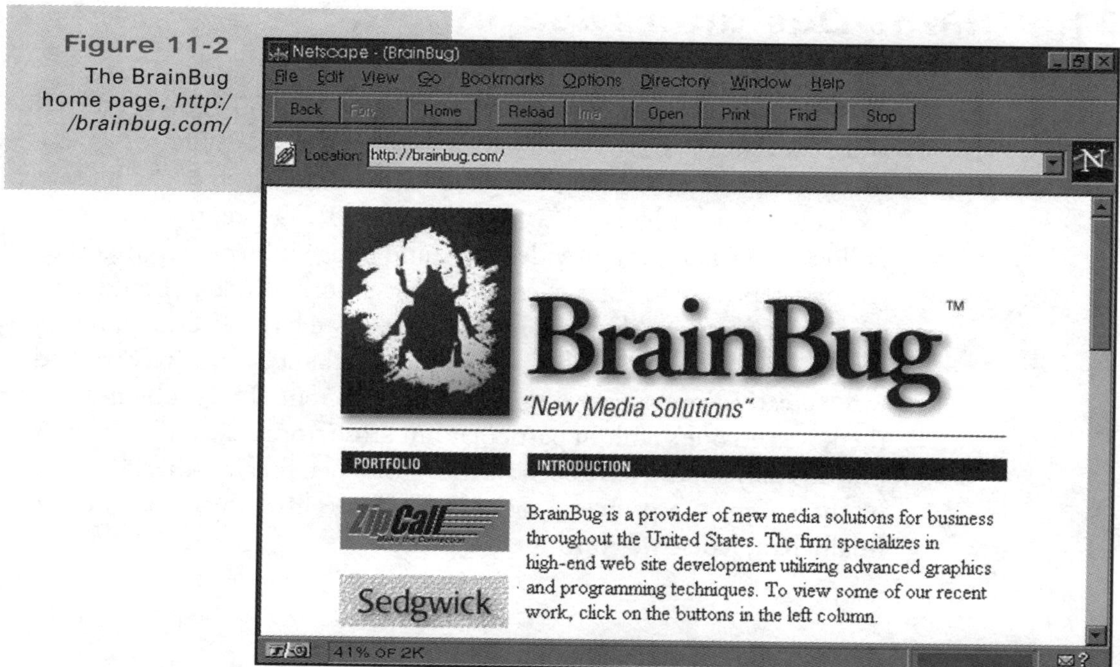

The Clients

With locations all over the southwestern and western United States, the Buffalo Exchange is a recycled clothing and fashion company. Using very high standards to select the clothing they buy, and targeting the youthful, trend-setting, hip market of 18–25 year olds, the Buffalo Exchange is a successful, growing business. It has a liberal image, focusing on issues such as the importance of recycling and promotion of diverse cultural interests.

Preproduction

One of the most critical problems faced during the development of this site was that preproduction was poorly coordinated. We discussed the critical nature of preproduction and its varied aspects in Chapters 7 and 8, and the Buffalo Exchange site serves as a very good example of why this level of the process is so critical. Let's take a look at specifics.

The Client-Designer Meeting and Obtaining of Content

The first meeting took place between Wil and the Ad agency, Pollock and Associates Advertising. Pollock had been responsible for a very successful print ad campaign that fully reflects the ideals of the Buffalo Exchange as described earlier (see Figure 11-3). The representatives at Pollock and Associates provided copy and image information that they felt best represented their client's interests. Normally this should have met all of the client-designer meeting needs we have described, but as it turned out, the principals at the Buffalo Exchange ultimately wanted more creative input regarding design and content. The problem here, then, was no one's fault in particular but arose from a lack of awareness of who really should have been sitting in the client chair—the ad agency or the company's principal owners. We'll see how this problem was finally handled as we continue the process.

Figure 11-3
A Buffalo Exchange print ad from the *Tucson Weekly*

Assessment of Client Need

Based on the information from the Ad agency, Wil assessed the clients' need. He addressed each concern:

- **Primary intent:** to create an image-setting presence on the Web for a growing company with a clearly defined audience
- **Short- and long-term goals:** to showcase the company's image, style, and commitment to its ideals of recycling and human culture. To update fashion news, create multimedia features of interest to the intended audience, and keep the site interesting and fresh
- **Intended audience:** Generation X—hip, trend-setting youth with an interest in fashion and environmental issues
- **Client image:** earthy, environmental, youthful
- **Unique aspects of the company:** interest in human diversity and environmental concerns, particularly recycling, as part of the fashion and image concept.

Planning

Based on the initial meeting and data obtained from the ad agency, Wil went to work planning the site.

- **Content.** Wil came to me with the data given to him. Together we worked out a fun way of presenting the copy that he had. We chose a monosyllabic "who, what, where" writing style, appealing to the unconventional, cool audience.

- **Size of site.** From the copy, we decided to break the site down into several sections that represented various aspects of the company's activities. We thought about an initial page that held the company's logo and set the image. Then we moved into the actual data and decided on about six pages' worth of content.

- **Navigation.** Wil always uses either image maps or buttons along with text navigation. His insistence on this approach is partially responsible for the acclaim he has received for handling large amounts of data—and in every case, be it smaller sites or larger ones, using both options has always been an excellent choice. In this case, he went with an image map and the related text option.

- **Look and feel.** Based on the information he had, Wil decided to go for an earthy, recycled feel, accentuated by our snappy, monosyllabic copy layout.

- **Graphic design.** Wil chose Matt and BrainBug to do the design, certain that the fun and trendy styles BrainBug is capable of would fit right into the clients' image. Matt and Michelle came up with a denim look for the front page, with images of literal buttons for navigation. Frames were chosen for the internal sections, appealing to the trend-setting nature of the site. The denim motif was repeated in the static left frame, designed for navigation. The content would be developed in the right frame, with a cream-colored, recycled-paper background, meeting the earthy, environmental, and youthful intent of the site (see Figure 11-4).

Figure 11-4 Renderings of the Buffalo Exchange site, version 1.0

- **Multimedia and programming.** Again, based on the previous marketing history of the company, Wil decided to use a Nanimation (a Netscape Animation—using a CGI script, this type of animation is currently viewable only with Netscape browsers) within the site as well as a programming function to have changeable data on the home page. The rationale here, again, was that the intended audience was trendy and would be into the fun of these implementations. We also had some fun images that would look good in an animated format. Hence, BuffaloVision was created (Figure 11-5). A mailto form was also developed for the site, as the clients have e-mail and were interested in responding to their clientele in that fashion.

At this point, Wil storyboarded the site and had BrainBug develop a mock-up based on his directions. The ad agency was contacted, and they came to an evaluation meeting along with the principals of the company.

Evaluation

"I got hit with blank expressions," Wil says, in describing the evaluation meeting. "My impression was that they were not impressed. I thought it was the site design, but it really turned out to be the content and the clarity of the logo." The content and direction, which were taken from the ad agency, apparently didn't match recent changes in the company, whose managers were still apparently unclear about what they really wanted their image to be. So Wil gathered up the new copy prepared by the owners, took notes on their comments, and went back to the drawing board.

BrainBug was contacted, and they redeveloped the site with a 70's retro and less earthy look and feel, as seen in Figure 11-6. When evaluation time came around again, the response was pretty negative. Many features were pleasing to the clients, especially the multimedia and programming functions that Wil had chosen. The colors and header designs, however, were not to the clients' liking. They had grown fond of aspects of the original design, as it turns out.

Frustrated, Wil put the site aside for a bit to take a breather and see if he could gain a new perspective. He then asked Michelle to try a few things with color and collage. These experiments were done on the main DesertNet server, but in another directory (see Figure 11-7). To the surprise and bewilderment of everyone at DesertNet, the clients contacted us, having actually found the work in progress! Fortunately, there were some facets of the test designs that the clients really liked, including the use of the logo shown in Figure 11-8.

Production

Now, incorporating various aspects from each of the given sites, Wil again went back to the drawing board. "At this point," he says, "I finally felt I had enough, knew enough, so I went for it." He gave instructions to BrainBug and then programmed and developed a site with all new graphics, based on what the clients were drawn to.

This time, he waited until the site was complete before showing it to the clients, as he felt that showing them a work in progress was part of the difficulties he was having. His instincts proved correct—the clients evaluated the new site and were very pleased.

Postproduction: Marketing

All DesertNet clients receive a listing on our search engine, Desert Links, shown in Figure 11-9. Besides indexing the site in our own search engine and other popular engines, we also have offered a banner advertising campaign for the Buffalo Exchange within the *Tucson Weekly* Online (see Figure 11-10).

Figure 11-5
BuffaloVision—a series of stills that make up the Netscape Nanimation for the Buffalo Exchange

Figure 11-6
Renderings of the Buffalo Exchange site version 2.0

Figure 11-7
The first hidden image in progress

Figure 11-8
The new Buffalo Exchange logo

Figure 11-9 The Buffalo Exchange listing on Desert Links

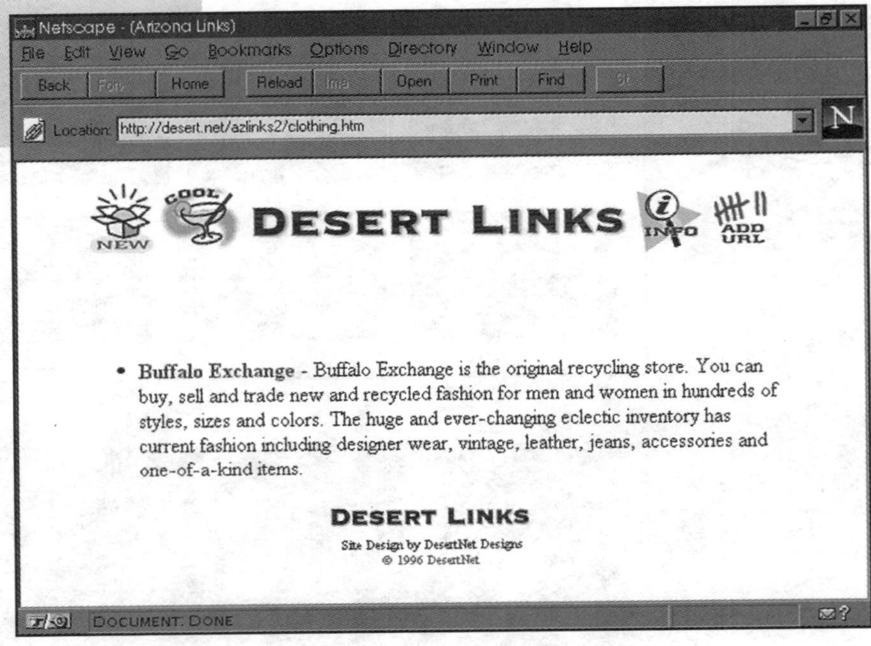

Figure 11-10 The ad banner for the Buffalo Exchange on the *Tucson Weekly* Online

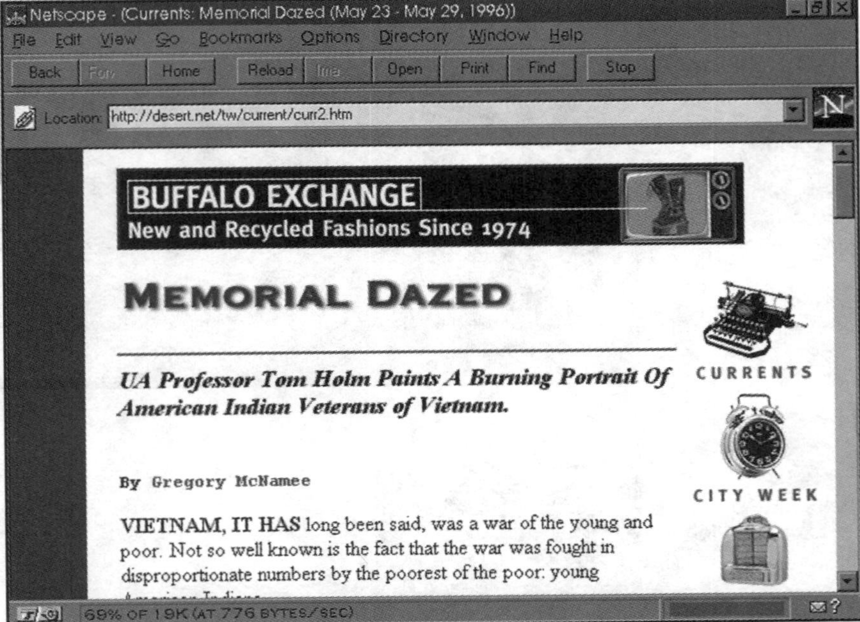

Postproduction: a Point to Ponder

The new Buffalo Exchange site is very well designed, with the stylish appeal we see in Figures 11-11 and 11-12. However, Wil, all of the team members at DesertNet, and members of the ad agency truly believe that the image it presents is contrary to the image the company has developed over the last decade. In a sense, there are contradictory elements being portrayed via the Web site as a result.

From a marketing perspective, it is interesting to ask whether the emergence of this slicker look and feel will affect the future image of the Buffalo Exchange. A request that the new logo look be used in upcoming print ads in the *Tucson Weekly* indeed reflects this shift and incorporation of the ideas that were presented in this new marketing medium. It brings to light an interesting question: how much effect will Web design have on existing print and other media?

Figure 11-11 The Buffalo Exchange home page, *http://desert.net/buffalo/*

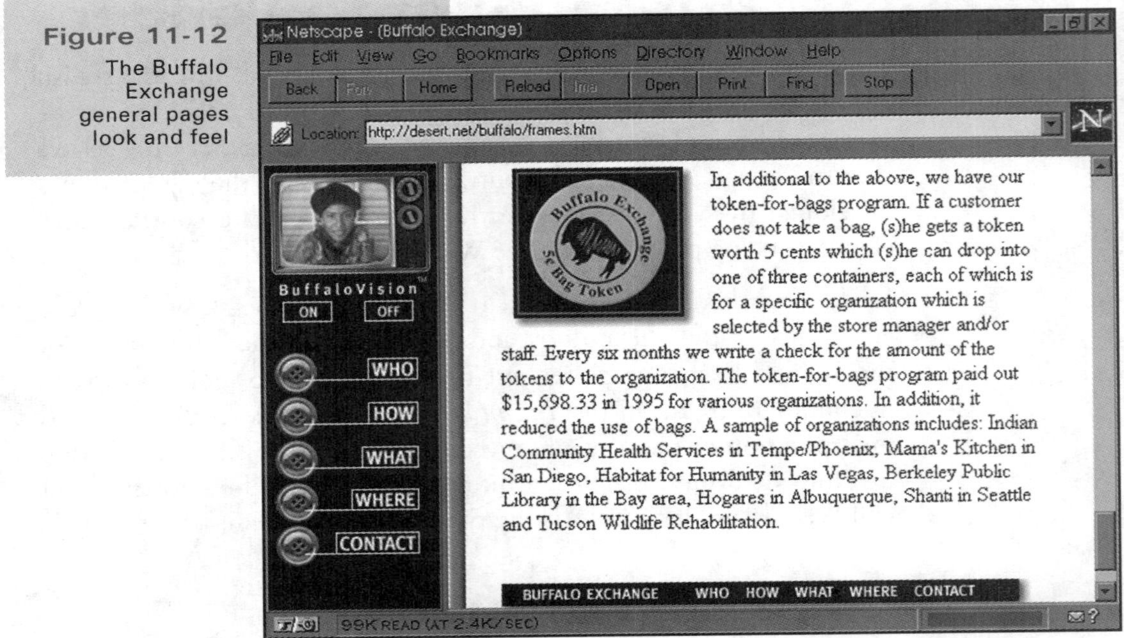

Figure 11-12 The Buffalo Exchange general pages look and feel

A Summary of the Challenges

The first and most pervasive problem with developing the Buffalo Exchange site was a failure in communication. We see from this example that this kind of situation can occur despite sincere, direct contacts. Instead of initially meeting with just the ad agency, we should have involved the clients, who wanted more artistic control, from the get-go. But who could have possibly known this? The ad agency had a long history of successfully marketing the company. The company itself had twenty years of successful advertising campaigns, and Wil assumed—not incorrectly—that his interpretations represented the clients' needs as he then understood them. What he did not know, and could not have known, was that the clients were actually unclear on how they wanted to be represented on the Web yet wanted to be involved artistically nevertheless.

The lesson here, then, is that a Web designer working with an ad agency must directly ask the question: who is the client here, the ad agency, or

its own respective client? One would certainly suspect that an advertising agency with a successful history in creating and maintaining a given company's image would be the client, but in this case, the principals wanted much more hands-on involvement, largely due to the fact that they were very interested in the technology of the Web. In the future, we know DesertNet will be much more thorough in digging for who actually makes final decisions as to the look and feel of a site.

The next problem was that Wil, thinking that he had enough information about the clients, went from the Web design meeting into his planning stages confident that the answers to the pertinent questions were there. Based on that, he went ahead and had a site designed. Wil feels he still had a lack of preproduction, that because he did not dig deep enough in that initial meeting, he went right through to production with information that was not in step with client need.

Another important realization was made during the second rendering of the site. The client was in the process of discovering its own changing image and self-perception. We did not give the client's management team enough of our jargon to best express themselves. Between all of the options they were faced with, the new ideas they were exposed to or—in this case—found, a new image was emerging, at least as far as the electronic company presence was concerned. Could better preproduction—particularly in the client-designer meeting and planning stages—have gotten this clarified *before* actual production on the site began? Wil thinks so, and I'm convinced that cases like this prove the point that the more time spent on a site before going to production, the more information will be gathered, and the less likely repeated site renderings will be.

The Buffalo Exchange is a site development experience that DesertNet learned a great deal from. We are, in fact, grateful both to Pollock and Associates Advertising and to the Buffalo Exchange for helping us learn so much about how we can be better prepared to deal with the potentially diverse needs of our clients. Also, we became well aware that the newness of the Web can both intrigue and confuse, and we better realized our responsibility to work very closely with our clients in the future to ensure their comfort.

"Money, time—so much of that was lost," summarizes Wil, "but the learning experience was really, really valuable."

Another Perspective

In later discussions regarding the lesson learned, Wil suggested that the Web design meeting should be thrown out of the process. This is a compelling thought—but I'm not convinced. Although as Web designers we are fully capable of creating Web sites that work for our clients, those sites are an extension of something very personal—and that something, in this case, the client's self-image—must be uncovered. I fully believe that the best-case scenario in which to find this out involves the initial meeting and subsequent relations with the client.

Interestingly, Dr. Joel Snyder, contributing editor to *Internet World,* has suggested that the client is a "member" of the team. My personal take is that this is the other extreme. Although its participation is certainly a critical aspect of the process, I do feel that there is a point when the client has offered what it can and needs to let the specialists do their job. I suppose it boils down to differing perspectives, and the best suggestion I have for Web designers in this new and often confusing field is to go with your own instincts and experience. This approach will not shake the foundational skills required of the Web design job: communications and organization.

chapter 12

Virtual Tour Guide II: Gadabout Salons

We've seen a Web site process example (the Buffalo Exchange) that was filled with learning experience—some of which was undeniably painful for the Web designer as well as for team members, clients, and client representatives. Lessons of this nature are not easily forgotten, nor should they be, for in fact they provide the foundation for stronger, more streamlined working styles.

Much as parents want their children to learn from the mistakes that a lifetime has lent them, so do we wish to offer up what we've learned learning from our experiences. The hope, as mentioned many times in this book, is to provide a model that will help Web design and Web designers by offering a foundation that can be modified, pondered, and ultimately used as a method that will be effective in a variety of scenarios. But learning doesn't only come from the tough stuff—it can come from the experience of mutuality. When a Web design process goes smoothly, there are lessons to be learned from examining what was done, how it was done, what was strong, and how we can bring those strengths into our next experience.

The Web Design Team

After the experience with the Buffalo Exchange, Wil told me that he was convinced that the most difficult lesson he learned was that he "didn't wear the Web designer hat well." I would disagree, because in reality, his daily job entails many aspects of Web design, and he has created quite a number of brilliant sites—often acting as a mentor and example for me. But the fact remains that his *love* is elsewhere—primarily in research, development, programming, and publishing.

We decided to departmentalize, and the Web design department at DesertNet became my domain, the publications department, his. As a result, my job has been to wear the Web designer hat daily. I, unlike Wil, really love this aspect of the business, and for a number of reasons. First, my strength has never been in programming, or actual design. Instead, I enjoy and excel at communications, layout, and the way a design will look and feel. Working with different clients on a daily basis stimulates me as well—one week it's a fine restaurant, the next it's a Spa and Salon like Gadabout. Like a good Web site, I thrive on fresh information, and the client variations in Web design please me greatly.

Perhaps the love of doing something is a part of doing it well. It certainly seems to be helpful. Nevertheless, the opportunity to work with Gadabout as Web designer was truly exciting to me. They are well-known in the Tucson area for their upscale, high-quality holistic spa and salon services. Having used their services for a number of years, I had a personal sense of what they were all about, and I knew that they have the image, the skill, and the quality of service to offer their clients.

Straz was my personal choice for art director—just as I understood Wil's instinct for the needs of the client, I knew that BrainBug had the slick look that image-oriented companies were going to demand. Gadabout has used the services of Sloan Imaging, which is responsible for many of their excellent print campaigns. Readers can enjoy some of Straz *and* Steve Sloan's work in the shape of this book's illustrated art. The two artists, while never having met and living 2500 miles apart, complement each other quite well, and Straz was able to bring out some of Steve's print-based influence (see Figure 12-1) within the work he developed for the Gadabout site. It's so refreshing to work in a field in which talents that otherwise would never have had the opportunity to co-create do so on a daily basis!

Figure 12-1
An example of Sloan Imaging's print work for Gadabout

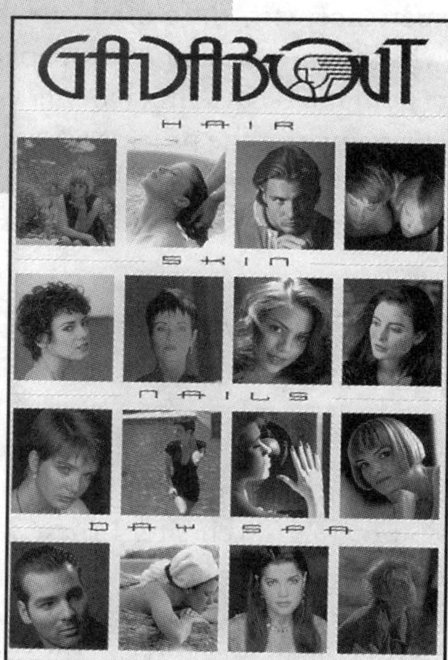

Ernest Padilla is the director of marketing and education for Pamela James, Inc., the parent company to Gadabout. There is no doubt that his creative eye and interest in the Web enormously influenced the tone and pace of this project. Ernest personally organized much of the copy and data. In this case, he has handled marketing as well, inasmuch as it pertains to non-Web-based activities. We handle the on-Web marketing in-house, and as with any DesertNet project, we have our own sysadmin and Web server.

The Client

Gadabout is, in one word, image. Whether it's beautifying hair, skin, and nails or providing clients with a full day of massage therapy and body wraps, the ultimate end is to make the client look good—and as an added benefit, feel good. Their services are very comprehensive, and while they are definitely on the expensive side of the beauty fence, the client benefits from personalized, warm, and wonderful service.

Preproduction

The preproduction process in the Gadabout case was a Web designer's dream. Unlike the experience with the Buffalo Exchange, it was very clear from the start who played each important part, demonstrating that Web designers are going to be in a much better position when they know *exactly* who the principals in the process are going to be. This was definitely a strong foundation for me, as well as for the team members later in the game.

The Client-Designer Meeting and Obtaining of Content

Ernest and I met in his office, where he is fully set up and connected to the Internet. We liked each other immediately and sat down to talk a bit about Gadabout's vision of their Web site. Ernest was extremely well-prepared, with a list of sites he really liked; materials including photos; promotional material designed by Sloan Imaging; and a file cabinet full of printed information on Gadabout's services, history, and products.

The fact that Ernest was so well-prepared had nothing to do with anything I did, but it brings up a major issue for the Web designer. That is, how do we encourage and create the opportunity for our clients to be well-prepared for our meetings? Many clients come to the Web designer without this much knowledge and interest in the Web, and we become in a sense their teachers and guides. To do this takes patience and consideration, and of course communication. I often told Ernest I wished all clients were like him, and then it occurred to me that although not everyone is going to function at this ideal level, I as Web designer bear a responsibility to give my client the tools, language, and opportunity to interact with me at the most beneficial level attainable.

Assessment of Client Need

After our discussion, drawing on the extensive information I had received from Ernest, I sat down to address the needs process:

- **Primary intent:** to create a slick, image-oriented presence on the Web
- **Short- and long-term goals:** to showcase Gadabout's products and image within the fashion industry and to the general public. To keep content fresh by offering something to the client and the Web community
- **Intended audience:** The primary audience is the fashion industry, which has a growing online presence. The secondary audience consists of potential clients for products and services.
- **Client Image:** classic, stylish, contemporary, very high-class
- **Unique aspects of the company:** a proprietary line of cruelty-free, all-natural hair care products. Community involvement through a nationally recognized program, Image Up! An interest in humanitarian issues such as AIDS, health and well being, and the environment

Planning

I was very confident that I had a strong feel for the direction of the site, and so I began playing around with fun wording and navigation. Before

I actually went into planning, I gave Straz a call and hashed out ideas with him. I wanted to be sure that my ideas were in line with his take on the materials. Going back to the interactive model, I have found that calling on the instincts of team members at key points in the process really helps. There is no formula for knowing when input at this point is going to be helpful or distracting; the answer really is, in my experience, based on instinct and experience. In this case, instinct served quite well, as Straz and I were able to combine energies with the strong data we had and come up with a very attractive concept.

- **Content.** We had a lot of written information on Gadabout's history, products, and activities. We organized this information into sections. Because Gadabout wanted to put the focus on relationships with their clients, I came up with a We/You theme to match their material, as shown in Figure 12-2, the Gadabout home page at http://www.gadabout.com/spa.

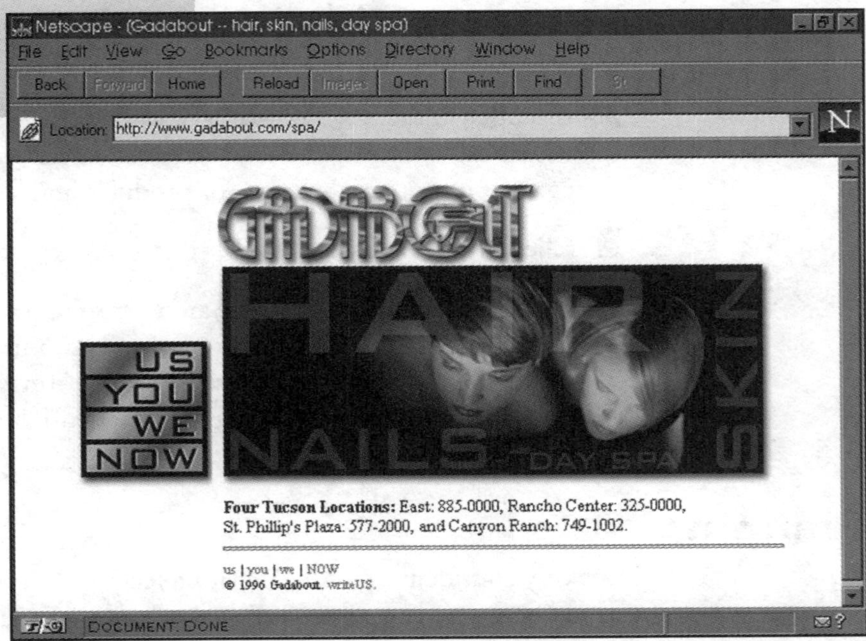

Figure 12-2 The Gadabout home page

- **Size of site.** The copy was fairly extensive. There was some concern about how to best balance it, but Straz came up with the great idea of laying the site content out like a fashion magazine. This created a situation in which the content was *required* to maintain the site's look and feel. Fortunately the information was interesting and comprehensive enough that we didn't find ourselves having to detract from the site's content by stretching the copy to fit our design needs.

- **Navigation.** To this day I'm not sure the decisions we made with navigation were entirely on the money, but it was a different and fun approach, and nobody has complained. On our main page, we offer four options, based on the We/You theme. Inside the site, however, navigation breaks down into more detailed pages. Compare the front page as shown in Figure 12-2 with an internal navigation bar in Figure 12-3. From the main page, you can get to only four pages, whereas from within the site you can navigate anywhere. Web designers are often challenged with situations like this, in which design and structure compete for dominance.

HOME US YOUSKIN YOUHAIR WEDO WETALK NOW

Figure 12-3
The Gadabout navigation bar

- **Look and feel.** Straz thought of using tables to create a magazine-style layout, with fashion photographs underscored by fun language. We chose colors based on classic industry design of white-and-black, with burnished gold accents from the Gadabout print material (Figure 12-4) designed by Sloan Imaging.

- **Graphic design.** We went high style all the way, including a full-color pallet for the graphics and fashion photos—a decision we would not necessarily have made if we weren't certain our competitive audience was going for total Netscape enhancements. The site is completely text accessible, but I shudder to think what our graphics look like in 256 colors. This is a perfect case of audience defining the design decision. It was an incredibly freeing

sensation just to be able to go for our ideal design, untethered by browser and bandwidth constraints. This doesn't mean we created images that are impossibly huge, but we definitely took advantage of some technological leeway as far as the graphics were concerned (see Figure 12-5).

Figure 12-4 The cover of the Gadabout menu, by Sloan Imaging

Figure 12-5 An example of a Gadabout internal page

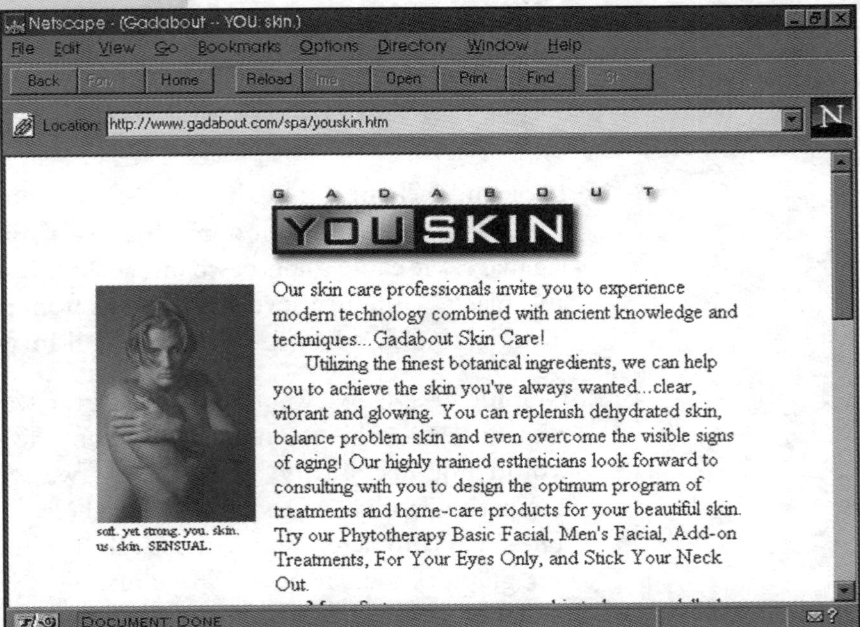

- **Multimedia and programming.** Ernest wanted to be accessible to anyone who would write, and he also wanted to be able to gather information on the types of individuals accessing the site. We created a simple, interactive feedback page, as shown in Figure 12-6. Otherwise, we chose to let the layout and photos on the site be the design focus. We sincerely felt that anything else would detract from the look and feel of the site.
- **Maintenance and open-ended design.** To keep things fresh, we decided to have a page called NOW, shown in Figure 12-7. Each month, Gadabout offers a special available only to people who see it on the Web page—this is called the NOWFeature. On the same page, we have a NOWLink. Each month, Ernest recommends a different link. Sometimes it's to another fashion site; sometimes it's to an educational site about HIV; sometimes it's related to animal rights and ecology. Interestingly, this is a point where people can jump off Gadabout and splash right into another part of the Web.

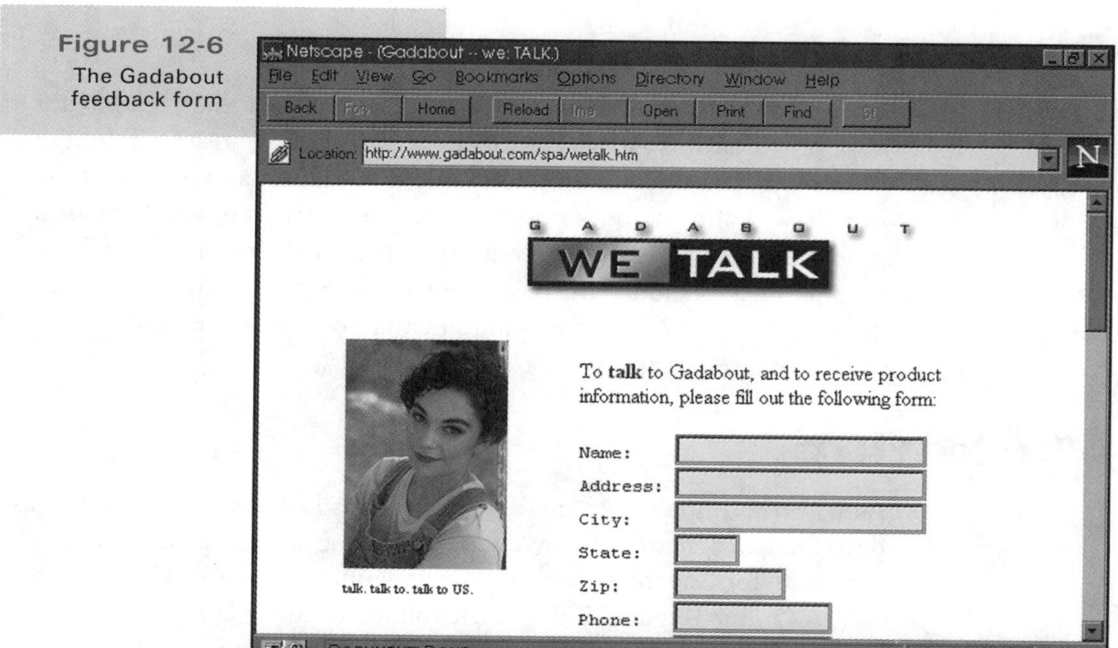

Figure 12-6 The Gadabout feedback form

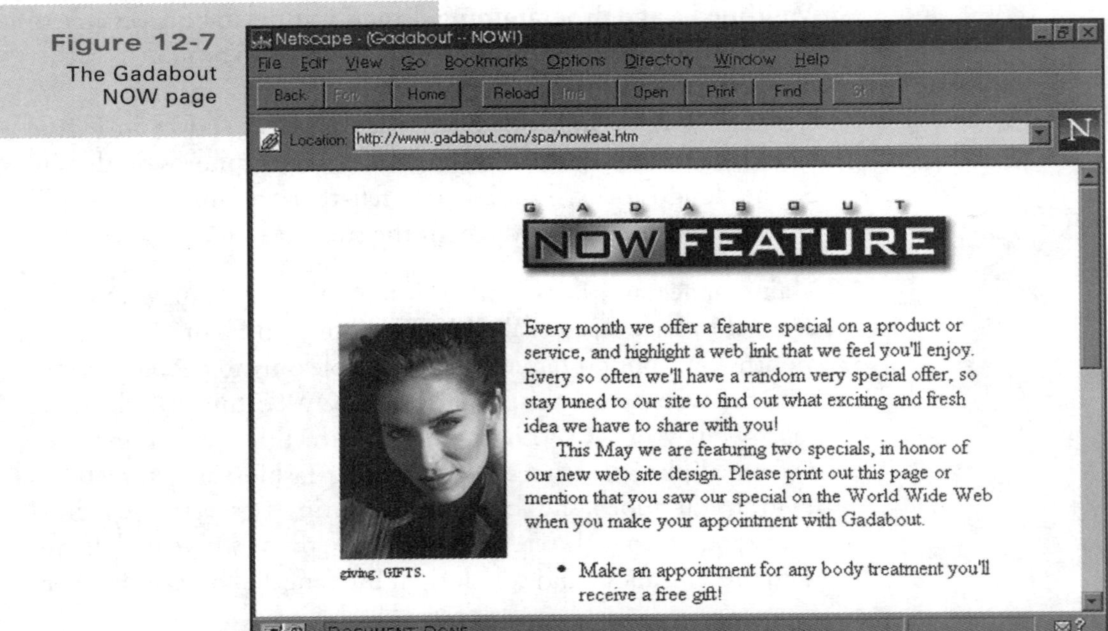

Figure 12-7 The Gadabout NOW page

Evaluation

There was nothing I showed Ernest along the way that he did not respond to enthusiastically. In fact, we got such a positive response from our original mock-up that we just went ahead and produced the site. It was almost too simple! By the time we were through with production, he had only a few comments to make toward improving the site. These included the placement and size of the company's 1-800 number (Figure 12-8) and making sure that there was an e-mail contact to him on every page.

Marketing

As with the Buffalo Exchange, we perform all of the site indexing as described in Chapter 10. We also are doing a high-profile banner campaign for Gadabout, with a series of banners throughout the *Tucson Weekly* Online (Figure 12-9). As with all our clients, Gadabout receives a listing in Desert Links, DesertNet's own search engine.

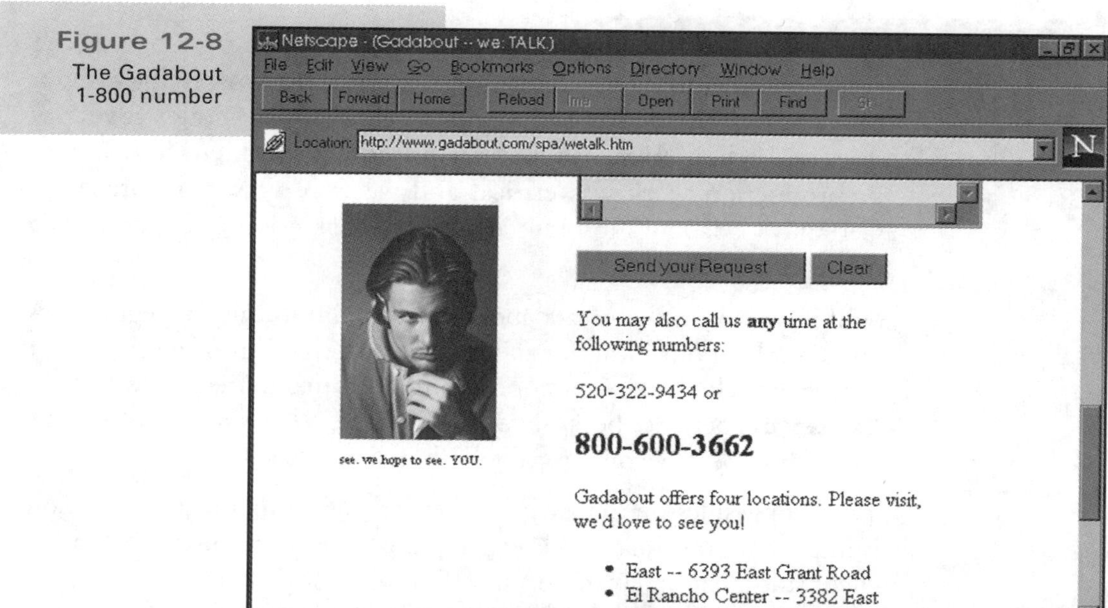

Figure 12-8
The Gadabout 1-800 number

Figure 12-9
A series of ad banners for Gadabout

Here we have another case in point in which the Web site design has influenced offline marketing options. During a conversation about illustrations for this book, Steve Sloan mentioned that Ernest had contacted him and asked him to adopt principal ideas from the Gadabout site for use in future print campaigns. I believe there is no finer compliment—to the Web designer, to the graphic designers, to the design team at large—for if this occurs, it certainly indicates that they have pleased the clients and met their needs immeasurably.

Lessons Learned

Gadabout went from preproduction to production to marketing without a hitch. In fact, it is to date probably the smoothest site we've ever done. Much of this can be attributed to the fact that, again, preproduction work was critical and we were very, very prepared. Certainly Gadabout's absolute certainty of their vision and desires made my job a breeze.

So if it was so easy, why talk about it? We point to this site regularly as an example of our ideal, for the very reasons that it *was* so easy. And I personally felt that it is a good example to juxtapose to the Buffalo Exchange experience because, while the results were similar, the lessons are both imperative ones for the Web designer.

The strongest lesson to take home here is not just that communication is important, but that *who* is wearing the hat of decision maker on the client side is extremely important. If, as with the Buffalo Exchange, the key personnel change in midstream, similar challenges may arise. Moreover, the role the Web designer can play as teacher to his or her client may make or break the process. In the case of Gadabout, my job was easy. Ernest was very well-educated about the Web, and his perception of how the company he represented should appear on the Web was very clear. There were no second guesses, because although we had certain artistic liberties and constraints, it was always clear what they were.

Next, the quality and type of data obtained from Gadabout matched the image they wanted to portray, and there was a significant amount of it. This helped avoid the problem we encountered with the Buffalo Exchange, because although yes, they gave us plenty of data—the sources were contradictory and the sense of image behind it, uncertain. Web designers must always make sure that what they obtain from a client sincerely represents that client's *current* image. Ask if you're not sure. And if somewhere along the line you lose confidence, ask again.

The amount of time spent in preproduction and in hashing out the details of the site with the graphic designer early on were strong components of why this site was successful.

We went from preproduction to production confident that we were doing *exactly* what the client wanted. Web designers are in a very good position when they feel this confidence. If at any time you do not, stop and ask why. Where is the weak link?

From preproduction to rendering, Gadabout took about seven working days, and some of those days were spent waiting for specific material. That's an astonishingly short turnaround time given the depth of this site, and it's something we are proud of and now use as an ideal to shoot for. Finally, the most important lesson learned from this experience simply restates our continual comment that successful production is based on two things: communication is the primary ingredient, and organization at the preproduction stage is the second. With these two factors as foundations, any snags along the Web design road will likely be much less harsh, time consuming, and money wasting than without them.

Send Us YOUR COMMENTS

Dear Reader:

Thank you for buying this book. In order to offer you more quality books on the topics ***you*** would like to see, we need your input. At Prima Publishing, we pride ourselves on timely responsiveness to our readers' needs. If you complete and return this brief questionnaire, ***we will listen!***

Name (First) ____ (M.I.) ____ (Last) ____

Company ____ Type of business ____

Address ____ City ____ State ____ ZIP ____

Phone ____ Fax ____ E-mail address: ____

May we contact you for research purposes? ❑ Yes ❑ No

(If you participate in a research project, we will supply you with the Prima computer book of your choice.)

❶ How would you rate this book, overall?

- ❑ Excellent
- ❑ Very good
- ❑ Good
- ❑ Fair
- ❑ Below average
- ❑ Poor

❷ Why did you buy this book?

- ❑ Price of book
- ❑ Author's reputation
- ❑ Content
- ❑ Prima's reputation
- ❑ CD-ROM/disk included with book
- ❑ Information highlighted on cover
- ❑ Other (please specify): ____

❸ How did you discover this book?

- ❑ Found it on bookstore shelf
- ❑ Saw it in Prima Publishing catalog
- ❑ Recommended by store personnel
- ❑ Recommended by friend or colleague
- ❑ Saw an advertisement in: ____
- ❑ Read book review in: ____
- ❑ Saw it on Web site: ____
- ❑ Other (please specify): ____

❹ Where did you buy this book?

- ❑ Bookstore (name): ____
- ❑ Computer store (name): ____
- ❑ Electronics store (name): ____
- ❑ Wholesale club (name): ____
- ❑ Mail order (name): ____
- ❑ Direct from Prima Publishing
- ❑ Other (please specify): ____

❺ Which computer periodicals do you read regularly? ____

❻ Would you like to see your name in print?

May we use your name and quote you in future Prima Publishing books or promotional materials?

❑ Yes ❑ No

❼ Comments & suggestions: ____

TAPE HERE

❽ I am interested in seeing more computer books on these topics

- ❑ Word processing
- ❑ Desktop publishing
- ❑ Databases/spreadsheets
- ❑ Web site development
- ❑ Networking
- ❑ Internetworking
- ❑ Programming
- ❑ Intranetworking

❾ How do you rate your level of computer skills?

- ❑ Beginner
- ❑ Intermediate
- ❑ Advanced

❿ What is your age?

- ❑ Under 18
- ❑ 18–29
- ❑ 30–39
- ❑ 40–49
- ❑ 50–59
- ❑ 60–over

SAVE A STAMP

Visit our Web site at **http://www.primapublishing.com**

and simply fill out one of our online response forms.

PRIMA PUBLISHING
Computer Products Division
701 Congressional Blvd., Suite 350
Carmel, IN 46032

PLEASE
PLACE
STAMP
HERE

Part IV

Web Design Technology in Practice

chapter 13

An Overview of Web Design Technology

In part one and two of this book, we explored some new media theory and looked at the crux of the challenges that face Web designers today. In part III, we went step by step through the process of creating Web sites and looked closely at case studies of successes and near failures. This part of the book takes a closer look at the distinct disciplines of Web design, using this book's multidisciplinary model.

It would be impossible to thoroughly investigate these disciplines without writing full-length books on each of them. However, this section does show how it is possible to get a good feel for current industry trends, current thinking, and issues within the individual disciplines. This chapter specifically sets up a series of pointers to key ideas necessary for the Web designer. Each of these key ideas is then discussed in greater detail in a chapter of its own.

For each discipline of Web design, then, the chapters in part IV offer brief discussions of specific baseline concepts. Bear in mind that much of this information is young and therefore amounts to little more than opinion born of experience. Accordingly, *Professional Web Design* attempts to back these opinions with examples and with their underlying rationales, while acknowledging fully that your experiences may be quite different and yet still serve you well.

In the final part of the book, "Web Design Resources," you'll find a series of appendices that correspond to the chapters in part IV. The appendices provide an overview of resources for each discipline—including Web sites, books, courses, and any related, relevant materials. The intent is to offer resources where Web designers can get a closer look at the ways things are being done currently and expose themselves to the varied opinions that exist. Web designers will make up their own minds, of course, on the basis of experience and exposure. These chapters and associated references should be thought of as starting points in the Web design journey, as well as places to go for advice and guidance while working in a particular discipline.

The Disciplines

As the foundation of our Web design paradigm, we've used these seven disciplines:

- Content and copy writing
- HTML
- Graphic design
- Multimedia
- Programming
- Systems administration
- Marketing

If you are currently a designer in the field, it is likely that either you are performing all of these tasks completely on your own or you are outsourcing them as necessary. Or perhaps you have developed a different, effective model of your own. Regardless of the situation, the information and concepts in this section have been broken down into what appear to be the most logical strata of Web design disciplines. The true art of Web design is in finding ways to *merge* this information both conceptually and in terms of workplace efficiency.

Content and Copy Writing

There's a reason that we chose this discipline as our starting point: without content—or with faulty, poorly written content—a Web site is doomed to failure. Content is the pivotal factor in Web design—it is the *what* in *what is our intent?* Copy is the language that conveys the content, and since language is the primary vehicle of communication, its importance cannot be stressed enough. Quality writing—which is rare enough—is imperative for good commercial Web site design. Poor writing, inappropriate voice, awkward style, bad spelling, and grammatical inaccuracy does not only look bad but can outright offend, as the self-proclaimed Grammar Cop shows us in Figure 13-1.

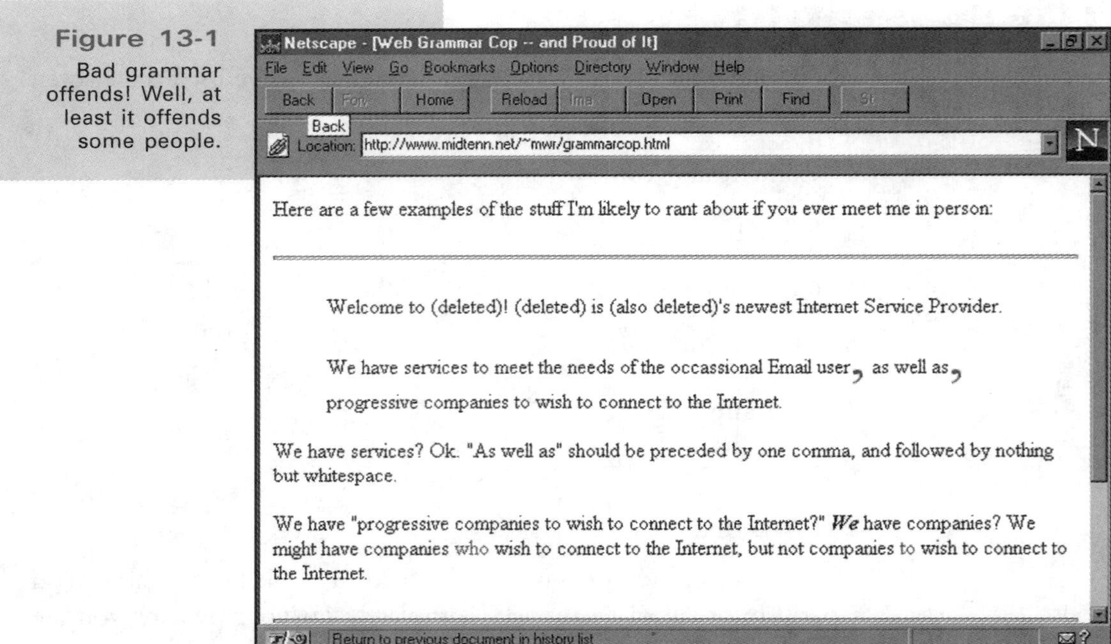

Figure 13-1 Bad grammar offends! Well, at least it offends some people.

As you polish your own judgment of good content and your copy writing skills (or as you look for competent writers to outsource your work to), keep in mind the following major points, which are examined in detail in Chapter 14:

- **Precision content is imperative.** Clear thoughts, written simply and to the point, are the foundation of strong Web site copy. This is true for both marketing-oriented sites and content-based informational sites. This is not to say that less is necessarily more, but that the attention span of Web visitors is often short. People want their information, they want it short and sharp, and they want it *now*. As the site's copy writer, to best ensure that your visitors get what they want, get to the point!

- **Appropriate voice can make or break a Web site.** If your company is reaching out to an alternative or hip audience, à la Dispatch (Figure 13-2), then fun with language is fine. On the other hand, if you are appealing to a more conservative audience, flippant language won't fly. A sincere approach is best, as with the Flagstaff

Festival of the Arts, which caters to a broader audience of mature individuals and families (Figure 13-3).

- **Words must work in concert with graphic and other elements.** If there is a lack of balance among a site's words, graphics, and other media, sensory overload ensues. This results in unattractive sites that people don't visit for very long. Words must enhance the site. They are not superfluous or there just because "words are important." Many will argue the opposite—that graphics must be used only to enhance words. Both are extremes that point to the significance of balance, as suggested in Figure 13-4.
- **Grammar, spelling, copy editing!** Nothing reveals a designer's interest (or lack of interest) in maintaining long-term clientele than the way he copyedits his sites. Yes, we are all human and can overlook things from time to time; it happens. But major embarrassments can be avoided by exhaustive copy editing in the postproduction phase, and there are some general rules of thumb when writing for Web sites, which we'll be examining in detail in Chapter 14.

Figure 13-2 A hip writing style for the Dispatch site

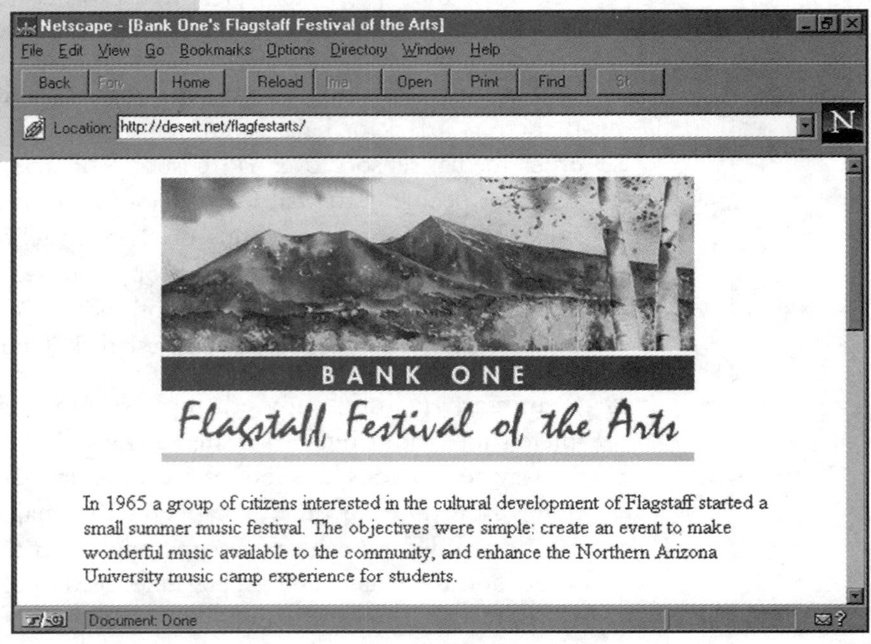

Figure 13-3 An attractive but sincere approach for a broader audience

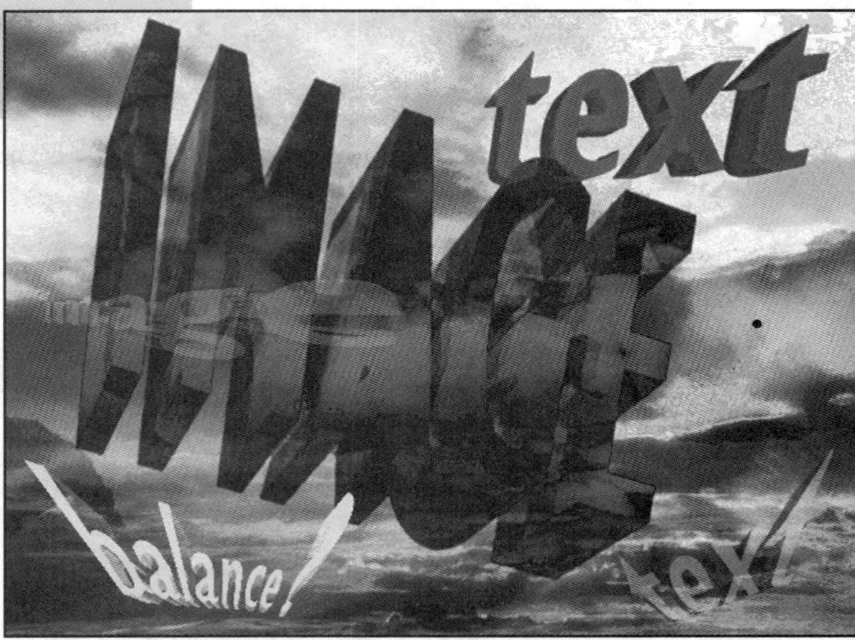

Figure 13-4 A question of balance

Hypertext Markup Language

Knowledge of HTML isn't a concern only for Web design professionals but also for technical writers and professionals in a growing number of fields, such as journalists. To do their jobs better, many people are finding good HTML skills to be an asset. Of course, for the purposes of our discussion, the most obvious application for HTML is Web design. We are already seeing the way Intranets—internal networks using Web-based standards—are employing all of the important facets of Web design. This indicates that knowledge of HTML can enhance one's professional journey, no matter where in the world it might take one.

HTML *is* an evolving language, and this evolution has become more rapid as needs have arisen for standards in step with Web designer requirements. Currently, draft version 3.2 represents the latest in HTML tags, but many browsers do not support them, so people currently avoid many available enhancements that will eventually empower their design work.

Some focal points of HTML that we'll discuss in Chapter 15:

- **Clean code is paramount.** This simply means that HTML coders (whether it's you, a member of your team, or both) should decide which book they're going by and stick to it. Not only is consistent, clean code nice, but it prevents specific Web browsers from having to parse "creative," or lazy, code.
- **HTML style should be consistent.** Create style sheets for your company and adhere to them. If you prefer all your code to be capitalized, then make sure that all your tags are capitalized. If the <p align=center> tag excites you much more than <center>, use it, but use it consistently. Neither is wrong or right, so choose a style and stick to it. Inconsistency looks sloppy (see Figure 13-5). Consistent presentation and style allow less room for mistakes—particularly when you have more than one coder working for your outfit.

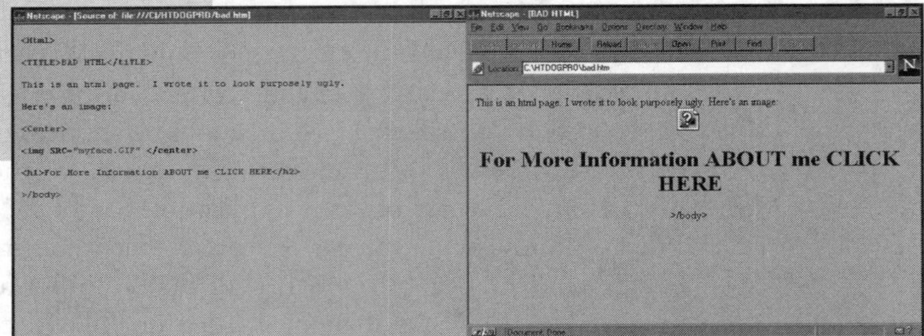

Figure 13-5 An example of inconsistent code and its varied results

- **Learn how to use tags that optimize loading, speed, and accessibility.** There are quite a few HTML tags and tag arguments that simply *must* be employed when designing professional Web sites. Examples of these include image attributes such as width and height, the "alt" tag, the <title> tag, and other tags that will optimize your code.

- **Check your syntax!** Just as copy must be copyedited, code should be edited as well. Go over finished code with a fine eye. Make sure that you've closed what you've opened, if the tag requires it—and most do. Also, be certain that there are no forgotten angle brackets, misspelled tags, and the like. Your browser may be forgiving, but others won't. There are good tools available to check HTML, many available right in popular editors, others available on the Web. There's a list of resources in Appendix B—be sure to check there for more information on HTML applications.

Graphic Design

As mentioned already, balance is an essential element in creating excellent Web sites. Graphics—which many still argue must adhere to very limited, strict rules—are truly important to the long-term survival of Web design. Learning how to use graphics wisely, effectively, and—most important—appropriately, is a critical element of Web design. Chapter 16 looks more intently at some of the primary principles included here:

- **GIF and JPEG.** Each of the two important graphic formats used for Web design has unique features, enhancements, and challenges. It is important that Web designers understand these differences in order either to render appropriate graphics themselves or to be able to discuss the details of a site with the graphic designer. The way that graphic formats are employed will have tremendous effects on load time and appearance—both extremely important considerations in professional Web design.

- **Color management systems.** How color is controlled is quite often determined by the browser, combined with an individual's computer graphics card and monitor. With a good knowledge of color management, a graphic designer can make strong choices based on the Web designer's instructions. As discussed in part III of this book, if you are going for a broad audience, you must tailor the site's content to that audience. If you have leeway in audience and are going for a high-bandwidth, cutting-edge look and feel, then there's more freedom. Knowing the parameters of color and how to manage it with regard to the Web is extremely empowering for the Web design professional.

- **Background patterns and colors are key to design.** As depicted in Figure 13-6, poor selection of background patterns results in an inability to read the content. To avoid this, knowing how to keep patterns interesting without having them interfere with a page's copy is important. With an understanding of color management, both the Web designer and the graphic designer can make appropriate decisions on a site for the intended audience.

- **Good tools are critical to graphic design, but good tools don't make a good graphic designer.** Doing the job with the wrong set of tools makes the job difficult if not impossible, and the results are poor at best. Knowing about hardware and software that assist the graphic designer is important to the success of any design. By the same token, having the right hardware and software doesn't automatically make someone a good designer! For detailed resources, check Appendix C.

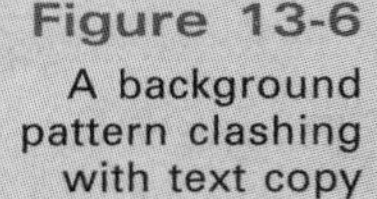

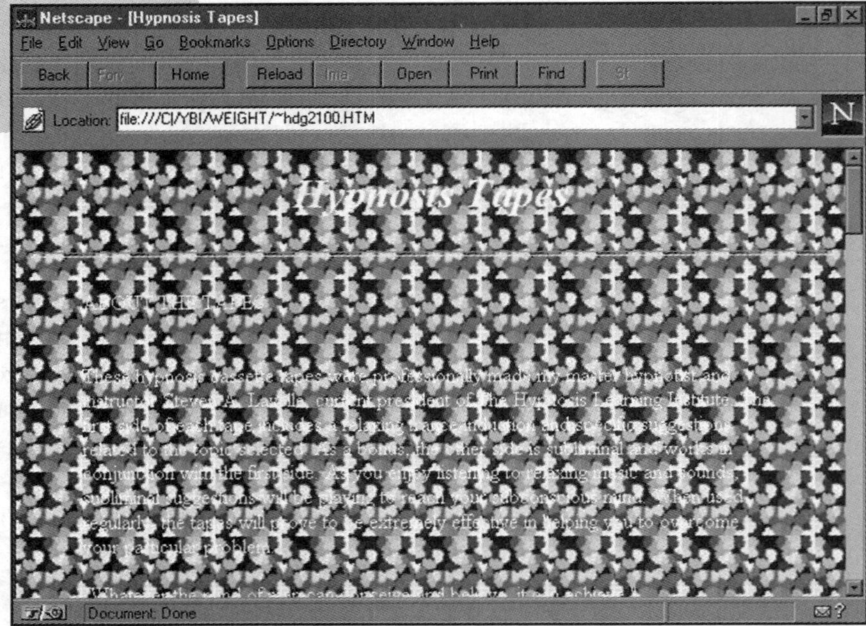

Figure 13-6 A background pattern clashing with text copy

Multimedia

With advances being made in this area daily, it is becoming quite the challenge to keep up not only with *what* can be done with multimedia on the Web but also with *how* it can be done. With emerging languages and scripts such as Java, JavaScript, ActiveX, and Visual Basic Script, as well as the implementations of VRML, QTVR, and Shockwave, the future of multimedia on the Web is exciting.

For the purposes of this book, the discipline of multimedia is defined as the art of adding specific media to a Web page design that are more than graphics and text. This means non-GIF animation, audio, and video. In Chapter 17, we will discuss some of the delivery issues and, as ever, the importance of making sure that audience is *always* considered before one adds multimedia options.

- **Viewing method and access are the primary considerations for multimedia use.** How is the multimedia "event" going to be viewed? Does it spawn an external application via a browser that your site's visitor may or may not have on a personal machine? Does it rely on plug-in software? Does it run in-line? These questions all must be answered before a Web designer chooses to use multimedia on a site, because the answers will affect how many people will actually be able to access the information.

- **Until multimedia platforms are in-line and common, it's best to not place them on index or main pages—with very few exceptions.** Because of multimedia access issues, it's wise to design your Web site so that it offers its welcome content without being impeded by a multimedia event. One exception to this rule of the road is when the site demonstrates multimedia technology or is only for a very specific audience that is capable of viewing that technology.
- **Non-GIF animations.** There are several ways to accomplish such animations—the most popular is called "Nanimation," which is short for Netscape Animation. Nanimations can only be viewed with Netscape browser version 1.1 and later. Basically Nanimations run on Common Gateway Interface scripts, which send to the server for information. They are not for the bandwidth-impaired but can definitely be enjoyable and quite usable.
- **Audio.** Audio can be handled via downloadable media that pull up a helper application to run. This takes time, but for sound bites of importance, as in music, it is a good way to do things. Real Audio is real-time streamed audio that requires a player but operates very quickly and is excellent for voice applications. Finally, both Explorer 2.0 and above and Netscape 3.0 and above offer some in-line audio features that are definitely the precursors of full audio for the Web.
- **Video.** Limitations of video Web production are largely due to bandwidth restrictions. Nevertheless, some preliminary video technologies exist and are certain to improve over time.
- **VRML.** Virtual Reality Modeling Language allows for the creation of virtual environments that can be controlled by the end user. Its future applications are interesting but yet to be proven.

- **QTVR.** Quick Time Virtual Reality utilizes wide-angle still photography, seamed together to create virtual worlds. It is much more manual and immediate than VRML, as it creates virtual worlds that can be based on realistic concepts as well as purely conceptual ones.

Be sure to check Appendix D for detailed resources on multimedia applications for the Web.

Advanced Programming for the World Wide Web

Advanced programming makes up a very specialized area that includes programming for multimedia development, creation of forms, and other interactive aspects of the Web. In fact, interactivity—especially as the technology evolves—will largely become the domain of programmers.

Several key languages and scripts are employed currently to make up the panorama of Web-oriented programming. They include Java, JavaScript (see Figure 13-7), Visual Basic Script, ActiveX, and Common Gateway Interface—which is not itself a language but a gateway from client to server, where scripts or programs written in languages such as C or PERL are called upon.

Each of these languages will be introduced as a central concept in Chapter 18, with a programmer's resource toolbox in Appendix E. Web designers are encouraged to become familiar with as much as possible of the jargon and as many as possible of the applications of the various technologies discussed in this chapter, since much of the Web's future is dependent upon them and familiarity makes it easier for the Web designer to interact effectively with programmers when hiring out-of-house help.

Systems Administration

Systems administration is the truly technical side of the Web design profession, and there are very specific considerations a Web designer must be aware of when selecting and working with systems administrators. We'll look closely at some of the ways Web designers can deal more effectively with systems and their administrators in Chapter 19, and we'll provide related resources in Appendix F.

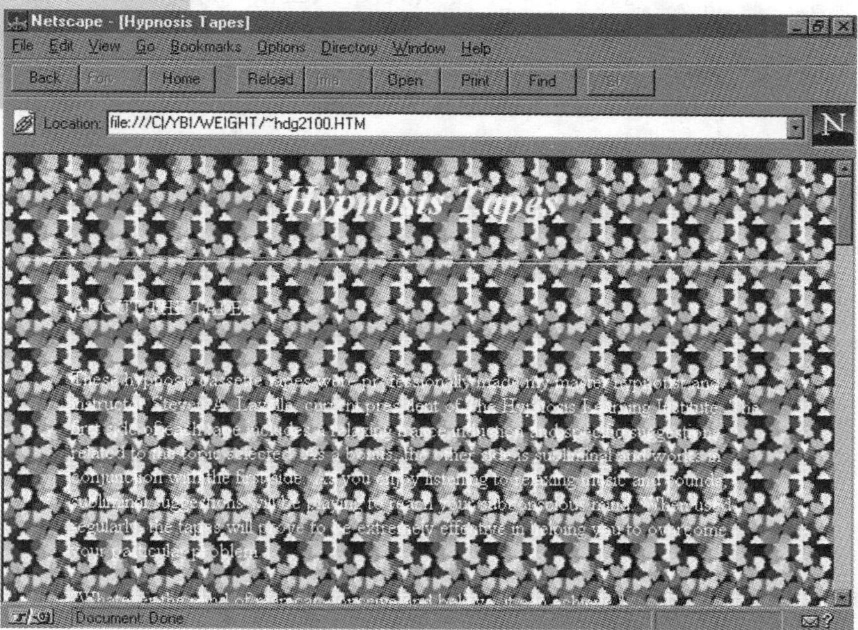

Figure 13-7 An example of JavaScript code

- **What type of Web server is best?** Without starting a holy war, we will discuss a few of the most popular Web servers available, and their common advantages and disadvantages.
- **Learn some tech jargon!** It is only through hard personal experience that I am even discussing this topic. However, Web designers—many of whom are strong in communications and creative endeavors rather than highly technical ones—need to be able to accurately communicate with their tech-oriented sysadmins, who have a language all their own. This ability in itself will empower a Web designer to get the most mileage out of a relationship with the sysadmin.

Web Site Marketing

What if we built a Web site and nobody came? Easy answer: we've failed to create a viable product for our client. This is why site marketing is so critical. Not all sites require aggressive marketing; sometimes a lighter touch is necessary. What about company standards, and image?

How do we balance the relationships between designers, clients, and audience? Again, the relationship of audience to the developed site is critical. A few areas we cover in Chapter 20 (offering related resources for in Appendix G) include:

- **Company standards.** This topic includes setting up ways to create a consistent image so that clients, and potential clients, have easy access and understanding of your company's services and directives. This in turn helps develop both company reputation and esteem.
- **Benefit and value.** Why should clients go with your company rather than another? What is it that you offer that no one else can, and how do you express this in a positive yet proud way?
- **The importance of offline advertising.** If you live in the United States and watch television or listen to radio, you've likely seen or heard URLs being advertised in these media. Encourage clients to use their URL in all the outside advertising they do—whether it's print ads, television, radio—even T-shirts, mugs, and novelty items should contain an URL!

Pulling It All Together

The Web designer holds the principal responsibility of pulling all these disciplines together in a balanced, harmonious fashion in order to create dynamite sites. This is a compelling notion, and it relates to the central model offered in this book. "Web weaving" is a term used with some frequency in the field, and it seems highly accurate to apply it to this most precise of Web design elements. In fact, the weaving of these elements is the true test of the professional Web designer's ability. If a site, incorporating most if not all of these disciplines, balances various media, is esthetically appealing, is technically precise, offers interesting content, and—most of all—is visited regularly, then the Web designer has succeeded in weaving a fine Web indeed.

chapter 14

Content and Copywriting

Perhaps it is a result of general problems with literacy, or perhaps there is simply a lack of concern with the importance of writing. Whatever the reasons may be, not only is writing in general—and writing for the Web in particular—frequently poor, but few resources seem to be dedicated to changing that fact.

As a Web designer, you (and your team's writers) must remember that audience is the most critical player, because without audience, there'd be no need for the work you are doing. It is essential that the writer put the audience first, yet this is a point that many writers lose sight of or never even consider. This is especially important when writing *to* a specific market, as is common in commercial Web design.

The true meaning and value of a site's content is most likely to be found in its words. Imagine yourself as the audience. If the information that you are looking for isn't made immediately clear, as in Figure 14-1, you'll find it time-consuming and confusing to search the site for the information you need. If you, as the writer, haven't made that information accessible, you've essentially failed at the task and disappointed the audience.

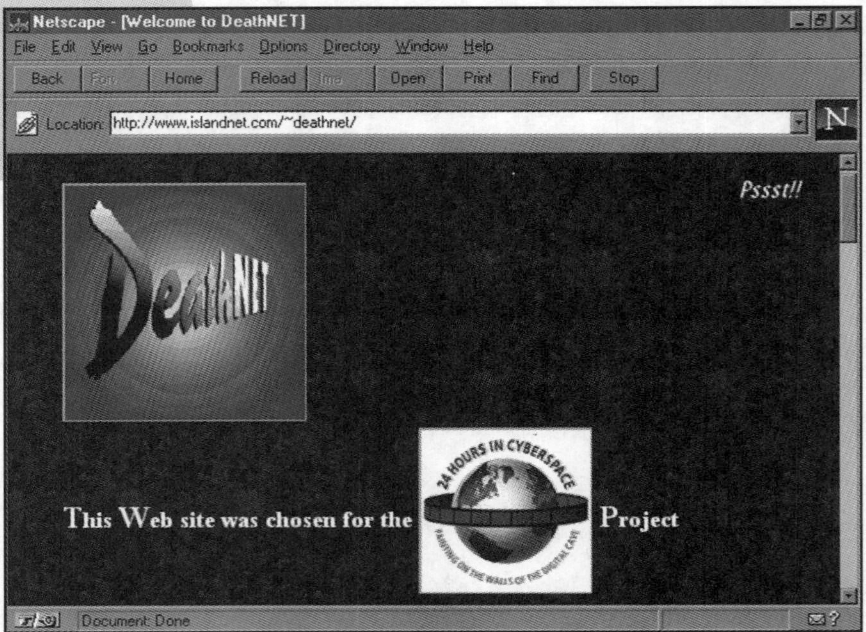

Figure 14-1 The intent of this Web site is nowhere to be found on this page!

Know Thy Audience

No matter what other points are covered in this chapter, remember this above all: the success of your Web design—and, ultimately, your success as a designer—hinges on how well you understand your audience. This understanding forms the foundation of a site's physical expression (colors, graphics, navigational tools, overall layout) but also provides a base from which you can create the site's language. All aspects of your site must be customized to meet your audience's needs, expectations, and tastes, and the effective Web designer understands this all-important point. The audience should be thought of as a personal critic, a customer, and hopefully a friend who spends a lot of time at your place. Knowing how to make and keep that friend happy and comfortable is paramount.

Dan Huff, editor of the *Tucson Weekly,* wastes no time getting to the crux of the issue. "Don't fake it—know your audience, because they all have built-in bullshit detectors." His point, though somewhat earthy in its expression, defines a critical starting point for a writer. The audience is going to know—consciously or unconsciously—whether certain language comes across as insincere or inappropriate. Both failings are deadly sins in writing, especially if you are trying to win your audience over, market a product, or sell an idea.

Writers can call on several techniques to help define the audience and speak to it appropriately. First, it helps to have the ability to write for a variety of audiences. Next, it's necessary to know how to organize data efficiently *in the context* of a given audience. Finally, the appropriate use of *voice*—essentially the tone you take with an audience—enables you to accurately and creatively interact with your Web site's visitors. In addition to these elements, there are several distinct methods for manipulating text for the Web that will enable you to be tremendously effective as a communicator. We will discuss these methods in detail throughout this chapter.

Diverse Skills Count

Having strong writing skills, or employing someone who does, is important to creating Web sites that are effective because a skilled communicator has evaluated the best way to communicate. In order to do that well, a mastery of language is of primary importance.

But what is mastery of language? Different disciplines require different types of skills. Writing great poetry might not demand excellent organization. If one is writing for children, sophisticated prose may get in the way; a simple, direct style is needed to communicate to that audience. When crafting instructional manuals, technical writers often neutralize voice in order to make instructions clearer and information easier to access.

Web designers may be called upon to do Web sites for poets, children, or technically oriented companies. The type of client coming through the portals of a Web design firm ranges from the small, home-based business to corporations with NASDAQ listings. The organizations represented on the Web are panoramic, vast, and varied. Accordingly, knowing how to write for a variety of audiences, or knowing the people who can do this, will give the Web designer an edge in creating successful sites.

Precision Content

If you have followed the guidelines as suggested in Part 3 of this book, you should have a large amount of information collected for any Web site you will design. This collection of information gives you an advantage, because it enables you (and your writer, if you have someone else providing writing services) to answer questions such as *what is the intent?* and *who is the audience?* instead of trying to figure out what sort of general information the site should provide. These questions, as well as the others examined in earlier chapters, can be answered now by using the client's information as the meat for the Web stew.

A Theoretical Case in Point

We have discussed the importance of precision content several times in this book. With the information-gathering process behind you, you should now be ready to take the broad, general information provided by the client and your own research and craft it into precise content. This is achieved by thoroughly examining the client's material and then culling the focus points from it.

Let's suppose that you're designing a site for a movie theater. This particular theater features independent films, and the audience is typically going to be people who have a greater interest in these more obscure films than, say, the average movie fan. They will likely be a well-educated audience, usually in their twenties or older.

The client has given you a lot of information on the history of the theater, the types of films typically shown there, a list of current film events and times, and pages of details on upcoming films. Since the client and his customers are avid fans of independent films, the client also has given you a huge quantity of minutely detailed information on film trivia, director biographies, and actor profiles.

Identifying the Site's Intent

In this case, when you focus on intent you'll find that it is "to provide information to people about our cinema, what's currently playing, and what's coming up." You'll also find that the need for the trivia and biographies, although interesting in their own right, is secondary. You can spice up the site by using a few important quotes from directors or interesting historical notes, but it is just that—spice—and not primary content. Also, the detail provided regarding upcoming films is lengthy, so with the goal of crafting precision content in mind, you decide to cut that detail into smaller, more easily used sections.

Again, audience and intent are the determining factors in *why* it is important to choose one feature over another as dominant. In this case, the audience needs to find out about the independent films playing at the cinema, and the client needs to make sure that his customers can get to that information. The interesting details such as history, amenities, and film trivia can all be used to enhance the site, either initially or later on. If the site's purpose were to feature independent film producers, directors, actors, and the like, then, yes, that would be a reasonable choice as a primary focus. In this case, it isn't, so our only justifiable option is to use that information as enhancement and promotion rather than static content.

Engaging the Audience

Once you've determined the site's primary content, you can then build the texture and options around it. Anticipate the audience; will they want to see specials, discounts, or free popcorn if they mention the Web site at the ticket office? What can you add to the site to bring people back? One idea would be to have a trivia contest; with all that great information, you could create a feedback form and ask a new question weekly. Then the client could have all the correct answers placed in a hat, and the first winner chosen could receive theater tickets or T-shirts and movie posters.

This is the area where Web writers really get to use their imaginations. There are all kinds of possibilities, but it is forever the writers' responsibility to bear in mind that the way they express their ideas will tremendously affect how the audience will respond to those ideas. In the case of the Cinci Cinema, we're dealing with an audience that is very likely college educated. As a result, keeping voice, grammar, and ideas consistent with that audience will be potent factors in how that audience will appreciate what you've done.

Finding the Right Style and Voice

Now that you have streamlined the plan and added some imaginative, fun aspects, you need to decide how to give your ideas some shape, using the information provided by the client. Examine that content. Is it too wordy, or full of run-on sentences? What about the voice? Is it strong, weak, or nonexistent? What can you do with this content to streamline it, give it appropriate personality, and keep it true to the intent of the site?

Let's suppose, for example, that the client gave you the following text, trying to describe the Cinci Cinema:

> *"The Cinci Cinema has been in existence for the last 25 years, and we are proud to show fine independent films for the discriminating audience, who enjoys only the best from their cinema experience. We have a beautifully restored theater located in the downtown arts district that is fully air conditioned for our customer's convenience, and we offer great snacks including pastries, and cappuccino, as well as the more traditional popcorn, candies and sodas. We are fully wheelchair accessible and are happy to*

> *accommodate all people, regardless of their special needs, and we'll go the length for you, since your having a great film experience here at Cinci Cinema is our reason for being. If you visit on Festive Fridays, we offer half off of our regular ticket prices for everyone! We're next to the 450 Gallery, right downtown, come see us soon!"*

This passage offers a lot of great information, but there are distinct problems with the style, including sentence length and wordiness. The text's voice isn't very mature, but it does try to communicate personally with the audience, and that is appropriate, given our intent. Also, there is an elegance *intended* in this paragraph, particularly in the expression of pride regarding the restored theater and the writer's desire to reach a select audience.

A few things the Web designer can do to make this material work include breaking down the paragraph into its most important points and rebuilding from there. I would personally decide to bring out the voice a little more, as I like the personal, proud point of view for this kind of business.

Let's list the main facts and sentiments of this paragraph, and let's group items by sections. In this case, items that focus on the building can go together, and those about services can be grouped together. This will help organize the data, although it is not necessary to stick to the order you create initially. Rather, the purpose is to create a point of focus for your writing. Your list might look like this:

- The Cinci Cinema has been in operation for 25 years.
- The owner proudly features films from independent filmmakers.
- The owner considers the audience to have discriminating taste.
- The Cinci Cinema is sincerely concerned that its customers have a comfortable and enriching experience while viewing films there.
- The Cinci Cinema is housed in a restored theater.
- The building is wheelchair-accessible.
- The building is fully air-conditioned.
- Food service features pastries and cappuccino as well as more traditional theater fare.

Now you can rewrite the paragraph with these main thoughts and sentiments in mind, and with the goals of ordering the information more appropriately while refining the voice of the text. Your recast version might resemble this:

> "*The Cinci Cinema has been featuring fine, independent films for 25 years. Located in a beautiful restored theater, we offer an environment as well as a film selection to appeal to the discriminating film fan. It is our pleasure to offer delicious pastries and cappuccino, as well as the more traditional fare. We are air-conditioned and fully accessible for your comfort. You'll find us in the downtown arts district, next to the 450 Gallery. Visit on Festive Fridays for discount admission!*"

What we end up with maintains the personal feel, yet it is written more smoothly. It makes a nice introduction to the site's eventual page. It is more refined, clear in its communication. In step with our theme, it is precise and strong in voice. These are all significant points in how writing, and especially writing for the Web, must be organized.

Voice Can Make or Break a Site

In the introduction to this section of *Web Design (*Chapter 13), we looked briefly at examples of how voice can make or break a Web site. We pointed to the Dispatch site, which is written in hip, fun language, and then to the Flagstaff Festival of the Arts site, which is more conservative. Dispatch is promoting online services to alternative newspapers, whereas the Flagstaff site highlights a yearly arts festival that is geared primarily to mature adults, with some family interest as well.

Two Distinct Voices

To find out exactly why voice is important, let's examine the welcoming copy from each site. Figure 14-2 shows how visitors are welcomed to the Dispatch home page.

Now, take a look at the Flagstaff Festival's welcoming copy (Figure 14-3).

Figure 14-2 Copy on the Dispatch home page

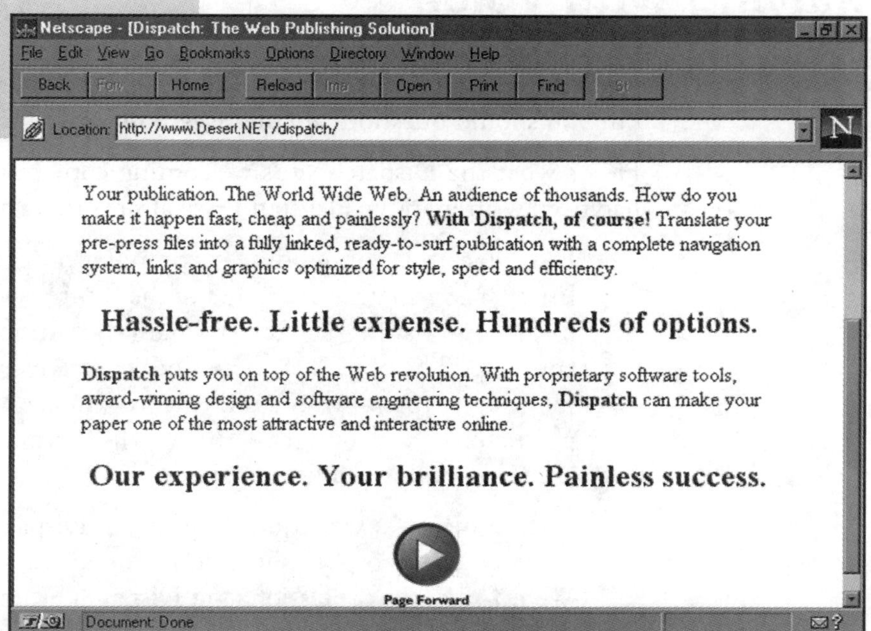

Figure 14-3 Copy on the Flagstaff Festival home page

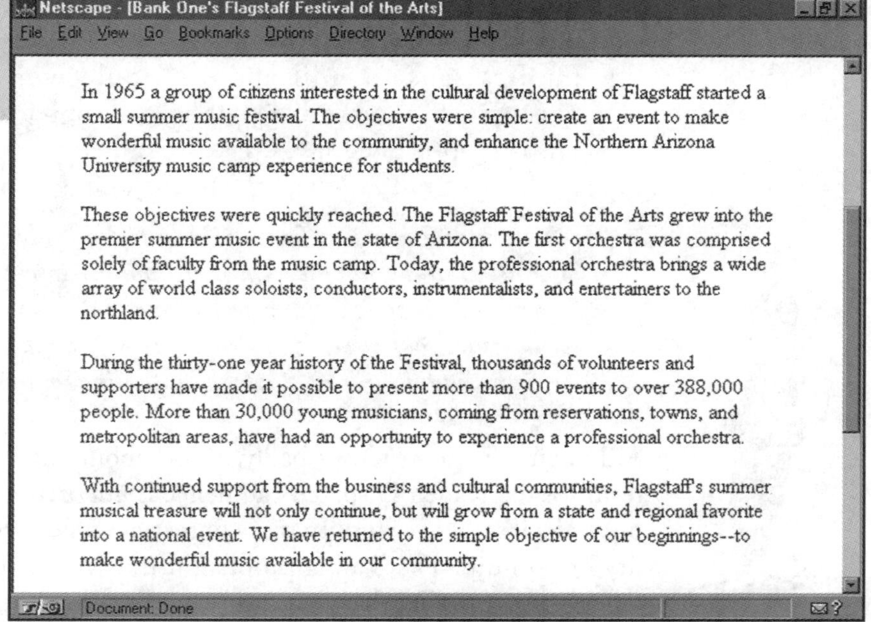

Playing with Voice

Okay, let's have some fun and swap the voices between these two sites. Keep the audience in mind as we do this! The copy might read well—but you should question whether it will *speak* well to its audience.

Here's what the Dispatch site's welcoming copy might look like, if it had been written in the Flagstaff Festival site's more conservative voice:

> In 1996 a group of publishers, computer programmers, and Internet consultants interested in the future development of online publishing started a small electronic publishing company. The objectives were simple: create a way to make wonderful programs available to the community of publishers, and enhance the world's experience when accessing online publications.
>
> These objectives were quickly reached. Dispatch grew into the premier Web publishing company on the World Wide Web. Today, the professionals at Dispatch bring a wide array of world-class programs, services, and products to the online publishing world.
>
> During the year-long history of Dispatch, hundreds of publishers have made it possible to present online publications to millions of people worldwide. An uncountable number of people have the opportunity to visit Dispatch-processed sites every week, there to experience the quality of a professionally produced online publication.
>
> *With continued support from the industry, not only will Dispatch's offerings continue, but they will grow from city-specific publications to regional, national, and international ones. We have returned to the simple objectives of our beginnings—to make the finest in electronic publishing available to our online community.*

Although this doesn't *read* badly, think about the communication in terms of the reader. Dispatch's audience is *alternative.* This passage has no sizzle; it's not very hip. In that context, it could easily be perceived as dry or ho-hum. That's a big problem if the Web designer's intent is to talk about a product that is cutting-edge, sizzling hot, and totally now.

Okay, now let's try changing the Flagstaff Festival's welcoming passage to the Dispatch's voice:

> *1965. Flagstaff, Arizona. A small summer festival.*
>
> *How do you improve cultural development in Flagstaff? With the Flagstaff Festival of the Arts, of course! Take your community and Northern Arizona University students and create a wonderful music event in our community.*
>
> Objectives achieved. Premier event. A professional orchestra.
>
> Flagstaff Festival of the Arts puts our community in touch with world-class music. With soloists, conductors, instrumentalists, and entertainers, Flagstaff Festival of the Arts makes your summer music festival experience one of the best in the northland.
>
> **Thirty-one years. Your participation. Return to simplicity.**

Imagine a conservative audience reading this. It's awkward, it doesn't flow, and it could even be perceived as insulting and ego-based. That voice is totally inappropriate to such an audience. It's okay to swagger a bit in the alternative world, but in a conservative setting that can come across as pompous and turn readers off to what is critical—communicating the product to the patron.

Writing on the Level

One way to annoy your friends—or your audience—is by speaking to them as though they aren't intelligent. As someone dear to me once put it, "no one likes to be mollycoddled." In general, people—especially those new to the Web—may need a helping hand here and there, but they catch on quickly. Learn to write on a level that respects the audience. This is done by using voice, as we've already exemplified, but also by using words that are in the common vocabulary without pandering to the lowest common denominator.

We go back to the issue of literacy that was introduced at the beginning of this chapter. There's a great paradox in the media, whether in print, television, or otherwise, that is pervasive and frightening. Publications typically do something referred to as "writing down." This means that publications research their demographics and determine the average reading level of their audience. This average typically falls around the 5th grade. Writers are then told by their editors and publishers to write to that average.

The advantage of this is obviously the ability to achieve a critical mass of readers, but the disadvantage is that literacy and advancement are not promoted. Isn't there a middle ground? I believe there is, and for this reason I encourage people to write *on the level* of an audience—not to the imagined, computed, demographic mean.

What's This Got to Do with Web Design?

Simply put: style has everything to do with Web design. The Internet, which grew out of academic, research, and military endeavors, still maintains a certain information-heavy environment. The Web, which this entire book's existence proves has become a commercial environment, is still an extension of that original environment. Even though it's gotten easier and easier to point-and-click through cyberdom, it takes some intelligence to maneuver through all of the issues surrounding computerized communications. Don't insult people by *writing down.*

Brock Meeks, of *Wired* magazine fame, made some powerful comments on these issues.

"*At this time and space the people that are on the Net and using it seem to have a particular bent. They're people that like to get their own information, they are inherently distrustful as to what is beamed to them through the TV or the* New York Times, *or* Washington Post. *They don't take news and info at face value, as they are seeking it out themselves. This sets them apart from the typical consumer.*"

Web Sites Are Closely Targeted

The most important point in this discussion is that Web writers must always be conscious of the diction level that is most appropriate for the site's intended audience. We want to be readable by everybody, but we especially want to cater to the demographic most likely to interact with

our site. It is a luxury, really, that Web writers can target readership and adjust diction and voice accordingly. Web sites, by their nature, typically have specific demographics, unlike broader-based publications and media like television or newspapers, which cater to all people.

Editing

No matter how content is developed, and no matter what voice the writer speaks in, if it is not edited well, the Web writer has missed the mark. Web designers need to know how to edit copy for style and voice as well as for grammar and spelling. If you don't feel proficient at this, then you need a staff member to do it, or you need to hire a professional copy editor to come in and give the site a going-over.

It is so terribly easy to miss simple things. Typos, spelling errors, double words, inappropriate use of a word (such as "there" rather than "their"), run-on sentences, split infinitives—the list goes on and on.

Be sure to check Appendix A, which is a comprehensive resource list dedicated to Web writers. Web sites, courses, books, and programs are recommended. Although many of these resources are to improve and assist with general writing skills, there are some resources specific to writing on the Web.

Technical Components of Web Writing

So far we've looked at content writing. But visual presentation is also a critical issue in Web writing. In the ideal instance, it's going to be up to the Web designer to determine who will take the prepared copy and fit it into the bigger picture (by breaking it up into hypertext documents or selected chunks of information). Knowing a few basic technical ideas will help the writer streamline this process.

Length of Text

One issue is how much text will actually be used, and how that text will be broken up into individual pieces. As a rule, a Web page should be *no more than three screens in length.* Why? Because a reader is quickly going to get bored scrolling and scrolling and scrolling down the page. The Web is built to navigate in hypertext, which—as we've discussed in our chapters about new media—involves dimension rather than linear structuring.

As a result, we need to determine not only how much information to put on a page, but how to place that information on a page. A good Web writer will trim the fat from the content to match the Web environment, but never at the cost of important content. He or she will also balance text with graphics, and here is a perfect example of where the Web designer must be conducting the team well. He or she must let the team members know how all of these components are interacting—in this case, graphics, text, and HTML.

Formatting

Look at the Dispatch example (Figure 14-4)—it's very clean and to the point, and it's broken up into bits of sharp data, which are sometimes centered and sometimes in traditional paragraph form. It never competes with the graphics, and vice-versa. In another instance, the Gadabout Site (Figure 14-5) has a lot more content, but look at how its placement on the page is very calculated. Part of this comes from an eye for design and an awareness of what is known as "white space." You'll notice that both examples place an emphasis not only on what is seen, but on where on the page it is seen, and very specifically where on the page there is *nothing but space.* As a result, it never seems as if there's as much on the page as there is, and reading the page is pleasurable rather than a chore.

To Write or Not to Write

To revisit our initial premise, literacy is the determining factor in writing, and this naturally flows into writing for the Web. Some Web designers will find that they prefer to do large amounts of copy writing themselves, particularly because of the need for cohesion between the various disciplines. However, not every Web designer will naturally fall into this role, and as a result, some may need to place the responsibility elsewhere. If there is one piece of advice I would give to pull this chapter

Figure 14-4
A close look at Dispatch's layout

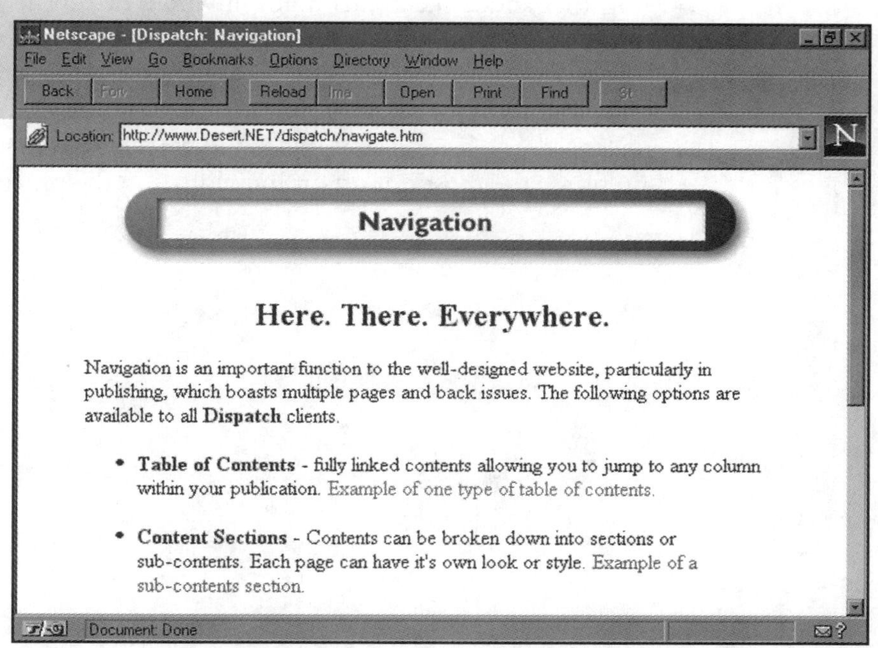

Figure 14-5
Text, graphics, and white space balance on Gadabout.

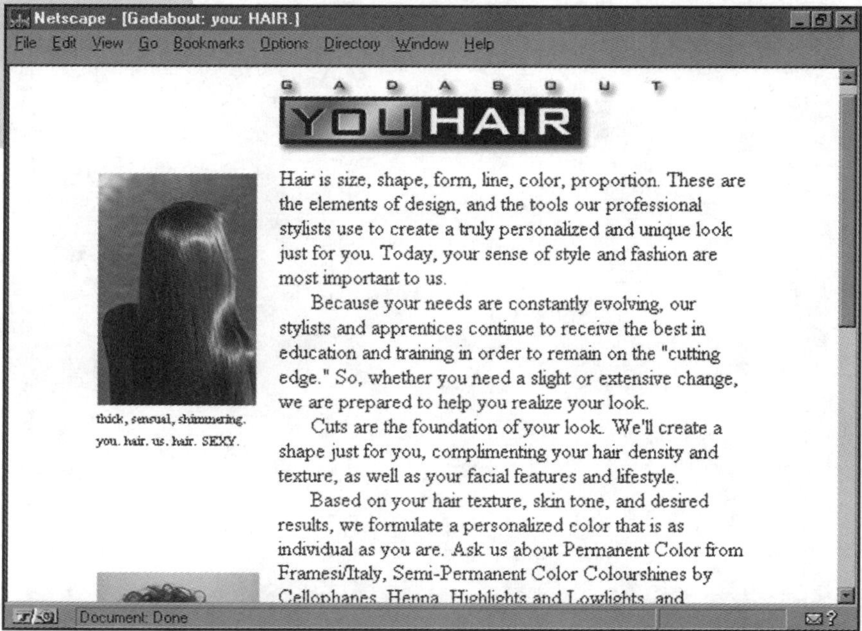

together and make a final point, it would be this: if you don't have the writing skills to begin with, either get them or get someone who has them, and *then* apply techniques for Web writing to that skill base. The end result will be an appropriately written, well-conceived site that is balanced in voice and appearance and that always shows that it is working to please the most important individuals in the process—the audience.

chapter 15

Hypertext Markup Language

There is a pervasive idea in current popular media that knowing HTML is equal to being a good Web designer. Just as having a good car doesn't make one a good driver, or having a recipe doesn't make one a gourmet chef, knowing a little HTML (or even a lot of it) does not necessarily make one a good Web designer. The two concepts of HTML and Web design must be separately defined because they are different jobs.

HTML is a straightforward script language that gives individuals *control* over how documents will look when viewed through a Web browser and how they will act with a server. HTML codes let the user position the text and images within a Web document, embed multimedia events, and designate when actions should be carried out by the server. What HTML does *not* do is create a Web design, which—as we've described repeatedly throughout this book—is a complicated and detailed process involving multiple disciplines.

Even though HTML is quite logical and fairly easy to grasp, it isn't necessarily easy to handle well. Years after learning this supposedly easy tool, I find myself constantly learning how to do things better. It's also important to mention that HTML is an evolving, emerging language (as expressed by Figure 15-1). New tags and arguments are added to the body of HTML at such a frightening rate that browser technology can't keep up, as we examined in the early chapters of this book.

As a Web designer, you need to constantly be aware of changing trends in HTML—even if you do little or none of the actual HTML coding for the sites you design. This is easy to do; by choosing a newsgroup or Web site that provides this type of information, you can stay current with the ways other designers are using HTML as a foundation for good design. Further, you and your team should develop strategies for long-term success by streamlining the HTML coding process—whether it be by creating custom templates, automating common routines, recognizing and avoiding common mistakes, or saving time in production. Such strategies are advantageous not only for the coder but for everyone involved in the process. A list of HTML-related information can be found in Appendix B.

Figure 15-1
HTML is an evolving, emerging language.

General HTML Concepts to Consider

The following is a collection of important general concepts about HTML as it is used currently. Consider adding these ideas to your general practice:

- ***Anything* coded must be coded for text-only access.** This translates to knowing how to include information within HTML coding so that anyone will be able to access your site's content *sans* graphics, whether they are using a text-line browser or a graphical browser with graphics turned off. "But Lynx is dead," you may have heard. "Everyone is going to be using a GUI browser now." Wrong. GUI access is very difficult for the blind, and you must accommodate this population, as well as others who prefer or require text-only access.

Text-only compatibility can easily be achieved with very few adjustments, such as the two below:

- **Always use the ALT argument.** This allows you to embed a text description of an image, so that the visitor can see the description if he can't or doesn't want to download the image (Figure 15-2).

Figure 15-2 The ALT tag argument in action

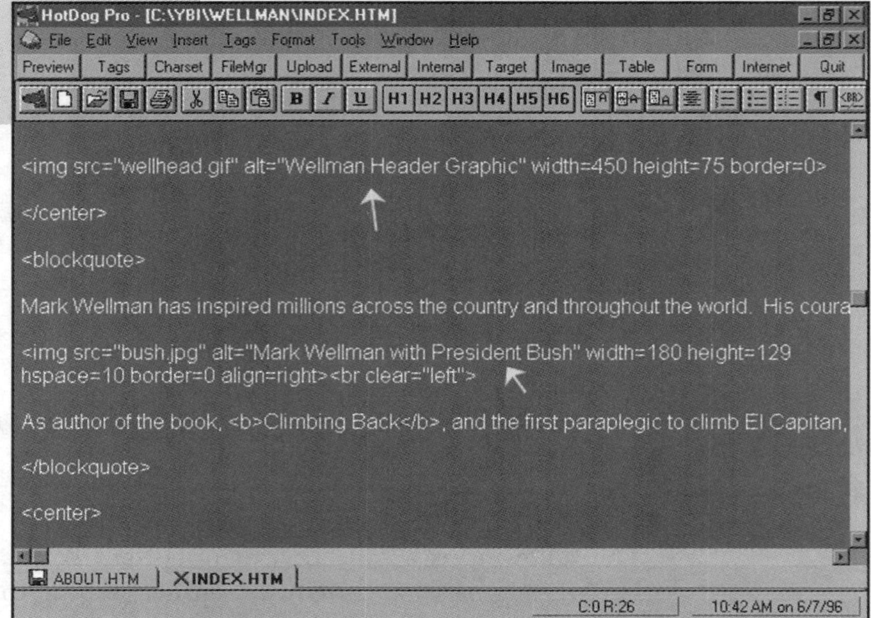

- **If you are using image maps, give text navigation options.** Simply mimic the choices on your map in some fashion in text links (Figure 15-3).
- **Be multi-browser aware.** Even though you may design only for Netscape, proof your work in other browsers. This will make you as a Web design professional more aware of the idiosyncrasies of individual browsers (see Figures 15-4 and 15-5). The differences among browsers mean a lot to Web design, for very frequently designs can be built on, or at least exploit, these idiosyncrasies.

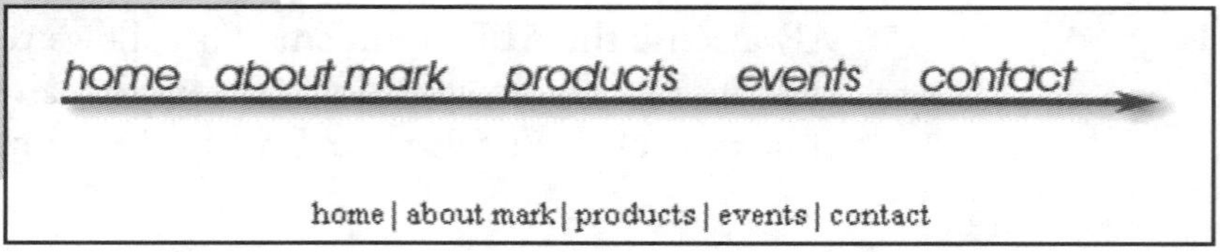

Figure 15-3 Text and image navigation options

home about mark products events contact

home | about mark | products | events | contact

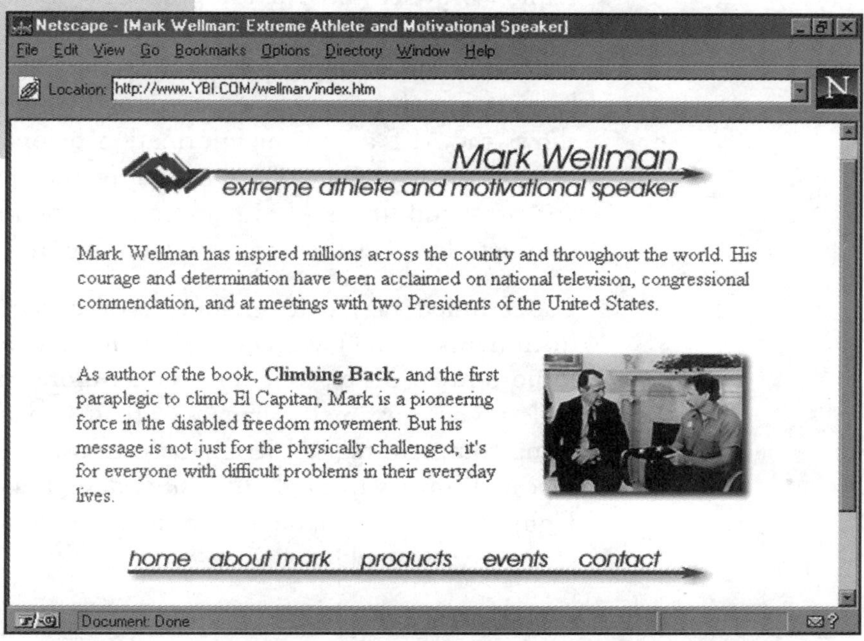

Figure 15-4 A site as viewed with the Netscape browser

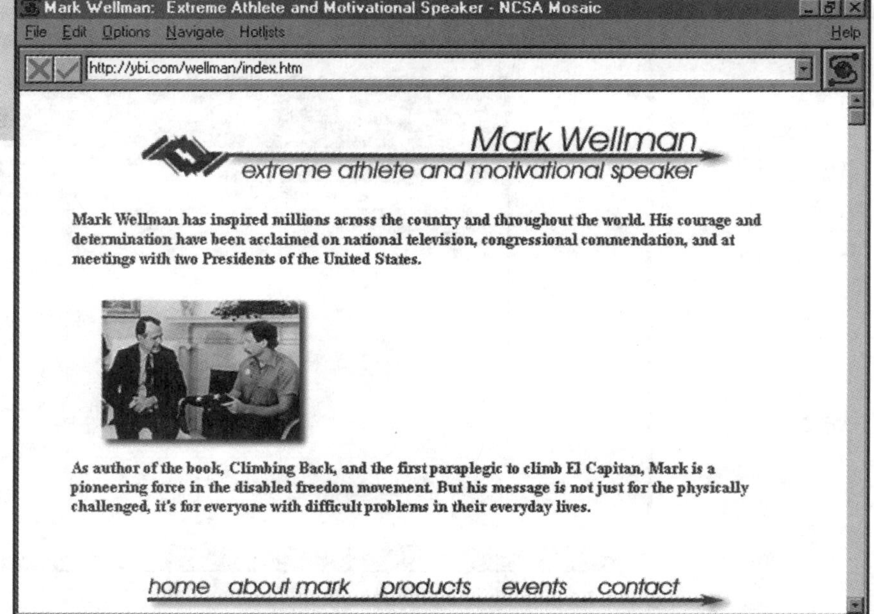

Figure 15-5 The same site as viewed with the Mosaic browser

- **Exploit browser idiosyncrasies.** Basically this means finding fun things that browsers do with HTML that can be put to design use. A current example is exploiting the ALT argument in the beta version of the Netscape Navigator 3.0 browser. This browser shows the ALT argument information before the graphic. The reader can read the ALT text before the graphic itself fully appears—and this is a fun place to hide comments, Easter eggs, or other playful elements, as shown in Figure 15-6.
- **Use comment tags to designate areas of code within your HTML documents.** As HTML coding gets more complex, it becomes important to make your documents more easily accessible to coders who must make changes or reuse code for new pages. By using comment tags to designate sections, headers, footers, and repeated images throughout a site's design, as demonstrated in Figure 15-7, you enable coders to get to those areas to make changes very quickly.

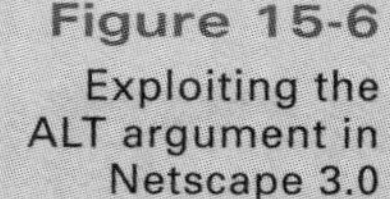
Figure 15-6
Exploiting the ALT argument in Netscape 3.0

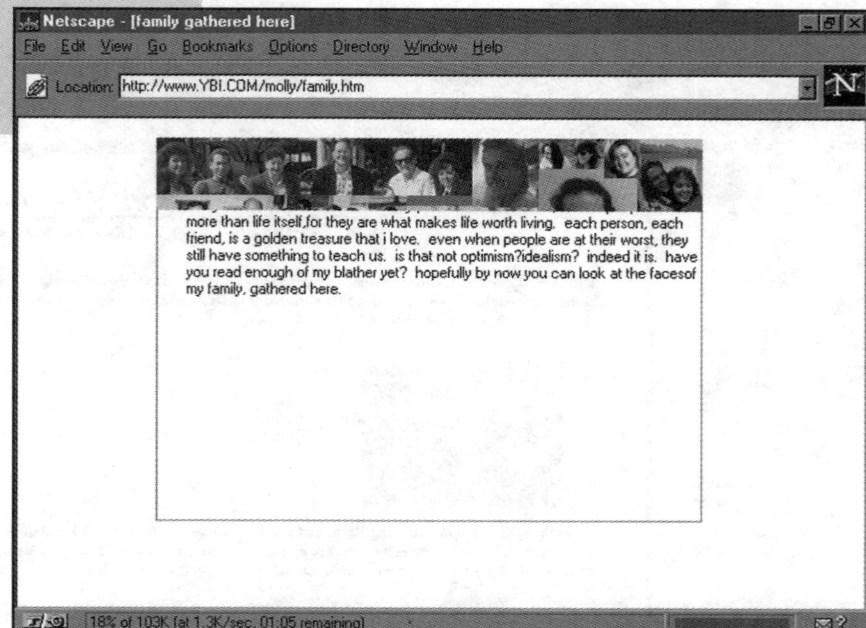

Figure 15-7
Comment tagging to designate HTML document areas

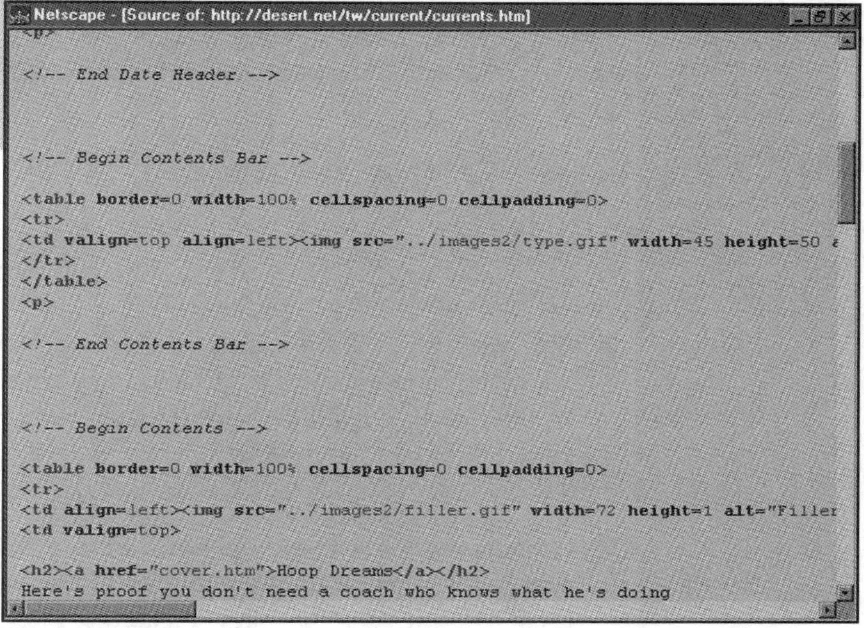

Netscape - [Source of: http://desert.net/tw/current/currents.htm]

```
<!-- End Date Header -->



<!-- Begin Contents Bar -->

<table border=0 width=100% cellspacing=0 cellpadding=0>
<tr>
<td valign=top align=left><img src="../images2/type.gif" width=45 height=50 a
</tr>
</table>
<p>

<!-- End Contents Bar -->



<!-- Begin Contents -->

<table border=0 width=100% cellspacing=0 cellpadding=0>
<tr>
<td align=left><img src="../images2/filler.gif" width=72 height=1 alt="Filler
<td valign=top>

<h2><a href="cover.htm">Hoop Dreams</a></h2>
Here's proof you don't need a coach who knows what he's doing
```

- **Use as many arguments for a tag as possible.** This helps override any browser or user defaults that designers have little or no control over. This is especially true for body tags (Figure 15-8) and image tags (Figure 15-9).

Figure 15-8
Using multiple arguments in the body tag. Each argument ensures a defined element rather than relying on a browser's default for that tag. 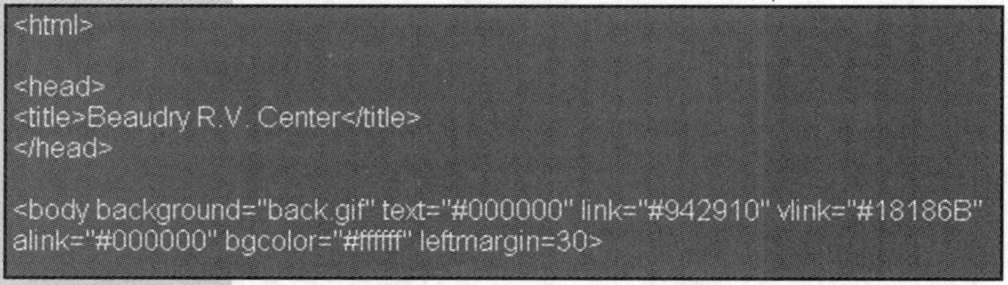

```
<html>

<head>
<title>Beaudry R.V. Center</title>
</head>

<body background="back.gif" text="#000000" link="#942910" vlink="#18186B"
alink="#000000" bgcolor="#ffffff" leftmargin=30>
```

Figure 15-9 Using multiple arguments in the image tag. This strengthens control over placement and sizing of graphics within the body of text.

```
<img src="basket.jpg" alt="Native American Basket" width=125 height=94
hspace=25 border=0 align=left>
```

- **Use meta tags!** We've discussed this feature in the context of marketing, and since it is an HTML tag, it's important to mention again. Meta tags definitely help search engines and crawlers identify your site, and the tags provide some content information for people who view source code (see Figure 15-10).
- **Comments, contact, and signature.** Place comments—including contact information and the names of team members and resources used—within comment tags (Figure 15-11). Sign your work—your signature says you are proud to have your name associated with it!

Figure 15-10 The META tag in action. This tag will help search engines find and catalog your page.

```
<meta name="molly does it really matter who?  A graphic word journey through the art,
poetry, and personal life of Molly Holzschlag">
<meta name="keywords" content="molly, molly who, molly holzschlag, biography,
poem, art, artist, graphic design, photography, pain, loss, grief, joy, writing, sex, sensuality,
beauty, depth, personal, journey, journal.">
```

Figure 15-11 Comments embedded into HTML

```
<!-- site by mainstay communications and desertnet designs:  molly@desert.net -->
<!-- web engineers:  molly holzschlag, scott convery -->
<!-- design director and online editor:  molly holzschlag -->
<!-- content provided by mark wellman -->
```

HTML for the Web Designer

As a Web designer, you may or may not be doing HTML coding yourself, depending on your situation. Whether you work on code yourself, hire the work out to others, or work within the team model, you should always know who is creating the HTML style for your company, and you should be instrumental in making style decisions. This allows for consistency, clarity, and quality control—all part of a Web designer's job. The following concepts will help you maintain strong HTML code standards within your operations.

Version Counts!

Currently there are three versions of HTML, with a draft proposal above 3.0. Having familiarity with the primary additions and changes at each level is important. How design comes together and how it is platform-compatible and portable are defined by what happens in the code.

Becoming familiar with HTML versions and drafts—and keeping up with changes—is a very helpful way to stay on top of design possibilities. There are countless resources on the Web and off, as mentioned earlier in this chapter and further described in Appendix B. With such accessible and thorough documentation of the history, dynamics, and evolution of HTML, staying current is quite easy.

Currently most coding is done somewhere between HTML versions 2.0 and 3.0, with elements being drawn from the current draft, and personal styles taking precedence over actual rules. As discussed thoroughly in earlier chapters of this book, there are incompatibilities between HTML tags and browsers. Nevertheless, it is fairly easy to create a strategy that streamlines the HTML coding process for your company's projects.

Cleanliness Is a Virtue

Clean code is something all HTML coders should aspire to. What this means is that coders—because of the various ways of coding HTML—should learn to write precisely, neatly, and in an organized fashion. Every coder develops a coding style, and that's good—if you know what that style is and stick to it as consistently as possible.

Here's an example of code that is sloppy:

```
<hTMl>
<TITLE>MY PAGE</title> <Body bgcolor=#FFFFFF>
This is my page. Thanks for being here. <p>
<hr>
</BODY>
```

First, we have an inconsistency in upper- and lowercase tagging. It may seem trivial, but inconsistencies like this look sloppy. So maybe they don't affect the browser, so what? Would it be wise to dress a child in a checkered shirt, shorts with one leg longer than the other, and one sock on, one sock off? Of course not! Although these items would be mostly covered, the poor child would be the laughing stock of the playground. So it is with consistency in HTML. It looks good, and it's good for your professional reputation to maintain a high-quality image. So what, you say? Nobody will see your code anyway? Think about it this way—if you want to work for another company eventually or to create very high standards for your own, make sure that you gain and maintain respectability among the brightest and best of programmers and coders—they will be looking closely at how you arrange your documents.

The next problem with this example is, simply, bad code. The `<body>` tag color element doesn't have quotation marks around it, nor are there head tags or a closing `</html>` tag. Here's the same example after being cleaned up:

```
<html>
<head>
<title>My Page</title>
</head>
<body bgcolor="#FFFFFF">
This is my page. Thanks for being here!
<p>
</body>
</html>
```

First, we have cleaned up the case problem, choosing to place everything in lowercase. I personally prefer all lowercase tags because it's neater to my eye. However, others might prefer uppercase. These are the kinds of choices regarding style that don't necessarily make a difference. What *is* important, again, is consistency. Choose a case and stick to it.

Next, we've followed proper HTML tagging techniques, with all necessary tags in this example in place. My personal style is to keep most tags on individual lines, because it gives me easy access to them in large or numerous documents. This is yet another case of individual preference; some people write multiple tags on one line, like this:

```
<head><title>My Page</title></head>
```

This is not incorrect per se, but to my eye it looks cluttered—which means I'll have a hard time getting to it quickly if I need to. Find out what works for you and your team members, and make it a consistent style.

Custom Style Templates and House Rules

Once the Web designer and the HTML coder have decided on a style, it's a good idea to prepare a custom style template. In commercial design, this can be enormously helpful not only because it gives the coder a prepared template to work with but also because it saves tremendous amounts of time. Certainly, coding will be different from site to site, but a general template is very helpful (Figure 15-12). Templates should include all of the elements of a standard site, sans text. You may want to develop a series for a variety of styles, including framed or nonframed sites, sites that exploit tables, and more simple, straightforward sites.

A list of house rules can also be tremendously empowering. Let's say your shop is flooded with business, and you require the assistance of an outside HTML coder. It's easy to send the person a style template and a list of rules that your shop follows. This makes the job much easier for the freelance coder. The same concept is extended to anyone you might be hiring into your company. Base house rules on elements that your company typically uses, much as we suggest you create custom templates.

Figure 15-12 One of DesertNet's custom templates

```
<!-- site by desertnet designs   sales@desert.net -->
<!-- design director:  -->
<!-- graphic design:  -->
<!-- director of web engineering:  -->
<!-- online editor: -->
<!-- content provided by  -->

<!-- Begin Header -->

<html>

<head>

<title></title>

</head>

<body bgcolor="#" text="#" link="#" vlink="#" alink="#" background="">

<blockquote>

<!-- End Header -->


<!-- Begin Footer -->

</blockquote>

<center>

<font size=2>

<a href="index.html"></a> | <a href=""></a> | <a href=""></a> | <a href=""></a> | <a href=""></a>

<p>

</font>

<font size=1>&#169; 1996 </font>

</center>

<!-- End Footer -->

</body>

</html>
```

Here is an example of the rules from the DesertNet list:

Images

Every image tag *must* contain regular syntax plus the following arguments:

- **ALT tag.** This tag is imperative for text-only browsing. Please use short but comprehensive descriptions for the related graphic.
- **Width and height tags.** These assist in optimizing graphic loading. Please always use width and height tags that are relative to the actual width and height of related graphics.

Custom Operations and Automation

If you are so fortunate as to be an excellent programmer, or to have one on staff, many applications can be customized for company needs. This step can be as simple as a program that codes data with your preferred specs automatically, or it can be more complex, as in the case of large data publishing programs. Knowing what your custom needs are and automating what you can are powerful ways to streamline the HTML process.

HTML Tools

Every HTML coder has a preference for his coding software. Some individuals like using text-based editors, such as Notepad in Windows (Figure 15-13). Others prefer full editing environments, such as Front Page or Netscape Navigator Gold. It is my opinion that the best choice lies between these extremes. The reason is simple. Unless you are an extremely fast and accurate typist, a simple text editor can be time-consuming for detailed coding projects. On the other hand, full packages often have their own style rules built in and offer little or no control over how to customize those options.

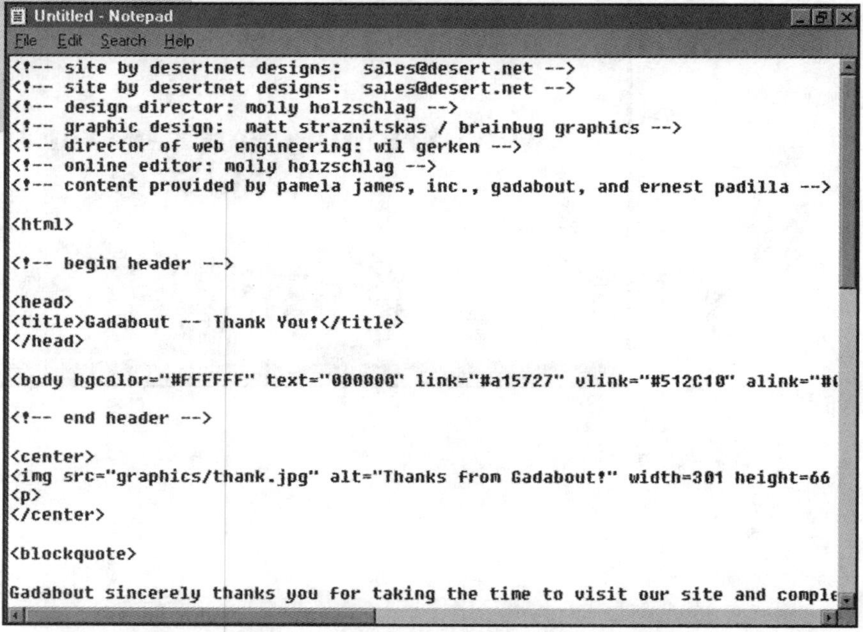

Figure 15-13 Coding in Windows Notepad

Untitled - Notepad

File Edit Search Help

```
<!-- site by desertnet designs:  sales@desert.net -->
<!-- site by desertnet designs:  sales@desert.net -->
<!-- design director: molly holzschlag -->
<!-- graphic design:  matt straznitskas / brainbug graphics -->
<!-- director of web engineering: wil gerken -->
<!-- online editor: molly holzschlag -->
<!-- content provided by pamela james, inc., gadabout, and ernest padilla -->

<html>

<!-- begin header -->

<head>
<title>Gadabout -- Thank You!</title>
</head>

<body bgcolor="#FFFFFF" text="000000" link="#a15727" vlink="#512C10" alink="#(

<!-- end header -->

<center>
<img src="graphics/thank.jpg" alt="Thanks from Gadabout!" width=301 height=66
<p>
</center>

<blockquote>

Gadabout sincerely thanks you for taking the time to visit our site and comple
```

There are two PC-based HTML editors that I use and that I sincerely feel support the middle-of-the-road option. One is HTML Assistant (Figure 15-14), and the other is HotDog (Figure 15-15). Both are available as shareware, but the professional versions of each offer excellent enhancements such as spell-checking and syntax review. These environments allow for individual editorial control over how the code appears, while offering tools and shortcuts that can help speed up the coding process. Not everyone will find using these, or similar tools for their preferred platform, best for their needs. However, having control and speed are two important considerations when coding.

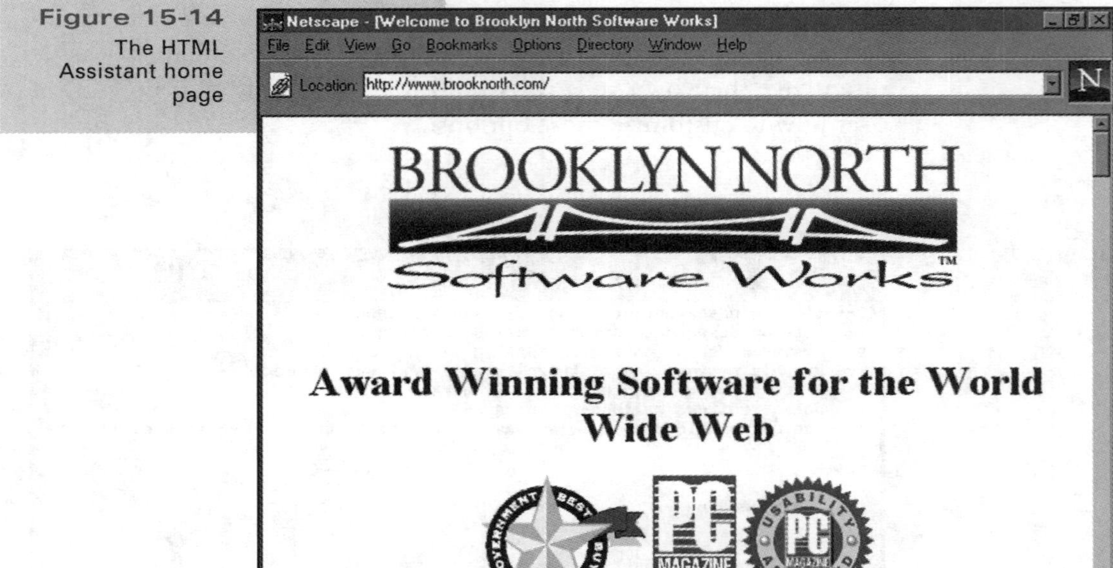

Figure 15-14 The HTML Assistant home page

WWW

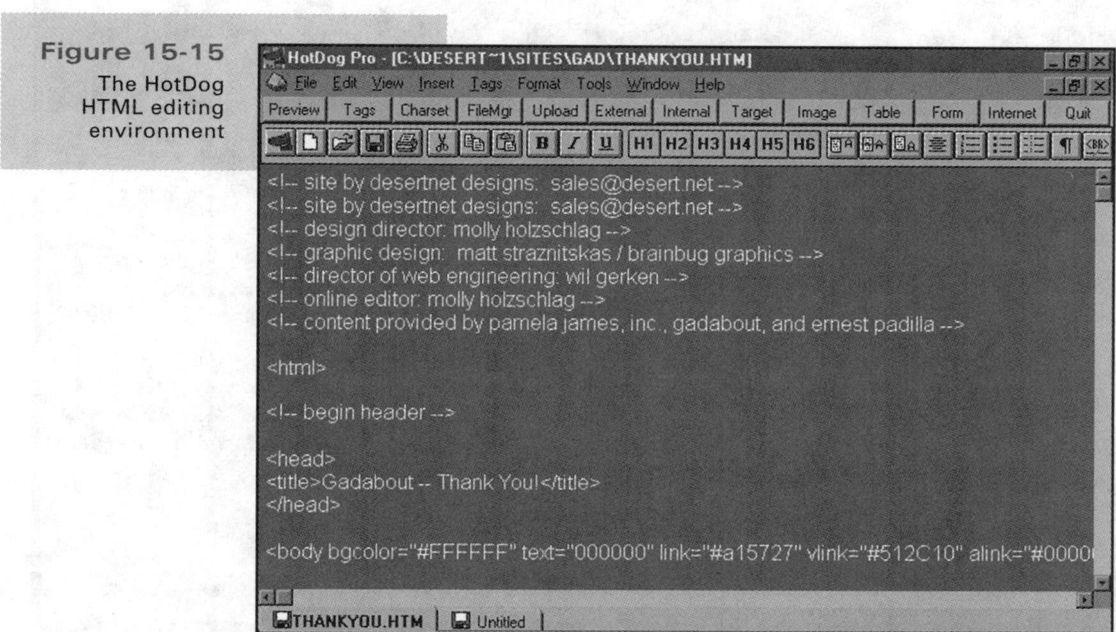
HotDog Pro - [C:\DESERT~1\SITES\GAD\THANKYOU.HTM]
File Edit View Insert Tags Format Tools Window Help
Preview Tags Charset FileMgr Upload External Internal Target Image Table Form Internet Quit
B I U H1 H2 H3 H4 H5 H6 ¶
<!-- site by desertnet designs: sales@desert.net -->
<!-- site by desertnet designs: sales@desert.net -->
<!-- design director: molly holzschlag -->
<!-- graphic design: matt straznitskas / brainbug graphics -->
<!-- director of web engineering: wil gerken -->
<!-- online editor: molly holzschlag -->
<!-- content provided by pamela james, inc., gadabout, and ernest padilla -->
<html>
<!-- begin header -->
<head>
<title>Gadabout -- Thank You!</title>
</head>
<body bgcolor="#FFFFFF" text="000000" link="#a15727" vlink="#512C10" alink="#0000
THANKYOU.HTM
Untitled
C:19 R:18
1:08 PM on 6/7/96

Figure 15-15 The HotDog HTML editing environment

What Now?

Rules and tools can make an organization strong. Primary concepts give a Web designer a lot to work with when communicating with HTML coders or deciding on coding practices. But how does this make a good Web designer? It doesn't, but it is an excellent starting point. Appendix B includes a wide range of resources to learn more about HTML specifics, a necessary step toward gaining mature control of the relationship between HTML and Web design.

What's the Point?

Wil Gerken
Web Engineer and Director of Publications, DesertNet

"What's the point? This is always the first and most important question I have about sites, designers, and projects. Are you creating a fancy business card, are you working with New Media, are you redefining the way people think, are you trying to represent everything you possibly can about this company or project, are you creating a new culture and personality that never existed in the real world, are you finally writing your mission statement and working it out in front of the whole world? What's the point?

How do you get users to return? How do you create a feeling of pride or trust that the user should get out of your site? How do you sell them something? How do you get them to bookmark you and tell their friends about you? How do you make them feel good about your site and what you are doing?

Advertising and marketing can only get you so far, if your site doesn't have something to say or create a mood, it isn't really doing anything but taking up space and getting one time visitors.

What's the point? Human creativity, culture, and humanity. Hire or become that web designer and they will make your site live, breathe, inspire, and interact.

That's the point."

Of Salad Dressing, the San Francisco Giants, and Freelancers

Dana M. Hunter
Webgal
`http://www.webgal.com`

A visit to Dana's site is never boring. With humorous updates on her weekend, interactive games such as "the great salad dressing debate" which requires people to go to their fridge and check how many different kinds of salad dressings they've got, and a "name that dude" contest, Dana's work exemplifies the importance of creating fun and interactive options for audience. Yes, that's a Giant's fly ball she's caught there in her picture, as her obviously happy dad looks on.

"I began life as a computer nerd, graduated to desktop publishing after being schooled in typography and typesetting (traditional) in London, England. After owning/partnering in several different advertising and publishing firms, I started freelance designing 5 years ago. Last year, while serving a season with the San Francisco Giants, as their designer, I took on the project of building their original web site. I left the Giants at the end of the baseball season to build sites on my own. I have produced over 20 sites in the last 6 months, and am contracted long-term for over half a dozen currently.

Being a "webmistress" covers a lot of skills—not just mastery of HTML or knowing how to send e-mail. It involves being a project manager, a designer, a typographer, with a knowledge of photography, color, printing, different platforms, computer languages, etc. It's up to us to continually remind others that this is a very high-tech position."

chapter 16

Graphic Design

Graphics on the Web excite, empower, and sometimes enrage. The field of Web graphics is one that is fraught with challenge, often due to the current bane of a Web designer's existence: browser inconsistency. Other issues play into the challenge, including bandwidth, hardware restrictions, and even an old-school attitude that there is little place—if any—for graphic design on the Web.

Many Web graphic artists understand these challenges and look upon the Web as an environment that excites them, because they view these restrictions as a way to stretch their imaginations and come up with clever alternatives. Some look upon the restrictions as boundaries to work within colorfully but conservatively; others constantly challenge those boundaries in order to demand that the medium and audience rise to the possibilities of the technology.

I personally am leaning toward the latter extreme, although as a commercial Web designer, I am constantly faced with—and reminded by my peers that I have to respect—those conservative boundaries, at least in specific instances. In certain circles, my beliefs may be viewed as impossibly idealistic, but I honestly believe that if we as designers *don't* push the envelope, then our audiences won't, and the technology won't reach beyond its limitations into the unimaginable. The evidence I offer to support my ideas is that the technology *is* advancing, and very, very rapidly at that. With that in mind, I believe that those of us who don't push the design edge—when and where we can—will be left behind in a pile of simplistic, forgotten Web work.

So what does this soapboxing have to do with Web graphics? Again, it's a field that's controversial and challenging, for the reasons we examine in this book and specifically in this chapter. The succinct message I'd like to express is that graphic artists working in this area must be able to grow with the future needs of the medium, which at this point in Web evolution (Webvolution?) conceivably means things beyond our present understanding. The artist will understand the constraints of the Web environment but will also willingly and deliberately work against them when and where it is possible and justifiable to do so. Artists have long been viewed as misfits and renegades, and the Web can often be a contemporary environment for acting out this natural rebellion.

Now let's move away from politics and into practice, so we can see for ourselves where the responsibilities, challenges, and possibilities for the Web graphic designer are.

Concepts and Interaction

The Web designer in our model is responsible for guiding the team. This critical relationship is especially important with the graphic artist. As we stressed in Chapter 14, the audience, along with the act of defining an appropriate concept and balance for the audience, is integral to successful communication. The same model is an absolute for Web art. Audience and intent of site reign supreme, and it is up to the Web designer to express this fact to the graphic artist, who should, in turn, provide graphic work that embodies the direction of the site.

When we look at what design is, we are looking at the combination of concept with realization. First we must conceptualize—examine our information and access our imaginations to bring forth ideas that are not only appropriate to our goal but contain visual grace and beauty. After that, we must go to the hands-on practical rendering of the concept—the realization of the site.

Site Layout, Look and Feel

Working closely with the Web designer, the graphic artist will help develop ideas about the way a site will be laid out. Whereas the Web designer will focus on new media issues such as interactivity and nonlinear opportunities, the graphic artist will give input as to the way the pieces will fit visually. Together they will come up with a layout that balances great art, new media, and the needs of the client—all to meet, greet, and seduce the audience into the Web experience.

With information brought to the drawing board by the Web designer, the artist will think about the way a site should look and feel. Herein lies the conceptual journey. What about the site's intent and audience would demand a slick look and feel rather than a soft approach? Why should we choose to go with a minimalist approach, or an elaborate one? When should we adhere strictly to conservative boundaries, and when can we jump off and have some fun, using frames or unconventional layouts?

These are some of the questions that determine how concept becomes matter. Let's look again at Gadabout (Figure 16-1), which is a potent example of a very successful design layout that translates to the Web with total style. In that case, our site's audience is the fashion industry and the image-conscious. Right there we have good reason to go with high style. But by the same token, Gadabout never gets more elaborate then it needs to. It's actually a very simple layout, but it dazzles because its look and feel express glamour, and it draws a great deal of rich color from the pictures on the site. Again, our audience being a group that wants the best, bandwidth, browser platform, and color management issues became less important than design.

On another design level, we have a site like Penelope's (Figure 16-2). In this case, our audience is the individual with a taste for fine cuisine—and that could be someone from virtually *any* walk of life! In this case, a look and feel that reflected the French fare, drew on the feminine name, and addressed a broad audience represented the way to go. We knew we were on the money when a very critical male eye with

Figure 16-1 Successful concept layout

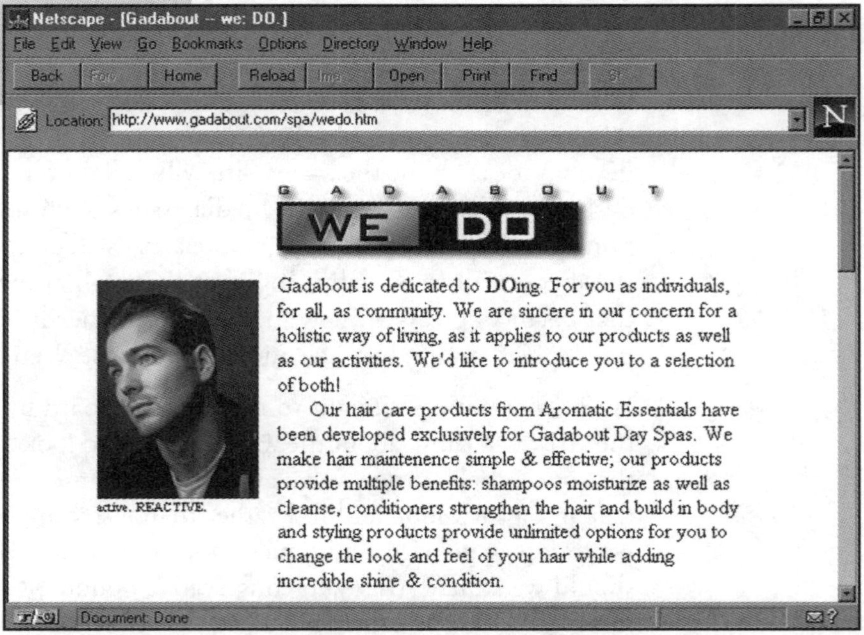

Netscape - [Gadabout -- we: DO.]

File Edit View Go Bookmarks Options Directory Window Help

Back Forw Home Reload Images Open Print Find Stop

Location: http://www.gadabout.com/spa/wedo.htm

G A D A B O U T

WE DO

Gadabout is dedicated to DOing. For you as individuals, for all, as community. We are sincere in our concern for a holistic way of living, as it applies to our products as well as our activities. We'd like to introduce you to a selection of both!

Our hair care products from Aromatic Essentials have been developed exclusively for Gadabout Day Spas. We make hair maintenence simple & effective; our products provide multiple benefits: shampoos moisturize as well as cleanse, conditioners strengthen the hair and build in body and styling products provide unlimited options for you to change the look and feel of your hair while adding incredible shine & condition.

active. REACTIVE.

Document: Done

minimalist inclinations said "hey, that's a great site!" We went low-bandwidth on this one without ever once sacrificing art because the designer and artist knew not only how to conceptualize but how to bring that concept into realization.

From Concept to Realization

So how do we move from ideas to reality in this challenging medium? There are several foundational techniques that must be learned. There is no way that—as with any of these disciplines—this book can teach you how to master this subject, but what we can do is impart enough information to get a Web designer and a graphic artist familiar with some Web art techniques. The Web designer, as the centripetal force within the design team, will then know how to express these Web graphic design fundamentals to artists and will work with them every step of the way, creating stunning Web graphic design that works in concert with all of the Web disciplines.

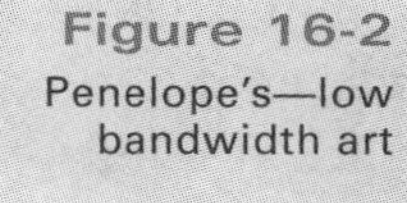
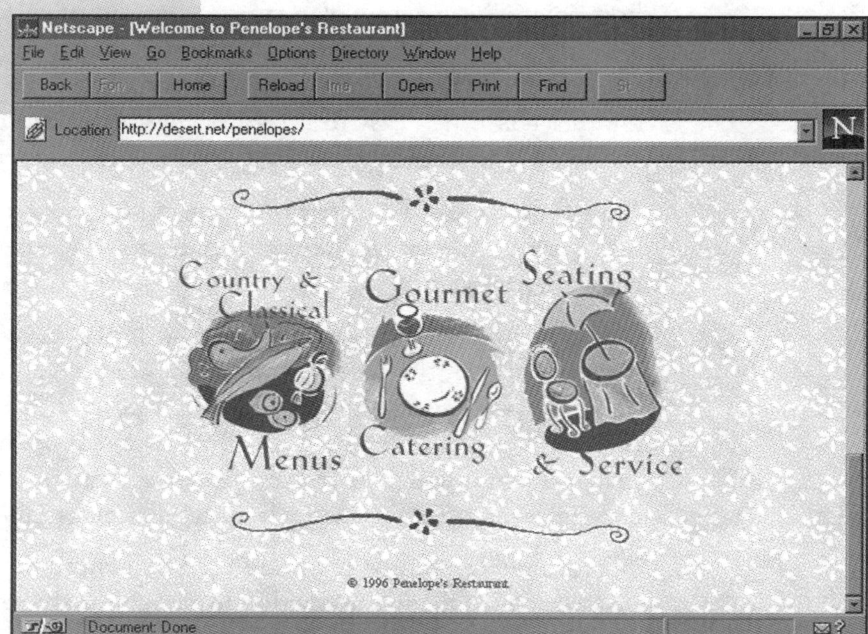

Figure 16-2
Penelope's—low bandwidth art

The Realization

Perhaps the greatest issue in today's Web environment is color management. This relates to the technical demands placed on Web art by computer graphics cards, computer monitors, and a browser's management of color. As in print design, fonts play a critical role in how designs come to life—or fail because they are inaccessible to the eye. Graphic file formats determine loading speed and loading style preferences. Transparency plays an enormous role in the use of shapes and backgrounds on the Web. Special effects, including the creation of dimension and awareness and use of light and shadow, are necessary to create designs that literally stand out from the rest. Choices of background color, texture, or pattern can make or break a site's success. Finally, the tools a graphic designer uses make a tremendous difference in the quality of his or her work.

Color Management

The only parts of the color spectrum that can ever be assumed to be reliably rendered lie at the polar extremes—black, and white. If a color management system—which is what a graphic artist will use to control how color is seen across platforms—runs out of colors in its palette, it will attempt to substitute one that is available or to replicate the color by *dithering*, which is mixing two different colors together to simulate another color. It is easy to imagine why this would cause problems—suddenly a new color appears to replace your original, intended color.

Matt Straznitskas, President of BrainBug L.L.C., has designed quite a number of our sites, including Gadabout. Matt has this to say about color management:

"Although today's computers can usually display in eight-bit (256-color) mode or higher, the specific colors that are used at any given time are not static. Choosing one color table out of the nearly infinite number of possibilities that can be displayed is a mission of a computer's color management system. Color management is therefore an issue that should concern everyone who is involved in creating graphics for the Web.

"Color management systems are used by computers to determine not only the colors that compose the current color table but also how colors are replaced in graphics that contain colors unavailable to the current table. This situation often arises when a computer that is displaying in eight-bit, 256-color mode runs out of available colors to display a particular graphic. In this case, colors are usually substituted for the closest alternatives currently in use. Unfortunately, this may not always result in a good-looking graphic.

"One way to attempt to circumvent color substitution is to create GIFs with the smallest number of colors possible. Since many computers accessing the Web can display no more than 256 colors, the number of available colors can drop fairly quickly once you consider the demands of the software being used. First, depending on the system software, up to 64 colors may be soaked up. Then, depending on the Web browser being used, another few dozen colors may be absorbed. A conservative estimate would put the maximum number of colors to be used in Web graphics at 160. But simply making graphics with 160 colors or less does not guarantee that color substitution will be avoided.

"For example, a scan of a kiwi and one of a banana result in very different color tables for each graphic, even if they are each reduced to a palette of 160 colors. If both of the graphics are put on a Web page side by side and a computer that is displaying in eight-bit mode attempts to render the page, it may run out of colors and resort to substitution once again. So what is needed are not only GIFs that contain 160 colors (or less) but GIFs that all pick from the *same* selection of 160 colors. This process of developing a single palette for a series of graphics is called *palette normalization* and can be accomplished with a program like Debabelizer.

"But even though restricting the number of colors and normalizing palettes are good techniques to increase the odds that Web graphics will be seen as intended, these techniques do nothing to alter the variations in color that occur among all the different display hardware combinations in use today. Some monitors shift all the colors to the red side of the color spectrum; others make everything bluer. Some may display things dark; others, light. The reality is that it is impossible for electronic publishers to have complete control over how their graphics will appear."

The DesertNet Approach to Color Management

Because of the difficulties in color management, DesertNet's designers have developed an approach to deal with the probability that what we see and what our audience sees may differ greatly. This approach is based on Wil Gerken's belief that people using hardware and browsers that are substandard are going to be used to seeing graphics that render poorly anyway. So even though we follow a palette while creating graphics, we are not too obsessive about the number of colors beyond what is reasonable—particularly in sites that are high-end. Where we've started to get meticulous is in dealing with background and text element colors. If these colors are not true, at least to the browser's palette, then they will be unreadable. If that happens, our audience is lost, and we may as well hang up our Web design hats and venture forth no more.

The Evil Windows-Netscape Palette

The Windows 8-bit color system found in 16-bit Windows programs (not Windows 95) and the Windows Netscape browser create an unfortunate combination that results in a 216-color palette—not a 256-color palette as some might naturally be inclined to believe. As a result, it is currently important to use this palette for text elements. Many choose also to use it for their graphics, but as I've mentioned, DesertNet decided not to go in that more conservative and very restrictive direction. Either choice is a logical one, but the former isn't visionary. The bottom line is that, either way, at least be consistent within a site, and you'll end up with some modicum of consistency for those on the outside, looking in.

It is a good idea for every Web designer and associated Web artist to have access to this palette. Using it, and using it wisely, will avoid trouble all around. Until the PC world is up to snuff with 24-bit color, it's the Web design graphics prophylactic. Yes, Windows 95 dominance in the PC market will make a huge difference, since no machine worthy of supporting it will have substandard surfing stuff. Until then, please practice safe color management, at least as far as content elements are concerned.

For a wonderful essay on color management and its implications, check out http://raven.ubalt.edu/features/desiRes/color/ (Figure 16-3). This site was created and developed by Stuart Moulthrop and Nancy Kaplan of the University of Baltimore, School of Communications Design. To grab a Netscape 216-color palette, visit http://www.chass.ncsu.edu/~extension/allcolors.latte (Figure 16-4). More resources on this and other important graphic design issues on the Web are located in both Appendixes C and D of this book.

Fonts

Fonts are collections of individual characters within a typeface. Different typefaces have unique values for size, weight, and other individual characteristics. Although font faces bear little importance for the current HTML–derived text elements of a page, there are some considerations to be aware of. Fonts are *very* important in the graphic elements of a page, and understanding some fundamentals can empower designers.

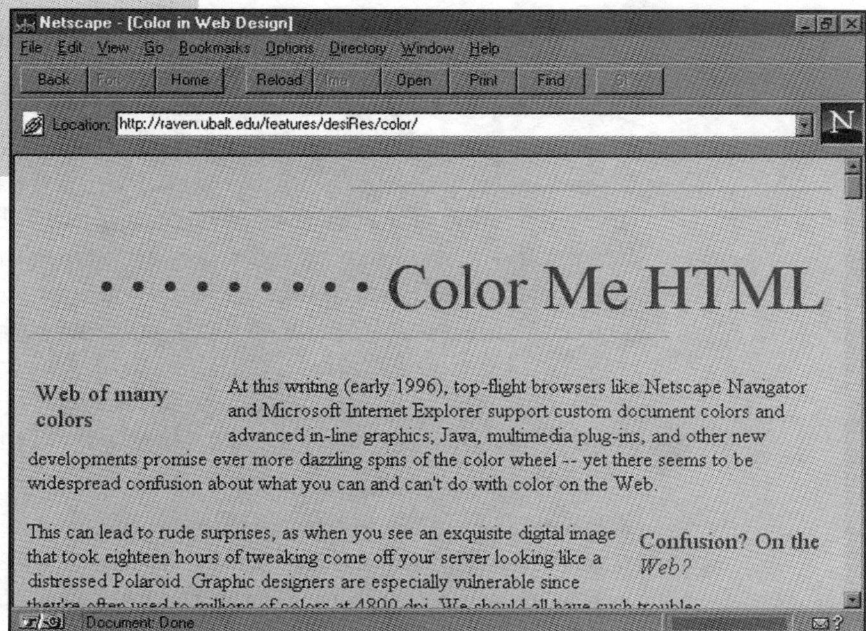

Figure 16-3 Color management concepts from the University of Baltimore

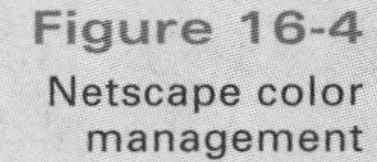

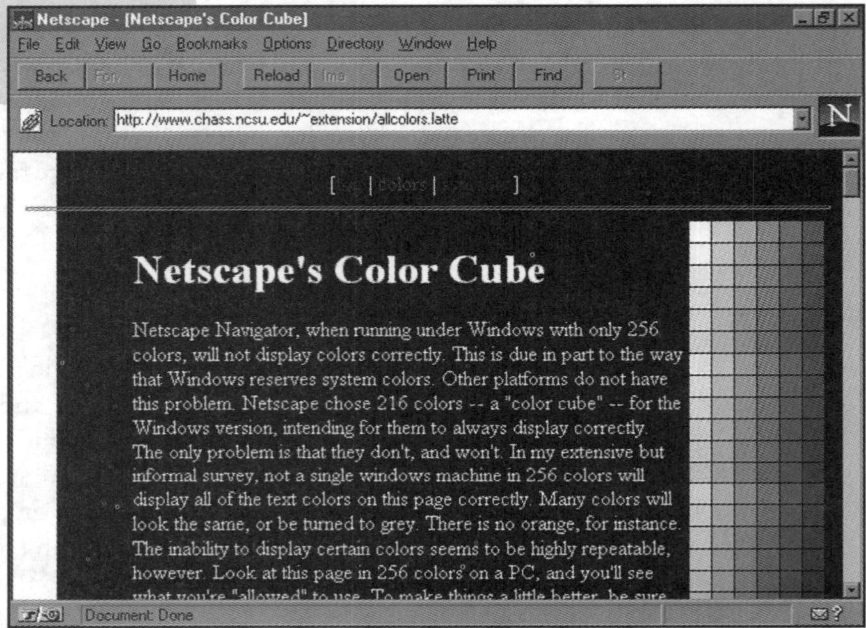

Figure 16-4 Netscape color management

HTML-Derived Text Elements

Some browsers, including Netscape 2.0 and above and Internet Explorer 2.0 and above, allow for the use of font size and color arguments (Figure 16-5). This allows for HTML-driven changes that will override browser defaults and allow design aspects to be carried into the text elements of a Web page. Internet Explorer allows actual font faces (Figure 16-6), such as Times New Roman or Courier fonts, to be defined in the HTML. This is still a feature, not a standard. Unless the user changes his or her default font, typically a Times face will be used for the proportional (text) font, and Courier, for the fixed (preformatted) font (Figure 16-7).

When choosing to define font attributes in a page, limiting font color to headers and enhancements rather than applying it to the strict text is the conservative way to play. Even then, it's wise to choose, as we've noted, from the Netscape palette. Font sizes are great for shrinking fonts for information that will appear consistently on every page, such

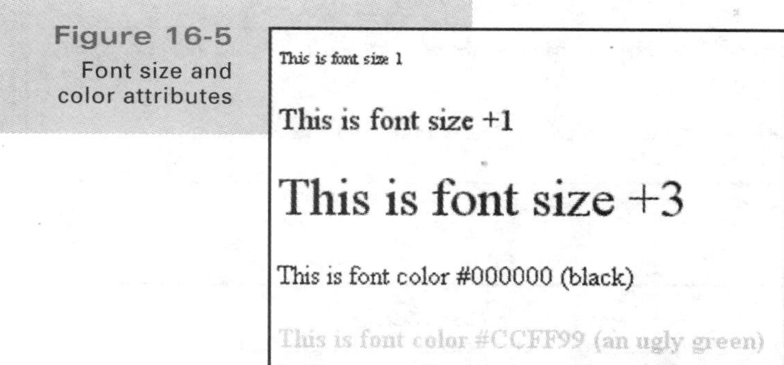

Figure 16-5 Font size and color attributes

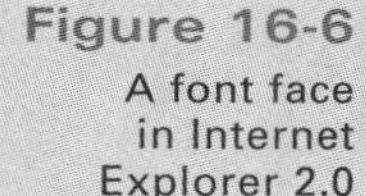

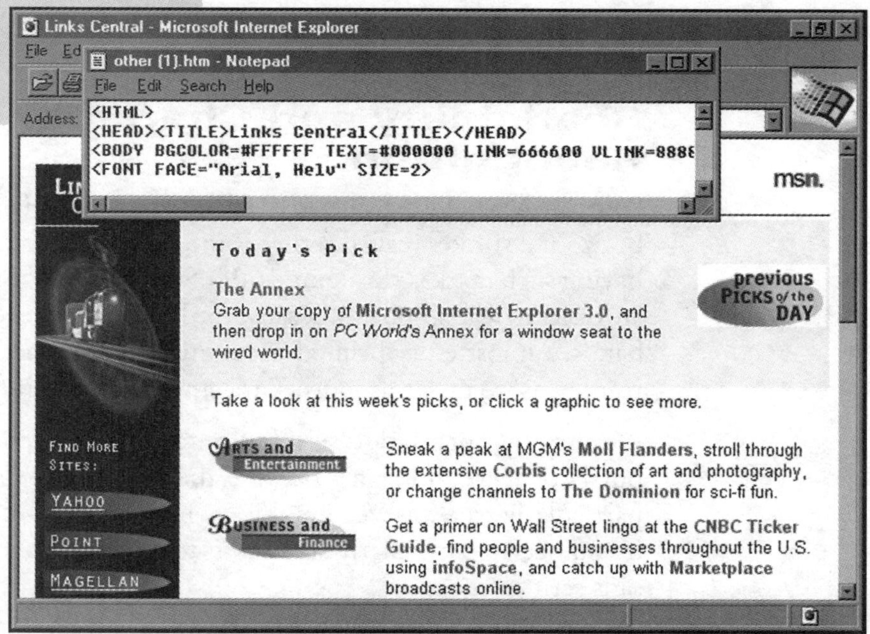

Figure 16-6 A font face in Internet Explorer 2.0

as the copyright and the design company identification shown in Figure 16-8. They also work well to create stylish headers or to make text larger if readability is an issue. More font attributes will quickly be brought to the table as browsers quickly mature, and it will be both exciting and nightmarish to imagine how Web designers will choose to use them within designs.

Figure 16-7 Proportional and fixed font defaults in Netscape

This text appears in the Times New Roman font, the proportional font default in Netscape for Windows 95.

```
This text appears as Courier font, the fixed font default
in Netscape for Windows 95.
```

Figure 16-8 Copyright and design identification using font attributes

© copyright 1996 Mark Wellman
Site Design by MainStay Communications & DesertNet Designs

Readability and Character Recognition

Fonts are generally considered to fall into two major families: *serif,* having horizontal strokes (called serifs) at the ends of letters, and *sans serif,* not having such marks (see Figure 16-9). Studies have shown that serif fonts are easier to read, probably because the lines of type tend to create horizon bands. Almost every printed page, including, in fact, the type you are reading as we take this journey together, is in a serif font.

On the other hand, sans serif fonts are good choices for headers, short bursts of text, and signs, because they are easy to recognize. This is particularly true for Web graphics, which need to be small. As a result, if you need a particularly small font to read well, choose one from the sans serif category.

Another important font readability issue is antialiasing. When fonts get to be larger than nine or ten points, use an antialiasing feature to improve legibility and overall graphic strength. Antialiasing basically shades pixels around the edges of the font character, making it appear smoother and less jagged, as demonstrated in Figure 16-10. If you're having a problem with jagged, hard-to-read fonts, try doing the same graphic over using these techniques, and see if it doesn't improve the look.

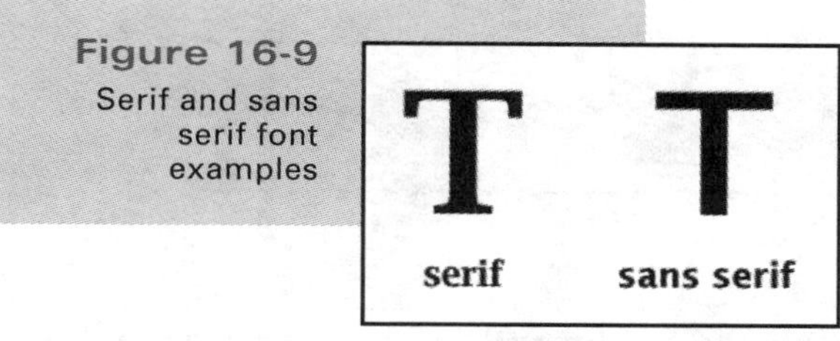

Figure 16-9
Serif and sans serif font examples

Figure 16-10
Aliased versus antialiased fonts

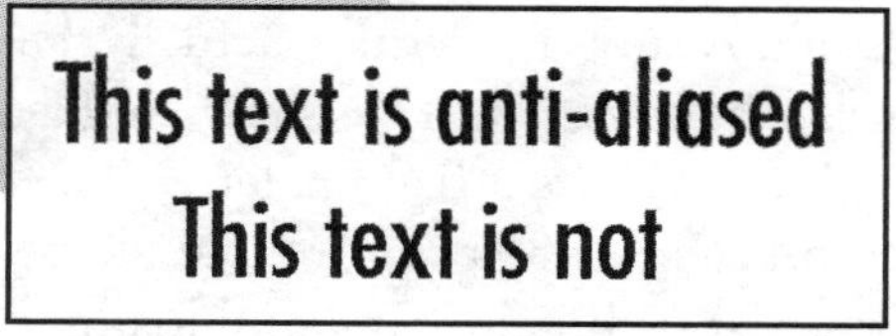

This text is anti-aliased
This text is not

Graphic File Formats

On the Web, we are concerned with two graphic file formats, GIF and JPEG (JPG). These file types offer different levels of color management and quality of appearance. Artists are likely to use both due to the specific features of each, so it's good to become familiar with them. Almost all browsers support both GIF and JPEG, although GIF was the more popular Web graphic format until fairly recently. JPEGs are now also very popular, because of their special features.

GIFs

GIF is the CompuServe Graphics Interchange Format. It is platform independent—meaning that it can be viewed on multiple platforms such as the Mac and the PC. GIFs give more control in terms of palette by indexing the colors and allowing control over what number of bits will appear in the final product (see Figure 16-11). For graphics that must be small and contain only a few colors, using this technique is the answer to bandwidth concerns. GIFs also can easily be interlaced for progressive rendering, and, as we will see in the next section, GIFs are used for transparent graphics. These qualities play into why GIFs are so popular.

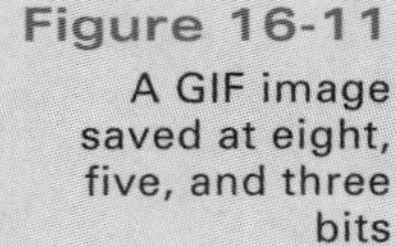

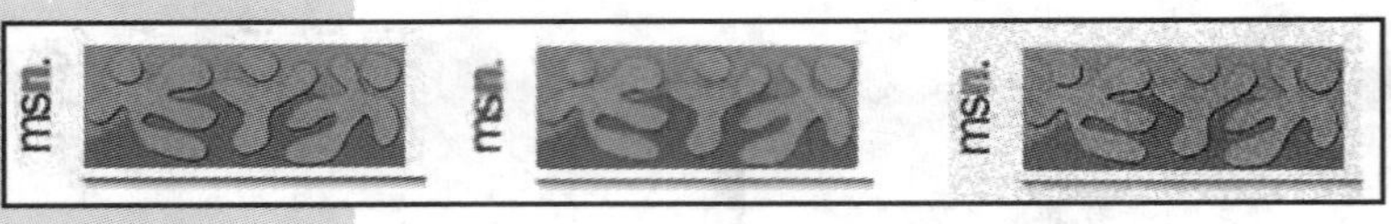

Figure 16-11 A GIF image saved at eight, five, and three bits

On the downside, GIFs are themselves limited to 256 colors, so they are not a great choice for photographs, particularly when a lot of gradation occurs in the picture. A sunset or vista—actually, any realistic image—will typically translate poorly as a GIF (as shown in Figure 16-12). Instead, use GIFs for graphics that use a fixed palette. Recent excitement over GIFs has focused on the GIF89a feature that allows designers to stack images and enclose data while looping and loading them. This allows for the creation of an animated graphic in the form of a single GIF that can be interpreted by Netscape. Obviously there are many other important considerations, so be sure to check Appendixes C and D for more detailed references.

Figure 16-12 GIF and JPEG images of a sunrise

JPEG

JPEG stands for "Joint Photographic Experts Group." This file format is the choice when creating graphics that demand true color, such as photographs. JPEGs are not restricted to the 256-color palette and therefore allow for stunning, 24-bit, high-resolution images that compress fairly well. They do, however, typically take up more memory than GIFs and are therefore larger in size. This equals longer download time, but a clever artist can learn techniques that help optimize JPEGs yet help retain their high-quality appearance.

There are currently some tools on the market that allow JPEGs to be progressively rendered, but this technology is quite young and therefore slow to catch on. Also, JPEGs load differently than GIFs, and designers need to take in to account how this occurs, particularly from browser

to browser. Finally, JPEGs cannot be transparent, and this creates limitations on certain shapes of images, as we will soon see.

Transparency

Transparency is a technique necessary under specific circumstances in Web design. Basically, transparency is used when a nonrectangular graphic is going to be placed on a colored or textured image-based background, as in Figure 16-13. When we create a transparency, the browser will replace the transparency color we've selected with the background image used for the entire page, as we see in Figure 16-14.

Figure 16-13 The black portion of this graphic is the transparent color.

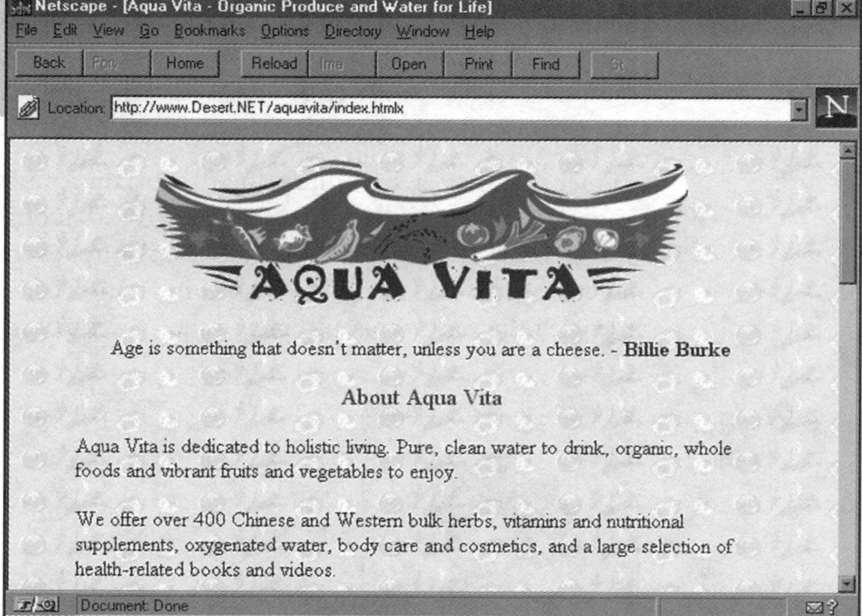

Figure 16-14 The same header has been placed on a background.

As mentioned, currently only GIF89a can support transparency creation. When creating a graphic to be rendered in part transparent, select the GIF89a export utility in Photoshop, or use another, third-party plug-in such as Box Top's PhotoGIF for more control.

Two helpful hints when creating transparencies:

- Make sure the color or theme of the background doesn't appear elsewhere in the image, as the color chosen will drop out *everywhere* within the graphic.
- Use only a solid color for the transparency to create a smooth look. Mixed colors will create grainy, uneven tones.

Transparency is an important technique. It has confused a lot of good artists and designers, but it is quite easy to do. Most importantly, the results help create good design, and learning transparency techniques will increase design ability. A great deal of information on this technique is available, and quite a few resources can be found in Appendix C of this book.

Effects—Creating Dimension

Creating *dimension* on Web pages is important because visually it provides texture. Without dimension, certain designs will appear flat or uninteresting. It takes a refined eye to determine when to use dimension, but when used appropriately, it contributes to visually exciting designs.

Dimension is created by one primary substance, and that is light. Light, how it touches and shadows an object, gives that object its dimensional appearance, as shown in Figure 16-15. Awareness of light and how to use it is not learned in a day—it is a combination of a skilled, experienced eye with the right tools and techniques necessary to pull it off.

Figure 16-15
Light creates dimension.

Simple techniques can create the appearance of dimension. One common choice is the drop shadow, which pulls images and text off a page and makes them appear to be floating above the page (Figure 16-16). Another use of light is in creation of dimensional curves on an object, as in Figure 16-17, or indentation of an object. These techniques should always be used appropriately, but how to determine appropriateness will lean heavily on the artist's eye. Typically, until bandwidth and programming for the Web become more stable and standard, subtle dimension tends to be the wisest choice.

Figure 16-16 Drop shadow creates the illusion of dimension.

Molly Was Here

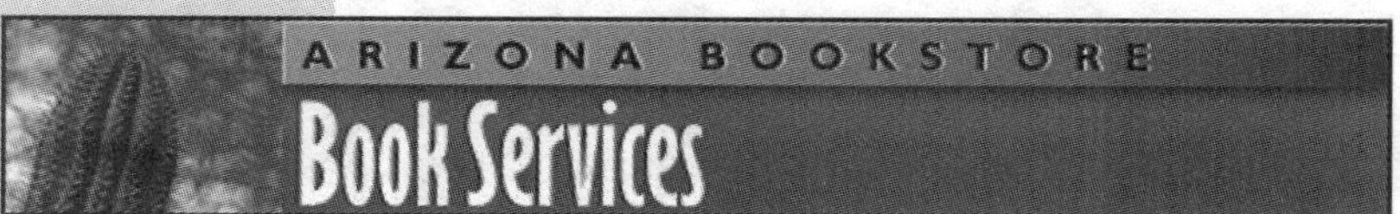

Figure 16-17 Light creates dimensional curves.

Backgrounds and Consistency

When support for backgrounds in browsers became available, the Web changed its face—as it often has—overnight. As time has passed, people have become more adept at using background colors and graphics, but the original problems that created ugly pages still exist.

These problems center primarily on poor and inconsistent color choices, the use of clichéd backgrounds rather than one's own original styles, and using backgrounds with text and text colors that detract from the readability of the text. This is a big no-no, and Web artists are encouraged to make sure everything they create is readable (Figure 16-18).

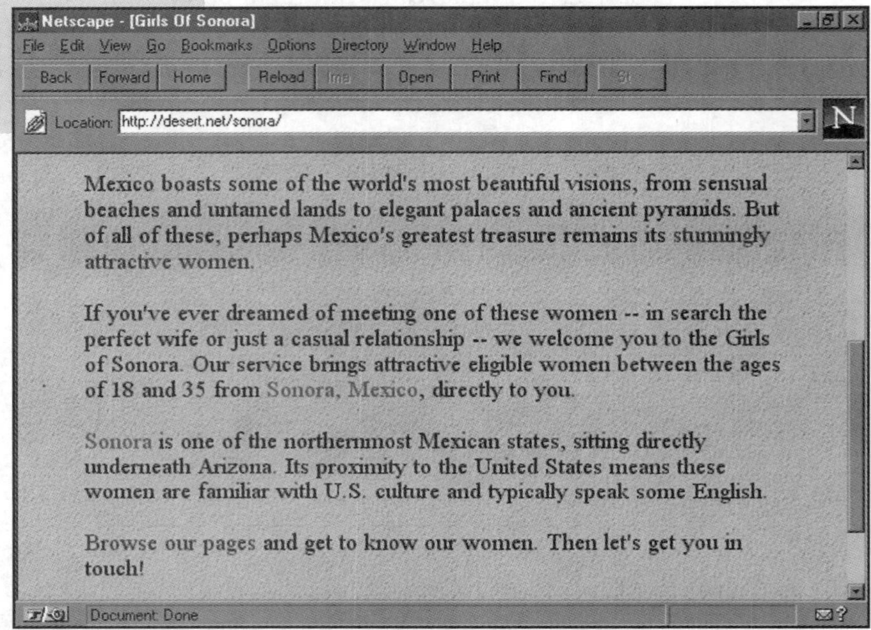

Figure 16-18 Readable text on a textured background

Some good rules of the road include avoiding colors that are too bright, avoiding background colors defined by the browser via the bgcolor element that are not within the Netscape 216 color palette, and finally creating background images that attract, rather than repel, the eye. Another good style call is creating a single palette of color and backgrounds for a site. Moving from page to page on the same site with a lot of inconsistent changes is bad design, plain and simple. I should always know what site I'm on because of the graphic consistency, style, and colors.

Resolution and Screen Width

This one is short and sweet. Remember this: the most commonly used graphics monitor is at 640 × 480 screen resolution, not more. Design to that size. The *only* time you shouldn't is when creating a background image that has a vertical element, as in Figure 16-19. This element will begin to repeat at the pixel point where the graphic ends (Figure 16-20). In this case, design a thin but wide background.

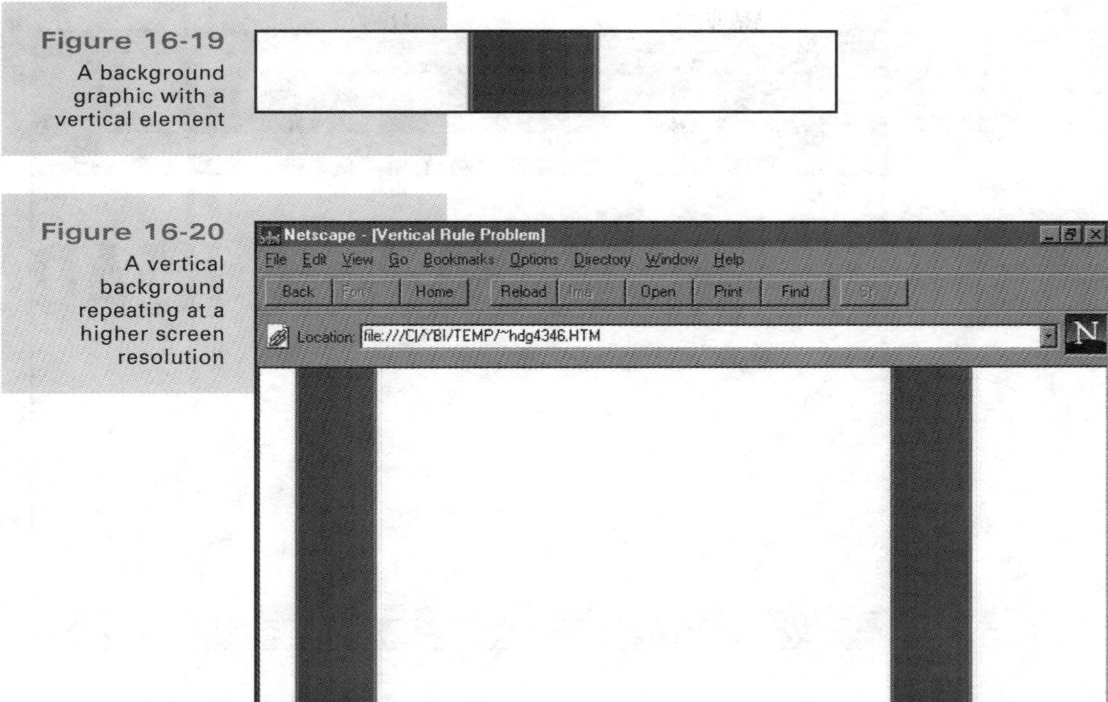

Figure 16-19 A background graphic with a vertical element

Figure 16-20 A vertical background repeating at a higher screen resolution

One of the ugliest things I've ever seen in design is when poor planning forces a horizontal scroll bar on my browser's interface (Figure 16-21). There are few, if any, true justifications for doing this. Please be aware of width and height constraints and adhere to them. You'll make me happy, but more importantly, you'll avoid creating problems that scream "ugly" or "amateur!"

Graphic Design Tools

Tools do not the designer make, but without the right tools, anyone undertaking any project will be at a disadvantage. There are many options out there for graphic designers, but there are some very specific choices that will enhance a Web artist's work.

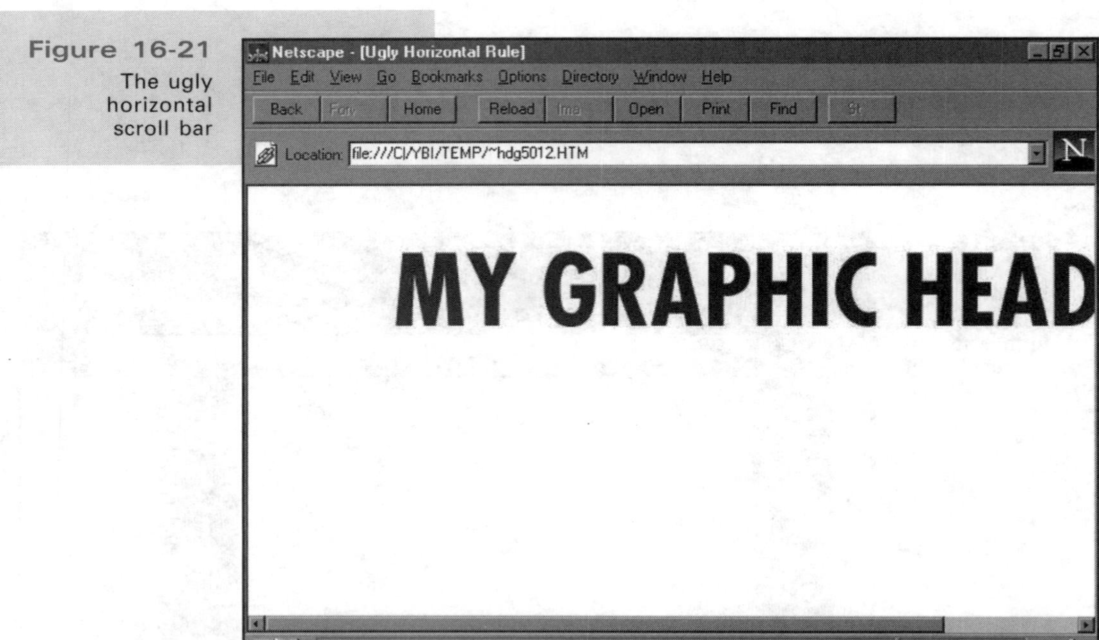

Figure 16-21 The ugly horizontal scroll bar

Photoshop is the program of choice for two-dimensional, static graphic development for the Web. Among other things, recent versions offer layering, which allows the artist to isolate different portions of the graphic. This is invaluable, because changes then can be made to the graphic with very little effort.

Photoshop also offers text antialiasing and good export filters for GIF89a. It also has good JPEG management. If a designer wants more control, then additional filters and tools can easily be downloaded as shareware or purchased commercially to plug right into Photoshop. One example is Kai's Power Tools. These tools make Web graphics development faster and easier. Learn more about them, as well as general tips and tricks for Web graphics, at Web site http://the-tech.mit.edu/KPT/.

Web designers will make sure their graphic artists have complete libraries of stock photography and clip art as well as mountains of fonts. All of these are quite expensive, but they are invaluable tools, and the successful design group is going to find a way to ensure that they are on the shelf. Again, check out Appendix C for a variety of resources to get started.

Web Graphic Design on the Move

In the next chapter we will be looking at multimedia on the Web. Many aspects of multimedia rely on the sense of a good graphic designer, especially with applications such as Web animation and the creation of virtual worlds. Here is more fodder for this chapter's opening arguments that Web designers and artists have to be ready to push the line. Knowing where that line is on the Web is a daily chore, but the artist truly involved in Web graphics is going to spend that time and know that line. He or she will challenge it, have fun with it, especially when there's no good reason not to do so. Please the audience, and they will respond with enthusiasm. Without that, it wouldn't be worth the long hours, tremendous precision, and significant learning curve that Web graphic design demands.

World Wide Woman

Deborah A. Howard
2 COW HERD
http://www.2cowherd.net/

"As one of very few ISP owners who is also a woman, I am getting tired of being the only woman at technical seminars. I keep proselytizing the power of the WEB to everyone to encourage deeper participation from more folks, especially women."

Deb Howard is the wearer of the proverbial many hats. She is owner, head designer, staff manager, and responsible for overseeing marketing, client management, and the company's general administration.

Strengths: Creative (great page layouts), flexible (come up with the perfect client solutions to tough Web problems), driven (when I say I will get the job done, I'm not just whistling Dixie), hard-working (my marketing director, with due deference to James Brown, has dubbed me, "The hardest Working Woman on the Internet").

Weaknesses: Creative ("this will look great if I just change this..."), flexible ("sure, you can totally ignore your written obligations under our contract, abuse my good nature, and make unlimited changes for no charge—absolutely!"), driven ("just one more page, honey, then I'll come to bed"), hard-working (need to play WAY more!).

Comments: *"I'd like to see more women online, more women ISPs, more women web designers: I see a real need for inclusion and direction taking for this medium. More people of color, more economic equality: I worry about the growing gap between the technology have's and the technology have-not's, and worry about Cyber "Surfdom" becoming Cyber "Serfdom."*

The InfiNet Jot of It

Heather Champ
Web Designer
http://www.jezebel.com

"I've had the opportunity to design a fairly high traffic site, having designed Infinet's Cool Site of the Day with different design elements which were online from August of last year to earlier this spring. It's interesting to see the comments of people who come through the site. With traditional design mediums there is limited feedback. With the web, feedback is as easy as a "mailto:" link. But given that there really isn't that much "discussion" as much as flaming mail, you have to take things with a grain of salt.

What I enjoy most about web design is that after years of having to work within the budgetary constraints of printing costs, color, number of colors, well within reason, is no longer an element that limits the designer. I created my home page in august of 94. I wish that I has saved the many variations of my page, from the gray, to overwhelming backgrounds to something somewhat more restrained

There are many days when I sit at my computer amazed that I get paid to design and develop web sites. Then there are the other days, full of computer and network nuttiness and I wonder why I'm doing this. :-)"

chapter 17

Multimedia

Multimedia has been a hot topic for several years now. The concept, in the form of solid, salable content, became overwhelmingly popular in the form of interactive CD-ROMs. The impact of these CDs, which cover everything from learning-oriented programs for children to adult interactive entertainment, has been so enormous as to literally change the home PC itself.

People buying a new home computer in the contemporary market are automatically presented with "multimedia" machines—in other words, machines that are capable of providing them with a complete mix of media. Typically this refers to powerful handling of audio and video, and to the associated hardware necessary—graphics and sound cards, monitors, speakers, high-speed CD-ROMs, advanced computer architecture—all to make these multiple media sing.

This is mostly good news for the Web world, and it has in fact been part of and party to the burst of interest in the Net, since many of these computers come with modems and communications software. The bad—or let's say challenging—part of the multimedia home PC phenomenon is that people have been spoiled by the higher-tech, local interactivity they're used to receiving from CD-ROMs. Thus when they get on the Web and find the experience to be rather different, it can be disappointing or confusing.

More Fiber, Please

Our biggest problem with creating fast access multimedia on the Web is bandwidth. The technologies exist to create the media—we see that daily with our televisions and with computer programs. But once we have to start squeezing all of the complicated data through the copper wire leading into most people's homes and offices, we end up bottlenecking. Even very high-speed data transmission via satellite or fiber optic cable—while good for the general flow of data—still will end up as a traffic jam when it has to step down to the limited bandwidth that enters most commercial and private environments.

In months and years to come, dramatic changes will occur that will lead to much better multimedia handling on the Web. In fact, the Web itself will likely change exponentially with the technology and bandwidth capabilities. Cable modems and fiber optics will bring about a merging—what is referred to as a "convergence"—of the many technologies that currently exist, giving rise to a new, unnamable but wholly exciting prospect.

Multimedia and Web Design

In order to create more stable multimedia for the growing tastes of our audience within current technologies, Web designers have had to lean heavily on the work of visionary programmers and computer scientists. These individuals are figuring out ways of compressing and managing the typically voluminous data that such media engender. The hope is to reach the low-bandwidth consumer in some fashion that is more acceptable than what we had—well—yesterday! It's a constant struggle, and this is the reason why so many Web-based languages and techniques have cropped up in the past few years—to meet the needs of consumer demand in a setting of changing technology.

The major components of Web multimedia exist to enhance the interactive model we already have with hypermedia text and graphics. Add to this model audio, animation, and video, and we have an environment that basically mimics a CD-ROM in its intent. Now throw in the fact that we can interact on a human level with others via the Net, and we get quite excited when experiencing technologies such as PowWow, an interactive, multimedia online interface.

This chapter will look briefly at some of the multimedia technologies available and how the Web designer needs to approach them. With emerging programs and new science to match our emerging and new media needs, this is easily the fastest growing—and most unstable—realm of online development.

How Multimedia on the Web Is Managed

There are several methods of managing data to reach the audience in a usable fashion. Some methods are more effective than others; very few

are truly ideal. Again, however, as techniques become more advanced and as more of these applications are built into the browser, we'll see better performance from multimedia applications.

Spawned Applications

In the instance of a *spawned application,* we will click on a button or select an option that will begin downloading the event to our computer, as shown in Figure 17-1. Once the download is complete, the browser will *spawn*—call upon and initiate—an external program known as a *viewer* or *helper application* that is necessary to run that particular media event (Figure 17-2).

The advantage to this process is that it allows multimedia to be played or viewed at all. The disadvantage is length of download; very often large amounts of data take time, and time means patience. There can be problems with downloads—from the client or server end. If little Johnny picks up the phone while Mom is downloading the latest audio clip from Z-City Dragons, the line could drop and with it the data requested. Servers can and often do choke, and the Net itself can slow to a crawl. Just yesterday I was at a popular site downloading the latest beta version of some software when my throughput dropped to zero and my browser sat immobilized for goodness knows how long before I noticed it.

Viewers (or helper apps) need to be set up in a browser by the user, as shown in Figure 17-3. Sometimes, as in the case with Netscape's Audio Player (NAPlayer), the program and the viewer are downloaded and set up together. If a viewer *isn't* resident on your machine, or if it is but is not pointed to by the browser, then the helper app won't run. Finally, helper applications typically load separately from the browser, popping up a dialogue window through which the event can be viewed (Figure 17-4).

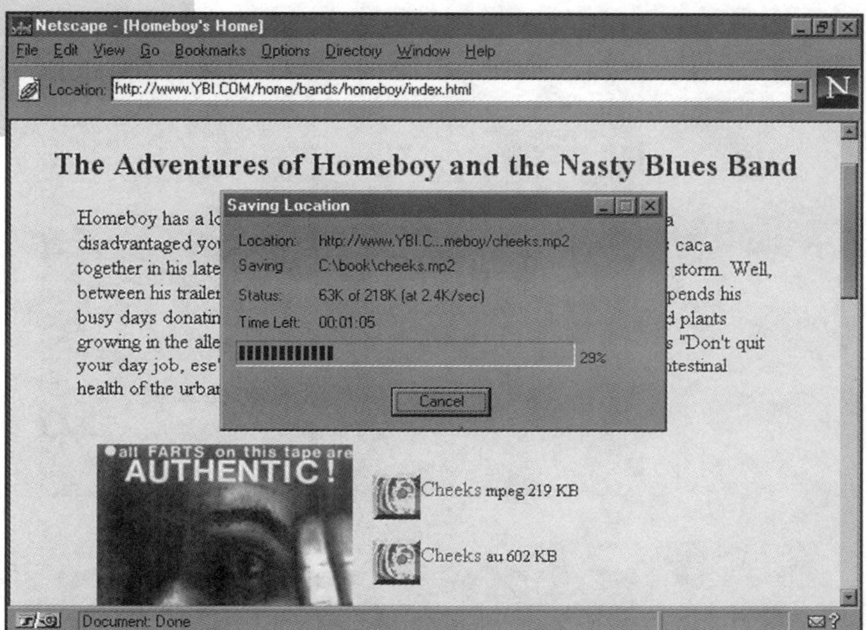

Figure 17-1 A media event downloading to a local computer

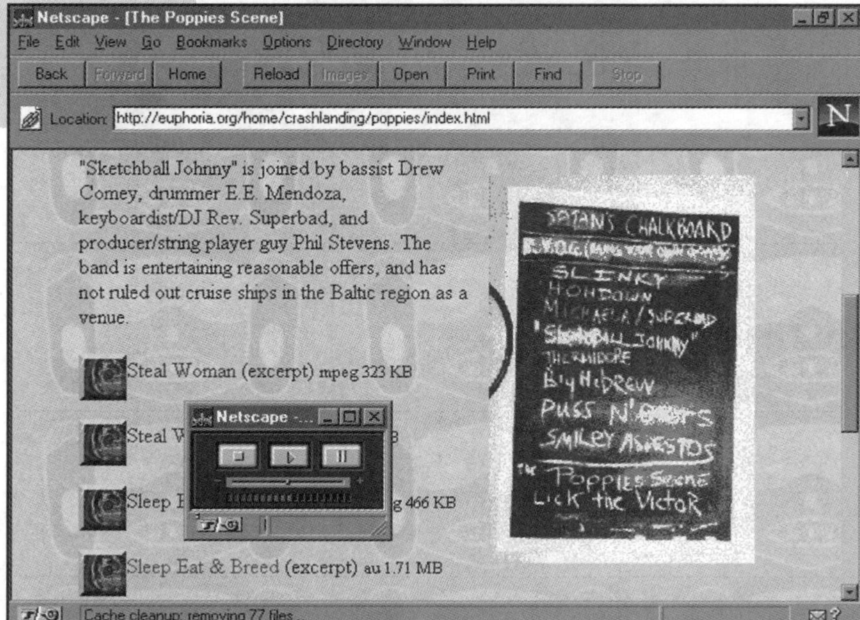

Figure 17-2 A spawned helper application

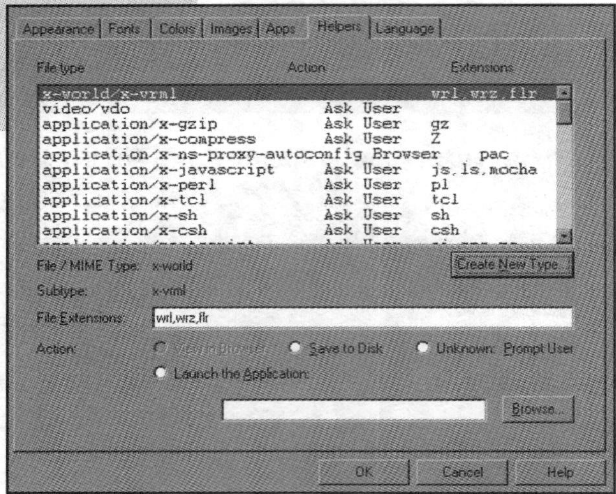

Figure 17-3 Setting up helper applications in Netscape

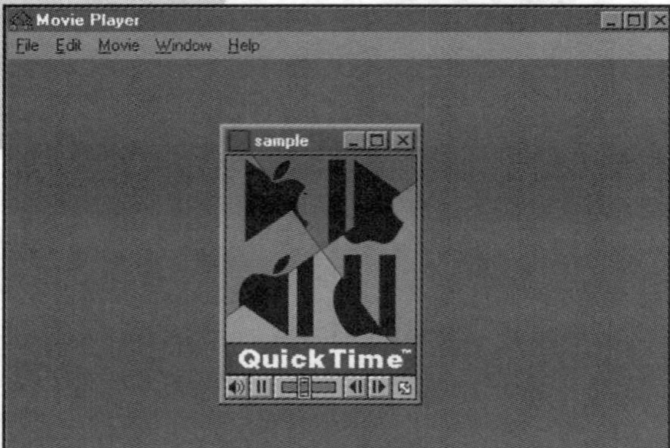

Figure 17-4 A separate viewer's dialog window

In-line Events

Basically an *in-line event* means that whether an application is downloaded and spawned by an external program or dealt with by the browser itself, the program will run *in-line.* Either the media event is visually seamless with the rest of the Web page—appearing as part of the production—or, as in the case of Real Audio, the information is *streamed* to your machine and then spawns a viewer that will play it (Figure 17-5).

Figure 17-5
The Real Audio player

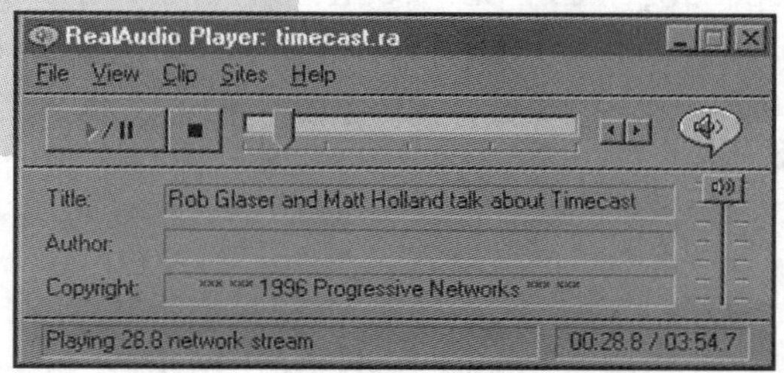

If the operation sounds very similar to downloaded and spawned events, it is, and it really is conceptually the same. The safe comments regarding spawned versus in-line media would be that in-line media are trying to creating the illusion that the events occur as part of the page. Also, in-line media tend to have been developed with browser technology in mind, whereas helper applications are independent from the browser. Sometimes, as is the case with Apple's Quick Time viewer, what began as a general multimedia application is now being applied to Web events and redeveloped as in-line technology (Figure 17-6).

Figure 17-6
The Quick Time developer's page

Another aspect of this in-line technology is browser-mediated, HTML-dependent functions. These things include animated GIFs, which we touched upon in the last chapter and will look at more closely here. Internet Explorer version 2.0 has allowed for in-line sound events using the <embed> tag for some time now, and Netscape 3.0 has created an in-line sound option using this tag as well (Figure 17-7). Other in-line technologies involve calling upon the server and a compatible browser to perform multimedia events via Common Gateway Interface programming, as is the case with server push-pull animations or live-action cameras (Figure 17-8), which DesertNet employs with some frequency.

Interdependent Media

It's also important to mention another type of package available that involves the use of proprietary interfaces, where instead of a browser, a separate program is used while connected to the Net to retrieve or use the information provided. Two good examples of this are PointCast Network and PowWow.

PointCast is a news network that requires a separate user interface, downloadable from their home page at http://www.pointcast.com/ (Figure 17-9). This allows a newsfeed, completely customized by the user, to bring up-to-the-minute news and information to the user's desktop. What is particularly interesting about PointCast is that it can act independently of a browser, it can call a browser such as Netscape if more information is requested regarding a given piece of information, *and* it is available as a Netscape 2.0 and above plug-in!

PowWow is a fascinating software package that focuses on interaction between individuals. You can create art (Figure 17-10); speak vocally with other participants; and quickly exchange pictures, sounds (Figure 17-11), and other programs with any individual in a session with you.

Perhaps the coolest thing about PowWow is that you can actually go Web surfing with other people online, looking at sites interdependently with your browser while chatting in another window via the PowWow software. How packages like these will fully interact with Web browsers in a less segregated fashion remains to be seen, but the suggestion is

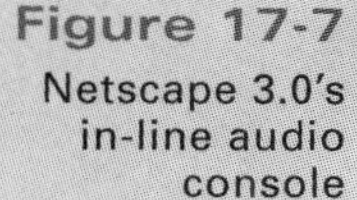

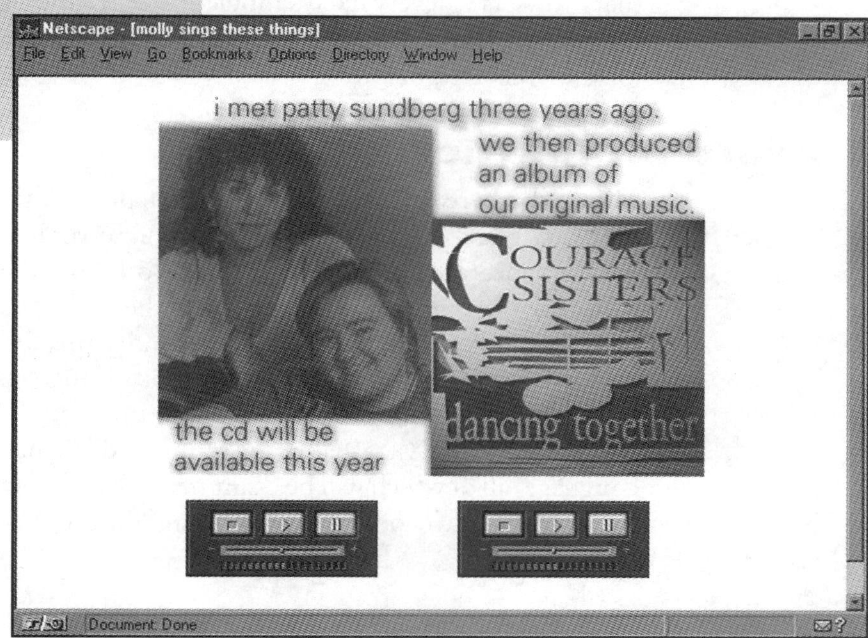

Figure 17-7 Netscape 3.0's in-line audio console

Figure 17-8 The now-famous Club Congress club cam

that browsers will very likely embrace these technologies at some point, forming a single package that will create an entirely new level of challenge for the Web designer.

Toward Integration

Although there are still delays with many multimedia events and problems due to a wide range of client and server issues, the trend is for in-line appearance and speed features to follow the lead of the CD-ROM or other mature multimedia rather than assume the form of spawned applications. In fact, the need, and desire, for better multimedia choices has itself spawned a new generation of languages and applications entirely built around the Web and Web browsers. These include Java, JavaScript, ActiveX, Visual Basic Script, and Virtual Reality Modeling Language, all of which will be examined in closer detail in the following chapter, where we look at programming for the Web.

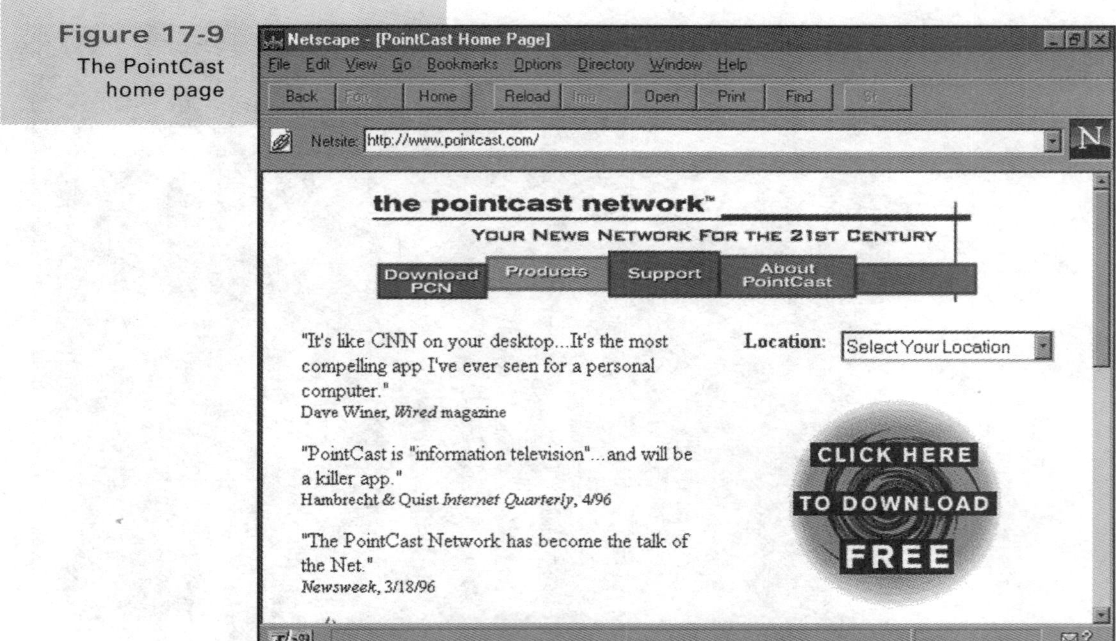

Figure 17-9 The PointCast home page

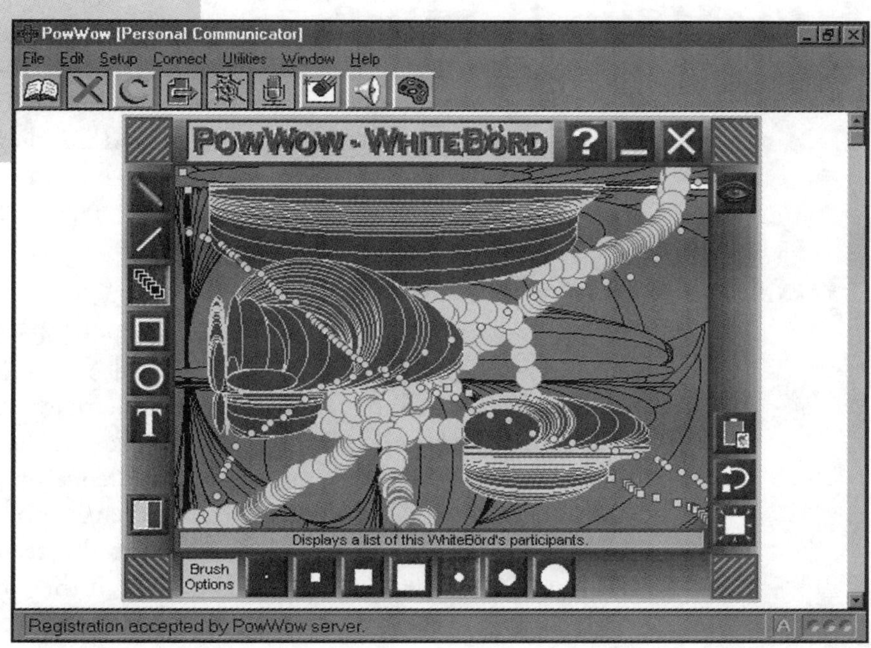

Figure 17-10 Co-creating art with PowWow's whiteboard feature

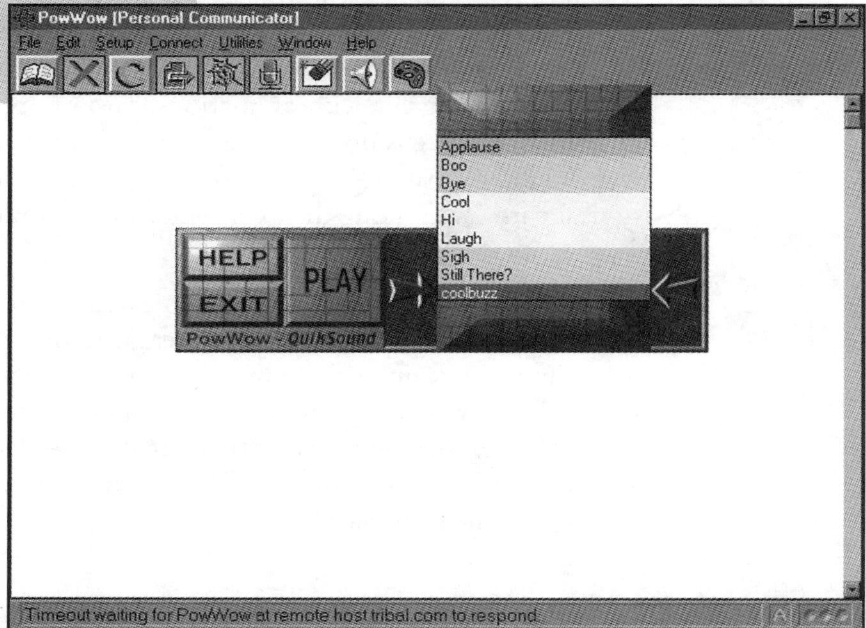

Figure 17-11 PowWow's QuikSound

Web Design Choices

Web designers need to weigh the need for multimedia heavily with the intent of their presentation. As with every other discipline, we are intrinsically linked to both the audience and the client, both of whom undoubtedly want the most interesting but the most reasonable application for the job.

The Challenge of Multimedia

Because of the diversity of browsers and the varied levels of audience skill, knowledge, and interest in these add-on, plug-in technologies, and because of the limitations of the technologies themselves, we run into a problem using these various resources in current commercial design. We don't want to alienate our audience by challenging them with something they cannot support, don't have, or may have no interest in having, and yet we also want to push the technologies, as I've mentioned before, to the cutting edge so that they improve.

Use and Abuse

A good Web designer will understand when it is appropriate to use varied technologies, and when staying away from them is imperative. The one thing to definitely avoid is overusing technologies. Getting to a page and being hit with animations, Java Script, runmovies, and options all at once is not only overkill, it's damning. There's no faster way of killing an audience than giving them too much sensory matter to deal with, or crashing their computer. Aside from those unfriendly aspects, it's just plain ugly.

Keep multimedia balanced with intent, and use it to enhance—not detract from—a site's direction. Another great rule to remember is only to use multimedia on a site's home page if there's really good justification for it—let's say you're doing a site about animation, or you're an arts-oriented magazine, or you want to sell that particular technique. If the site you are working with is purely commercial, leave the bells and whistles off the front page.

Web Multimedia Options

A Web designer needs to be aware of the details we've just discussed—the how and why of multimedia on the Web. The next step is to become familiar with common multimedia options and how to use them. For the purposes of this book, we'll look at some popular ways to create animations and implement audio, at the current video options available, and at VRML, QTVR, and complete multimedia plug-ins such as Shockwave.

In the following chapters, we look a little more specifically at present and upcoming programming aids that will push multimedia on the Web to a new level. Don't forget to check the appendices, particularly Appendix E, for multimedia resources that will give Web designers serious about using these technologies good starting points for further research.

Animation on the Web

There are currently three primary ways to do animations on the Web. A wonderful format that has become exceedingly popular in recent months is animated GIFs. We touched on this subject briefly in the last chapter, and we'll learn a little more about them here. Next, we have server push-pull, which basically relies on a Common Gateway Interface script that processes images and pushes them back to the client. Finally, Java has been used to create fun animations, but as with most aggressive Web technologies, its use is still limited to sites that have a specific need or interest in them.

Animated GIFs

The *animated GIF* format is supported by Netscape 2.04b and above. It is unclear at the time of this writing if Internet Explorer 3.0 supports them. This type of animation is very useful in creating fairly small or contained animations. It exploits certain aspects of GIF89a technology and enables the graphics designer to manipulate the technology and create compact, server-independent animations that are quick and attractive (see Figure 17-12).

Figure 17-12 Separate images within a single GIF animation. The second frame appears after several seconds, and then the sequence continues to loop.

The technology is fairly in-depth, and for those interested in understanding exactly how it's all put together, I recommend visiting one of Royal Frazier's excellent sites, where he describes the process in detail. The address http://members.aol.com/royalef/index.html will get you to the top level, and then you can follow the links to the mirror site closest to your own.

Making animated GIFs is actually quite simple. There are several programs that can be extraordinarily helpful. The GIF Construction Set (GIFcon) comes in 16- and 32-bit applications for Windows OSs. GIF Builder is the recommended version for Macintosh. Visit the Frazier sites for complete information on not only how to construct animated GIFs but where to acquire these programs.

Server Push Animations

A *server push animation* requires interaction between the browser and the server. As a result, it can appear slow, with a lot of jerking motion and inconsistent speed. Still, these animations can be used in remarkable and fun ways.

What is required of this process is a script residing on a server that is set up to process a series of images prepared and defined by the animator. Each image will then be sent back to the client and appear as a moving sequence, as in Figure 17-13. Once the script is in place, it is easy to call upon it to make animations of this type; however, some commercial ISPs do not allow for custom CGI scripts and may not have this script, known as *runmovie*, or another like it available. Because of the other forms of animation that rely less on the server, this form is declining in popularity, but I have a personal taste for it, and I believe it will continue to be used in new and clever ways.

Java Animations

Animating with Java requires knowledge of the language but offers the author a lot of flexibility. What's especially impressive about Java animation is that individual frames within the animation can be tied to individual audio files. This enables in-line, seamless multimedia for browsers capable of interpreting Java. For more information on the creation of Java Applet animation, visit http://colos-www.prz.tu-berlin.de/~testcolo/JavaApplets/. This site gives a step-by-step tutorial about the various aspects of animating with Java (Figure 17-14).

Figure 17-13 Sequential frames in a runmovie/server push animation

Figure 17-14 A Java animation by Andreas Krebs, featuring rotating words.

Web Audio

Audio on the Web is a growing and exciting area in Web multimedia. We have options that range from simple sounds to use for fun in-line via the HTML <embed> tag (supported by Internet Explorer 2.0 and above, and Netscape 3.0), to streamed audio from Real Audio, to downloadable sound bites that will spawn an audio player—which with Netscape is built right into the browser.

I spoke with Phil Stevens, owner of Crash Landing Records (Figure 17-15), a 24-track digital studio here in Tucson. Phil and I work closely on both Web- and music-related projects, including Euphoria World Wide Music, http://euphoria.org/home/. PBS recently covered our work for their syndicated show *The Internet*, and we had a lot of fun sharing both Web technology and tunes with them.

Figure 17-15 Audio and Web engineer Phil Stevens in his studio

Phil has this to say about audio on the Web:

> *"Here's a synopsis of my thoughts on audio. First, know when to use sound files and when to skip them. With music, stick to excerpts, and edit well. For example, a verse and a chorus of a pop-style song should suffice. Long introductions and fadeouts of musical selections can be trimmed. With spoken content, edit out rambling and digressions from the main topic, if possible.*
>
> *"It's important to keep the quality high. If you don't have the tools or knowledge, outsource the work! If you're doing it yourself, use the best source material you can, such as a CD, an original master, or a good cassette. Keep your recording levels as high as*

possible without overloading. So, in common editing software, see that peaks go to the top but don't 'square off.' Don't try to raise volume on samples recorded too low because you'll just raise the hiss along with the content, so rerecord higher instead.

"Quality high, yes—but make sure to keep the file size low. Here are a few ways of doing that:

- *8-bit AU good, cross-platform (22K sampling frequency (fs) for high-res music, 11 for low-res music or high-res speech, 8 for average speech (phone grade))*
- *MPEG Layer-2 for shrinking down more—not as available across-platforms, but quality/size is much better than with linear AU, WAV, or AIFF (which are all very similar, by the way)*

"Now, with streaming solutions like Real Audio, you have a technology that is good for speech but really mangles music content. Newscasting is an appropriate application for Real Audio, but to get quality music, I wouldn't use it. It also is a serious server bandwidth hog—10 RA 2.0 streams will eat a T1 for lunch!

"MIDI is often overlooked as a musical 'soundtrack' resource. MIDI typically offers very economical file sizes and relatively well-standardized instrument designation. MIDI can also be packaged into Java applets for full multimedia effects. One major con with MIDI is that there is no way to do vocals or handle 'real' instruments.

"Check out the help page on Euphoria. It's there as a Web resource, and it's got some great audio information, as well as links to applications and further reading, http://euphoria.org/home/help/help.html."

Web Video

Just as there is streaming audio, there are now products that stream video and simultaneous audio using in-line plug-in technologies. One such product is CoolFusion (Figure 17-16), which is currently available as a plug-in for Windows 95 and is bundled as part of the Netscape 3.0 versions for both Macintosh and Windows platforms. CoolFusion technology will be available for Internet Explorer 3.0 as well and will comply with ActiveX-aware applications. At 28.8, it's still a long download, but it's a glimpse into an interesting future. For more information or to check out CoolFusion, visit http://www.iterated.com/coolfusn/cf_home.htm (Figure 17-17).

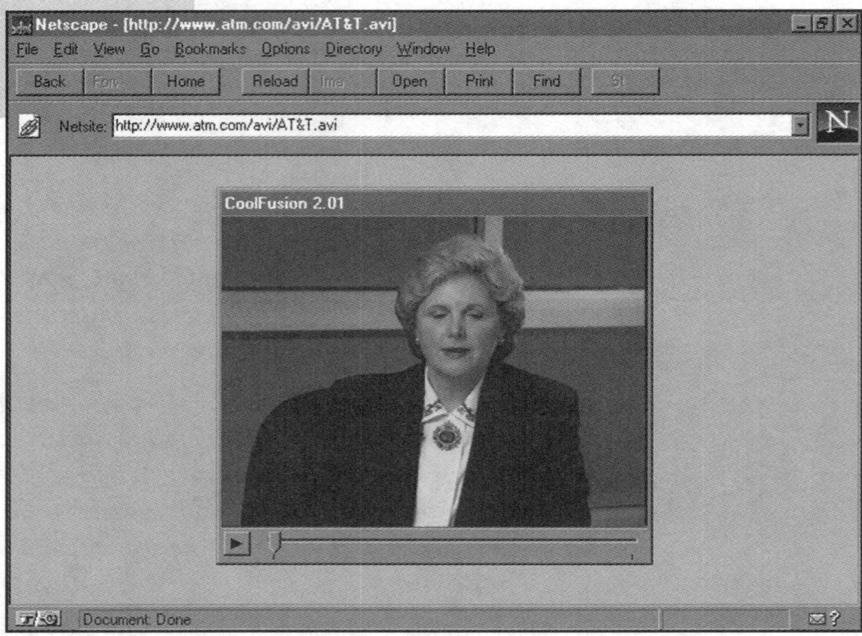

Figure 17-16 Streaming video with CoolFusion

Other video options include creating downloadable MPEG or AVI files and spawning a helper application to view them. The issues that dominate audio handling of this type are applicable here as well. Use video only when really necessary and keep the quality as high as possible but the file size as low as possible for strong video applications that don't take forever to download.

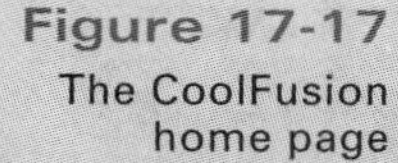

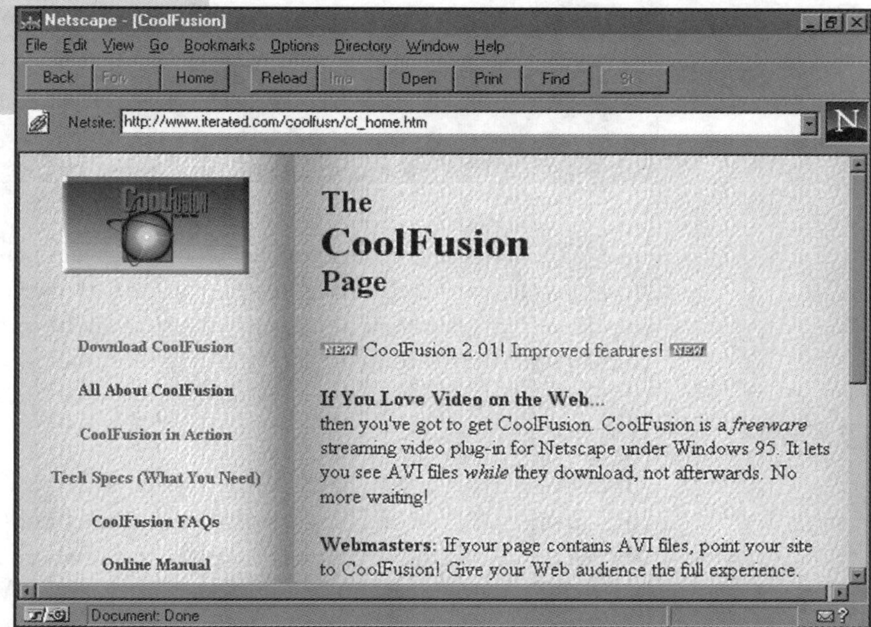

Figure 17-17
The CoolFusion home page

Virtual Worlds

In the future it will be easy to imagine widespread need for VR (virtual reality) applications that use programming languages and plug-ins to delineate and define the creation of virtual, three-dimensional worlds.

VRML

Let's say, for example, you wanted to allow a company's widget to be displayed so that the prospective widget buyer could look closely at it from a variety of angles. With a virtual reality application such as VRML, designers can create three-dimensional renderings of the widget and program it so that clients can access the rendering—moving it to the desired position, zooming in and out—all from the comfort of their own office, as shown in Figure 17-18.

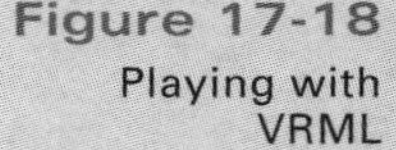

Figure 17-18
Playing with VRML

The Web design advantage for this technology lies primarily in product demonstration and comparable applications. However, VRML is more applicable to geometric renderings than to realistic photography. For that QTVR seems to be the technology of choice.

QTVR

Developed by Apple, QuickTime Virtual Reality is a powerful and intriguing tool for creating virtual panoramas and objects. As with VRML, you can move around the panorama, which is a scene created with still photographs and sewn together with QTVR programming applications. With objects, the individual can interact with the VR by clicking and dragging images such as three-dimensional representations of products and the like.

QTVR files are actually quite small and can be rapidly downloaded; the QuickTime player will spawn to play them. Netscape 3.0 offers in-line support for QTVR. Popular uses for the Web include the ability to show real rooms, streets, and the like. For example, if I'm showcasing a car, I can show the inside of that car in detail, allowing the viewer to look closely at various details. DesertNet has developed QTVR for the Club Congress, where we are creating panoramas of a number of the club's rooms. Look at the panorama of the club's Red Room, as shown in Figure 17-19.

Shockwave

Perhaps the most comprehensive multimedia package available, Shockwave allows for the creation of entire user interfaces that include animations, in-line video, links to URLs, sounds, and interactive

Figure 17-19
Panoramic views of the Club Congress's Red Room

navigation components. Shockwave presentations are created with MacroMedia's Director. This is an interesting and important direction for multimedia development on the Web, largely because it is representative of the CD-ROM-style interface we discussed earlier and expresses one possible face of the Web as bandwidth, browser, and platform issues become more stable (Figure 17-20)

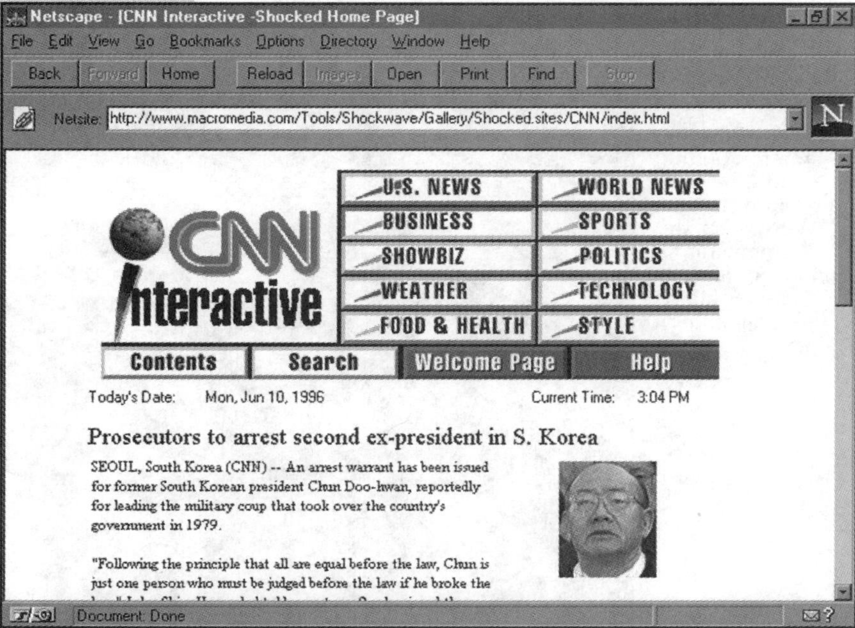

Figure 17-20
A Shockwave page. A page using this technology is referred to as having been "shocked."

Back to Square One

This chapter provided an overview of issues and examples of multimedia applications on the Web. As Web designers, however, we must return to the question of whether any of these choices are appropriate for our clients. From my experiences, the answer is "usually not."

The only items that DesertNet employs regularly in commercial design are GIF animations and server animations, the latter only very deliberately and even then, only occasionally (Figure 17-21). The reason lies primarily in the fact that in commercial media—unless the client is highly motivated to use these advanced but problematic technologies—the audience will not be as involved in our sites as they potentially can be.

This is not, of course, to discourage the use of these and like technologies. As I have already clearly mentioned, I believe that their use is important. At the very least, the Web designer interested in the future possibilities of the Web should become as familiar with these emerging technologies as possible.

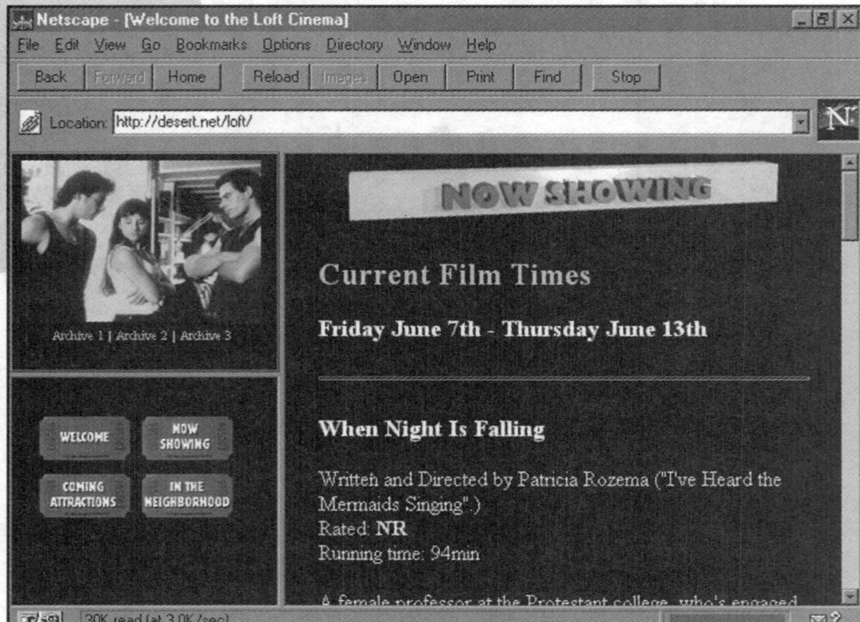

Figure 17-21 A runmovie animation on the Loft Cinema's pages. In this case, such an application, mimicking film, is conceptually justified.

By the time this book reaches publication the Web will be ready—because of the impending push against Netscape by Microsoft Internet Explorer and related ActiveX technologies (Big Browser, if you will, see Figure 17-22)—to undergo changes that we can only fantasize about. Until we see what comes of the programming languages and browser opportunities available, it is wise to learn all you can, practice where it's safe, but create commercial sites with deliberation and conservatism where multimedia of this nature is concerned.

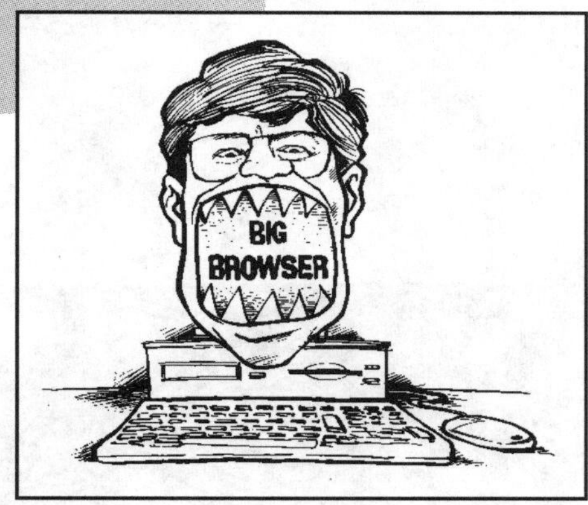

Figure 17-22
Big Browser

The Art of the Designer

Ms. Amatul H. Hannan
ToolBox Productions
http://web.mit.edu/ahannan/WCA_HTML/AHannan.html

"I'm a Black Lithuanian Scottish and Irish American woman, living and working in Boston M.A. My interests are mentoring under-served youth, low income communities and access issues, and the social transition from consumer to producer."

Also interested in multimedia literacy, Amatul focuses her personal as well as professional interests on work with urban youth, artists, and performers. Preferring the Web for delivering poetry or artistic ventures, Amatul is also interested in the educational uses of the Web medium.

She began her media studies as an independent video artist. Her interest in community led her to become a youth mentor at the Boston Computer Museum's Computer Clubhouse.

Now a solo Web designer participating in regular partnerships with artists, her Web design strengths include creating graphics and writing original material. "Most sites are too cold, too corporate, with not enough use of art."

Amatul hopes for continued breakthroughs in using the Web as a "visual language." She would like to see better character sets available more inexpensively, and better connectivity in the form of wireless or cellular Internet for the former Soviet Union, China, Africa, and European/American inner city areas—built right into the walls of all new infrastructure.

Writing the Web

Dan Huff
Editor, The Tucson Weekly
http://desert.net/tw/

Web journalism emphasizes the importance of all web design elements, but particularly is a showcase for the true uses of new media. It's interesting to see what happens to people, particularly highly creative ones, when they are offered a new way to do something they love. In this case, we see an editor of an alternative newspaper enlivened by the possibilities that the web offers both from the conceptual stance, to the possibilities for writers in the new media realm.

When speaking with Dan about the web, there's a certain idealistic spark that comes over his typically cynical attitude. "There are no rules." He says. "None. Nobody knows where it's going. We will be surprised.

Words are very powerful. But a few words and a well done graphic or photo are ten times as powerful. Poets can make things visual they have an inherent idea how words and ideas have to speak to us emotionally. With the web you've got people there with an attention span of 7 seconds. If they're not involved, they're gone."

For aspiring web writers, Dan suggests that they Pay attention to popular music. Pay attention to rhythms, lyrics, visual art, good graphics. If you're a true writer, you'll pursue things emotionally.

"Some day in the future our language might become technological hieroglyphics. People in this era think linearly. People in the future? Who knows?"

chapter 18

Advanced Programming

A Web site comprising nothing more than clean HTML documents and attractive graphics may deliver all the results you need. Good content, presented appropriately, can stand on its own without needing tinsel draped all about. If the site's interaction with surfers is nothing more than a "drop us a line" mailto: command, you may not need to know anything about forms, processing data, and authentication. And simple sites requiring low maintenance probably aren't candidates for dynamically generated pages. But chances are you'll need or want more somewhere along the way.

Fortunately for the designer, a growing collection of tools is available to customize, manipulate, animate, and otherwise turn a Web site into almost a living entity. From the basic applications of HTML forms and CGI to VRML, ActiveX, and Java, the Web programming arsenal provides a potent means for putting together knockout presentations, collecting data, and automating sites. Just as object-oriented tools allow software developers to move away from reinventing wheels, the generation of code for Web use has already moved away from shell commands and toward application programming interfaces (APIs).

This progress will allow faster coding, and the "smart" development environment will do more low-level housekeeping work so that the finished executable is lean, clean, and ready for the Web. As a Web designer, the more options that exist for high-speed, fun applications that don't require all of the fancy extras we discussed in the last chapter, the more fun you're going to have creating dynamic, interactive, and unique Web sites.

Programming is a highly skilled field, so much so that some programmers spend their entire professional lives focused on the mastery of one language. Typically, programmers are important members of the team, since their typically meticulous, in-depth way of thinking can bring clarity and ideas to many aspects of Web design.

As with every individual discipline within Web design, the basic rules of the field always apply. If you're doing it yourself, make sure you have the time to focus on the specific skills involved, such as writing code or scripts for your Web site. If you do your own programming, you must be able to work that code and those scripts, debugging where necessary and streamlining where possible. The other, strong option is to get

familiar with some of the aspects of Web programming and hire specialists or outsource more detailed programming jobs to individuals capable of writing, reviewing, and debugging code.

The Originals—Forms and CGI

The simplest examples of programming for the Web are HTML forms. A form is the means by which user input at the browser can be entered, put somewhere, and acted upon in some way. There are basic tags that specify text input, check boxes, and "do something" buttons (see Figure 18-1).

Once the form has been filled out, a browser then submits the form's contents to its destination, where the server then follows instructions in order to process the information. The instructions are directed to the Common Gateway Interface (CGI), which tells the server's host processor to run certain code acting on the input and deliver the resulting output (see Figure 18-2).

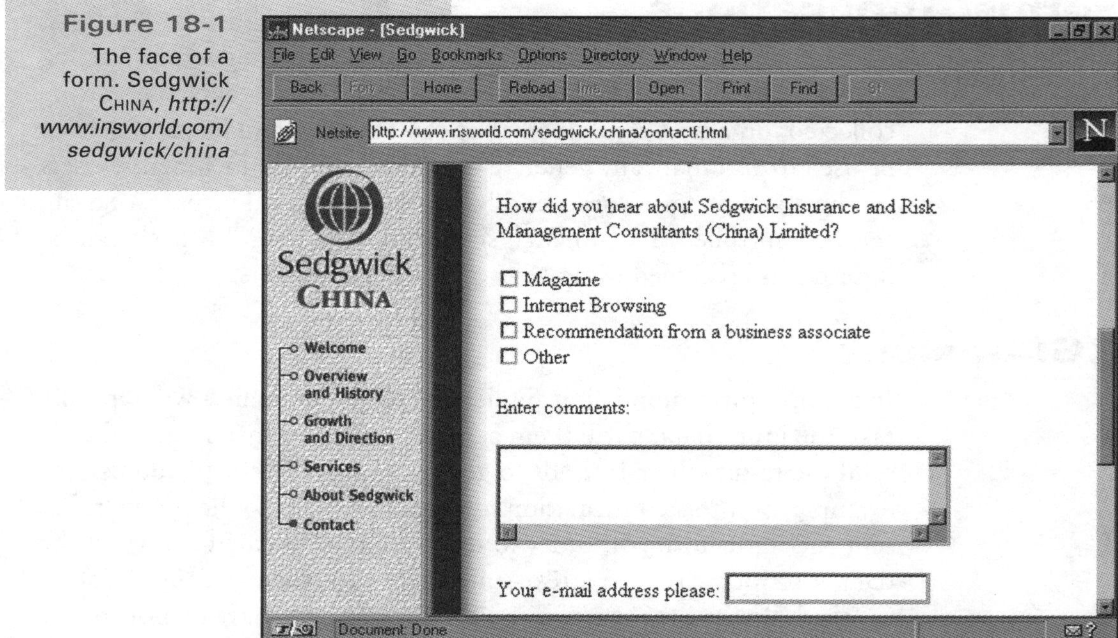

Figure 18-1 The face of a form. Sedgwick CHINA, *http://www.insworld.com/sedgwick/china*

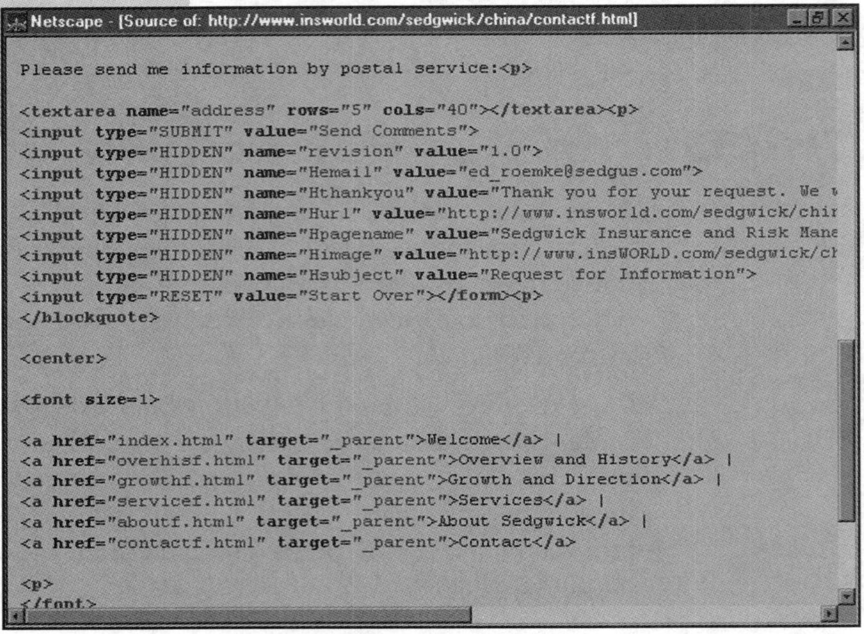

Figure 18-2 The CGI behind the form, Sedgwick CHINA

Netscape - [Source of: http://www.insworld.com/sedgwick/china/contactf.html]

```
Please send me information by postal service:<p>

<textarea name="address" rows="5" cols="40"></textarea><p>
<input type="SUBMIT" value="Send Comments">
<input type="HIDDEN" name="revision" value="1.0">
<input type="HIDDEN" name="Hemail" value="ed_roemke@sedgus.com">
<input type="HIDDEN" name="Hthankyou" value="Thank you for your request. We w
<input type="HIDDEN" name="Hurl" value="http://www.insworld.com/sedgwick/chir
<input type="HIDDEN" name="Hpagename" value="Sedgwick Insurance and Risk Mane
<input type="HIDDEN" name="Himage" value="http://www.insWORLD.com/sedgwick/ch
<input type="HIDDEN" name="Hsubject" value="Request for Information">
<input type="RESET" value="Start Over"></form><p>
</blockquote>

<center>

<font size=1>

<a href="index.html" target="_parent">Welcome</a> |
<a href="overhisf.html" target="_parent">Overview and History</a> |
<a href="growthf.html" target="_parent">Growth and Direction</a> |
<a href="servicef.html" target="_parent">Services</a> |
<a href="aboutf.html" target="_parent">About Sedgwick</a> |
<a href="contactf.html" target="_parent">Contact</a>

<p>
</font>
```

Forms Applications

Many useful applications can be written using forms and CGI—catalog orders and comment logs are obvious examples. A database can be collected, organized, and queried by these means, and its contents can be used to automatically generate or update HTML documents. Users can be asked for passwords, and levels of access to all or parts of a site can be controlled. Documents, sites, and even the Web itself can be indexed and searched using keywords and parameters.

CGI Basics

In a simple form submission application, CGI commands will typically take the input data, parse them according to their meaning, and then send the result where it needs to go—to someone's e-mail address, for example, or into a confirmation message to be sent to the browser that sent the input form. In order to do more sophisticated things to the data, a script written in a text-suited language such as PERL is often invoked. By the time you're into PERL scripts, you have demonstrated a fairly serious commitment to programming, and these are not the waters for beginning swimmers!

A potential drawback of the shell-based CGI model is the demand placed on the CPU by multiple scripts. On a busy site with several forms requiring processing, the load can be enough to distract the Web server from its main task—sending documents when browsers request them. This slows response and makes the site appear sluggish to users, even if the pages are short, the graphics, optimized, and the connection, speedy.

APIs to the Rescue

Thanks to the rapid growth of Web development resources, designer-friendly alternatives are appearing on the scene. Several server packages now offer toolkits and "wizards" to guide the creation of back-end code without requiring knowledge of CGI or scripting. An additional advantage to this model is the ability of the API environment to optimize the code and produce a faster, less CPU-intensive executable.

Other features showing up in the server-companion arena include database-driven applications that allow nonprogrammers to manage large amounts of information and deliver it in HTML format through the use of templates, instead of inserting the tags manually. This can free a solo designer from the chore of plugging in hundreds of angle brackets and allow him or her to concentrate instead on the big picture, or it can facilitate the creation of turnkey Web sites that update themselves with user input.

Motion and Modeling

Some contemporary methods of creating animated images on the Web involve server push or client pull of frame lists, analogous to "flip books" of static images. We've seen examples of these throughout *Web Design.* The resources consumed by these techniques tend to be steep in terms of processor and bandwidth usage, and they perform erratically on slower modem connections.

In addition, little interactive control is available. The movie runs its course and then quits, without giving the viewing user the ability to scroll or change the animation's speed. We are able to start and stop runmovies via HTML code, but this is akin to only being able to turn your computer off and on—and it doing whatever it wants to, offering no fun and games to you, the user. This linear and passive model goes against the interactive ideas that new media hold high.

Fortunately, as Web browser technology improves, animation features are being added in the form of plug-ins, as described in Chapter 17. We've looked at two virtual world options, Apple's Quick-Time Virtual Reality (QTVR) and Virtual Reality Modeling Language (VRML). QTVR that involve seaming multiple photographs together to create panoramic views. VRML, on the other hand, is an evolving programming language—currently about to enter its second draft. VRML packages a series of geometric or rendered art together with a user navigation control. In a VRML "world," one can spin around, stop, back up, and move up and down all with simple mouse movements (see Figure 18-3).

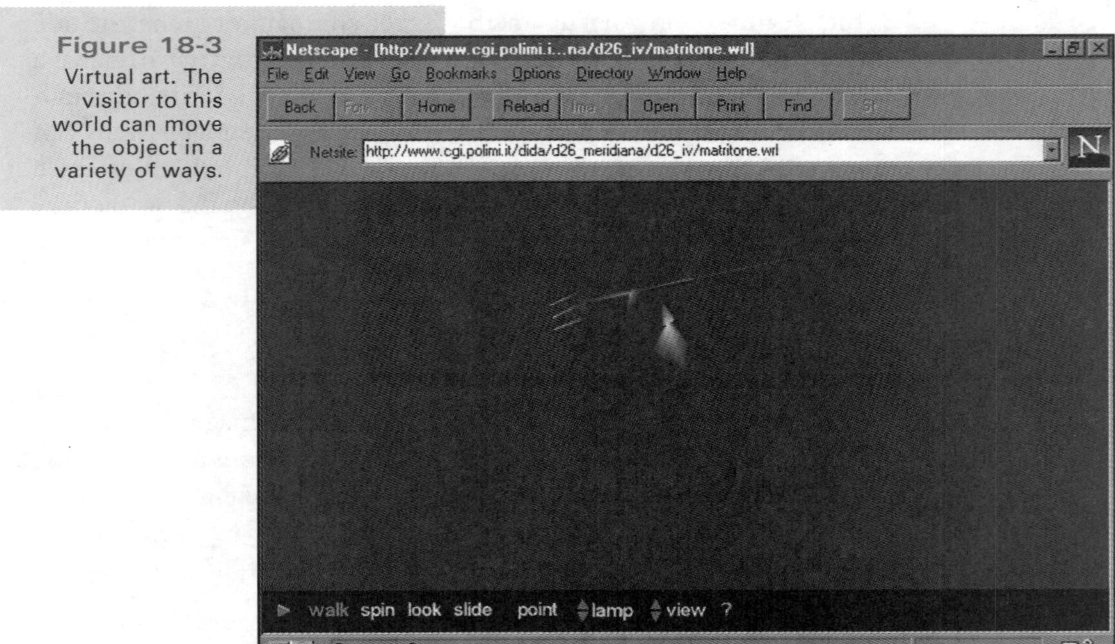

Figure 18-3 Virtual art. The visitor to this world can move the object in a variety of ways.

When VRML goes down in Web history, Mark Pesce will be counted among its founding fathers, since his vision has shaped so much of the reality in VRML. Mark described the early history of VRML in a keynote address for the World Wide Web Developer's Days in Darmstadt, Germany, 1995:

> *"Early in 1994, working with Tony Parisi, I developed a three-dimensional equivalent of HTML and a "helper app" which could work in conjunction with an HTML-based Web browser. We called the application 'Labyrinth.' In February of 1994, looking through the Web pages at CERN, we found that Tim Berners Lee believed that a perceptualized Web would be an important step toward a rich Web. Over a series of e-mails, we found ourselves invited to present our work in Geneva, at the First International Conference on the World Wide Web.*
>
> *"At the conference, Dave Raggett and TimBL had organized a 'birds-of-a-feather' session to discuss 'Virtual Reality Markup Languages and the World Wide Web.' It was clear that there was intense interest, at CERN, NCSA, and other places, to provide some more perceptualized interface to the Web. While our work was preliminary, it was also clear that a more industrial-strength approach to a VRML (as it was now called) was necessary.*
>
> *"With plenty of help from Brian Behlendorf, the sysop for Wired magazine, and the blessing of Wired (who donated server space and bandwidth) we established a mailing list for interested parties. To our pleasant surprise, within a month we had two thousand people worldwide eagerly engaged in a discussion of what VRML should be.*
>
> *"In the very early days, we confronted two issues directly: first—should we 'reinvent the wheel' or adapt an existing, even commercial implementation as the basis for VRML? The consensus of the list membership was that an existing solution would be preferable to something 'hacked up' by us. It would also bring us to an implementation phase considerably faster. We asked the list members to nominate candidates and, after a*

three-month process, settled on the ASCII format of Silicon Graphics' Open Inventor language. They agreed to place this data format into the public domain and further contributed QvLib, a C++ class library which can be linked into any VRML application and is used to parse VRML into an internal object representation. This work, by Gavin Bell and Paul Strauss of SGI, is a core technology of VRML and forms the basis of something that has become as integral to VRML as libwww is to the Web.

"The second and more vexing issue concerned scope. While HTML grew organically out of a community's needs for a hypermedia system where none existed previously, the same could not be said for virtual reality. Films, from Brainstorm to Lawnmower Man, and implementations as varied as 'Dactyl Nightmare' and 'PLACEHOLDER' gave their own rendering of the feature set essential to a virtual world. The Web provided some guidelines for a minimal feature set, but beyond that lay a gray area of possibilities so broad they could easily choke any development effort in language wars and other semantic skirmishes. For this reason the consensus of the list membership is that VRML in its 1.0 specification is not highly interactive but merely replicates the functionality of HTML in its ability to 'inline' objects and 'anchor' objects (down to the polygon level) to other items within the Web. As we well know, even that limited interactivity gives HTML and VRML a very broad range of possibilities."

Although VRML may not be an application that the Web designer is currently employing in commercial Web site design, the important thing to remember about it is that it *interacts* with other items within the Web. This provides a very rich atmosphere for potential uses of it and other virtual reality applications such as we've examined with QTVR. The point is that programming for the Web is not only about forms; it is about vision, dimension, and the creation of interactivity within visual dimensions through computer languages (see Figure 18-4). Nothing is more compelling in my mind than the possible uses—interactive art, object display, and the creation of entire environments—that virtual reality offers designers and their clients in years to come.

Figure 18-4
An example of VRML code

Netscape - [Source of: http://www.cgi.polimi.it/dida/d26_meridiana/d26_iv/matritone.wrl]

```
#VRML V1.0 ascii

Separator {
   WWWAnchor {
name "d26melod.wrl"
description "MERIDIANA"

    Separator {
        Info {
            string      "matritone.iv.1"
        }
        Translation {
            translation 15 283.57 0
        }
        Coordinate3 {
            point       [ -14.751 -8.493 0,
                              -16.014 -10.238 0,
                              -16.857 -12.163 0,
                              -17.398 -15.292 0,
                              -17.579 -17.639 0,
                              -17.097 -19.263 0,
                              -16.496 -21.309 0,
                              -16.746 -23.962 0,
                              -16.857 -24.089 0,
                              -17.412 -25.16 0,
                              -17.761 -26.408 0,
                              -17.88 -27.748 0,
                              -17.761 -29.087 0,
```

Heating Up the Brew

One of the biggest buzzes to hit the Web in the past year has been Sun's Java programming language, which allows developers to package objects with a self-extracting piece of streamlined, platform-independent code. The package gets sent to the browser, where it is "unzipped" and automatically run. The objects in the package are typically images for an animated sequence, but they may also include anything from audio samples, to graphing or chart-plotting data, to graphics that change appearance when the mouse pointer moves over them.

The compactness of Java applets allows far speedier-appearing animations than server push can afford, and Java has a vastly lower cost in terms of server overhead; most of the display work gets done by the client machine after the package is delivered. But animations are only one of many uses for this powerful language, and many new releases of server software are incorporating integral API-type support for creation of Java modules.

Microsoft, not wanting to be outdone as it jockeys for pole position in the Web platform races, has been promoting its VBScript, a Java-like set of extensions to its popular Visual Basic language. At the same time they are developing ActiveX, an object-oriented front end for VBScript, Java, and other high-level languages. A great deal about the future of these languages can be learned from a visit to Microsoft's home pages, http://www.microsoft.com/. There, the Web designer can seek out current, breaking news about Microsoft's technologies, which there is a lot of buzz but few current examples and models to share.

Bug Patrol

A course in computer programming fundamentals is obviously beyond the scope of this book. If you have a background in any high-level language, then the transition to designing applications for a Web site will probably be a simple one. On the other hand, novices won't be out of luck, because many big software manufacturers are going out of their way to make everyone an object-oriented maven before we can all blink.

But no matter how intelligent the tools become, programming axioms will always ring true. A few reminders came my way from Phil Stevens, whom we've already met in earlier chapters, and who has been programming since he was too young to remember. These can keep you sane as you or your team members hack away. They are offered in the spirit that programming is going to be a big part of the Web designer's life, and so remembering these ideas when coding, or wondering why your programmer won't talk to you just yet, will help get you through the day.

- When coding, expect and test for incorrect input, user error, and misprocessed forms.
- Use comments liberally. You just may have to come back and debug you own code.
- When the only tool you have is a hammer, everything starts to look like a nail.

- For back-end code, consider how much of a burden you're going to place on the machine. There may be a less CPU-intensive solution.
- For packaged executables, be considerate of the end user. Don't load a page down with a dozen twiddlies, twirlies, flashers, and beeping nuisances.
- If you're new to programming, have a guru check out your code before you install it on a live site. The system you don't crash may be your own.

A Living, Breathing Organism That Runs, not Crawls

The Web is already alive and crawling. Proof of its life is its growth cycle, which can be viewed without a microscope. Evidence of its breath can be heard world 'round as people ooh and ahh their way through the technology. That it crawls is a reality both fans and Web designers are all too aware of as they wait for graphics to load, and as they glimpse the possibilities through the often visually clunky but conceptually exciting end-results of Java or VRML.

This is not to say that Web programming is free of its temper tantrums. Certain problems with Java have sent programmers, Web designers, and the watching public into a frenzy of concern over what it can do to people's machinery, and the machinery of the Web itself.

Nevertheless, I believe programming is going to be the growth hormone the Web needs. Clever programming has in a sense become the workaround for bandwidth restrictions, and as a result, we're going to be empowered by the end results. Concise programs that have been built for speed and accuracy will lend their spirit and strength so that this crawling organism will one day shake off the silk strands it has become tangled in and run, leading the way toward a whole lot of yet unknowable fun for Web designers and Web fans alike.

Audience, Audience, Audience!

Kim Silk-Copeland
The Discovery Channel, Canada
http://www.discovery.ca

I became interested in the World Wide Web in the fall of 1993. I found the Web fascinating—a huge storehouse of information without organization or authority: at best, a librarian's playground; at worst, a living nightmare. The challenge was set. I wanted to participate in the development of this new and exciting medium. Through teaching myself to "surf the Net" and learning HTML, I am lucky enough to be managing and constantly recreating one of Canada's most respected web site"

Kim sees herself from two very different angles. One is as a user of the web, the other is as a web designer. This perspective is especially strengthening to her awareness of the importance of the web audience. I believe that every web author must consider their audience first and last when designing and maintaining their web site. By remembering who they are designing for, the mass volume of web sites out there would improve exponentially.

With strengths in usability of net sites, and organization of information, a visit to the Discover Channel's page demonstrates Kim's message that content must be presented sensibly in order for users can quickly find the information they need becomes clear.

Future hopes include more development in Java technology, uniform web-browsing capabilities, and of course that web designers will consider their audience before designing sites.

Who, What, Where, and Why

Thea Partridge
Thea ArtWorks
http://www.cyberbabe.com/

WebWitch Thea Partridge answers these questions.

Who?

"I am an artist and my chosen tool is the computer."

What?

"I started this exploration of the computer as creative tool in 1980, learning to program with PL1, using punch cards on a main frame computer at the University of Toronto. Since 1980, as a designer and artist, I have worked with computers. I have owned an Apple II, a DOS PC, a Lisa and of course a couple of Macs."

Where?

"Currently and very recently, Vancouver, BC is my home."

Why?

"Why, not?

I feel myself very fortunate to live in an age when analytic and logic skills can coexist and enhance the visual skills of color, space and line. The rhythms of design and the passions of the artist thrive well in this world of computer graphics."

chapter 19

Systems Administration

Once a Web site is produced, the next step is to put it on display for the world to see (and critique). The Web server, and the people and systems that support it, are the means by which HTML documents and all their accompanying media are delivered to the audience. As a Web designer, it is up to you to ensure that the quality and performance of the server your Web sites sit on are up to par. This, then, requires you to determine whether to have an in-house system set up or to outsource the process that will make Web sites come to life.

If server systems and their administration aren't already a part of your business, there are several considerations to be aware of. Cost of hardware, software, and network bandwidth are obvious primary factors. Web servers need to be powerful machinery, capable of running sophisticated software, and having advanced hardware features that allow for power networking. Security, reliability, and management of computing resources needed for a Web server are additional items that need to be addressed.

Learning the skills necessary to run a highly trafficked server smoothly requires tremendous effort. For the Web designer with a strong background in technical matters or a willingness to spend some time studying the fundamentals, systems administration is the means for exerting the most control over the technical management and maintenance of a Web site, but, as so often mentioned in this book, if you or your team do not have the resources to do this—don't. Find an individual or company that is capable of helping you make wise, informed decisions on how to address these issues.

Even if the choice is to go with an outside source, or to hire a team member willing to spend time under the hood making the machinery behind the design hum, it's smart to be able to talk shop with the mechanic. By understanding the basics of Web servers and their care and feeding, you can make better decisions regarding service provision. You also can avoid many of the pitfalls associated with growth or changes in your sites.

Web Servers

In its most basic form, a Web server is quite a logical system. A software program called a *daemon* runs on a computer attached to a network.

This program *sleeps,* consuming almost no system resources, until it receives a browser request for an HTML document. The daemon then wakes up, processes the request, and looks for the document. If it finds it, it then sends the document across the network to be displayed by a browser on the requester's end.

There are now dozens of server programs, or HyperText Transport Protocol Daemons (HTTPD), available for all common hardware and OS platforms. The costs range from nothing for public domain UNIX servers to hundreds or thousands of dollars for packages with bells and whistles such as secure transaction features, built-in search engines, and graphical administration tools.

Of course, when in common usage we speak of the Web server, we are often referring to the machine and operating system under which the HTTPD software runs, and even the means by which the machine connects to the Internet. All of these variables will influence the performance, complexity, reliability, and ease of dealing with the functioning Web site.

Hardware

If your Web design business plans on buying a system to run as a dedicated Web server, there's almost no such thing as too much CPU power or too fast disk access. Backup mechanisms should be a principal concern, as one electrical hiccup could cause the loss of months of content generation, design, and usage statistics. Multiprocessor machines will have the advantage of dealing with peak request loads and back-end executable scripts better than single-CPU boxes.

For disk space, be prepared to consider a configuration that provides faster transfer rates and lower data failure. And, as my friend Phil likes to say, "Don't plan on using your fancy 3-D rendering software or playing Duke Nukem" on the machine while the server is handling lots of requests.

The next step is to get a dedicated, high-speed network connection. A 56K frame relay is a minimum for Web service, and even this will support only around four or five simultaneous browser sessions before becoming visibly burdened. ISDN is faster but is notoriously difficult to set up and configure and economically unattractive for continuous connection. Above ISDN we begin looking at fractional to full T1 lines, which can cost well over a thousand dollars per month. And that's only for the bandwidth—there's still the cost of network hardware!

In addition to the network line, some sort of device must sit between it and the computer that hosts the server. Depending upon the type of connection, this may be a terminal adapter, a packet-switching device, or a router, which will also need to be configured for use. These are complex, highly specialized issues—well outside the knowledge base of the typically media-oriented Web designer—and it may be well worth it to engage the services of a qualified consultant to make sure the job gets done, and gets done well.

Common OS Platforms and Servers for the Web

The headings that follow introduce common operating system and server platforms for Web servers. Again, the point is to encourage Web designers to gain an understanding of the technology as it will relate to them. Web designers may have heard what UNIX, Windows NT, and Mac Platforms are, but until they gain some idea of the way they work, they will find it very difficult to communicate with the systems administrator to get the most out of the unique relationship that exists between the two ends of the Web design industry—the matter, and the means by which it is delivered.

UNIX

Since the Internet grew largely from interconnected mainframe-based networks, UNIX is by far the most common OS platform encountered in the server arena. The first HTTPD programs developed were created by CERN and the NCSA at UIUC. These are both public-domain applications, very widely used and well documented. The downside is that they offer very few of the extra features that many of the commercial solutions, such as Netscape's new generation of servers known as Suitespot (Figure 19-1), offer.

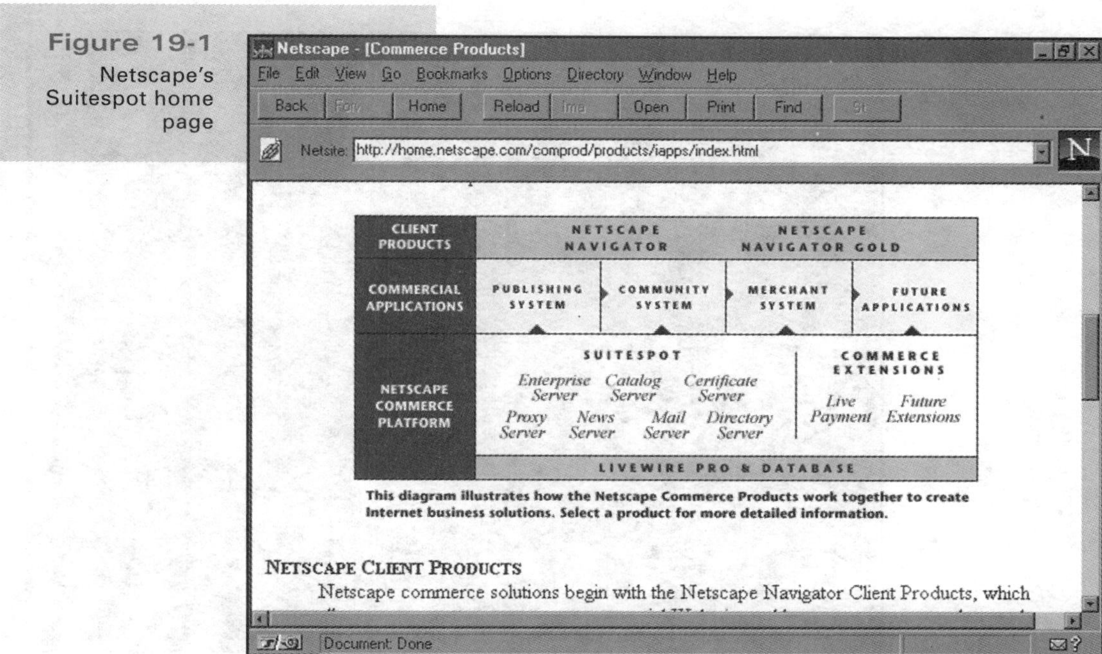

Figure 19-1 Netscape's Suitespot home page

The prevalence of UNIX on the Internet means that commercial releases of server software will continue to build on this foundation, but for many people the cryptic nature of UNIX commands is a deterrent (Figure 19-2). Administration of a UNIX-based server that is secure, efficient, and reliable can be a daunting chore for the uninitiated, but in capable hands the operating system is well-suited to the demands of the Web.

Windows NT

This is the industrial strength version of Microsoft's operating system (OS); it is rapidly becoming the platform of choice in many small and medium-sized corporate networks. Because of the current industry growth in the Intranet market, as well as the general ease of use and familiarity that Windows provides, many server solutions are available on NT. Also, the feature lists tend to be impressive and are growing practically on a daily basis.

Figure 19-2
UNIX commands from within a UNIX shell

```
telnet - azstarnet.com [default:0]
File  Edit  Setup  Help
 dirs [-l]                          echo [-neE] [arg ...]
 enable [-n] [name ...]             eval [arg ...]
 exec [ [-] file [redirection ...]] exit [n]
 export [-n] [-f] [name ...] or exp fc [-e ename] [-nlr] [first] [last
 fg [job_spec]                      for NAME [in WORDS ... ;] do COMMA
 function NAME { COMMANDS ; } or NA getopts optstring name [arg]
 hash [-r] [name ...]               help [pattern ...]
 history [n] [ [-awrn] [filename]]  if COMMANDS; then COMMANDS; [ elif
 jobs [-lnp] [jobspec ...] | jobs - kill [-s sigspec | -sigspec] [pid
 let arg [arg ...]                  local name[=value] ...
 logout                             popd [+n | -n]
 pushd [dir | +n | -n]              pwd
 read [-r] [name ...]               readonly [-n] [-f] [name ...] or r
 return [n]                         select NAME [in WORDS ... ;] do CO
 set [--abefhknotuvxldHCP] [-o opti shift [n]
 source filename                    suspend [-f]
 test [expr]                        times
 trap [arg] [signal_spec]           type [-all] [-type | -path] [name
 typeset [-[frxi]] name[=value] ... ulimit [-SHacdfmstpnuv [limit]]
 umask [-S] [mode]                  unalias [-a] [name ...]
 unset [-f] [-v] [name ...]         until COMMANDS; do COMMANDS; done
 variables - Some variable names an wait [n]
 while COMMANDS; do COMMANDS; done  { COMMANDS }
bash$
```

Advantages of the NT platform include relative ease of setup, excellent security features, and a growing market share that ensures lively applications development and support. A downside can be the hardware resources demanded by the operating system. All in all, with the type of technologies that Microsoft is working on for the Web, the NT platform will likely become a dominant one in the Web service field (Figure 19-3).

Macintosh

For do-it-yourself Web server setups, the Macintosh platform is the easiest way to go. TCP/IP implementation has been native since the release of System 7.5, and many administrative tasks can be accomplished through simple mouse clicks. However, communication speed limitations can bog down a Mac server, since most 680*x*0 machines cannot support more than 64 simultaneous socket connections. Also, the release of Apple's Open Transport Protocol for Power PCs has been plagued with difficulties. If you don't foresee a lot of traffic, it's certainly an option, but at present it's simply not a serious contender for busy sites.

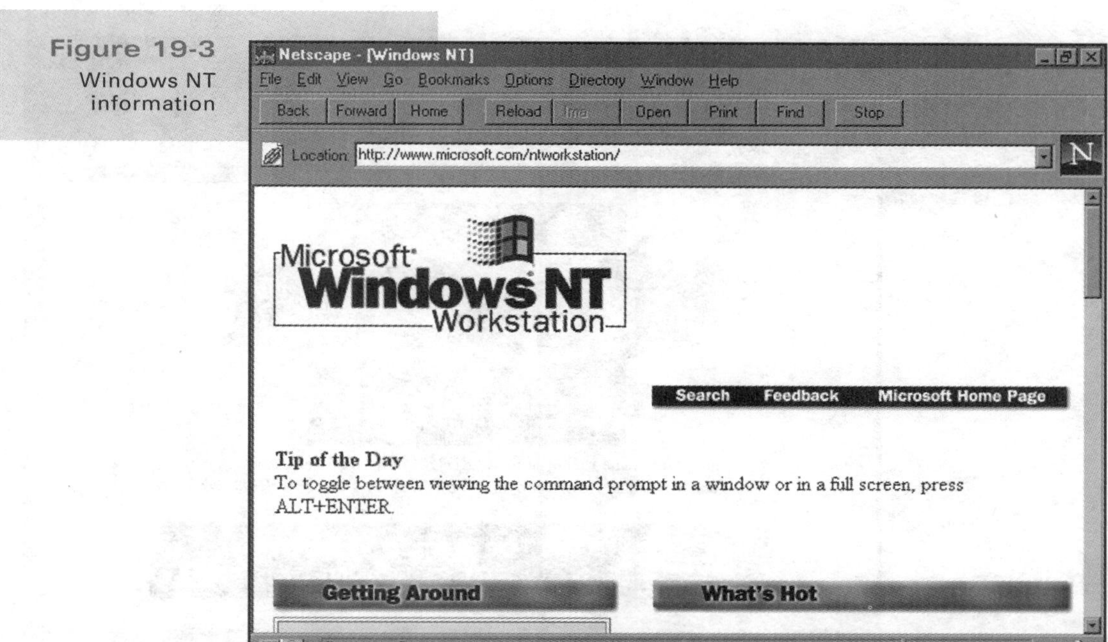

Figure 19-3 Windows NT information

A few others should be mentioned by name, as they each offer a variety of features that may be important to your particular needs. These include Netscape Netsite and O'Reilly Website (Figure 19-4). There is a great deal of information available on these servers all over the Web. Check Appendix F for more resources. The bottom line is that, regardless of what is chosen, the selection of Web server software should be based on its compatibility with your hardware configuration and operating system, its documentation, and whether its additional features fit your needs.

To Serve or Not to Serve

If this discussion has piqued your curiosity, you may find it worthwhile to learn more about the technology involved. However, if you, like me, cringe at the thought of having to put a lot of time and energy into systems administration, choosing someone or somewhere else to run servers is a good idea. At DesertNet, we've developed an interesting blend. We have our own servers, running at a remote site, with dedicated

Figure 19-4
O'Reilly's Website home page

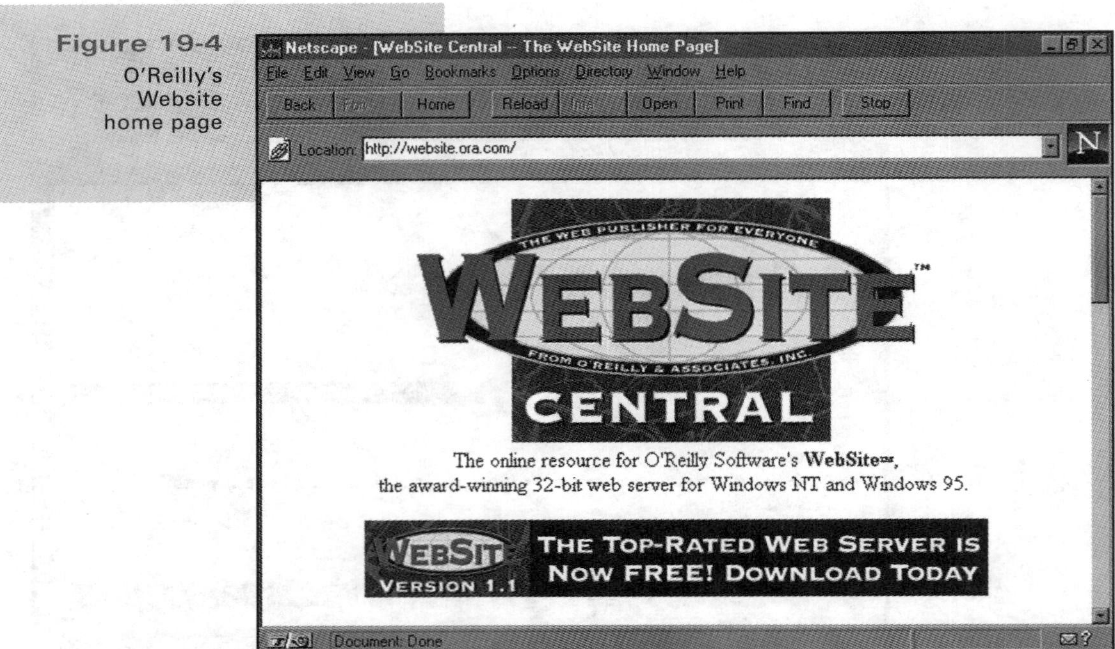

systems administrators. We very rarely have to be concerned about how those servers are operating. We consult where necessary and request different items, but thanks to the quality service we receive, the headaches are avoided.

Outsourcing Systems Administration Services

If the choice is not to serve, then consider outsourcing the responsibility to a Web service provider. Bear in mind that there's a lot of variation in the levels of service offered, and even more in the expertise of the purveyors. How do you determine the type of service and provider that will meet your present and future needs, and what can you expect from the relationship? We've offered a few guidelines that will hopefully aid you in making this critical decision.

Beware the Cottage ISP

One indicator of the explosive growth of the Internet, and the WWW in particular, is the number of Internet Service Providers (ISPs) setting up shop all over. All one needs, it seems, is a good, fast machine, a bank of modems and phone lines, and a network connection, and voilà! Instant cash cow. Remember when, early on in this book, we laughed a bit at the FlyByNite.com Web design model? That model is a direct outgrowth of the way ISPs have cropped up like so many mushrooms after a good, hard rain.

When we add to our FlyByNite model the ability to sell Web page design and hosting services, the ISP can become a potential solution in the Web designer's search for a home for his or her sites. But problems often come of choosing the local ISP who happens to have the best rates this week, and some of the headaches that can result are the type for which no panacea exists.

Many ISPs, in their zeal to attract dialup customers and Web sites, sell their services, lines, and bandwidth on too thin a margin or even below their actual cost. A few months or a year down the road, when the bills are too steep to pay, and disgruntled users are leaving in droves because of endless busy signals, they go belly up. Suddenly their Web server clients have to find new provision and may have to change URLs and script parameters to cope with a new IP address and system policies. Or perhaps the ISP places its Usenet newsfeed and mailserver on the same underpowered machine hosting all of its clients' Web pages, and the overloaded system creaks and groans under the strain.

Other stressed-out ISPs may skimp on tech support, hiring college students who may understand how to write code and explain Internet technicalities but can't cope with the volume of calls coming in. Do you want a business relationship with an enterprise in these circumstances? My earliest work in the Web design field was overrun with difficulties because of an ISP like this. It literally took an aggressive attorney to settle the score between us, and the entire experience has obviously left a bad, bad taste in my mouth.

The 800-Pound Gorillas

At the other end of the ISP scale are the giants of the marketplace. These companies are typically regional or national in scale, and they usually have the resources to deal with growth and support issues. They may have a package offer for Web site hosting, with options such as virtual domain aliasing, mail accounts, and FTP access for maintenance. They may also offer secure transaction processing and script debugging, and they may even have staff available for consulting on specific customer issues. Their business models tend to be more sound than those of some of the startups, but they can just as easily be plagued with crashing systems, insufficient capacity, and ineffective support if they aren't careful.

How Do I Know What to Choose?

The whole business of Internet service provision is still shaking itself out, and the best strategy is to ask as many questions as possible and run some tests on your own. Do some surfing—go to the Web sites of the various companies whose services you are considering. How fast do the pages load? Do you get server timeout messages? If you've got the tools and the know-how, run network utilities such as ping and traceroute to see just where the packets are going. This will give you some idea about their infrastructure, and whether they can handle a high request load. Also, talk to their existing clients. There's probably no better way to gauge the ability of a service provider to handle your needs than to talk to someone whose needs are being handled by that provider.

When you ask questions of your potential Web service provider, here are things you should consider:

- What are the network connection and the maximum bandwidth?
- What is the hardware configuration? Are there regular upgrades?
- What is the OS?
- What is the backup policy? How close are backups to being fail-safe?
- How easily and quickly can you reach someone if you have a question?

- If you will be dialing in to do maintenance, do they have a no-busy guarantee?
- Is there someone available to debug or optimize back-end code?
- How many clients does the provider currently serve, and may you contact them?

Once you've got your provision solution figured out, then it's just a simple matter of setting your material onto the Web server and seeing your sites come to life. But in order to do the best job you can, and to help your provider do its best, it helps to know just *how* to talk to its representatives.

Having a Web service provider takes some of the systems administration burden off the Web designer's shoulders. But if you intend to run your Web sites like the well-oiled machine you've designed them to be, learn these technical points as thoroughly as possible.

Talk the Tech Talk

When I asked our systems administrators what they would like to see go in this chapter, one of the first things they said was "teach those Web designers how to talk!" Being a creative bunch, those of us in Web design are unlikely to be as concerned with the difference between the meanings of words such as *standard* and *convention.* For the people who have learned computers as a science, language is an absolute. There can be no straying from the technical, scientific meaning. Therefore, it's important for Web designers to learn some of this language:

- **IP addresses and domains**. Every location on the Internet has its own unique address, called an IP number. It looks something like "127.0.0.1" and provides an unambiguous way for all other locations on the Internet to refer to it. A domain name is a human-readable address, such as "server.hostname.com" (see Figure 19-5), that is translated into an IP address by the central nameservice database of InterNIC. Your site may have its own fully qualified domain, have an aliased domain, or be a branch of your host's Web server directory. It's important to know which it is and understand how it works.

- **POP and SMTP**. These are the protocols used for dealing with e-mail. If you are using mailto:, or any sort of mailbot-type script, on your site you should have a working knowledge of what goes on in a mail session.

- **FTP**. This is how you will most likely be putting files onto the server. Find out whether your server needs you to specify file types when they are transferred—HTML files need to be put in ASCII format, whereas graphic and multimedia files will usually be binary (Figure 19-6).

- **Telnet.** In order to do maintenance on your site, it is often easiest to telnet directly to the server and issue commands (Figure 19-7). For instance, you can move a large multimedia file by a simple RENAME command in a telnet session rather than spending half an hour or more uploading it to the new directory via FTP.

- **Directory paths and aliasing.** A Web server may host more than one site, or it contain different versions of a site's content depending on where the browser requests come from. In order to make this work, there will actually be different path names at the server level than what the "world" sees.

- **MIME types.** When an HTTPD server delivers a document, it needs to know what type of file it is sending in order to make sure the browser executes the proper action when it is received. The MIME extension tells the software about the content of the file. If you are dealing with multimedia extensions you may need to talk with your systems administrator to set the server up for a particular file type (Figure 19-8).

Figure 19-5 Numeric and alphabetical domains

```
NS.OPUS1.COM          192.245.12.50
NS1.ACES.COM          192.195.240.1
```

Figure 19-6
FTP in action

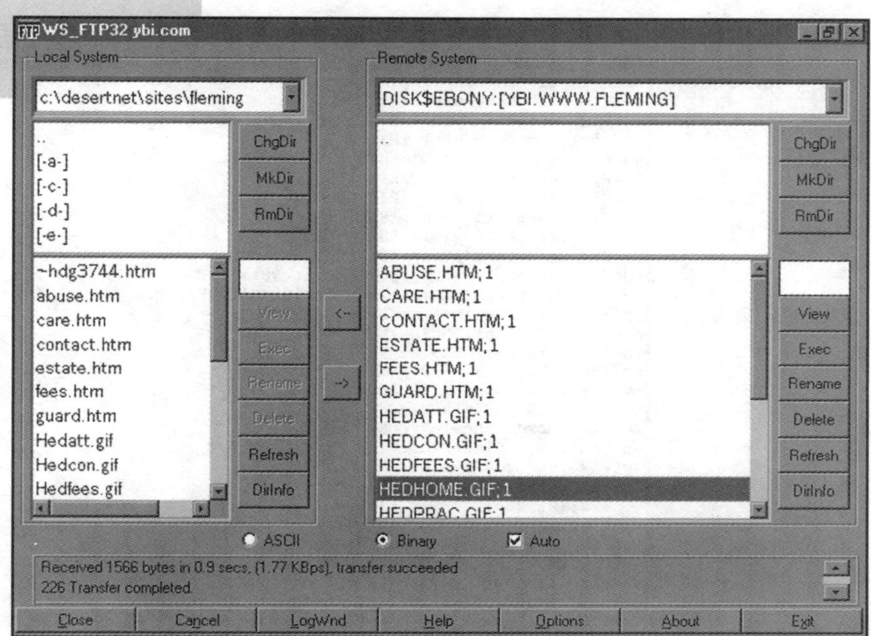

Figure 19-7
A telnet session

telnet - ybi.com [default:0]
File Edit Setup Help

```
$ set def [www]
$ dir
%DIRECT-E-OPENIN, error opening DISK$EBONY:[WWW]*.*;* as input
-RMS-E-DNF, directory not found
-SYSTEM-W-NOSUCHFILE, no such file
$ set def disk$ebony:[ybi.www]
$ dir

Directory DISK$EBONY:[YBI.WWW]

AQUA-VITA.DIR;1      AURORA.DIR;1         AWARD.GIF;1          AYBI.LST;1
AYBI01.GIF;1         AYBI02.GIF;1         AYBI03.GIF;1         AYBI04.GIF;1
AYBI05.GIF;1         AYBI06.GIF;1         AYBI07.GIF;1         AYBI08.GIF;1
AYBI09.GIF;1         AYBI10.GIF;1         AYBI11.GIF;1         AZBOOK.DIR;1
BACKTO.GIF;1         BBIMAGE.MAP;1        BOOK.DIR;1           CFIDS.DIR;1
CINDY.DIR;1          CULTHD.GIF;1         DEMOS.DIR;1          DNAHD.GIF;1
DND.DIR;1            EB.HTML;1            ECONHD.GIF;1         FLEMING.DIR;1
GWP.DIR;1            HUGH.DIR;1           INDEX.HTML;1         ITCHYTICKLE.DIR;1
LINUS.DIR;1          MAINSTAY.DIR;1       MAINSTAY.MAP;1       MOLLY.DIR;1
NAN.HTML;1           NANIMA.DIR;1         NIDET.DIR;1          NIDET.MAP;1
POETRY.DIR;1         POINTSHD.GIF;1       RAINER.DIR;1         ROBOTS.TXT;1
RULE.GIF;1           RUN.DIR;1            SSVEC.DIR;1          TALKHD.GIF;1
THIS.GIF;1           ULC.DIR;1            VALERIE.DIR;1        WANNA.GIF;1
WEHD.GIF;1           WELLMAN.DIR;1        WILDHD.GIF;1         WORK.DIR;1
WWW.DIR;1            YBI.GIF;1            YBICULT.HTML;2       YBIDNA.HTML;2
YBIECON.HTML;1       YBIMENU.GIF;1        YBIMENU.MAP;1        YBIPOINT.HTML;2
YBISITES.HTML;3      YBITALK.HTML;3       YBIWE.HTML;2

Total of 67 files.
$
```

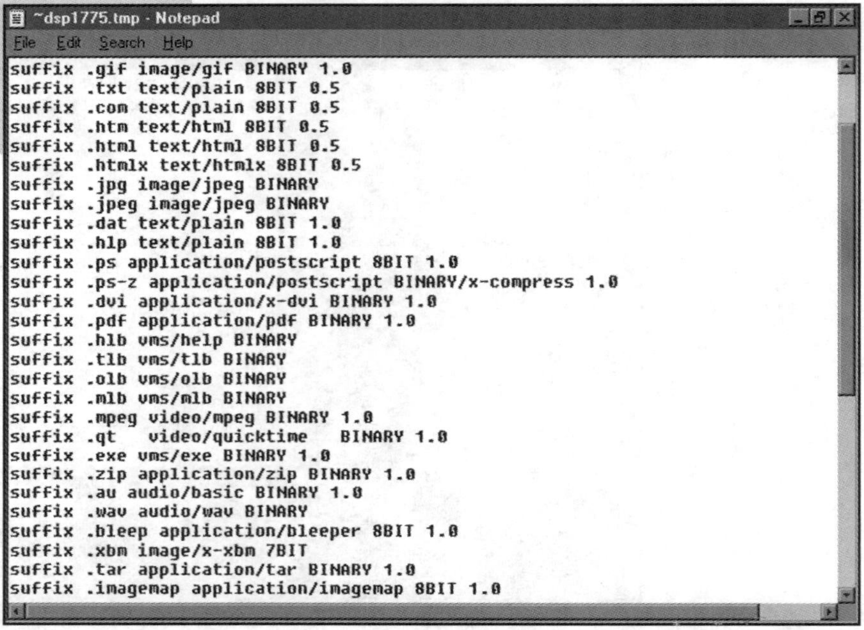

Figure 19-8
An HTTP configuration file with MIME types described

```
~dsp1775.tmp - Notepad
File  Edit  Search  Help
suffix .gif image/gif BINARY 1.0
suffix .txt text/plain 8BIT 0.5
suffix .com text/plain 8BIT 0.5
suffix .htm text/html 8BIT 0.5
suffix .html text/html 8BIT 0.5
suffix .htmlx text/htmlx 8BIT 0.5
suffix .jpg image/jpeg BINARY
suffix .jpeg image/jpeg BINARY
suffix .dat text/plain 8BIT 1.0
suffix .hlp text/plain 8BIT 1.0
suffix .ps application/postscript 8BIT 1.0
suffix .ps-z application/postscript BINARY/x-compress 1.0
suffix .dvi application/x-dvi BINARY 1.0
suffix .pdf application/pdf BINARY 1.0
suffix .hlb vms/help BINARY
suffix .tlb vms/tlb BINARY
suffix .olb vms/olb BINARY
suffix .mlb vms/mlb BINARY
suffix .mpeg video/mpeg BINARY 1.0
suffix .qt   video/quicktime   BINARY 1.0
suffix .exe vms/exe BINARY 1.0
suffix .zip application/zip BINARY 1.0
suffix .au audio/basic BINARY 1.0
suffix .wav audio/wav BINARY
suffix .bleep application/bleeper 8BIT 1.0
suffix .xbm image/x-xbm 7BIT
suffix .tar application/tar BINARY 1.0
suffix .imagemap application/imagemap 8BIT 1.0
```

- **Sockets and connections.** When a graphical browser requests an HTML document from a server, several files may be contained in the page (that is, as in-line images). Most browsers open multiple connections, also referred to as sockets, to get several things at once. In situations where many browser requests are hitting the server at once, too many connections can degrade server performance. In addition, some servers "keep alive" a browser connection for a specified amount of time, assuming there will be more activity. If you have forms that require users to spend time filling them out, you may want to specify the keep-alive interval to avoid tying up server resources.

- **Code integrity.** If you are running CGI scripts or any other type of back-end processes as part of your Web site, you need to make sure that they don't do things that might affect server performance. Ask your systems administrator to review your code to make sure it is clean and well-behaved.

- **Internet etiquette.** If you plan on promoting your site by means of e-mail or Usenet postings, make sure you follow conventions regarding acceptability of your activity. One poorly thought-out newsgroup post could result in enough e-mail traffic to bring many service providers to a grinding halt. It never hurts to ask in cases where you're unsure of the propriety of an announcement or advertisement.

- **Acceptable use policies.** Although the debates about commercial content on the Internet have been rendered moot in most instances, many ISPs have policies about what type of content and activity is or is not acceptable on their system. You should have a copy of your provider's AUP in writing and refer to it whenever there is a question of propriety.

Ready to Serve

With these fundamentals, the Web designer is in a good position to make decisions regarding how he or she will manage the serving of sites. Remember, we can write, do HTML, create stunning graphics, juggle multimedia, and code terrific programs, but without Web server service, we have no site. Furthermore, if we make choices that are not optimal for our needs, we will end up with problems that can detract from our goals. Stunning work is nothing without equally stunning technical stability.

Designers and Publishers

Marianne Wroe
CamWeb Communications
http://www.campuscafe.com

With more and more news and magazine formats appearing on the web, the distinction between web designers and publishers is narrowing in scope. Marianne is the web designer for the Campus Cafe, an online magazine out of Toronto that is well-worth a visit.

"I was a boring history student . . . could be the first five words of my biography. I always liked computers for playing games, editing essays etc., but never realized the true fun of them until the spring of 1993 when I began experimenting with email and online chatting programs. from there it was a natural progression to web browsing, with Lynx! I saw an ad in the university paper for "volunteers wanted for online version of campus paper" in the fall of 1994, and signed up right away. Week after week we worked updating the campus paper. I loved it!

At that point I began working on my own page and applied to community college for Interactive Multimedia. To enhance my application, and to make a potentially boring essay much more enjoyable, I did my last term 4th year history project as a web page.

After graduation from my history BA and from the Interactive Multimedia program, I realized web design was my one true love in this world, and spent one hellish week of unemployment before landing this job I love and look forward to each day. I realize its a possibly tenuous position being a web designer (will the web exist in five years?) :) but I wouldn't trade it for any other job!"

chapter 20

Marketing on the Web

As the Web grows bigger and vaster, and information sources become layered, it becomes increasingly challenging to get your Web sites seen. And if no one sees your work, how are they going to know about the fabulous design services you offer? Web marketing, then, is an activity that involves not just the promotion of what you as a Web designer create but the projection of your company's image as a Web design firm. It is of particular importance in this transitional time to create an environment that current and potential clients will find comfortable and reliable.

The pressures that this need puts on a Web design company can be immense. First, you need the clients—how do you get them? It's one thing to hang up the FlyByNite.com shingle, another to be really dedicated to doing the best overall job of self-promotion, production, and complete, comprehensive postproduction—the marketing of Web sites.

There are straightforward techniques and a variety of philosophies that a Web designer can pick up to begin this journey. Learning them can create a basis for the development of your own individual strategies. Everyone's experience is going to be different, and because of that, marketing—which so appears to be an external activity—is actually based on a system of very personal experiences. In this chapter I'll share some experiences from my work as a Web designer with DesertNet, and I'll introduce some practical concepts for both self-promotion and the marketing of Web sites. It is my sincerest hope that this will stimulate Web designers to study their own experiences and learn for themselves what methods will work for their given model.

Company Standards and Self-Promotion

I believe that there is no such thing as shame when it comes to promoting your services. This is not to say that bragging, or putting down others, is an appropriate way of presenting oneself, but having pride in what you do is a powerful thing. I've often been astonished at how, when people truly put their minds to a task, they not only succeed but excel. In my own life, I've found that pride is wrapped up in setting goals and meeting the responsibilities and challenges involved in those goals. It's a good thing to have self-confidence and to back up that confidence with quality service. The combination is very strong and practically ensures success.

Seek out opportunities. Tell people about what you are doing, and let them know how to get in touch with you. For the Web designer, this means being fully accessible electronically—e-mail, FAX, phone numbers, and, of course, a Web site. If you're just starting out, you may want to do some free or low-cost work for businesses within your own and your coworkers' circle of family and friends, in order to develop a professional portfolio. Add to that business cards, brochures, and eventually full media kits, and you'll be well on your way to creating not only a strong self-promotional toolbox but a unified company presence. Once you have that, and once you've made yourself accessible via various forms of advertising such as yellow page ads and advertisements in local and—if you can afford it—national trade and other magazines, then the next step is to set standards for your company.

Service Standards

Service standards encompass the process of creating lists of services you are able and willing to provide, how you will provide them, how you will follow through on the service-client relationship, and how much the company will charge for those services. There are so many things to consider, including overhead costs such as advertising, salaries, insurance—the list goes on and on.

One of the most difficult challenges for me in this arena has been determining what services to offer, when to bend for a client, and when not to bend. In the first years of setting up any business, researching competitors is a helpful way of forming service standards. In Web design, this is a very difficult thing to do, because there is no current stability in the market. Independents may be charging 100 dollars—or even less—per Web page, whereas large ad agencies and design companies charge hundreds of thousands, sometimes millions, of dollars for Web site design. And here's the funny thing—what you might get from the independent could conceivably be far superior in quality.

So how do you set a standard? Start by clearly delineating what kind of services your company is able and willing to provide. Are you going to offer Web server services along with design, as we discussed in the last chapter? What about other services such as mail, mail-to-fax, or other ISP-based services? Determine what you have to offer, and what you want to offer.

Next you'll need to determine what costs are necessary to meet overhead, and then you can look beyond that to profit. The most important thing here is not to sell yourself or your partners short. This field is extremely demanding, as this book has clearly explained. Because of this, self-worth, pride in quality, and what the market will bear all play into how you should create standards for your company and your market.

There are those that will always attempt to undercut a competitor. This is the nature of the free-enterprise systems in which most readers of this book are operating. My way of coping with this is knowing that if I'm charging more than they are, then I have extensive skills and resources to bring to the job, and these more than justify the fees associated with the services my company offers. In this context, it's easy to realize that those undercutting my company are not actually competitors but are actually selling a different product to a completely different market.

I implore you as a serious Web designer to consider the importance of charging money equivalent to the worth of your time. Not only are there the issues of personal pride involved, but the push exists within the field to create some standardized costs. This is a huge issue, and I wish that it were one that could be easily addressed by saying "charge X amount" for your services. The only way a company can determine that is by evaluating individual overhead costs, combining that with a reasonable profit margin, and factoring into that what the market will bear locally, as well as nationally.

Designers, Clients, and Audience

Once a standard is set and clients begin asking for services, it is important to express to clients what Web design can and will do for their companies. Obviously this will mean different things for different people and organizations. Some will want an information-based resource for their own organizations, such as we see with the National Organization of Elder Law Attorneys (Figure 20-1). Others will just want to be on the Web because it's the "hip" thing to do. Still others are looking for a point-of-sales for products.

A Web design company that is truly versatile will have ways of meeting all of these needs. However, knowing which of these clients you want to deal with the most helps streamline your company's practice and give you more consistent results. DesertNet's Director of Marketing, John Hankinson, synthesizes the relationship between Web designer, client, and audience: "I think the first thing that a company has to do is be consistent in anything it does, and then to figure out their direction. Who do they want to sell to? Qualify your client. Qualify their audience. Then follow through on consistently meeting needs."

How We Do Our Marketing?

The best way to start is to sit down and separate things into packages. DesertNet has three design packages and three co-related presence and

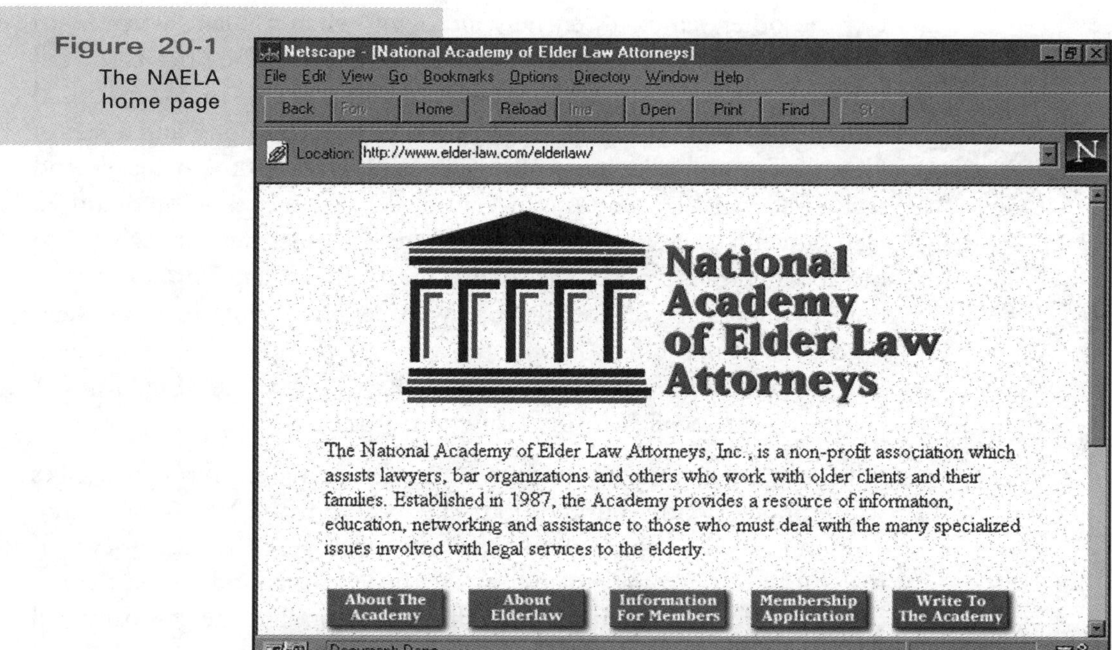

Figure 20-1 The NAELA home page

marketing packages. The first package includes just what clients will get in terms of actual site design including layout, graphics, and content. The related packages help a client promote their sites on- and offline through presence (how they'll sit on our server) and Web site marketing options, as we'll explore in just a bit.

One reason we break up our design and marketing is to give the client the greatest flexibility. Many clients come to us with an existing Web site and just want marketing. Others want just design, having their own means to market their site or no need for mass marketing as they are seeking to provide information for their own individuals, as again we see with NAELA. These clients are what we consider Inter-Intranets, a term I coined to describe organizations seeking to provide information over the Internet that is really of an intraorganizational nature.

Another reason we have strict packaging is so that both the client and the DesertNet organization know exactly what is being bought and sold. There are no questions and very few openings for clients to haggle. There's nothing more understandable then a client wanting to get a great deal.

On the other hand, it's entirely annoying when a client attempts to create a package of his or her own and recommend the price tag. I call this the "soup can" phenomenon. Imagine going into a national supermarket and pulling a can of generic mushroom soup and a can of Campbell's mushroom soup off of the shelf, going to the manager, and saying "Gee, I like the taste of Campbell's but the value of Brand X. Can you mix these into this Tupperware container here and give it to me at a mid-range price?". It sounds funny, but it happens, and there's nothing more difficult for the nice Web designer trying to meet client needs than attempting to come up with a way to bend for the client. The bottom line is that you shouldn't have to—and having clear-cut price structures will help to clarify your position.

Whatever your company decides to do, designing a series of packages will empower both you and your clients. From the Web design end, everything will fit quite neatly into one package or another—even if that package is a complete custom site, because it is understood that, at that level, that is what is necessary for the client, and the company will

be paid in kind. The client, on the other hand, will have very clear options, and this creates a good, solid relationship. The sales directive is set, the company knows its personal standards, and these can be communicated to the client in a realistic fashion.

Based on the model created, it is then important to get the options clear in the minds of both staff members and the client. Putting together a media kit that describes the options, as shown in Figure 20-2, and the company's qualifications, is a necessity. Setting up some internal training for sales staff can really assist both sales personnel and the staff at large—it keeps everyone on their toes (Figure 20-3). Next, get the details of the company's standards and responsibilities down in writing, and have an attorney help you work up a reasonable service agreement (Figure 20-4). Clearly delineate your company's offerings and responsibilities, and the responsibilities the client has to you. Finally, make sure everyone signs the dotted lines—and the checks—and gets down to work.

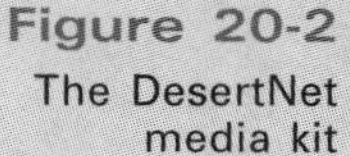

Figure 20-2
The DesertNet media kit

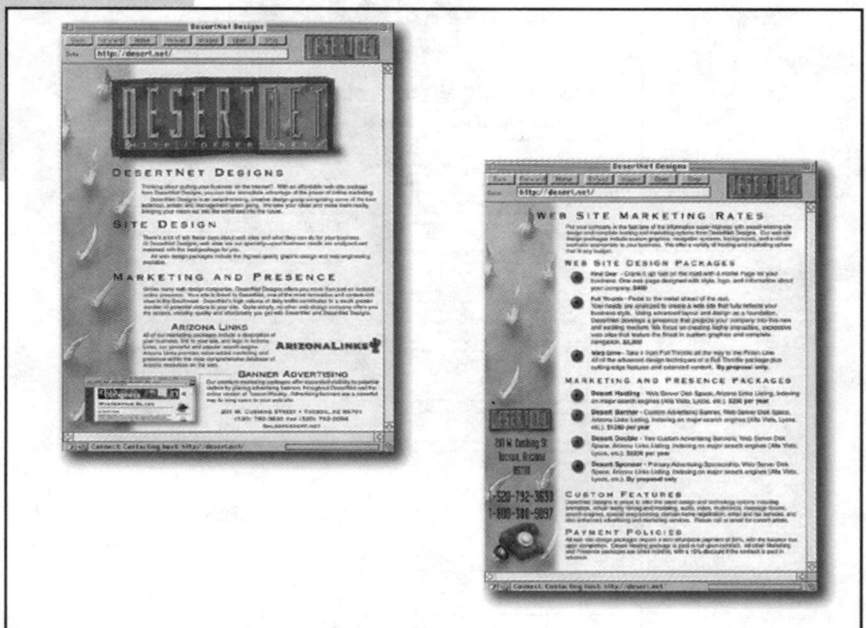

Figure 20-3
A DesertNet staff review

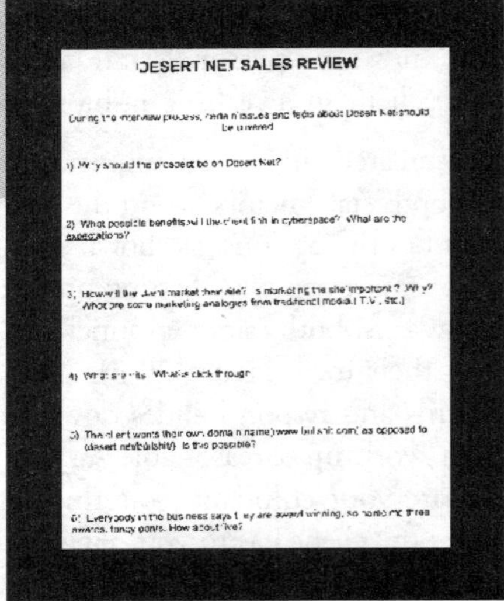

DESERT NET SALES REVIEW

1) Why should the prospect be on Desert Net?

2) What possible benefits will the client find in cyberspace? What are the expectations?

4) What are hits. What is click through

Figure 20-4
The DesertNet service agreement

World Wide Web Design Service Agreement

The service provider, also known as DesertNet, and the client, also known as THE LOFT agree to the following:

Client

DesertNet

2-27-96

Date

Client Information

Value and Benefit

We're all clients sometimes, and we know that shopping for value is important to us. We want to buy products that meet our needs—whatever those are—and don't fail us. The cost is a big issue, but there are few people that will purposely pay for bad products. There is a great deal of truth in the old saying "you get what you pay for."

It's important to help clients understand what they are getting—beyond the data delineated in the service agreement. How will this service benefit them? Why is your company the best one for the job? Why do you charge more, or less, than other companies doing Web design? John Hankinson helped me to understand value and benefit much better when he told me the following:

> *"Basically benefit and value are the starting point for where you structure your price. By establishing this, you are creating self-worth. Once you've established that there is a value to the quality of your service, you can be more confident in answering client questions. Look at Mercedes Benz. It's a supremely well-crafted vehicle, we all know that. Why? They don't market themselves, they market an image. Therefore the client doesn't say 'I'm only going to give you ten thousand dollars for this car, because that's what I'd pay down the street at Ford.'*
>
> *"Others will market toward affordability. Neither approach is wrong, but consistency is the key. DesertNet goes for Mercedes; we're asking for the dollar benefit, but we're going to give you all of these other values—incredible art, high-profile sites, full marketing, lots of hits. Sure, we're hot. We know that, but we have to change that into a sales package, a positive structure that doesn't put down others but transfers our knowledge, our self-worth—our value."*

Follow-Through and Follow-Up

Follow-through and follow-up are of critical importance for image setting and client relations. We have established our standards, our benefits, and our value. Now we need to follow through and provide them, and continue our commitment to each of these three elements.

Here the labor-intensive, quality-control aspect of the Web design business is really put to the test, with Web sites that adhere to the image and standards set by the company.

Well, easy for her to say, you may be thinking! Frankly, it *is* easy to say, but it isn't easy to do. I have often set standards that were more optimistic than I could or did reach. I have all too often had to look at something I've done and to go back and fix it because it just didn't meet the standards set. This is part of follow-through—being able to honestly assess the work, and realizing that we all have the potential for both great success and occasional failure.

When failure occurs, it's wise to look at what went into that and take the lessons home. We exemplified this in the virtual tour of the Buffalo Exchange, and I have learned a great deal from Wil as he took the time to examine where the failures were and meticulously correct them. Just this week I miserably failed with a site design. My first thought was "screw it, the client is happy," but then I went back, after encouragement from my caring peers, and evaluated what I could improve. It hurt, sure, but in the end I learned a great deal about the value of follow-through. If only by impelling us to reach out to our very best, this self-evaluation is what makes us get better and better at what we do.

Finally, we need to follow up. This is an essential part of creating, maintaining, and growing a company's image. Keeping up with your clients will keep them happy and also create a general reputation for your company that ensures your stability and efficiency. We turn again to John's wisdom:

> *"Realize that it is not our client's job to remember that they are still there. Mailers, follow-ups, constant reminders to people that your company plays a valuable role in their company's success is part of your value. Don't ever think 'Hey, we've arrived, we don't need to keep this image up.' Look at Microsoft. They're the king of the hill, and they don't quit. A lot of companies take the approach that people should come to them. No, you don't do that. You can always hire more people to meet client demand, but you can't undo a bad reputation."*

I think John's regular use of the words *constant* and *consistency* speak very strongly to the issue of creating strong company values and image. Again, personal experience—and time—are going to play into the way a consistent style is developed. It doesn't happen overnight, but knowing that it's an important goal will give the Web designer a great deal of strength in terms of how to begin planning structure, or how to reevaluate existing practices.

Marketing Web Sites

The company image is set, the clients are coming in because they've heard of the great work you do, you're creating Web sites on a regular basis that meet the standards set. How do you make sure your Web sites are seen, used, and visited time and again? There's no way to absolutely ensure this, but there are some very good techniques that can be applied to get your Web sites a lot of attention.

As we discussed in an earlier chapter, this practice should be looked upon as part of a site's postproduction. By working it into the vision of Web design, we create a long-term relationship with our sites—like children, they need regular attention and consideration. Besides that, we are duty-bound to our clients to give them the best value, and if marketing is part of that value, we need to make sure we do the work. The analogies that fly around DesertNet are rather funny, but they all ring true when it comes to why commercial Web sites must be marketed.

- Not marketing your Web site is like setting up a business in a dark, scary alley.—*Wil Gerken, Web Engineer, Director of Publications*
- Would you get phone service for your business and not list the number?—*Julie Boyce, Sales Representative*
- A Web site without marketing is the equivalent of spending $20,000.00 on a TV commercial, and then never airing it.—*John Hankinson, Director of Marketing*
- Remember the peaceniks? They said, "What if we gave a war and nobody came?" Well, we'd have no war. So what if we built a Web site and nobody came? We'd have no Web site!—*Yours Truly, Web Design Director*

How to Make It Happen

We've already introduced such online marketing techniques as link sharing, site tagging and indexing, announcement of sites, domain registration, and banner advertising. The technical aspects of doing these things are well-documented in the production chapter of this book. It will give the Web designer a lot of good points to start with in terms of the technical mechanisms.

Also, we touched upon the importance of carrying the ball off the Web court and into other media. Encourage clients to get those URLs up on TV spots; into radio and print ads; onto promotional items such as T-shirts, mugs, pens—whatever your client's company uses to promote themselves. The idea is to *cross-promote*, making sure that one promotional campaign enhances another. We see this with growing frequency all around us. One client, in fact, placed their URL on the film marquee that resides over a busy street. We like that! There's something totally fun about driving down the road and seeing a DesertNet URL up there for all to behold.

But make no mistake, this isn't frivolity. This is the way people will become familiar with what an URL is, what it means, and what all the things it stands for could do for their company. Sly, yes, but that's part of marketing—shifting the view of the masses toward a sense that they *need* a specific product.

Branding, name recognition. It's an essential. It's why Pepsi and Coke are household words, even when someone is referring to the can of generic cola in the refrigerator and not—and don't pardon the pun—the real thing. The very fact that the "real thing" works is because, through its marketing, Coca Cola made it its very own. This is what we want to do with Web design in the commercial arena—make our sites the real thing. Name them, bring them to life, and they will serve your client, and your company, very well.

Final Words

I hope you have found the concepts in this book helpful to you in your unique quest. In many ways I feel that I have given a great deal of quality information that will be practical as well as thought-provoking for Web designers interested in the professional aspects of the field.

All too often, as with this chapter, I am reminded of how much is missing from this book—details that are relentlessly practical and not so idealistic and theoretical. I am comforted knowing that the information herein is of critical importance for the Web designer, who can use the many resources recommended in this book as a way to fill in the areas of practical step-by-step, how-to-do-HTML, or graphics, or multimedia, or Web programming.

Finally, I sincerely hope that the information here will help create a starting point for future publications and resources dedicated to the emergence of Web design *as a profession.* It has so much value, both from the personal sense, to the broader applications as they relate to the creation and marketing of a new media, and a new culture in this—the information age.

Appendices

Web Design Resources

appendix a
Writing Resources

Web Sites

Bricolage

`http://bel.avonibp.co.uk/bricolage/etc/masthead.html`

Bricolage is a monthly publication that tracks writing-related information and developments on the Internet. Each month's issue will carry a small number of articles about one or two particular features of interest. This e-zine is very helpful to online writers. All of the features are directly relevant to writers who work on the Web.

Inklings

`http://www.interlog.com/~ohi/ink/inklings.html`

"Inklings is a free electronic newsletter for writers. It includes reports about new resources for writers on the net, market information, writers' tips, interviews, and useful articles. Inklings is published every two–three weeks (usually closer to two weeks). Issues are approximately 28–30K in size and are available by e-mail subscription and on the Web."

The Internet Writer's Guideline Listing

`http://www-wane-leon.scri.fsu.edu/~jtillman/DEV/ZDMS/`

This site lists a variety of online 'zines, contact information for each, and submission specs for written materials.

Jack Lynch's Grammar and Style Notes

`http://www.english.upenn.edu/~jlynch/grammar.html`

This is an excellent resource focusing on rules of grammar, offering clear and concise rules and explanations. Lynch makes comments on style as well as recommendations on usage.

John Hewitt's Writer's Resource Center

http://www.azstarnet.com/~poewar/writer/writer.html

Mr. Hewitt has placed 14 informative articles written either by himself or by other experienced writers on this helpful site, which also includes links to consumer magazines, book publishers, writers' markets, and more.

Magazine and Newspaper Editors' Resource List

http://www.tfs.net/personal/tgoff/erlist.html

Writers will find this extensive list of reference guides, libraries, publishers, newspapers, advertisers, and professional associations to be highly relevant.

Online Writery Writing Resources

http://www.missouri.edu/~wleric/writehelp.html

This site has links to helpful sites for writers, including style guides and online writing labs.

Publishers' Catalogues Home Page

http://www.lights.com/publisher/

This site lists the home pages of hundreds of publishers from many different countries.

Promoting Your Writing

http://www.interlog.com/~ohi/inkspot/promotion.html

The site includes links to extensive authors' directories, Web publishers, and writers' marketing sites.

Writing at University of Missouri: Online Writery

http://www.missouri.edu/~wleric/writery.html

"A place for writers to talk to other writers." Tutors are available.

Technical Writer's Page

http://user.itl.net/~gazza/techwr.htm

This page provides a concise description of the field of technical writing, together with links to resources for technical writers.

The Write Page

http://www.writepage.com/

This site has extensive listings describing books of different genres, as well as helpful links to topics of concern to all writers.

Writers' Resources on the Web

http://www.interlog.com/~ohi/www/writesource.html

This site is part of the WWW Virtual Library. It features links to resources for a number of genres, has a couple of dozen links related to the craft of writing, and includes information on selling one's writing.

Writing Resources and Writing Labs on the Net

http://owl.trc.purdue.edu/resources.html

This site includes links to online reference works, style guides, professional organizations, and more. A good starting point.

Resources Specific to Web Writing

Guidelines for Web Document Style & Design

http://sunsite.berkeley.edu/Web/guidelines.html

How to make your on-line presentation information accessible and readable

http://137.229.14.99/jb493/pages/JB493readability.html

Special Topic: Online Journalism. School of Journalism and Communication, Duquesne University

http://the-duke.duq-duke.duq.edu/dept/online.htm

UMass Cybered: Course for Web Writers

http://www3.umassd.edu/Public/catalogue/Tissuesindesign.html

Writing for the Web, Part II by Jack Powers

http://www.electric-pages.com/articles/wftw2.htm

Listservs and Newsgroups

A-WRITERS

Back issues can be obtained via ftp from: ftp://ftp.samurai.com/pub/lists/a-writers/

A-WRITERS (also known as @WRITERS) is a free e-mail newsletter for writers on the Internet. It encourages reader submissions and publishes leads on magazines that are seeking authors. To subscribe to @WRITERS, send the following command in the body of an e-mail message to majordomo@samurai.com:

```
subscribe a-writers
```

bit.listserv.techwr-l

This is the newsgroup for technical writers. The group is also available as a listserv. To subscribe, send the following command in the body of an e-mail message to listserv@listserv.okstate.edu:

```
subscribe TECHWR-LYour Name
```

digerati

Contact: digerati-request@ai.mit.edu

"Purpose: Increasingly, creative writers (poets, novelists, short story writers, etc.) are bypassing the mainstream media establishment and publishing their work directly on the World Wide Web."

The list considers both technical and practical challenges of being a writer who publishes on the Web. The Web site is http://www.ai.mit.edu/digerati/digerati.html; it has an extensive listing of resources for Web writers.

To subscribe, send the following command in the body of an e-mail message to digerati-request@ai.mit.edu:

```
subscribe digerati
```

Freelancers

Contact: nitefall@idirect.com (Brandi Jasmine)

"Purpose: A discussion and networking group for professional freelance writers, and their publishers and editors."

http://www.idirect.com/oracle/oracle-a-policy.html. To subscribe, send the following command in the body of an e-mail message to freelancers-request@idirect.com:

```
subscribe
```

mediapub

Media Authoring and Publishing Mailing List. To get the info file, send the command "info mediapub" in the body of an e-mail message to majordomo@flux.mindspring.com. The list also deals with concerns of multimedia authors.

misc.writing

http://vanbc.wimsey.com/~sdkwok/mwfaq.html

This address yields the misc.writing FAQ. Misc.writing is a large and sometimes noisy newsgroup. Many regular contributors are published writers, and their insights are invaluable.

ONLINE-NEWS

This is a "public Internet mailing list on electronic publishing." To subscribe, send the following command in the body of an e-mail message to majordomo@marketplace.com:

```
subscribe ONLINE-NEWSYour Name
```

The list owner is Steve Outing, outings@netcom.com or owner-online-newspapers@marketplace.com.

rec.arts.prose

Rec.arts.prose is afflicted to a certain degree by spammers, but it generally serves its purpose as a place for writers to post their prose pieces and receive feedback and commentary.

WRITE Writers Internet Exchange

Topics are similar to a closed newsgroup in which the members post their original work and critiques of other members' work. The members e-mail their submissions to WRITE@camcat.com for distribution to the full membership list. Failure to submit three on-topic posts each month will automatically cancel membership. Participation is important! Subscription: send your human-readable request to join or leave to jkent@camcat.com The owner is Janet Kent, jkent@camcat.com.

Description from List Info File

Writer's Workshop

Topics: The WRITERS list is an open, unmoderated electronic workshop for discussions of the art and craft of writing and sharing of works in progress. As might be expected, writers tend to write quite a lot, so be prepared for plenty of mail. Subscription: the workshop is self-serve— send e-mail to listserv@mitvma.mit.edu (or listserv@mitvma.mit.bitnet) with the message:

```
SUBSCRIBE WRITERSyourfirstname yourlastname
```

Description from List Info File

Courses, Seminars, Learning Resources

General Writing Courses on the World Wide Web

http://ernie.bgsu.edu/~skrause/WWW_Classes/

This site is a general resource for online writing courses with some excellent pointers to Internet-specific courses. Presented on a "no frills" page, the resources here list present resources and upcoming plans regarding online classes in writing, rhetoric, and literature that "in some fashion have to do with the World Wide Web."

John Hewitt's Writers Festivals Page

http://www.azstarnet.com/~poewar/writer/pg/festival.html

This site lists three summer writing conferences to be held in Wisconsin, Iowa, and Florida.

Writers Calendar

http://screenwriter.com/insider/WritersCalendar.html

This site provides information about several dozen writers' conferences being held in different states and in Canada.

Writers Classified: Events

http://www.inkspot.com/~ohi/inkspot/msg/msgmisc.html

Look here for descriptions of over a dozen upcoming American and Canadian workshops and conferences.

Writers' Conferences

http://www.inkspot.com/~ohi/inkspot/conf.html

This page provides a list of about seven upcoming conferences and workshops.

Writing Courses and Workshops

http://www.inkspot.com/~ohi/inkspot/courses.html

This list features a wide range of writers' courses and workshops. The offline courses outnumber the online ones.

The Writing Workshop

There are ongoing workshops in several different genres. To get detailed information, send the following command in the body of an e-mail message

to listserv@psuvm.psu.edu:

```
subscribe WRITING Your Name
```

You will receive information about joining the appropriate workshops and the requirements for membership.

Books

The Elements of Hypertext Design

Marc Demarest

SAMS, September 1995

ISBN: 1575210290

A manual covering hypertext layout and design, the book presents a balanced point of view.

The Elements of Hypertext Style

Bryan Pfaffenberger

Ap Professional, 1996

ISBN: 0125531427

More of an HTML resource, the work includes some excellent concept and layout style elements that are important for Web writers to understand.

From Paper to Online Publishing: a Guide for Planners and Decision Makers

Book and two disks

Larry Bielawski

Bk/2 disks Edition

Prentice Hall Computer Books, 1995

ISBN: 0133537498

The book covers issues regarding the differences between paper and online publications, including technical information and some layout and design issues.

The Web Is the Message : Ten Key Principles of Effective Web Publishing

Bryan Pfaffenberger

Ventana Press, 1996

ISBN: 1566043700

This book is described at http://www.netscapepress.com/promotion/tensecrets.html. The author, a writer who has published dozens of computer texts, interviewed the founders of today's top Web sites to determine fundamental principles for succeeding at Web publication.

World Wide Web Handbook : Retrieving, Writing, and Providing Hypertext and Hypermedia Documents

Flynn, Peter

Van Nostrand Reinhold, April 1995

ISBN: 0442020384

The book covers how to deal with writing for the hypertext environment.

Other Resources

In Search of the Perfect HTML Page

`http://cctr.umkc.edu/user/mhiggason/mainhtml.htm`

A look at theoretical and practical issues that arise when writing for the Web. An onsite tutorial and style guide are included. The links to discussions of hypertext writing philosophy at http://cctr.umkc.edu/user/mhiggason/philbib.htm are interesting and thought-provoking.

Internet Writer Resource Guide

`http://bel.avonibp.co.uk/bricolage/resources/lounge/IWRG/index.html`

This site includes practical advice about submitting manuscripts to Web publishers, as well as theoretical and visionary articles about Web publishing.

World Wide Writers Groups

`http://www.writepage.com/groups.htm`

Writer's Resources

`http://www.jazzie.com/ii/writing.html`

This site includes links to general writers' resources, links to sites discussing proper usage and citation of Internet resources, writing-related FAQs and more.

appendix b

HTML Resources

The following resources all offer a wide range of information on Hypertext Markup Language.

World Wide Web Sites

The HTML Reference Manual (From Sandia National Laboratories)

`http://www.sandia.gov/sci_compute/html_ref.html`

More of a technical manual, this site is a great reference for HTML authors who want quick information. The HTML Reference Manual is a quick reference for authors who require technical details about HTML. The site offers many links to other HTML and Web design–related resources.

HTML Writers Guild

`http://www.hwg.org/`

I've been a member for a long time now, and I'm still not sure what the benefits of membership to the HTML Writers Guild—an association open to all individuals who have "an active and ongoing interest in authoring for the World Wide Web"—really are. However, the Web site includes instructions for accessing various Web-related e-mail lists, as well as links to tutorials, shareware, and graphics related to HTML.

InfoBON's HTML Guide by Dr. Clue

`http://www.cnw.com/~drclue/Formula_One.cgi/HTML/HTML.html`

Don't let the design of this site put you off center, the content is, despite all visual evidence to the contrary, very high quality. The HTML tutorial provides an "HTML 101" environment for the novice. Other tutorials cover topics including CGI programming and advanced HTML.

Web Development CyberBase—HTML

http://www.hamline.edu/personal/matjohns/webdev/html/

Includes links to HTML tutorials, thorough information on Netscape extensions, Web-development resources, reference and style guides, and a dozen or so HTML syntax checkers.

NCSA—a Beginner's Guide to HTML

http://www.ncsa.uiuc.edu/General/Internet/WWW/HTMLPrimer.html

The HTML primer is a great place for HTML coders to start, but it also offers solid and practical information for all skill levels of those interested in HTML. Of particular note is a straightforward discussion of images and tables. This site covers the fundamentals, but it is also a good reference for advanced HTML authors. The site includes some basic discussion of images and tables.

The Web Developer's Virtual Library

http://WWW.Stars.com/

Considering itself to be the "Webmaster's Encyclopedia of Web Development and Software Technology," the site allows Web designers to learn how to use meta tags, the workings of search engines, updated information on the latest HTML information, and Common Gateway Interface facts. The site boasts a lot of links to helpful tools and programs.

World Wide Web Consortium's HyperText Markup Language—HTML Working and Background Materials

http://www.w3.org/pub/WWW/MarkUp/MarkUp.html

The World Wide Web Consortium is the standard-setting body for HTML. Web designers will gain a great deal of insight into the evolution, emergence, and future of HTML at this site. The WWW3 site offers details on the most current specification, upcoming events, plans, most recent announcements regarding HTML, and other links to Web-related resources.

World Wide Web FAQ

http://www.boutell.com/faq/

Glancing at a FAQ (Frequently Asked Questions list) for specific topics is always a good place to start before venturing into the fast lane. Check this FAQ before posting on Web-related newsgroups or mailing lists. Available in a number of languages, it also answers many common HTML questions.

Yale/CAIM WWW Style Manual

http://info.med.yale.edu/caim/StyleManual_Top.HTML

Undoubtedly one of the best one-stop Web resources on HTML and Web design, this site carries information that goes far beyond the basic HTML tutorial. Focusing instead on the details of what goes into making a good Web site design, it offers a wealth of information on how to create navigation systems, create appropriate page lengths, and lay out material in a comprehensive fashion.

Mail Lists (Listservs) and Newsgroups

ADV-HTML

A moderated list with strict discussion protocols, the ADV-HTML list offers a very high level and quality of information. This is not a list to ask basic questions. Geared for more advanced comments, it can be a valuable resource for both the experienced HTML coder and the novice open to learning advanced coding techniques and standards.

To subscribe to ADV-HTML, send the following command in the body of an e-mail message to listserv@ua1vm.ua.edu:

```
subscribe ADV-HTMLYour Name
```

alt.html

With considerably lower traffic than comp.infosystems.www.authoring.html, alt.html offers very similar content.

comp.infosystems.www.authoring.html

This newsgroup is extremely high-volume, but a user with a good newsreader will find it to be very valuable. The newsgroup is famous for its flame wars and opportunists, but an aware consumer can avoid falling into battle and stick to the critical information. This newsgroup is for discussion of HTML issues specifically. Other Web-related conversations are discouraged.

HTML-L

Unlike ADV-HTML, this is an unmoderated discussion list. It is generally quite friendly to new coders. The list is high-volume, and the level of discussion tends to be aimed toward the HTML coder just starting out.

To subscribe to HTML-L, send the following command in the body of an e-mail message to listserv@vm.ege.edu.tr:

```
subscribe HTML-LYour Name
```

HTML Writers Guild: Mailing Lists

http://www.hwg.org/lists/index.html

hwg-news (Mandatory for all hwg members)

hwg-main "Discussion of all aspects of creating Web services"

hwg-main-digest "As above, but in digest version"

hwg-basics "Basic HTML, including inline images"

hwg-business "Marketing, contracts, ethics, sales, etc."

hwg-ops "Guild-related business"

Netscape

This list is for discussion of the Netscape browser and its related extensions to HTML. Often plagued by a low signal-to-noise ratio due to browser wars, the list remains a valuable resource for Web designers interested in understanding the Netscape browser and how to use its enhancements. To subscribe to NETSCAPE, send the following command in the body of an e-mail message to listserv@irlearn.ucd.ie:

```
subscribe NETSCAPEYour Name
```

Spiderwoman

Spiderwoman is a list supporting women Web designers, and it covers all Web-related issues, including HTML, graphics, and CGI programming. All are welcome to join. The level of expertise is frequently expert, and the list can be a very valuable resource. The list is unmoderated and high-volume.

To subscribe to Spiderwoman, send the following request in the body of an e-mail message to majordomo@lists.primenet.com:

```
subscribe spiderwoman
```

Web-Consultants

The Web-Consultants list is aimed at individuals who make their living in some discipline of the World Wide Web. HTML issues are discussed, but the special feature of this list is that it focuses on business and programming issues.

You can find out how to subscribe to the Web-Consultants list and the Web-Consultants Jobline list at http://just4u.com/webconsultants/mlists.htm.

www-html

This list has wide-ranging, intelligent discussion of current problems and upcoming features of past and future HTML specifications. "This is the public mailing list for technical discussion among those interested in enhancing the Hypertext Markup Language (HTML) or building systems that support HTML. It is explicitly intended for the collaborative design of new systems, software, protocols, and documentation which may be useful to the HTML developer community."

To subscribe to www-html, send the request "subscribe" (without the quotation marks) in the body of an e-mail message to www-html-request@w3.org.

Books

The HTML Sourcebook: a Complete Guide to HTML 3.0

Ian S. Graham

2nd Edition

John Wiley & Sons, 1996

ISBN: 0471142425

The "Introduction to HTML" at `http://www.utirc.utoronto.ca/HTMLdocs/NewHTML/htmlindex.html` forms the basis of this book.

Teach Yourself Web Publishing with HTML 3.0 in a Week

Laura Lemay

2nd Edition

SamsNet, 1995

ISBN: 1575210649

Complete Teach Yourself HTML Kit

Laura Lemay

SamsNet, 1995

ISBN: 1575210630

Laura Lemay's books are renowned for their clear presentation and approachable style. You can view chapters of her books at http://www.lne.com/web/.

HTML and CGI Unleashed

John December, Mark Ginsburg

Book & CD-ROM Edition

Sams, 1995

ISBN: 0672307456

Any book about the Web can become dated very quickly. But the excellent information in this book, ranging from theoretical aspects of Web design to complex CGI programming in several languages, will continue to serve readers well.

HTML, CGI, SGML, VRML, Java

Web Publishing Unleashed

William Robert Stanek

Book & CD-ROM Edition

Sams, 1996

ISBN: 1575210517

Sams's books have a very good reputation for their comprehensive and careful treatment of the subject matter. Although I haven't seen the book, the title is disturbing, as I wonder if the author could give quality treatment to all of those subjects.

The Webmaster's Guide to HTML: for Advanced Web Developers (J. Ranade Workstation Series)

Nathan J. Muller , Linda L. Tyke (Illustrator)

Book & Disk Edition

McGraw Hill, 1995

ISBN: 0079122736

Web Programming Secrets with HTML, CGI, and PERL

Ed Tittel, Mark Gaither, Sebastian Hassinger, Mike Erwin

Book & Disk Edition

IDG Books Worldwide, 1996

ISBN: 156884848X

Conferences and Events

An In-Depth View of Forms, Tables, and CGI

http://WWW.Stars.com/Seminars/

This site is an online version of a presentation given at the WWW4 conference in Boston. A complete list of the tutorials given is available at http://www.w3.org/pub/Conferences/WWW4/Tutorial_Abstracts.html

General Events Information

http://conferences.calendar.com

This site lists a number of upcoming events concerning all aspects of the Internet and Web development. A handy search engine allows the reader to search by event, location, or keywords.

Mecklermedia / Internet World Events

A complete list of the events sponsored by Mecklermedia (*Internet World*) is available at http://events.iworld.com. One such conference held yearly is "Web Interactive '96."

Location: New York, New York

Date: July 31–August 2, 1996

URL: http://www.iworld.com/shows

Contact: Ann Zmitrovich (annz@mecklermedia.com)

Phone: 203-341-2967

Softbank Expo's Upcoming Event Calendar and Product Fact Sheet

http://www.sbexpos.com/sbexpos/public_relations/product_fact_sheet.html

Softbank provides NetWorld+ Interop conferences to meet the educational needs of Internet professionals at a number of locations around the globe. Tools, technologies, and applications for both Internet and Intranet applications are featured. Also check http://www.interop.com.

Using HTML to Design and Structure Information

http://www.sol-sems.com/creatwww.html

Nancy Hoft teaches this two-day seminar. Users begin with the basics and progress through all aspects of creating an HTML page, including advanced features and tips on how to publicize the finished site.

"Web Design and HTML Authoring"

http://www.webacademy.com

This four-day course is offered on various dates between June and September 1996. webacad@webacademy.com Location: Cupertino, California.

"The Web Academy provides hands-on training in Web design, HTML authoring, and JavaScript at sites in the Silicon Valley area. Web page creation, usability and performance issues, graphics techniques, imagemaps, forms, and CGI scripting are covered in a comprehensive four-day format. This training is designed to expand and improve job skills for those involved in presenting information (inside or outside corporate firewalls) and anyone involved in Web site creation and enhancement."

"Web Developer Canada '96"

Location: Vancouver, Canada

Date: September 16–18

An intensive three-day high-level conference and exposition of the latest, state-of-the-art products. URL: http://events.iworld.com Contact: Ann Zmitrovich (annz@mecklermedia.com) Phone: 1-800-MECKLER

Other Resources

WebTechs Validation Service

http://www.webtechs.com/html-val-svc/

Check the validity of your Web pages before you release them on the public. This site catches errors that are all-to-easy to make but difficult to see.

Yahoo

http://www.yahoo.com/Computers_and_Internet/Software/Data_Formats/HTML/

Yahoo offers this expanding list of HTML resources, tutorials, and tools.

appendix c

Graphic Design Resources

The following resources focus on how to understand the special realm of Web graphic design. Tips, tools, and other information are readily accessible through these resources.

Web Sites

The 3-D Café

`http://www.baraboo.com/3dcafe/`

"The Internet's Ultimate Resource for Graphic Artists," this site has high-quality clip art in 19 different categories, ranging from aircraft and weapons to plants and animals.

Creating Graphics for the Web

`http://www.widearea.co.uk/designer/`

This guide is short but useful. Learn some basic design and Photoshop tips.

Graphics Formats for the WWW

`http://www.w3.org/pub/WWW/Graphics/`

The official word on graphics formats still comes from the WWW Consortium. This is a good starting point to learn the technical details of displaying Web graphics, and it can also serve as a useful refresher. The page also has links to several other sites that provide basic technical information.

Adobe

`http://www.adobe.com`

Corel/WordPerfect

`http://www.corel.ca`

Corel and Adobe products are often used by Web graphic designers. These sites provide the latest downloadable patches as well as product support and relevant information.

David Siegel's Net Tips for Writers and Designers

http://www.dsiegel.com/tips/tips_home.html

David Siegel is a leading-edge Web designer whose concise advice should be taken seriously. If you learn by example, check out David Siegel's High-Five sites at http://www.highfive.com, where the best-designed sites on the Web are singled out for acclaim.

Kai's Power Tips and Tricks for Adobe Photoshop

http://the-tech.mit.edu/KPT/

This is an excellent resource for all graphic designers who use this premier package.

Paintshop Pro

http://www.jasc.com/index.html

Paintshop Pro's Web site showcases the popular graphics shareware program, which is available for download and evaluation. The site also provides links to Web development information.

Royal Frazier

http://members.aol.com/royalef/index.html

Royal Frazier's now-famous page details how to do animated GIFs using the GIF89a format, and it provides links to resources to assist in the task.

Web Developers Virtual Library

http://www.stars.com/Graphics/

As usual, the Web Developers Virtual Library proves an indispensable resource to just about any Web-related topic. The page offers links to several sites of interest to Web graphic designers. The step-by-step demonstration of how to build your own 3-D graphics for the Web is at http://WWW.Stars.com/Graphics/3d-demo.html.

Web Graphics FAQ

http://www.cis.ohio-state.edu/hypertext/faq/usenet/graphics/fileformats-faq/faq.html

This FAQ covers general graphics format questions, image conversion and display programs, graphics file formats, and tips and tricks of the trade.

Listservs and Newsgroups

alt.corel.graphics

Like the other Usenet newsgroups mentioned, this forum is a helpful source of information.

comp.graphics.misc

This group is not specifically Web-based, but like the first-mentioned newsgroup it has a high level of discussion often important to Web graphic designers.

comp.graphics.apps.photoshop

This newsgroup, devoted to discussion of Adobe Photoshop, provides useful info for graphic artists of all types, but Web designers will find many of the topics helpful and informative.

comp.infosystems.www.authoring.images

This is an excellent resource for the graphic Web designer. Knowledgeable experts like Royal Frazier (of GIF89a animation fame) respond to inquiries. The signal-to-noise ratio is high, but as on most Usenet newsgroups, there are flamewars and off-topic discussion.

Corel

`http://www.corelnet.com/corelnet/newtalk/newtalk.htm`

Corel-sponsored Web-based discussion groups, these are similar to e-mail lists, but they are available on the Web. A wide variety of discussion forums are available, including one devoted to Corel products and the World Wide Web.

Direct-L

"The DIRECT-L list was formed to provide a forum for discussions of the software program MacroMedia Director for the Macintosh."

To subscribe to DIRECT-L, send the following command in the body of an e-mail message to LISTSERV@uafsysb.uark.edu:

`subscribe DIRECT-L`*`Your Name`*

Graphics

The Graphics mailing list discusses the history, theory, practice, and techniques of graphic design. To subscribe to the Graphics mailing list, send the following command in the body of an e-mail message to listserv@ulkyvm.louisville.edu:

`subscribe graphics`*`Your Name`*

Lynda's Homegurrl Web Design List

"The purpose of Lynda's Homegurrl Web Design List is to host a dialog between visual designers working within the context of the Web. This is a place to share questions, tips, techniques, and job opportunities related to visual design on the Web." The author wrote the popular book "Designing Web Graphics."

To subscribe to "Lynda's Homegurrl Web Design List," follow the instructions available at http://www.lynda.com/webdesign.html

Photoshop

An e-mail discussion list about Adobe Photoshop for Mac or Windows or SGI platforms. To subscribe, send the following command in the body of an e-mail message to listproc2@bgu.ed:

```
subscribe PHOTSHOPYour Name
```

Books

Creating Great Web Graphics

Laurie McCanna

Holt Publishing

ISBN 1-55828-479-6

This book "gives basic step-by-step techniques so that the reader can create great, professional-looking graphics in just a few short steps, using either Photoshop or Corel PhotoPaint. Think you're not artistic? Not a problem! This book was written for people who want to create simple graphics easily, by following step-by-step examples." More information and sample chapters can be enjoyed at http://www.mccannas.com/book/overview.htm

Designing Large-Scale Web Sites: a Visual Design Methodology

Darrell Sano

John Wiley & Sons, 1996

ISBN: 047114276X

This book is described in more detail at http://www.connect.hawaii.com/hc/webmasters/books/sano1.html and http://www.dru.nl/bedrijven/broese/specials/eoug96/int7.htm.

It appears to be a useful guide for those who want to take a methodical approach to Web site development.

Designer's Guide to the Internet

Rick Albertson, Jeffrey Fine

Hayden Books, 1995

ISBN: 1568302290

Find a complete description at http://www.davison.net/books/desc/macmillan/internet.des.guide.html. Go to http://designers.zender.com/toc.html to see the table of contents and to read select chapters. The book appears to be quite theoretical in nature.

Designing Web Graphics

Lynda Weinman

New Riders Publishing

ISBN:1-56205-532-1

The author's Web site is at http://www.lynda.com. The table of contents is at http://www.lynda.com/dwg/dwg2.html and includes excerpts from many of the chapters. The book provides practical hints for making your Web graphics look their best.

Photoshop for Windows 95 Bible

Deke McClelland

IDG Books Worldwide, 1996

ISBN: 156884882X

As described at http://www.readmedotdoc.com/cat/cat50.html, this book was "written as the ultimate hands-on reference for artists, designers, and anyone who works with today's leading image editing software. Covers everything from Photoshop fundamentals to guru techniques."

Conferences, Courses, and Events

Adobe Internet Conference Overview

`http://www.adobe.com/events/aic/main.html`

Designing Effective User Interfaces

`http://cs.wpi.edu/~matt/courses/cs563/talks/smartin/int_design.html`

This Web page is related to the computer science and computer graphics courses taught by Matthew Ward. You can see an index of his online and offline courses at http://cs.wpi.edu/~matt/courses.

Eurographics 96

`http://www-syntim.inria.fr/eg96/presWWW.html`

This conference is held from August 26–30 in France. There will be a mix of seminars and tutorials on both theoretical topics and practical applications.

The MasterClass Series: Training in HCI (Human-Computer Interface)

`http://www.system-concepts.com/masterclass/`

Visit the Web site for up-to-date information on these courses.

Photoshop Unleashed

`http://microweb.com/idig/psun/PSUN.html`

Conferences are in September, October, and November in San Francisco, New York City, and Los Angeles. This is a three-day seminar discussing a variety of techniques that work with Photoshop.

Siggraph Online

`http://www.siggraph.org/`

Siggraph Online is the Association for Computing Machinery's Special Interest Group on Computer Graphics. The calendar of Siggraph events is at http://www.siggraph.org/calendar/calendar.html.

Web Design Seminars

Lynda Weinman, the author of *Designing Web Graphics* is presenting seminars in California and Illinois during the summer of 1996. You can also contact her to book a seminar. http://www.lynda.com/dwg/wds.html

Web Publishing Techniques

This conference will be held in New York, Dallas, and Chicago during the summer and fall of 1996. The conference will feature the world's top experts in Web design.

Other Resources

Computer User Groups on the World Wide Web

`http://annarbor.apcug.org/others/index.htm`

You can search by software product or other identifying feature to find a local user group that shares your Web-design interests.

appendix d
Multimedia Resources

This appendix focuses on multimedia resources specific to the creation of multiple media on the Web.

Web Sites

The Apple Quick Time VR Download Site

`http://qtvr.quicktime.apple.com/`

The Apple Quick Time VR player is available for both Windows and Mac OS as a helper app. It's an extension of the popular Quick Time movie video technology, which allows movement.

Internet Safari

`http://www.bloomfield.k12.mi.us/CompCntr/safari/Inet.html`

Internet Safari is a page created entirely by the students of Model High School as an interactive exploration of the Internet and an introductory tutorial. Both Mac and Intel versions of the safari are available. The page explains how to set it up and system requirements. This is an excellent site.

Jack Decker's Personal Audio-Video Home Page

`http://www.novagate.com/~jack/audiovid.html`

Jack Decker's personal audio-video homepage with extensive information on both audio and video over the Internet. It contains summaries and overviews of most of the products currently available. Extensive links and varied information.

Macromedia Shockwave

`http://www.macromedia.com/Tools/Shockwave/index.html`

Macromedia's Web site with links to many example sites and downloadable plug-ins for Windows and Mac. Macromedia is the premier plug-in, fully multimedia-ready package widely available on the Web. A site that uses this product is said to be "Shocked."

The MICE Multimedia Index

http://boom.cs.ucl.ac.uk/mice/

An index of multimedia links related to live conferencing. More limited in scope than most, it nonetheless offers very good coverage of this subset of multimedia applications.

Microsoft Internet Explorer

http://www.microsoft.com/ie/default.htm

The rival Web browser from Microsoft is a strong contender for eventual dominance, given the company's historical performance as market strategists and its strong economic base. It is still a distant second but is becoming an excellent product.

Netscape Navigator Plug-Ins

http://home.netscape.com/comprod/products/navigator/version_2.0/plugins/index.html

No discussion of multimedia is complete unless we discuss the primary engine that drives most current multimedia displays. This page is an extensive list of available audio and video plug-ins and "helper apps" for the Navigator Web browser, used by somewhere in the neighborhood of 70 percent of the users on the Net.

QTVR: a Practical Guide

http://www.sils.umich.edu/~mbonn/guide.html

A very handy explanation of how to make your own QTVR exploration, including equipment and techniques.

University of Geneva Multimedia Sources

http://viswiz.gmd.de/MultimediaInfo/

http://fourier.dur.ac.uk:8000/mm.html

The Index to Multimedia Information Sources from the University of Geneva is a very extensive and broad listing of information, software, standards, and other issues relating to multimedia.

Voice on the Net home page

http://www.von.com/

Maintained by an advocacy and interest group dealing with audio and video technology on the Net, this covers all products and issues, including possible U.S. federal intervention in Web-based telephony at the request of the common telephony carriers. This is a big issue on many of the audio pages, especially. Extensive links and resources, including commercial providers.

Listservs and Newsgroups

Image-L

Send e-mail to listserv@vm3090.ege.edu.tr with

```
SUB IMAGE-L Your Name
```

in the body of the message and a blank subject line. Imaging technologies, compression methods, etc.

Multimedia Discussion List

Send e-mail to majordomo@cleo.murdoch.edu.au with

```
subscribe multimedia
```

in the body of the message and a blank header.

news:clari.tw.new_media

This is a newsfeed dealing with multimedia and other new technologies.

news:comp.multimedia

This is a general multimedia newsgroup.

news:comp.os.ms-windows.programmer.graphics

This is a technical MS-Windows graphics programming list.

Voice on the Net (VON) Mailing List

This is a mailing list dedicated to broader discussion of all of the various audio/video products and technologies. To subscribe, send e-mail to majordomo@pulver.com. Leave the subject blank and in the body write:

```
subscribe von-digest
```

Web Multimedia Fusion

`http://www.emf.net/~mal/vcd-dev.html`

This offers subscription information for a multimedia list devoted to "discussions of Web multimedia fusion with an emphasis on audio and multimedia/Web integration."

Conferences and Events

Antares Virtual Reality

http://www.avrs.com/antares/edu.html

Educational software and classes are offered through Antares Virtual Reality Systems.

Asymetrix Seminars

http://www.asymetrix.com/events.html

Seminars are available from Asymetrix, a proprietary multimedia tool vendor.

CSU Master of Arts in Multimedia

http://monet.mcs.csuhayward.edu/mmm/

Pick up an outline for the Master of Arts in Multimedia Program at California State University at Hayward.

Imagination Online Creating 3D Images Seminar

http://www.ination.com/p0000037.htm

3-D imaging techniques are the focus of this tutorial. This company also has seminars on creating a Web site. The base address provides information on these services.

Texas A&M

http://mccnet.tamu.edu/Internet_Seminars.html

Descriptions appear for free seminars at Texas A&M on the second Tuesday of every month.

University of California at Berkeley

http://www-plateau.cs.berkeley.edu/courseware/

Descriptions are offered for courseware at UC Berkeley. Many lectures are broadcast on the Internet backbone.

Virginia Commonwealth University: Multimedia Seminars

http://www.vcu.edu/mdcweb/new/seminars/seminars.html

Find multimedia seminars at Virginia Commonwealth University.

Books

Designing Multimedia: a Visual Guide to Multimedia and Online Graphic Design

Lisa Lopuck

Peachpit Press, 1996

ISBN 0-201-88398-8

This is an artist's guide to multimedia with lots of full-color photos and screen shots so that you can see what the author is talking about[emdash]a beautifully illustrated how-to guide with case studies of actual multimedia projects from conception and design through completion, with step-by-step explanations of the tradeoffs between different design decisions and tools. She pays close attention to user interfaces and dynamic interactions that may be challenging new concepts for the graphic designers for whom this book is written. Useful for both Mac and Windows platforms.

Multimedia: Making It Work, Second Edition

Tay Vaughan

Osborne, 1994

with CD-ROM

ISBN 0-07-882035-9

An overview and tutorial of multimedia for a wide audience, it does touch on more advanced topics but does not overwhelm with excessive detail. A very practical hands-on tutorial.

The CD-ROM contains practical examples, graphics, and exercises for the lessons.

Multimedia Power Tools, Second Edition

Peter Jerram and Michael Gosney

Random House, 1996

with CD-ROM

ISBN 0-679-76346-5

This contains shareware and freeware utilities for generating multimedia elements for both Mac and Windows platforms. Good information to have in arm's reach, although almost all the actual software is available for downloading on the Internet.

Multimedia Systems Design

Prabhat K. Andleigh and Kiran Thakrar,

Prentice Hall, 1996

ISBN 0-13-089095-2

This advanced book covers the design of distributed multimedia systems using a variety of compression/decompression tools, design methodologies, and implementation techniques. Although the book is tutorial in nature, the authors never lose sight of the rapidly changing environment of advanced multimedia systems and present a sound basis for handling further developments.

Shockwave for Director User's Guide

Sasha Magee and Noel Rabinowitz

New Riders Publishing, 1996

with CD-ROM

ISBN 1-566205-595-X

This covers animation for the Web using Shockwave. The CD-ROM contains sample code and demonstrations, the Afterburner file compression tool, and a Lite version of the DeBabelizer batch graphical tool. The book covers lingo, movies, vertical movies, animated logos, game, animated buttons, and more.

Other Resources

MULTIMED-Request@URIACC.URI.EDU

This is an e-mail-based multimedia course.

appendix e
Programming Resources

This appendix is dedicated to Web-based programming resources.

Web Sites

Aereal Serch

http://www.virtpark.com/theme/cgi-bin/serch.html

Aereal Serch is a search engine especially tuned to Web programming and multimedia sites. Enter search criteria and be instantly gratified with a list of VRML and other multimedia sites meeting your criteria. Aereal also maintains a "Top Ten" list that changes periodically.

Earthweb's Gamelan Java Directory

http://www.gamelan.com

The directory offers links to examples, newsgroups, tutorials, you name it. This is a great resource for Javaheads and fun to browse even for casual nonprogrammers as it points to many "fun" demonstrations.

The Java Message Exchange

http://porthos.phoenixat.com/~warreng/WWWBoard/wwwboard.html

The Exchange is a message board devoted to Java development. If you like message boards and need occasional "help from the experts," this is the place for you.

The JavaScript Index

http://www.c2.org/~andreww/javascript/

This is a great source of links to the JS world: tutorials, example pages, you name it. This is the magnum opus of a dedicated Javahead and shows both his knowledge of the field and his dedication to it in every link and reference.

The Microsoft Internet Developer's site

http://www.microsoft.com/intdev/welcome.htm

Look here for information on Visual Basic Script, Microsoft's proprietary answer to Java and JavaScript; ActiveX (a proprietary "industry standard" interface formerly called OLE), that lets the user transparently interface to and control Java, VBS, or other programming languages; Explorer 3.0; and other hot topics. It's interesting that there is so little information (that I've seen anyway) about ActiveX and VBS outside of Microsoft. I guess it's not quite "an industry standard" yet. I have seen a few corporate sites that claim to support AX, but even they don't have much to say. There's nothing much in the bookstores, either, so this is either a groundfloor opportunity or another Betamax, take your pick.

The Microsoft "Jakarta" Site

http://www.microsoft.com/visualc/jakarta/

Jakarta is an unreleased visual Java development tool. Check back frequently if you want to know what Microsoft's left hand is doing to sabotage the efforts of its right hand's insistence on reinventing wheels.

Netscape's JavaScript Authoring Guide

http://www.netscape.com/eng/mozilla/Gold/handbook/javascript/index.html

This is an introduction to JavaScript using a frames-based JavaScript application. Not only does it tell you how it works, but you can take it apart to see how it works for yourself. A very cool demonstration of technical mastery in a very slick presentation.

Netscape JavaScript Link List

http://www.netscape.com/comprod/products/navigator/version_2.0/script/index.html

The Netscape JavaScript link list includes links to many outside reources and examples. Netscape has incorporated Java/JavaScript into the heart of its Navigator browser, and the company has a vested interest in seeking out the brightest and best examples and tools that can be found on the Net. This is an excellent place to start looking for information, with online tutorials on just about everything connected with Web development as well.

Netscape's JavaScript Tutorial

http://www.netscape.com/comprod/products/navigator/version_2.0/script/script_info/tutorial/main.htm

This introduces a complex application that builds graphics and presentation-style reports in response to user mouse clicks. Another slick effort from a company that wants you to be fascinated with its capabilities.

PERL Manual and Searchable Index

http://www.cs.cmu.edu/htbin/perl-man

Virtual Cities Repository

http://www.vir.com/~farid/ctrepos.htm

The Repository is a collection of 3-D models of actual cities using a variety of rendering tools, VRML, QTVR, 3DS, DXF, and so on. Very cool.

VR for the People

http://gnn.com/gnn/wr/sept29/features/vrml/index.html

VR for the People is an online publication dedicated to VRML. Controversial and irreverent, it doesn't shy away from such topics as "teledildonics" (which I will leave up to your imagination) and from tweaking SGI (just a little) about its dominance of the standard.

VRML Futures Forum

http://vag.vrml.org/

This forum is a standards body dedicated to guiding the development of the next generation of VRML specifications.

The VRML Repository

http://www.sdsc.edu/vrml/

This is an extensive and impartial collection of materials and pointers dealing with VRML from the San Diego Supercomputer Center. It contains a bibliography of periodical references, many of them available on the Net, and pointers to many other sites.

VRML Resources

http://vrml.wired.com/

This is a general VRML site with many links to other resources. It contains an open forum and conference for the discussion, design, and implementation of VRML worlds, as well as a mailing list.

VRML Resources from Silicon Graphics

http://webspace.sgi.com/

A general VRML site from Silicon Graphics, arguably the major contributor to the standard and a dominant player with its WebSpace product. It contains a beta version of a downloadable VRML driver for Win95 and WinNT, Cosmo Player, as well as extensive links to other resources.

The World Wide Web Consortium

http://www.w3.org/pub/WWW/

The World Wide Web Consortium is an industry-funded standards body with tons of information about graphics and multimedia formats. It is home to several general-interest mailing lists and of primary interest to developers.

Listservs and Usenet Newsgroups

CGI List

This is a Common Gateway Interface discussion.

Send e-mail to listserv@vm.ege.edu.tr with:

```
SUB CGI-L Your Name
```

in the body of the message and a blank subject line.

JavaScript Talk

http://www.farhorizons.com/jstalk/jstalk.html

It offers subscription information about the JavaScript Talk mailing list.

JavaScript Mailing List

Send e-mail to javascript-request@netural.com with SUBSCRIBE in the body of the message and a blank subject line.

news:comp.lang.java

This is a Java newsgroup.

news:comp.lang.javascript

This is a JavaScript newsgroup.

news:comp.lang.perl

Check this for Perl information and discussion.

news:comp.lang.basic.visual

It offers MS Visual Basic general news.

OpenDoc Standards and Java Discussion

`http://www.cuesys.com/lists/jod/`

The page offers subscription information about a mailing list dedicated to combining the OpenDoc and Java standards.

Strong-Java Mailing List

`http://www.entmp.org/cgi-bin/lwgate/STRONG-JAVA/`

This offers subscription information about the STRONG-JAVA mailing list. Beginners are strongly discouraged.

VRML Standards

To join the VRML standards discussion, please subscribe to the www-vrml mailing list. Send e-mail to majordomo@wired.com with no subject and, in the message body:

```
subscribe www-vrmlyour e-mail address
```

Conferences, Learning Resources, Organizations

Algorithm Incorporated

`http://www.algorithm.com/virtual/virtual.html`

Self-paced training software from Algorithm Incorporated covers a variety of Web and VR topics. Very good for self-motivated individuals.

Association for Women in Computing

`http://www.halcyon.com/monih/awc.html`

Local chapters sponsor technical and career seminars and networking meetings. Check chapter pages for seminars and meetings in a given area.

Interface Online Training Center

`http://www.iftech.com/iti/itioltc.htm`

It offers classes and online tutorials in C/C++ programming, along with other programming resources.

SIGGraph 96

`http://www.siggraph.org/conferences/siggraph96/siggraph96.html`

Team WebGrrls

http://www.women.org/

Team WebGrrls offers in-house training in Net issues including programming and other Internet-based technologies.

Women Online

http://women-online.com/

Women Online is Amy Goodloe's training and consulting service for women.

Books

Beyond HTML

Richard Karpinki

Osborne, 1996

ISBN 0-07-882-198-3

An overview of many technologies "beyond" straight HTML coding, it covers Java, JavaScript, VRML Shockwave, VB Script, Acrobat, Digital Paper, RealAudio, TrueSpeech, and Streamworks.

CGI Programming on the World Wide Web

Shishir Gundavaram

O'Reilly & Associates, 1996

ISBN 1-56592-168-2

This is a thorough book on CGI programming from a very respected publisher of standard texts in the UNIX world. It includes a list of online resources and a FAQ. It uses PERL as its scripting language and contains many typical examples of use, including a guestbook, dynamic hypermedia documents, database applications, and gateway interfaces.

Danny Goodman's JavaScript Handbook

Danny Goodman

IDG Books, 1996

with CD-ROM

ISBN 0-7645-3003-8

It covers Mac and Windows platforms. The CD-ROM contains graphics files, sample code plug-ins, the Crescendo audio helper app, and the Shockwave video helper app.

Learning Perl (the Llama Book)

Randal L. Schwartz

O'Reilly & Associates, 1993

ISBN 1-56592-042-2

This is an excellent tutorial on Perl.

Programming Perl (the Camel Book)

Larry Wall & Randal L. Schwartz

O'Reilly & Associates, 1991

ISBN 0-937175-64-1

This is the definitive guide to PERL, and it comes with a handy reference card. PERL has lots of fans, but few support Web sites have the friendly tutorials and user groups that you see for many other Web tools. This stems, I'm sure, from its UNIX background. These books from O'Reilly, a well-known name in UNIX circles, help make up for the dearth of palatable information.

Teach Yourself Java in 21 Days

Laura Lemay and Charles L. Perkins

Sams, 1996

with CD-ROM

ISBN 1-57521-030-4

Here is yet another of Laura Lemay's excellent and well-crafted tutorials on Web design. Her previous volumes have been very popular among beginning Web designers for their clarity and scope, and this book follows in the tradition set by the earlier volumes, focusing on an advanced topic of Web page design. Highly recommended.

Using CGI: Special Edition

Jeffry Dwight and Micael Erwin

Que, 1996

with CD-ROM

ISBN 0-7897-0740-3

A *huge* book with applications covering almost anything one can think of, from a WAIS indexer and DB engine to audio and video servers, robots, and Web crawlers, it provides a clear explanation of how to keep *most* spiders out of directories where they don't belong, how to do server includes, and much more. If you don't break your arm lifting it off the shelf, it's a great resource.

VRML: Flying Through the Web

Mark Pesce

New Riders, 1996

with CD-ROM

ISBN 1-56205-521-6

A concise overview of VRML with short hands-on test drives of actual sites and tools, it was written by a cocreator of VRML and an evangelist for the technology. Fun to read. Check out:

`http://www.mcp.com/newriders`

appendix f Systems Administration Resources

The following resources are for individuals interested in learning more about the technical end of administering Web sites.

Web Sites

How to Set Up and Maintain a WWW Site: the Guide for Information Providers

`http://www-genome.wi.mit.edu/WWW/resource_guide.html`

This page is an online resource associated with the book of the same title, How to Set Up and Maintain a World Wide Web Site: the Guide for Information Providers by Lincoln D. Stein, Addison-Wesley Publishing Company, ISBN 0-201-63389-2.

Jeff's Unix Vault

`http://www.NDA.COM/~jblaine/vault/`

This is a very complete listing of online UNIX resources.

SAGE (System Administrator's Guild)

`http://www.sage.usenix.org/sage/sage.html`

The Guild is a professional organization for sysadmins, and the site features good links, especially to SAGE mailing lists and resources.

Sven's Operating Systems on the Web page

`http://www.lfbs.rwth-aachen.de/~sven/OS-Projects/`

This is a very thorough compendium of current research and publications about Web operating systems, mainly UNIX and UNIX variants such as MACH.

Tony's Unix Administrator's Home Page

http://www.efs.mq.edu.au/unix_admin/

Very much a work in progress, it is nonetheless a good resource that should get better in time.

The Unix Guru Universe

http://www.polaris.net/ugu/

Called the Official Homepage for UNIX System Administrators (no one is sure why it's official) it is an excellent resource with many links. One could spend hours here just browsing everything, but a searchable index helps cut to the chase.

Unix System Administrator's Resource Page

http://www.stokely.com/stokely/sysadm.resources.html

This is a very good collection of links.

The UnixWorld Magazine Online Homepage

http://www.wcmh.com/uworld/

The electronic counterpart to a widely read magazine, it links to other online magazines and resources as well, so check this one out thoroughly.

University of Texas Computation Center UNIX Resources

http://www.host.cc.utexas.edu/cc/services/unix/index.html

This is a thorough UNIX resource repository.

The Web Master's Page

http://gagme.wwa.com/~boba/masters1.html

This is a very thorough reference page on creating a Web presence.

Listservs and Newsgroups

This is a broad field, and there are groups for every taste. Since the topics tend to be unique to each system, there are a bewildering array of specialized newsgroups available, and some are hostile to newbies. A word of advice: read quite a few posts in the newsgroup to get a feel for the tone of the people who post before posting anything, and try to keep your question focused on topics the group seems to care about.

alt.sysadmin.recovery

Not a technical group—this is more a place where sysadmins go to vent, be weird, etc. If your site is ugly or stupid, this is the place you will be made fun of as well. You will find little or nothing of information value here, but if you like gossip and chatter, this is the place to visit.

comp.unix.*

Here is the hierarchy for general UNIX discussion.

comp.security.*

In this hierarchy, check out comp.security.unix. Security is a big issue on the Internet, and this is where you will find the systems administrators who are worried about it, as well as a significant portion of the hackers who subscribe for very different reasons. This is a good place to ask questions, but be cautious, as with any newsgroup, about quickly following unconfirmed advice or giving out too much information.

news:comp.sys.unix

This is a general group for UNIX systems administrators.

news:comp.sys.*

More narrowly focused groups fall in this hierarchy.

news:comp.infosystems.*

Many groups in this subheading are relevant to systems administration.

news:comp.infosystems.www.providers

Of particular interest for Webheads with discussions about server design, server bugs and workarounds, HTML, page layout, and other information you might need to set up or maintain your Web server. Look at others in news:comp.infosystems.www.* for anything that looks interesting.

news:alt.*

There are several groups of interest, including news:alt.hypertext, which deals with concepts and high-level issues such as the best tools to use, and news:alt.html, which more specifically focuses on, logically enough, html questions. You'll have to be selective here, though, as there are (at last count) almost 4000 groups under this header.

NT-ISP

For providers working on the Windows NT platform. Write to lists@windowsnt.com.

SAGE Women's Systems Administrator's Mailing list

http://www.usenix.org/sage/mail/sage-bof-women

A list for women in the field, it offers support and technical information.

Systems Administration: General Lists

http://www.ugu.com/sui/ugu/

Many specialized mailing lists are available on this site. Look down the list and choose the one (or more) that seems closest to your needs.

Seminars and Learning References

The Australian 85321 Systems Administration home page

http://mc.cqu.edu.au/subjects/85321/

It's an online course with very good list of links.

Caltech Systems Administration

http://dontask.caltech.edu:457/OSAdminG/CONTENTS.html

Check here for a very thorough online systems administration tutorial.

Introduction to UNIX System Administration from Ohio State University

http://sunos-wks.acs.ohio-state.edu/sysadm_course/sysadm.html

This offers an introduction to UNIX administration.

Linux Systems Administration, Indiana State

http://www.uwsg.indiana.edu/linux/mdw/LDP/gs/node155.html#SECTION00600000000000000000

USAIL Independent Learning

http://www.uwsg.indiana.edu/usail/

A UNIX systems administration independent learning center, it also have good links to other sites and online courses.

R870: Unix System Administration—a Survival Course, University of Washington, Seattle

http://www.washington.edu:1180/R870/R870.html

UNIX System Manager's Manual (SMM) for the 4.4 Berkeley Software Distribution

http://www.eecs.nwu.edu/bsd/smm/index.html

Techweb

http://techweb.cmp.com

It has lots of handy tidbits of technically oriented information and up-to-date news to help you stay on top of the industry.

Training On Video

http://www.trainonvideo.com/

A video course on Unix systems administration and a few other courses of interest are available here.

UNIX Help for Users

http://www.eecs.nwu.edu/Unixhelp/

As the title implies, this is a general overview of UNIX and a reference manual for new users, but it is a good resource for sysadmins as well, as they can deflect a lot of questions by telling users to check out this site.

Books

DNS & Bind

Cricket Liu

O'Reilly & Associates, 1993

ISBN 1-56592-010-4

This is only one of several books you'll need if you are stuck with the job, er . . . given the opportunity of administering the UNIX mail system. The other primary source is Sendmail by Brian Costales with Earl Allman & Neil Rickert, published by O'Reilly & Associates, 1993. These books cover configuring the basic tools that get mail from user A to user B with as few bounces or detours into a sysadmin's dead.letter mailbox as possible. Sendmail covers the configuration files and rules needed to send messages on their way as well as receive them, whereas DNS & Bind covers the distributed directory service that makes e-mail as we know it today possible. These are fairly heavy reading but essential.

Essential System Administration

Aileen Frisch

O'Reilly & Associates, 1991, 1995

ISBN 0-937175-80-3

This book addresses the nuts and bolts of UNIX systems administration, starting with a short discussion of file systems and processes and covering day-to-day activities in a logical manner. Start-up and shut-down share a chapter, and from there the book covers managing user accounts, security, managing system resources effectively, automating common tasks, e-mail, TCP/IP, printing and spooling, usage accounting, and ever so much more fun stuff. If you are a dedicated system freak, this is the book for you. If you are a user who just wants to get your work done and mind your own business, you might want to look just a little further on the bookshelf.

Managing Internet Information Services: World Wide Web, Gopher, FTP, and More

Cricket Liu, Jerry Peek, Russ Jones, Bryan Buus & Adrian Nye

O'Reilly & Associates, 1994

ISBN 1-56592-062-7

This is the fun stuff. The book covers Gopher and WAIS, which have little of the pizzazz of the graphical Web services but are nonetheless important to know about as they are still widely used in academia, as well as HTTP and FTP, which are the most frequently encountered services in casual browsing on the World Wide Web. There is a brief but thorough description of how to set up Web HTTP and FTP servers, how to administer mailing lists with majordomo, and lots of other cool stuff, some of which is of mainly historical interest but for which you would gladly sell your collection of early Silver Surfer comic books if you run into the need to manage them. Highly recommended.

UNIX Power Tools

Jerry Peek, Mike Loukides, Tom O'Reilly, et al.

O'Reilly & Associates, 1993

with CD-ROM

ISBN 0-679-79073-X

This is an excellent collection of accumulated advice from the UNIX gurus for aspiring acolytes, containing tips and tricks, wisdom, freeware utilities, abstracts from other O'Reilly books, warnings, and other tidbits from the vast store of information in circulation among sysadmins. Highly recommended.

Unix System Administration Handbook

Evi Nemeth, Garth Snyder, Scott Seebass, Trent R. Hein

Prentice Hall, 1995

with CD-ROM

ISBN 0-13-151051-7

You should also probably have a book or two or three on the shells most often used at your site, whether the ubiquitous sh (Bourne Shell), csh (C Shell), tcsh (an enhanced C Shell), bash (Bourne-Again Shell), ksh (Korn Shell), or any of the other flavors one finds and discovers passionate devotees surrounding. O'Reilly publishes books for each, so check out their Web site at http://www.ora.com/.

If your site offers the X Windows Graphical User Interface in any of its incarnations, you will need still other books, such as the X Window System Administrator's Guide from O'Reilly. O'Reilly has a Web site, http://www.ora.com, that will give you a tantalizing glimpse of more information in one place than you can shake a stick at. O'Reilly is a sort of standard in the UNIX world. There may well be other good books on any given subject, but everyone is at least familiar with the ORA offerings, which are almost always well written and thorough. Plan on spending a significant portion of your salary on books.

Other Resources

Tech Speak

For learning that tech jargon, check out:

```
http://www.yahoo.com/Reference/Dictionaries/
Computing_Dictionaries/Jargon_File_The/
```

Here's a good reference for new systems administrators or those who want to be able to communicate with them.

Web Site Software by Server Type

```
http://www.ora.com, http://www.netscape.com, http://
www.microsoft.com.
```

These sites will point you toward all the tech specs on their vast and varied services.

index

C

N

O

P

Q

R

S

T

U

V

W

Y

Z

License Agreement/Notice of Limited Warranty

By opening the sealed disk container in this book, you agree to the following terms and conditions. If, upon reading the following license agreement and notice of limited warranty, you cannot agree to the terms and conditions set forth, return the unused book with unopened disk to the place where you purchased it for a refund.

License:

The enclosed software is copyrighted by the copyright holder(s) indicated on the software disk. You are licensed to copy the software onto a single computer for use by a single concurrent user and to a backup disk. You may not reproduce, make copies, or distribute copies or rent or lease the software in whole or in part, except with written permission of the copyright holder(s). You may transfer the enclosed disk only together with this license, and only if you destroy all other copies of the software and the transferee agrees to the terms of the license. You may not decompile, reverse assemble, or reverse engineer the software.

Notice of Limited Warranty:

The enclosed disk is warranted by Prima Publishing to be free of physical defects in materials and workmanship for a period of sixty (60) days from end userís purchase of the book/disk combination. During the sixty-day term of the limited warranty, Prima will provide a replacement disk upon the return of a defective disk.

Limited Liability:

The sole remedy for breach of this limited warranty shall consist entirely of replacement of the defective disk. IN NO EVENT SHALL PRIMA OR THE AUTHORS BE LIABLE FOR ANY other damages, including loss or corruption of data, changes in the functional characteristics of the hardware or operating system, deleterious interaction with other software, or any other special, incidental, or consequential DAMAGES that may arise, even if Prima and/or the author have previously been notified that the possibility of such damages exists.

Disclaimer of Warranties:

Prima and the authors specifically disclaim any and all other warranties, either express or implied, including warranties of merchantability, suitability to a particular task or purpose, or freedom from errors. Some states do not allow for EXCLUSION of implied warranties or limitation of incidental or consequential damages, so these limitations may not apply to you.

Other:

This Agreement is governed by the laws of the State of California without regard to choice of law principles. The United Convention of Contracts for the International Sale of Goods is specifically disclaimed. This Agreement constitutes the entire agreement between you and Prima Publishing regarding use of the software.